JAMES JOYCE

ATE DUE

097

JAMES JOYCE

A Collection of Critical Essays

Edited by
Mary T. Reynolds

Prentice Hall, Englewood Cliffs, New Jersey 07632

Library of Congress Cataloging-in-Publication Data

James Joyce : a collection of critical essays / edited by Mary T.
  Reynolds.
     p. cm.—(New century views)
    Includes bibliographical references.
    ISBN 0–13–512211–2
    1. Joyce, James, 1882–1941—Criticism and interpretation.
I. Reynolds, Mary T. II. Series.
PR6019.O9Z63356   1993
823'.912—dc20   92–16520
                                                CIP

Acquisitions editor: Phil Miller
Editorial assistant: Heidi Moore
Editorial/production supervision and interior design: Joan Powers
Copy editor: Ellen Falk
Cover design: Karen Salzbach
Prepress buyer: Herb Klein
Manufacturing buyer: Patrice Fraccio/Robert Anderson

© 1993 by Prentice-Hall, Inc.
A Simon & Schuster Company
Englewood Cliffs, New Jersey 07632

Printed in the United States of America
10 9 8 7 6 5 4 3 2 1

ISBN 0-13-512211-2

Prentice-Hall International (UK) Limited, *London*
Prentice-Hall of Australia Pty. Limited, *Sydney*
Prentice-Hall Canada Inc., *Toronto*
Prentice-Hall Hispanoamericana, S.A., *Mexico*
Prentice-Hall of India Private Limited, *New Delhi*
Prentice-Hall of Japan, Inc., *Tokyo*
Simon & Schuster Asia Pte. Ltd., *Singapore*
Editora Prentice-Hall do Brasil, Ltda., *Rio de Janeiro*

Contents

A Note on the Essays

All omissions from the essays reprinted here are indicated with an ellipsis (. . .). Footnotes have not been regularized to a single style. When notes have been eliminated, the remaining notes have been renumbered.

Citations in the text to Joyce's works have been regularized to the standard editions, which are listed with standard abbreviations as "The Joyce Texts" in the Bibliography. All such primary source abbreviations, with two exceptions (Richard Ellmann's biography, *James Joyce*, and *Ulysses*), will refer to the work without distinguishing between its various editions.

References to *Ulysses* have been edited to specify uniformly the page location in both the 1961 Random House edition and the 1986 one-volume (Gabler) edition, and these citations are followed by the episode and line numbers as they appear in the one-volume edition. Thus a citation to lines in the "Sirens" episode reads (*U* 1961:333; *U* 1986:273; 12–1493), identifying line 1493 in episode 12, page 333 in the 1961 Random House Vintage edition and page 273 in the one-volume Gabler edition.

References to the Ellmann biography will identify the 1959 edition as *JJ* and the revised 1982 edition as *JJ II*.

Introduction

Mary T. Reynolds

James Joyce is perhaps the quintessential twentieth-century writer. His contemporary appeal is extraordinary, and the essays in this volume help to explain the phenomenon through a many sided account of Joyce's mastery of his craft. Criticism and scholarly investigation of his work, which effectively began in 1922 with the first reviews of *Ulysses*, saw a significant broadening in the last quarter of the century. Some vigorous debates developed. The state of Joyce studies, as shown by the range and diverse styles in this collection, is above all vigorous, eclectic, lively.

The centennial of Joyce's birth, in 1982, was given due celebration around the world, and the volume of publications reached flood stage. In Dublin, Joyceans gathered for the week-long biennial Symposium, which traditionally ends on Bloomsday, June 16, the day on which *Ulysses* takes place. On this occasion there was a reenactment, in 1904 costumes, of the "Wandering Rocks" episode of *Ulysses*, in which a procession of the Lord Lieutenant of Ireland drives across Dublin and in which all the leading characters of the book are involved. The youthful Lord Mayor took the part of the former colonial ruler, and costumed Dubliners joined enthusiastically with Joyce scholars, stopping traffic in central Dublin for several hours. During the week a statue of Joyce was raised in Stephen's Green, the park between Trinity College and University College, Dublin, and several plaques were placed on buildings associated with Joyce's life or with his novels. When one of these was fixed on one of the houses where Leopold Bloom lived, in *Ulysses*, a local resident earnestly assured the party of scholars that another nearby house had been the actual residence of these fictional personages.

All this academic and popular enthusiasm is inspired by a short list of only six volumes. Joyce began as a poet, with a little book of thirty-six lyrics that was published in 1907 as *Chamber Music;* thirteen additional poems appeared as *Pomes Penyeach* in 1927, and the two volumes are now combined in *Collected Poems*. He wrote one play, *Exiles*, which has been performed many times, often to indifferent reviews; but it has also been enthusiastically received, most notably in a 1980s production by Harold Pinter. Joyce's *Dubliners* revolutionized the art of the short story, and his first novel, *A Portrait of the Artist as a Young Man*, similarly changed the writing of longer narrative. *Ulysses*, the novel generally considered his masterpiece, was more strikingly innovative still, and his last work, *Finnegans Wake*, remains mysterious half a century after publication. The record is in many ways unmatched. Whatever else may be said, however, it is clear that Joyce is greatly valued by many readers and by other writers and that he changed the course of Western literature. His works have been translated worldwide, most recently into Chinese. Many writers have acknowledged their debt, directly or indirectly, as for example, Jorge Luis Borges, in a poem describing *Ulysses*[1]: "One of the days of man contains all days / of Time, from that unknowable, initial / day when time began . . ." and in Seamus Heaney's contribution to the present volume, a poignant evocation of Joyce as precursor. As Ezra Pound said, "the best critic is the next fellow to do the job."[2]

I

What was James Joyce like? Richard Ellmann called him "one of the most rarefied minds of the century," but a few brief paragraphs cannot convey the essence of this man.[3] There is no scarcity of fact, rather the contrary, and indeed Hugh Kenner warns against over-reliance on what he calls the Irish fact. Ellmann's great biography, Brenda Maddox's biography of Nora Joyce, the four volumes of Joyce's letters, and numerous memoirs by his brother Stanislaus and by Joyce's friends provide a mass of information.

He was born February 2, 1882, in Dublin, the oldest of ten children, into a middle-class Catholic family that declined in his childhood from relative affluence to severe poverty. The hungry children and the drunken, spend-thrift father, Simon Dedalus, in *A Portrait* and *Ulysses* are drawn from life. Joyce was educated in Jesuit schools on scholarships, and at Belvedere preparatory school he won several prizes in the highly competitive annual national examinations. A Protestant boy equally gifted might have gone to Trinity College, Dublin, and his Catholic equivalent from a wealthier family might have gone to Oxford, as did Joyce's friend Oliver Gogarty, the model for Buck Mulligan in *Ulysses*. Joyce instead attended University College, Dublin, where he took little interest in his studies and failed to win an honors degree. But he read widely outside the required curriculum. He had come into conflict with the narrowly doctrinal views of his Jesuit teachers, some of whom are satirized in the autobiographical novel *Stephen Hero*, but there is no doubt that they recognized his brilliance. In his first year, at age seventeen, he wrote an essay on Ibsen that was published in the *Fortnightly*, a

[1]Robert Lima, trans., "James Joyce," *James Joyce Quarterly* 10, no. 2 (1973), 285. Reprinted by permission of the *James Joyce Quarterly*.

[2]Forrest Reid, ed., *Pound/Joyce* (New York: New Directions, 1967), 197.

[3]Richard Ellmann, *James Joyce* (New York and London: Oxford University Press, 1959; new and revised edition, 1982), 159. I have relied on the biography by Ellmann for all information about Joyce's life.

prestigious London journal. Other essays which still stand as evidence of his aesthetic principles were written for the College Literary Society. In 1982 the Jesuits set a bronze tablet over the door of University College, commemorating its three most illustrious names: Cardinal Newman, Gerard Manley Hopkins, and James Augustine Joyce.

After graduation Joyce went to Paris hoping to study medicine, supporting himself by giving English lessons and book reviewing, but he could not pay the fees, and when his mother fell ill he returned home abruptly. When she died, the family she had held together disintegrated. Now Joyce entered a very troubled period. Oliver Gogarty encouraged Joyce in dissipation, and he became a figure of scorn in Dublin intellectual circles. Nevertheless, between 1902 and 1904 he wrote the poems of *Chamber Music*, had a couple of them published, and published three short stories; he also wrote most of the chapters of *Stephen Hero*. Then Joyce met Nora Barnacle, fell in love, and with her left Dublin for the Continent in October 1904. The date on which *Ulysses* takes place, June 16, 1904, memorializes the joining of their lives.

He found a teaching post in the Berlitz School in Trieste, and here he spent ten productive though difficult years. The couple's first child, a son named Giorgio, was born in 1905. Joyce's brother Stanislaus, and later their sister Eileen, came to Trieste, and the family lived on the edge of poverty. Joyce worked for six months in Rome as correspondence clerk in a bank, and he spent a shorter period in Dublin where he organized that city's first cinema. He wrote "The Dead" in 1907 while convalescing from rheumatic fever, and his second child, Lucia, was born at this time in the paupers' ward of the Trieste hospital. *Chamber Music* was rejected by seven publishers, and a contract for *Dubliners* was signed in Dublin but abrogated in 1912; fortunately, when the printer destroyed the proof sheets, Joyce obtained one copy by a ruse. Out of these frustrations came two long satiric poems, "The Holy Office" which satirized the Irish Literary Revival, and "Gas from a Burner" which denounced the treatment of *Dubliners*. Joyce nevertheless persevered, and the Trieste years saw the publication of *Chamber Music*, the completion of *Dubliners*, the revision of *Stephen Hero* into *A Portrait of the Artist*, most of the writing of *Exiles*, and completion of the first three episodes of *Ulysses*.

When the outbreak of war in 1914 drove Nora and Joyce out of Italy, they came to rest in Zurich, where Joyce finished *Exiles* and *A Portrait of the Artist*, and wrote the greater part of *Ulysses*. He came into correspondence with Ezra Pound, and now two books were published, *Dubliners* and *A Portrait*. He had the good fortune to attract the patronage of two wealthy women, first Mrs. Edith Rockefeller McCormick and then Harriet Shaw Weaver, and after 1917 he was free from the burden of giving poorly paid English lessons.

After the 1918 Armistice, the Joyces returned briefly to Trieste and then on the advice of Pound they moved to Paris. Stanislaus, who had been interned during the war, resumed teaching in Trieste; Eileen, who had married, now lived in Prague. The publication of *Ulysses* made Joyce a celebrity, and he immediately began the writing of *Finnegans Wake*. Now the family's medical problems, which had been present for many years and had grown acute in Zurich, became critical. Joyce had eleven major eye operations, and eventually glaucoma left him nearly blind; his teeth never had proper attention; and he suffered from an undiagnosed ulcer that finally caused his death. The great misfortune of Joyce's adult life was that his daughter Lucia developed acute schizophrenia.

The onset of war in 1940–41 once again drove the Joyces to Zurich, this time with Giorgio and his son, Stephen, but Lucia had to be left in France in a mental hospital. Less than two weeks after their arrival in Zurich, Joyce was hospitalized with a perforated duodenal ulcer, and he died in the early hours of January 13, 1941. Nora survived him by ten years, and they are buried together in the Fluntern cemetery in Zurich.

II

Criticism, the art that produced the essays in this book, is only an inspired and expert reading of a literary work. One of the pleasures that Joyce, like all great artists, gives his readers is a never-ending stream of new discoveries. After fifty years of reading Joyce, a fresh look at a paragraph can subtly change its meaning, with a ripple effect through an entire chapter or even the book. As late as 1979 Hugh Kenner, whose work on Joyce goes back to 1950, adds a footnote to his little guidebook to *Ulysses* saying that another critic has convinced him that in the Martello tower scene in the opening chapter Stephen's unspoken words. "It is mine. I paid the rent." (*U* 1961:20; *U* 1986:17; 1–631) do not refer to himself but "are to be read in Buck Mulligan's voice, between invisible quotation marks, as words Stephen can already hear Mulligan speaking when he demands the key."[4] This reading changes the view of the quarrel that is such an important feature of *Ulysses*.

Joyce's innovative writing and the candid naturalism of his novels made him a center of controversy, and the first response to his work was bewilderment. More than most novelists, Joyce rewards careful reading, and especially re-reading, to understand his methods. For example, in *A Portrait of the Artist as a Young Man*, Stephen Dedalus (the same young man who reappears in *Ulysses*) as a child in boarding school has a dream while he is sick in the infirmary. But is this really a dream, or is it a vision? He sees the arrival from England of the dead Nationalist leader, Charles Stewart Parnell, an event that

---

4Hugh Kenner, *Ulysses* (London: George Allen & Unwin, 1980; revised edition, Baltimore: The Johns Hopkins University Press, 1987), 54.

did happen in October 1891, the year in which this chapter is set. The details are exact; how can this be, in an age before radio and TV? Joyce always plays fair, and a careful reader will remember (or find, by looking back three pages) that the Jesuit Brother in charge of the infirmary had been asked by an older student "to be sure and come back and tell him all the news in the paper." So when Stephen's fever makes him delirious, his mind combines the rise and fall of firelight in the room with the sound of waves "talking among themselves as they rose and fell," and the child sees the waves, the pierhead, the entering ship, the multitude of people who fell on their knees moaning and crying out, "Parnell is dead!" (*P* 24, 27). In fact, Brother Michael is reading the newspaper to the two sick boys, and Stephen, the sicker of the two, in whose family Parnell is a great hero, hears the reading and faithfully registers the scene. This is a key to understanding Stephen, for Ireland's colonial status and the effect of Parnell's death are important aspects of *A Portrait* and *Ulysses*. Joyce might have written these pages as an overt reading of the newspaper. But that is not his method.

Each of the essays in this volume represents in one way or another some aspect of the main currents of thought about Joyce's work. Taken together, as an introduction to Joyce, they supply information about the writer, the milieu in which he wrote, and the construction and narrative techniques visible in specific writings. What has been left out—most notably his poems, his critical essays, and his letters—can be reached through the bibliography. The essays reflect critical views and patterns of taste that develop as succeeding generations encounter Joyce, and such development will certainly continue beyond the twentieth century. Joyce radicalized literature, and his fiction helped also to radicalize criticism.

Large questions have not received final answers. Is Joyce's view of the world and of human life optimistic or pessimistic? Can any moral or spiritual values be discerned from his language and his expressive devices, or from the movement of plot and development of character? Why exactly did he attach *Ulysses* to Homer and, as we now know, also to Dante and Shakespeare? Are the Homeric parallels helpful or necessary in understanding *Ulysses*? Joyce "explained" *Ulysses* to friends by circulating a detailed diagram, which he called "the schema," of correspondences chapter by chapter with episodes of the *Odyssey*, with narrative techniques such as soliloquy and dialogue, with parts of the human body, with arts and sciences (theology, history, chemistry), with colors. But Joyce left very few critical writings and none that, as with T. S. Eliot, directly explain his own work. So readers and critics continue to ask questions and argue about answers, and behind all the models of analysis there remains the basic question: How can *Ulysses* (and Joyce's other books) continue to give such intense and lasting enjoyment? Here, the critical verdict is little more than an abstract and intellectualized version of the common reader's reaction writ large.

III

Four important movements of criticism can be found, all showing the effect of one basic division of opinion that began with the publication of *Ulysses* in 1922 and continues to the present day. This division stems from the question of whether the virtuosity of technique in all Joyce's works is and should be the primary element of value, or whether the important factors are representation of character and event, and similar human elements of the story or novel. The close of the century finds a large body of criticism based on the idea that brilliance of technique and style are central constituents of value.

The publication of *Finnegans Wake* reinforced the impression of radical virtuosity that began with *Ulysses*, and this seemed to be confirmed by Joyce's statements to friends, such as Stuart Gilbert, Frank Budgen, and others, like Harriet Weaver to whom he wrote of "the task (in *Ulysses*) I set myself technically in writing a book from eighteen different points of view and in as many styles." Harry Levin said in 1944 that Joyce's real secrets were matters of literary technique. He deplored the early symbolist critics who were fascinated by Joyce's "schema": "Joyce's exponents are still suffering from an excess of hierophantic zeal, a belief that what must be so laboriously decoded must somehow contain a message of mystic profundity."[5] Harvard's Gaelic scholar, John V. Kelleher, agreed, and added:

> Joyce's originality lay always in his use of language and not in his use of themes, for he discovered no new themes and never professed to. Parts of the *Wake* simply do not repay the reader's effort, let alone Joyce's in composing them. But where he succeeded, he succeeded so magnificently and with such undeniable rightness that no one, who has read and begun to understand the book, can doubt that a revolution in the use and conception of language dates from its publication.[6]

The early symbolic-mythological view of Joyce's work continues to influence criticism, in studies of formal patterns of every kind. Richard Ellmann's *Ulysses on the Liffey* (1972) used Joyce's schema to reveal a subtle balance of synthesis and antithesis in character and event that moves toward a construction of triads as intricate as Dante's *Divine Comedy*. In Joyce's complexities, Ellmann concluded, "Art has been shown to be a part of nature and all its processes natural ones."[7] Michael Seidel, in *Epic Geography* (1976), shows that Joyce's use of the *Odyssey* parallels went so far as to superimpose a Homeric geography on the map of Dublin. Seidel's warrant came from a book by Victor Bérard, in which Joyce expressed keen interest, that identified the location of Ulysses's adventures as routes along the Mediterranean coast that Homer took from seafaring manuals used by Phoenician sailors. Michael

---

[5]Harry Levin, in his review of Joseph Campbell and Henry M. Robinson, *A Skeleton Key to Finnegans Wake*, in *New Republic*, July 24, 1944.

[6]John V. Kelleher, "Joyce Digested." *Accent* 5, no. 3 (Spring 1945), 181–86.

[7]Richard Ellmann, *Ulysses on the Liffey* (London: Faber & Faber, 1972), 175.

Groden, in *Ulysses in Progress* (1977), studied the composition of *Ulysses* from the surviving manuscripts and came to the conclusion that Joyce had not initially intended to write in eighteen different styles, but changed his mind at some point after the first chapters had been written. Subsequently, a number of critics have speculated about the varied styles of the eighteen episodes and about Joyce's reasons for the decision. Karen Lawrence, in her essay in the present volume, describes the initial style of the first six chapters as the norm of the book and contrasts the aesthetic of *Ulysses* with that of *Dubliners*.

A second major movement began in 1956, with Hugh Kenner's argument, in *Dublin's Joyce*, that he had found a pervasive irony in Joyce's work. This view was supported by the discovery of an autobiographical "first draft" of *A Portrait*, and publication of this long fragmentary manuscript as *Stephen Hero* revealed for the first time an ironic point of view toward Joyce's youthful artist. Kenner's book was opposed a few years later by S. L. Goldberg's *The Classical Temper* (1961), in which Goldberg assembled evidence that Joyce could not have so completely repudiated his characters. These opposing views continue in somewhat modified form as a critical debate: an insistent view of Joyce as ironist on one side, and on the other a humanist view that emphasizes Joyce's comedy and finds his major works subtly permeated with optimistic affirmation.

A third approach to Joyce developed from the infusion of European literary theories that brought such methods as structuralism, deconstruction, psychoanalysis, and a post-structuralist combination of the three.

A fourth main current has its source in the historicity of Joyce's works. One element of this critical family comes from the Marxist concentration on class divisions and other economic aspects of life in colonial Ireland, though the connection with Marxist theory seems tenuous. An influential group of critics today, however, directly address Joyce's political views as they appear in his fiction. Of course, these four movements tend to overlap and shade into each other.

Events, no less than the clash of ideas, shaped these critical developments. While Joyce was alive, an authorized—indeed, closely supervised—biography was written by Herbert Gorman in the early 1930s, with some access to Joyce's letters, and by 1935 Sylvia Beach, the publisher of *Ulysses*, had assembled and catalogued manuscripts and other materials that she had collected over the years and planned to sell. But scholarly use of Joyce's manuscripts, with revelations that forced new readings in many areas of his fiction, began only when the various manuscripts became available in American and British libraries. Striking disclosures began with the *Stephen Hero* manuscript, acquired by Harvard in 1938, and continued with the acquisition of the Gorman papers at the University of Southern Illinois at Carbondale, and the large and very important collections that came to the British Library in London, to Yale, Cornell, and the State University of New York at Buffalo in the 1950s.

A significant watershed was the year 1959, when Richard Ellmann's biography, *James Joyce*, revealed the extent to which Joyce's fiction was a reflection of events in his life. No single book has had a greater influence on Joyce studies. Between 1957 and 1969, three volumes of Joyce's letters (unfortunately not in chronological sequence) were published, the first edited by Stuart Gilbert, the second and third by Ellmann; but in 1975 Joyce's most important letters were brought together in Ellmann's edition of the *Selected Letters*. In the 1960s these and other manuscript materials compelled critical reassessments and produced two decades of vigorous debate. When the *James Joyce Archive* collected all Joyce's manuscripts in a 63–volume facsimile edition, published between 1977 and 1980, Joyce's entire workshop became available.

IV

Ulysses is central to interpretation of Joyce's work.[8] His books are all connected with it, and with each other, not only by the Dublin setting and by reappearance of characters, but by subtle elements of context. Seventy years after its publication, there is still a division of opinion on such basic questions as what the book is "about," whether it can be called a novel, whether it is a modern epic or a mock-epic, whether its diverse styles contribute to or diminish the book's value. Similar questions are asked about *Finnegans Wake*.

The first critical models for understanding *Ulysses* were set by T. S. Eliot's and Ezra Pound's reviews. Before *Ulysses*, it was taken for granted that the

---

[8]There are now two editions of *Ulysses* with many different readings, a few of which can significantly change the book's interpretation. The first printing of *Ulysses* (1922) had many errors, and new ones appeared in every subsequent printing. In 1973 an international committee of scholars was formed to work toward an accurate text. Hans Walter Gabler, Professor of English at the University of Munich and editor of the facsimile edition of *A Portrait of the Artist*, became editor of the proposed new *Ulysses*.

Professor Gabler prepared a critical and synoptic edition that was brought out by Garland Publishing Company (New York) in 1984. This was a considerable achievement, but controversy began soon after the edition appeared. Several scholarly conferences were organized to discuss a long list of alleged errors and arbitrary changes, and the principal issues were eventually identified in a series of published papers and books. These are listed in the Bibliography (page 236).

The publishers of *Ulysses* (Random House, New York; Bodley Head, London) and the Joyce Estate needed to have an edition with enough new material to justify a fresh copyright, and in 1986 the Random House/Vintage edition of 1961 was replaced by a new one-volume edition, based on the three-volume Gabler edition of 1984 and subtitled "The Corrected Text." Controversy continued, however, and in June 1990 the former 1961 edition of *Ulysses* was republished by Vintage Books.

There is now in preparation (1992) another new edition of *Ulysses*, edited by Professor John Kidd, of Boston University; this project will start with the 1922 (Paris) first edition as copytext, an important decision that was rejected by Professor Gabler. *Ulysses* is a complex work; the circumstances of its composition and first publication were somewhat chaotic, leaving a confusing record and an incomplete mass of manuscripts, typescripts, and proofs. None of Joyce's other works present such severe editing problems.

"meaning" of a novel could be found through close examination of character and plot. Eliot and Pound saw that Joyce had written a novel that encompassed the tradition but went beyond it to a new narrative form, not experimental but stunningly innovative. Eliot decided that Joyce's use of the mythical approach, through hundreds of parallels with the *Odyssey*, was an ordered commentary on the anarchic futility of the modern world. Eliot did not fully explain this insight. Pound, more interested in Joyce's virtuosity and more responsive to his comedy, emphasized the Flaubertian naturalistic constructions in *Ulysses*. Two additional major presences in *Ulysses*, Dante and Shakespeare in addition to Homer, were perceived by S. Foster Damon. Edmund Wilson placed *Ulysses* in the movement of European modernism, in *Axel's Castle* in 1932. Wilson took exception to the complicated patterns in *Ulysses*, saying in effect that it was too complex to win readers. Wilson has been proved wrong. For many it was indeed considered a difficult book, the property of the academy. But the Random House edition of 1934 opened up the American market, and in 1941 Harry Levin's comprehensive interpretation of all of Joyce's works in *James Joyce: A Critical Introduction* raised the curtain on American interpretation in a little book that has never lost its freshness.

Subsequently, an important critical model shifted attention to the centrality of the artist. Joyce creates an artist figure most notably in the character of Stephen Dedalus in *A Portrait of the Artist as a Young Man*. In *Ulysses* a slightly older Stephen reappears and, as one critic puts it, goes through the worst day of his life on June 16, 1904. Has Joyce shown a genuine artist, or is Stephen an artist manqué? Will the young man, who clearly has not had time to mature in either novel, eventually become the successful creator of his own literary work? Joyce also puts an artist figure at the center of his play, Richard Rowan in *Exiles*; and in *Finnegans Wake* he devotes a chapter to Shem the Penman. In *Dubliners*, there are less comprehensive portrayals of men of artistic sensibility or temperament, including Gabriel Conroy in "The Dead," Little Chandler in "A Little Cloud," and Mr. Duffy in "A Painful Case." Taken together, there is great ambiguity in Joyce's treatment of his artist-figures. Most intriguing of his vignettes is the portrait of Leopold Bloom, whose discourse is banal but whose inner thoughts reveal discerning judgment and much originality of expression. Bloom's status is perhaps validated by the comment of a character in the tenth chapter, "Wandering Rocks," who says "seriously" of the man who has just been presented as a ridiculous figure, "He's a cultured allroundman. . . . He's not one of your common or garden . . . you know . . . there's a touch of the artist about old Bloom" (*U* 1961:235; *U* 1986:193; 10–580).

Another influential critical approach opens up the problem of aesthetic distance and develops the view that Joyce's fictional world is controlled by parody and irony. Hugh Kenner's Joyce has the moral vision of a writer detached from his creations, Kenner insisting that the author's likes and dislikes, preferences and antipathies, are expressed through technique. S. L.

Goldberg, arguing in *The Classical Temper* against Kenner's interpretation of Joyce's characters, saw in *Ulysses* a complex irony and a positive role for Leopold Bloom that Joyce rendered by hundreds of small details of speech and thought. The problem received a sustained discussion by Wayne Booth in *The Rhetoric of Fiction* (1961) and by Robert Scholes in his masterly 1964 essay, "Stephen Dedalus: Poet or Esthete?"

As close readings developed over four decades, the critic's conclusions occasionally seemed not to follow from the evidence he or she displayed. An early example is William K. Schutte's *Joyce and Shakespeare* (1957), a relentlessly ironic reading of Leopold Bloom, concluding that Joyce presents him as a pathetically limited little man who is a failure in all his human contacts. But at the same time Schutte carefully lists the evidence for Bloom's wit, his shrewd perception of relationships, his original way with language, demonstrating a quite different view of this uncommon common man. Some years later, in "Leopold Bloom: A Touch of the Artist," Schutte retracted his analysis and recanted his adverse judgment, to conclude that "Bloom is indeed an extraordinary man . . . whose essentially prosaic mode of thought can even rise to the poetic under stress of great emotion."[9]

An essay in the present volume, by A. Walton Litz, takes exception to Goldberg's explicit assumption that *Ulysses* is a traditional English novel, arguing that this is a narrow and reductive approach that fails to understand Joyce's mature art and "leaves out most of the structures and harmonies that give the work a special form and special impact." James H. Maddox, in another contribution to this collection, extends the argument by proposing that the radical change in styles that takes over midway in *Ulysses* was the result of Joyce's "long meditation upon the nature of language and narrative authority," and still more a result of his discovery of the character of Leopold Bloom. Maddox's essay sees the genius of the book precisely in its ability to combine basically novelistic concerns such as character and plot with a "metanovelistic concern with narrative authority."

In 1967 a special "*Portrait* Issue" of the *James Joyce Quarterly* (*JJQ*) reviewed the positions that had been taken, and in 1979 a different approach appeared. In another special issue of the *JJQ*, a "Structuralist/Reader Response Issue," James Sosnoski, invoking concepts taken from Roland Barthes and French literary theory, offered a critical model that could explain or reconcile the many conflicting readings of *A Portrait* and the ensuing controversy about aesthetic distance in Joyce's work. Sosnoski proposed that the "writer-oriented theory of criticism" had produced an oversimplified view that some of the readings are "wrong" and some are "right," and suggested instead a "reader-oriented" model with allowance for a more flexible and more complex analysis of relationships between writer, reader, context, and text.[10]

9William K. Schutte, *James Joyce Quarterly* 10, no. 1 (1972), 118–31.
10James Sosnoski, *James Joyce Quarterly* 16, nos. 1–2 (1979), 43–64.

Kenner's preference for unrelieved irony began a long controversy in which critics raised questions of irony and aesthetic distance in every corner of Joyce's writing. By the 1980s Kenner had changed his emphasis and softened his tone; but in this volume, in an essay that bridges *Portrait* and *Ulysses*, he shows that he has not swerved from the basic position that "what we make of Stephen . . . depends a good deal on whether he has the author's complete indulgence" and that "the calculated vagueness of *A Portrait* answers the imperatives of a nearly solipsistic novel." In Kenner's present view of *Ulysses*, however, where Bloom is "the hidden hero," he is described as "quietly witty . . . a man of ready tongue," and is even tentatively canonized as "a man who was never down for long, [whose] distinction is to have been fit to live in Ireland without malice, without violence, without hate."[11] Even so, irony enfolds them both, and the future of Stephen Dedalus seems to Kenner most likely to continue the pattern of June 16, 1904, the same downward movement that identifies the dissolute young men with whom Stephen spends this day.

V

Other critics stress Joyce's language, exploring its structures, its associations and polyvalent functions, and its origins. For Joyce, language is the fundamental human activity. His ideas anticipated a general development in the twentieth century, as philosophy shifted its primary concerns from metaphysics to epistemology and finally to linguistics. Some consider this a natural progression, moving from the question "How do we come to know the world?" to "How can we think?" and, ultimately, "How are we capable of thought?" Language is radically fundamental, and from the first page of "The Sisters," the child's musing over words, to the etymological palimpsest of *Finnegans Wake*, Joyce's preoccupations with language are given form in his fiction.

The essays in this collection all show, directly or indirectly, some aspect of this lifelong preoccupation. Denis Donoghue reminds us of the European origins of Stephen's diction in *A Portrait, Dubliners, Ulysses,* and *Finnegans Wake,* displaying the connection of Joyce's use of language with Wittgenstein's dictum that the world is "everything that is the case." For Donoghue, Joyce is able to make language "offer itself as a counter-truth to the truth of reality," creating a kind of second world of imagination and desire at the same time that his precise skill with a sentence (Donoghue instances Mrs. Mooney, in *Dubliners*) is able to "disclose a reality not itself linguistic." David Hayman's essay probes the European origins of Joyce's linguistic theory and practice, reviewing the evidence for his interest in Père Marcel Jousse, the Jesuit linguist whose ideas were already reflected in Joyce's writing when Joyce

---

[11]Kenner, *Ulysses*, p. 1 and Chapter 5, p. 43.

heard him lecture in 1931 in Paris. Fritz Senn's contribution, making the point that ambiguity in Joyce's writing is often deliberate and wilful, gives an example of his use of language to present "an erroneous universe on a local scale." Joyce's knowledge of Giambattista Vico is given a particularized treatment in John Bishop's essay, which is the first attempt to explain in detail what Joyce meant by saying, "I would not pay overmuch attention to [Vico's] theories beyond using them for all they are worth, but they have gradually forced themselves on me through circumstances of my own life." Bishop argues for a philosophical connection, for Joyce's recognition of "a vision of historical growth as intricate as the vision of personal growth that he represented in *A Portrait*."

The infiltration of European literary theory into traditional Joyce criticism, in the 1970s and 1980s, was principally but not exclusively centered on *Finnegans Wake*. Bernard Benstock's account of the Fifth International Joyce Symposium in Paris in 1975, where the French and Anglo-American participants "mostly ignored each other," gives a revealing glimpse of the first encounter of "French theoretical excesses" with more conventional approaches.[12] By the Ninth Symposium in 1984, the humanist and empirical paths were interwoven with modernist and postmodernist critical theory. In 1975 an opening address (in French) by Jacques Lacan drew an audience of 1300; in 1984 Jacques Derrida gave a three-hour deconstructionist reading (also in French) of *Ulysses*.

In the present collection Margot Norris's structuralist method offers an integrated interpretation of *Finnegans Wake* but rejects the novelistic approach. Bernard Benstock's contribution, taking the view that "it is impossible to investigate Joyce's language without explicating meaning interwoven with language," illuminates with many examples the comic constructions in the *Wake*. The essay by Jean-Michel Rabaté addresses one of the *Wake*'s crucial problems: Who speaks? How can the reader establish an identity for the subject? In a few cleanly written pages Rabaté shows how Joyce creates a basic narrative pattern (in this case, from a seven-line entry in one of his early notebooks) and artfully locks it into the book's web of interlocking correspondences. Maud Ellmann gives the "Sirens" episode of *Ulysses* a witty poststructuralist analysis inspired by Joyce's own virtuoso imitation of musical effects in this chapter, and by taking her title from a phrase in *Finnegans Wake*, ". . . signsigns to soundsense," she connects both books with Joyce's innovative use of styles to make "soundsense and sensesound kin again" (*FW* 121:15; 138:7). Jacques Derrida's essay, a radical annotation of language and thought, speech and writing, writing and translation, sets up resonances in a reading of *Finnegans Wake* that makes us think about how it is possible to think. Joyce, for this critic, is a lifetime obsession. Closing the collection, Derrida's lecture

12Bernard Benstock, ed. Introduction to *The Augmented Ninth* (Urbana: University of Illinois Press, 1989), 3–24.

spontaneously conveys this dimension of Joyce's powerful appeal, his continuing hold over generations of readers, the capturing of our imagination by his writing.

VI

The historicity of Joyce's fiction is the subject of a growing body of sophisticated discussion, using linguistic theory and occasionally also Marxist critical principles. Phillip F. Herring's chapter explains Joyce's use of ambiguity in "The Sisters" as a protective device that insulated from censorship Joyce's criticism of Irish society. Cheryl Herr, examining traces of popular culture in *Dubliners* and *A Portrait of the Artist*, argues for Joyce's covert representation of the economic matrix of Irish culture in 1904. In the short story "Grace," and again in *Portrait*, the emotional impact of a priest's sermon discloses a divided public image of the Irish Church in Joyce's day. The Irish dimension of Joyce's writing was for many years undervalued, even ignored. His works almost obsessively chronicle an Irish reality, and he wished to be known as an Irish writer. He announced his intention to write "the moral history of my country," but until the 1970s he was called apolitical, and indeed he encouraged this view of himself by consistently refusing public comment on political developments in Ireland and in Europe.

The discovery intact of Joyce's Trieste library changed all this in 1977, when Richard Ellmann brought together Joyce's reading and his writing in *The Consciousness of Joyce*. His early interest in socialism and his approval of Arthur Griffith's Nationalist writings were discussed by Dominic Manganiello in *Joyce's Politics* (1980), and Joyce's concern with history is now fully recognized. Fredric Jameson contributes to this collection an interpretation from history of the narrative pattern of *Ulysses* and its special demands for a cross-referencing reading that moves back and forth among the multiplied details of character and event. Joyce's epic of colonial Dublin, an economically backward community that Jameson views from Marxist perspectives, is given form by "a great flux" of anecdotes, of Dublin gossip containing concrete and visible images of life under imperialism. In fact, Jameson says, the rigid constraints (Joyce's word was "paralysis") on human energies under imperialism account for the flowering of those energies in the eloquence and rhetoric of the Dubliners in *Ulysses*.

Another aspect of Joyce's political views appears in a growing body of feminist writing, loosely associated with linguistic currents in Joyce studies. His female characters and their cultural setting are examined in a search for power structures, a venture that brought gender and sexual politics into Marxist-historically oriented analysis. Can women's writing be separated (and should it be?) from male-produced literary texts and theory? A more central concern is with the actual dimensions of gender-oriented literary theory. In the late years of this century, critics have analyzed both Joyce's female characters and, what is not always the same thing, the position of women in his fiction. Suzette Henke and Elaine Unkeles were the first to collect a group of essays on Joyce's female characters, in *Women in Joyce* (1982). The women in Joyce's life have also become part of such investigations. Feminism as a movement was extremely important in the years of Joyce's youth, achieving in England rights of property and the right to vote, and Joyce's affirmative reactions to women's emancipation are found both in his fiction and in Ellmann's biography. Brenda Maddox, in her biography of Joyce's wife, *Nora* (1988), summarizes with many revealing and amusing quotations the perspectives on Joyce that have come with, as well as from, the feminist movement. Bonnie Kime Scott gave these questions their first comprehensive theoretical treatment in her *James Joyce* (1987), from which her essay on *Exiles* in this volume is taken.

For French feminists the term *woman* is itself still problematic; Anglo-American critics focus on the social construction of sexuality and gendered behavior patterns. Jeri Johnson in a valuable essay compares the currents of French feminist theory with its Anglo-American counterpart.[13] Johnson and others find that the divisions in feminist readings reflect ambiguities in Joyce's texts themselves, and also Joyce's consistently negative comments on "women," which Ellmann aptly described as Joyce's leisure-hour misogyny. These, however, contrast with his fictional treatment of women and with his more serious comments on feminism, such as the dictum recorded by Arthur Power to whom Joyce said that "the greatest revolution in our time is in the most important relationship there is—that between men and women: the revolt against the idea that they are the mere instruments of men."[14]

Another dimension of historicity looks for traces of Joyce's views on the literary movements of his time. Did he include in *Finnegans Wake* a parodic critique of the modernism it transcended? Can *A Portrait of the Artist* be read as a critique of nineteenth-century aestheticism? Hugh Kenner notes the affinity of Stephen's style with Newman and Walter Pater, and other critics have shown the presence of Yeats (who is a presence in Joyce's work but never named) and D'Annunzio. The villanelle Stephen writes is clearly a product of fin-de-siècle aestheticism. In *Finnegans Wake*, the presence of all Joyce's previous works is significant, and Margot Norris believes that the *Wake's* "radical departure from modernism" signals "its potential for historical, political and aesthetic subversion." Extending this insight, she says:

> This is a time, I believe, when without losing the benefits of two decades of avant-garde theory that has taught us to be wary of the fictions we produce when we do

---

[13]Jeri Johnson, "Beyond the Veil: *Ulysses*, Feminism and the Figure of Woman," in *Joyce, Modernity and Its Mediation*, ed. Christine van Boheemen (Amsterdam: Rodopi, 1989), 201–28.
[14]Arthur Power, *Conversations with James Joyce* (New York: Barnes & Noble, 1974), 35.

read, interpret, and construct the critical history of texts and their periods, we can begin a historically grounded consideration of *Finnegans Wake*'s writing of the modernity, and the artistic crises within modernity, that produced it.[15]

[15]Margot Norris, *Joyce's Web: The Social Unraveling of Modernism* (Austin: University of Texas Press), 1992.

Part 1
THE ARTIST

James Joyce In and Out of Art

Richard Ellmann

James Joyce thought about his centenary, recently celebrated, long before it occurred to his readers to do so. He scrawled in a notebook on Bloomsday, the day of *Ulysses*, in 1924, "Today 16 of June 20 years after. Will anybody remember this date." His Stephen Dedalus in *Ulysses* asks the same question as he jots down lines for a new poem, "Who ever anywhere will read these written words?" Stephen also recalls, with a twinge, how before leaving for Paris he gave instructions that in the event of his death his epiphanies should be deposited in all the major libraries of the world, *including Alexandria*: "Someone was to read them there after a few thousand years . . ." The library at Alexandria having been burned centuries before, chances were slim that anyone would be reading his epiphanies there at any time. Still, if Joyce mocked such immortal longings, it was because he had immortal longings to mock. His brother Stanislaus, who drew a sharp line between fiction and fact, remembered that James had given him similar instructions for the disposal of his poems and epiphanies before leaving for Paris in 1902. No one will object to brave youths displaying youthful bravado. Flushed with talent or its semblance, they have all claimed with Shakespeare:

Not marble, nor the gilded monuments
Of princes, shall outlive this powerful rhyme.

Sometimes they've been right.

Joyce was convinced that a great future lay in store for him, and on the promise of it he allowed people to help him secure it. In 1904 he thought briefly that the moment had arrived; an Irish-American millionaire named Kelly seemed about to lend him money to start up a weekly magazine which was to be called *The Goblin*. Joyce said to his friend Francis Sheehy-Skeffington, who was to be coeditor, "I think I am coming into my kingdom." Unfortunately, millionaire Kelly withdrew. Eight years later the same phrase occurs in a letter from Joyce to his wife: "I hope that the day may come when

I shall be able to give you the fame of being beside me when I have entered into my Kingdom." That he was still borrowing "left right and centre" did not dishearten him. In 1907 his second child was born in a paupers' ward, but in that atmosphere Joyce confided to his brother, "My mind is of a type superior to and more civilized than any I have met up to the present." An empty wallet did not diminish his conviction of spiritual affluence. His confidence persisted as he grew older, and his putative kingdom continued to include the posterity for whom he thought his books would be required texts. When Max Eastman asked him why he was writing *Finnegans Wake* in the way he was, Joyce replied, with a brag intended to provoke a smile, "To keep the critics busy for three hundred years."

The first hundred of these three hundred years Joyce appears to have weathered quite well. His books are indeed studied all over the world and have their effect even on those who do not read them. If nothing else, writers in England as elsewhere have to choose when they start a novel whether or not to be traditional, whereas in the pre-Joycian past they could be traditional without scruple. Joyce does not lack for admirers; he does not lack for detractors either. His detractors are repelled by the Joyce fans who obsessively follow Leopold Bloom's trail around Dublin, or climb the stairs of the martello tower at Sandycove, or drink at the much refurbished Davy Byrne's. Still, such activities are not more pernicious, or cultic, than climbing Wordsworth's Helvellyn, or visiting Hawthorne's House of the Seven Gables in Salem or Proust's aunt's house in Illiers. If Joyce particularly inspires such pilgrimages, it is perhaps because we long to be on closer terms with this *scriptor absconditus*, this indrawn writer, in the hope of achieving an intimacy with him which he does not readily afford.

Another reason for seeing the places described in his books is that Joyce, although he transformed those places into words, did not invent them. He said, "He is a very bold man who dares to alter in the presentment, still more to deform, whatever he has seen and heard" (May 5, 1906). This was in connection with the book *Dubliners*. He was always trying to verify details of the city which lay almost a thousand miles from the table at which he was writing about it. How many feet down was the area in front of the house at 7 Eccles Street? What kind of trees were there on Leahy's terrace? Some of Joyce's flavor comes as a reward for this zeal. . . . He could quote with approval (May 16, 1907) Pater's remark, "Art is life seen through a temperament."

When Joyce was young so many subjects pressed urgently upon him that he had only to choose among them. As he grew older he needed more hints. He sometimes thought he must alter his quiet life so as to secure them. . . . For the main theme of *Ulysses* and of his play *Exile*, Joyce could rely on an incident which did not happen but which he briefly thought had happened. A onetime friend claimed in 1909 that Nora Barnacle, in the days when Joyce was courting her, had shared her favors with himself. But when Joyce was actually writing his novel and play five years later, he had trouble reactivating the jealousy he had once felt so intensely. His wife complained to their friend Frank Budgen, "Jim wants me to go with other men so that he will have something to write about." She seems to have failed him in this wifely duty. She did however oblige him to the extent of beginning a letter to him with the words, "Dear Cuckold," with the helpful aim of sharpening his pen for *Ulysses. . . .*

Still, closeness to life was not enough. Granted that he believed himself from earliest youth to be an artist, it was as an Irish artist that he wished to become known. To that extent he was and always would be a part of the national literary revival. Although he spoke of *Finnegans Wake* as a universal history, the universe is given a distinct Irish coloration, and in a way the whole book is an arabesque on the Irish ballad of that title. Similarly his first work, now lost, written when he was nine, was on the most Irish of subjects—the death of Charles Stewart Parnell. In his youth perhaps his most passionate literary enthusiasm was for James Clarence Mangan, whom he complimented as "The national poet of Ireland" and as one who (he said) "had the whole past of the country at the back of his head," an ideal he marked out for himself as well. "An Irish safety pin is more important to me than an English epic," he remarked. Yet it was not Ireland as it had been that attracted him, but Ireland as it might be. Joyce was affected by the talk of renaissance that was in the air, and in the earliest as well as the final version of *A Portrait of the Artist*, that is, in 1904 as in 1914, he ended by summoning in his imagination a new Irish nation.

The Irishness of his books was a distinguishing mark. *Dubliners*, he told his brother, was "a moral history of the life I knew" (May 5, 1907), and to his publisher Grant Richards he wrote, "My intention was to write a chapter of the moral history of my country." Joyce is often considered amoral; he regarded himself as a moralist. Stephen Dedalus concludes *A Portrait* with the words, "I go forth to encounter for the millionth time the reality of experience and to forge in the smithy of my soul the uncreated conscience of my race." Irony-hunters, who throng to Joyce studies, have been reluctant to take this expressed ambition of Stephen seriously. Joyce did so, however; in an earnest letter to his wife in 1912 he said, "I am one of the writers of this generation who are perhaps creating at last a conscience in the soul of this wretched race." His books move obliquely, even urbanely, toward this goal. In nine articles he wrote from 1907 to 1912 in a Triestine newspaper he presented his country's plight in more downright fashion. He offered these in 1914 to a publisher in Rome. They were not accepted: a pity, since they would have confirmed Joyce's "political awareness," a quality he valued in Turgenev. If he was not a nationalist of anyone else's school he was his own nationalist. His brother records a conversation they had in April 1907; Stanislaus argued against a free Ireland on the grounds that freedom would make it intolerable.

"What the devil are your politics?" asked James. "Do you not think Ireland has a right to govern itself and is capable of doing so?" As an Irish writer, Joyce in 1912 went to the head of Sinn Féin, Arthur Griffith, to secure his help in having *Dubliners* issued by an Irish firm. Griffith, later to be Ireland's first president, was powerless to help but received him with respect.

As Irish artist, Joyce could be contemptuous toward his literary compatriots, whom he derided as serving lesser gods than his own. He was nevertheless modest before his own art. He had many of the self-doubts that are often attributed only to lesser writers. Though his first book was verse, he did not pride himself greatly on it and even denied to Padraic Colum in 1909 that he was a poet. Of course he did not like it when others agreed with his estimate; Ezra Pound was one of those who deeply offended him in the late 1920s by urging him to file his new poems in the family Bible. Joyce published them anyway but hedged his claim for them by giving them the title of *Pomes Penyeach.* He considered lyricism to be a vital part of his revelation of himself in his art, yet he played down his lyrics like a man unwilling to risk all on that throw. He was sufficiently affected by the criticism of early parts of *Finnegans Wake* to consider turning the book over to James Stephens for completion. As to *Ulysses*, he said of it to Samuel Beckett, "I may have oversystematized *Ulysses*," though in fact Joyce had a Dantean skill in making what was systematic appear entirely improvisatory.

While he was writing his first book, Joyce owned up to uncertainties about the works with which he hoped to make his name. Of *Dubliners* he said to his brother, "The stories seem to be indisputably well done, but, after all, perhaps many people could do them as well." His autobiographical novel awakened even more misgivings. He had composed about twenty chapters of it under the title *Stephen Hero* when he abruptly announced to Stanislaus that he was changing the book's scope and redoing the early parts because they were not well written. When he had revised them, he was still dissatisfied. He decided to change the book completely; instead of having sixty-three chapters, as once planned, it would have only five. He would omit all its first part, in which he dealt with Stephen before he started his schooling. Instead he would begin at school. The name of his hero, Dedalus, would be changed to Daly. . . .

The decision to make the book into five chapters was to stand. Otherwise, the new version pleased Joyce little better. On December 5, 1907, he complained to Stanislaus, "The book begins at a railway station like most college stories; there are three companions in it, and a sister who dies by way of pathos. It is the old bag of tricks and a good critic would probably show that I am still struggling even in my stories with the stock figures discarded in Europe half a century ago." Stanislaus labored to reassure him. After all, there were not three companions, he said, but five. Sister Isabel died in the book because their brother Georgie had died in actual fact. Joyce conceded, "I didn't consciously use stock figures, but I fear that my mind, when I begin to write, runs in the groove of what I have read." This statement, recorded by Stanislaus, is the best hint we have that Joyce was determined to emerge from that groove, to stand literature on its head. He did just that, and evidently he intended it from the start.

These remarks prefigure the revisions he now made in *A Portrait of the Artist as a Young Man*. He eliminated sister Isabel from the book. No pathos, then. The opening scene at the railway station, evidently one in which Stephen arrives at Clongowes Wood College, is also left out. Joyce did not expunge Stephen's preschool days entirely, but he condensed them into three or four pages. The picture of infant consciousness, with shapes and touches and smells all distinct if not yet understood, and with words beginning to reverberate, was so astonishing as to provide William Faulkner with the technique for the equally admirable portrait of an idiot's mind in *The Sound and the Fury*. After this overture we might expect Joyce to take up the narrative in a sequential way, but there are telltale signs that he is not doing so. We gradually realize that Stephen has a fever, and that what we have been reading is not a history but a deliberate hodgepodge of memories of his earlier school days and holidays at home, rendered with the discontinuity and intensity appropriate to fever. Not until two-thirds of the way through the first chapter does Joyce change the tense, and when he does so he is signalizing not only Stephen's recovery from fever, but Stephen's apprehension of his own separateness as a recording consciousness. In *Ulysses* Joyce employs a somewhat comparable method by having Stephen recall the last two years of his life in a kind of fit, not of fever this time but of remorse.

Although his own life provided him with much material, he ruthlessly departed from it where he needed. The first chapter culminates with Stephen, unjustly pandied by Father Dolan, protesting to the rector. We know from Joyce's autobiographical recollections to Herbert Gorman that this incident was based upon fact. But this was by no means the only punishment Joyce received at Clongowes. The Punishment Book from that time is incomplete, but its surviving pages disclose no less than three other transgressions by Joyce in February and March 1889, at which time he was still only seven years old. He was given two pandies in February for not bringing a book to class, six in March for muddy boots, and four the same month for "vulgar language," an offense he would commit with growing frequency for the rest of his life. Since these three punishments were presumably meted out with just cause, Joyce ignored them and dealt only with the great injustice inflicted by Father Dolan. So Stephen became a victim, and a heroic one whose protest against unjust pandying at a Jesuit school could be a prelude to his larger protests in youth against Church and State.

During the year 1907 Joyce hesitated over keeping the name of Dedalus for his hero. If he changed it to Daly, he could write the book on the same realistic level as his epiphanies and stories of Dublin life. Call him Dedalus, and he would have to justify the oddity of this name for an Irishman; he would be able to do so only by connecting the contemporary character with the mythical artificer of wings and labyrinth. Some years later Joyce would speak of his art as "extravagant excursions into forbidden territory," and in choosing Dedalus over Daly he made such an excursion. In the last two chapters, instead of describing Stephen's movement outward from Ireland, Joyce represents also another movement, downward into myth. On a superficial level Stephen is dissociating himself; on a deeper level he is achieving an association with the Greek Daedalus, he is becoming himself a creature of myth. This decision led Joyce on to *Ulysses*. When asked why he had used the *Odyssey* so prominently in that book, Joyce replied, "It is my system of working." The method was established in 1907, when he threw Stephen Daly out and invited Stephen Dedalus in.

After he completed *A Portrait of the Artist as a Young Man*, Joyce had pretty well exhausted the possibilities of the artist-hero. For his next book he needed a new impulse. He was beginning to find it long before he used it, in 1907 also. In that year his remarks to his brother indicate that he was situating himself in relation to Ibsen, a figure he had idolized in his youth. "Auld Aibsen always wrote like a gentleman," he said, and added that he would himself not write so. On May 16, 1907, he commented, "Life is not so simple as Ibsen represents it. Mrs. Alving, for instance, is Motherhood and so on. . . . It's all very fine and large, of course. If it had been written at the time of Moses, we'd now think it wonderful. But it has no importance at this age of the world. It is a remnant of heroics, too." Joyce was very much opposed to heroics. "For me," he went on, "youth and motherhood are these two beside us." He pointed to a drunken boy of about twenty, a laborer, who had brought his mother into the trattoria where Joyce and Stanislaus were talking, while the mother was leading him home. The boy was hardly able to speak but was expressing his contempt for someone as well as he could. "I would like to put on paper the thousand complexities in his mind. . . ." Joyce was evidently imagining the dense consciousness that he would give to his characters in *Ulysses*. He went on, "Absolute realism is impossible, of course. That we all know. . . . But it's quite enough that Ibsen has omitted *all* question of finance from his thirteen dramas." Stanislaus took it upon himself to object, "Maybe there are some people who are not so preoccupied about money as you are." "Maybe so, by God," said his brother, "but I'd like to take twenty-five lessons from one of those chaps."

Given a writer so convinced that old ways would not do for him, *Ulysses* was from the start designed to break with precedents. "The task I set myself technically in writing a book from eighteen different points of view and in as many styles, all apparently unknown or undiscovered by my fellow trades-men, that and the nature of the legend chosen would be enough to upset anyone's mental balance," Joyce (whose mental balance was not upset) confided to Harriet Weaver. In this book he set himself as many difficulties as he could, knowing that his genius would be equal to them. There is the title itself, so abrupt in its insistence on a mythical background, which however is never mentioned as it was in *A Portrait of the Artist*. The author's silence about it is intimidating, yet the relation to the *Odyssey* is problematic, and its intensity varies from chapter to chapter, or even from page to page. Joyce felt at liberty to deal with Homer as highhandedly as Virgil had done, keeping the basic typology but varying and omitting and adding as his own book required. In the first episodes he realized his ambition of rendering the thousand complexities in the mind, and for the first time in literature we have all the lapses and bursts of attention, hesitations, half-recollections, distractions, sudden accesses or flaggings of sexual interest, feelings of hunger or nausea, somnolence, sneezing, thoughts about money, responses to the clouds and sunlight, along with the complications of social behavior and work. Joyce's power is shown not only in the density of sensations, but in the poetry and humor that infuse the principal characters and in the spirited irony of the narrator. Yet to mention these characteristics is to be put in mind of others. There is an extraordinary counterpoint between the first three chapters dealing with Stephen Dedalus and the next three dealing with Bloom. Not only is there an implicit parallel in their responses at the same hours of the day, but in the inner nature of the incidents that are described. So at the start of the first chapter, Buck Mulligan, holding a shaving bowl as if it were a chalice, claims to be transubstantiating the lather in it into the body and blood of Christ. Bloom makes an unspoken derisive commentary on this miracle when, at the end of the fourth chapter, he has a bowel movement and so in effect transubstantiates food into feces. Stephen ponders the way that states and churches alike have engaged in persecution and sadistic war, while Bloom thinks about the masochism which attracts devotees to confess and ask for punishment. A recognition of sado-masochism seems to bind the characters together, though they have not yet met. Then Stephen, as he walks along the strand and sees the debris heaped up by the waves, thinks darkly of the process of life as one from birth to decay to death. In the parallel passage in Bloom's morning, he attends a funeral, and is put in mind of the process from death through decay to new birth. What we thought were two parallel lines prove to be a circle.

As the book proceeds, the circle is itself questioned and sometimes mocked. And the reign of order gives way to the reign of chaos. The physical universe, so glancingly built up in all its multiplicity in the early episodes, begins to lose its plausibility. Space and time, once so distinct, are shaken almost out of recognition. The reader like the narrative is caught up in the agitations and images of the unconscious mind. Our daytime selves are almost overwhelmed by this night. Yet in all the disorder Joyce keeps as firm a hand as he had when all was order in the early chapters. At the end he gives us back our world, somewhat the worse for wear, based no longer upon primal certitude but upon affirmation in the face of doubt, as the universe hangs upon the void. And while he prided himself on his novel's physicality, and ended with a supposedly fleshly monologue, what we recognize in reading Molly Bloom's soliloquy is that she is no fleshlier than Hamlet, and that for her too the mind affects everything. In it she acknowledges grudgingly that her husband, who recognizes her wit and musical talent and inner nature, is a better man than her lover Blazes Boylan. She pays Bloom the ultimate compliment, one a man rarely hears from a woman, "I saw he understood or felt what a woman is." Penelope recognizes Ulysses not by his scar but by his imagination. Although Joyce said jocularly of Molly that she is the flesh that always affirms, she is not to be identified with unconsciousness, or Mother Nature, or fertility. Her amorous career has been limited. She has copulated a little, she has ruminated a great deal. Bodies do not exist without minds. Molly may not be capable of impersonal thought, as Bloom is, but she has a good sharp practical intelligence. She is in fact cerebral too—a great and unexpected tribute from a writer who in life said many unpleasant things about women.

Joyce thought of his books as way stations on a psychic journey. His last book, *Finnegans Wake*, was an even more "extravagant excursion into forbidden territory," since it invaded the region of language itself, a region which other novelists had left inviolate. Dante obligated Italian literature to use the vernacular instead of Latin. Joyce's invention of *Finnegans-Wake*-ese was not intended to change literature so fundamentally, though it has had its imitators. Rather he wished to find an adequate medium to describe the world of night, the world of dream, the world of the unconscious, the world of madness. In such an atmosphere neither shapes nor events nor words could be intact. As he wrote in a letter, "One great part of every human existence is passed in a state which cannot be rendered sensible by the use of wideawake language, cutanddry grammar and goahead plot." Every person experiences this other state, but Joyce also envisaged a "universal history" in which he would represent the night world of humanity. This night world has always been associated with dark fantasies, but no one had described its work. The principal work of the night shift of humanity—its involuntary, accidental, half-conscious labor—is the perpetual de-creation and re-creation of language. The tongue slips, no one knows why. We go to sleep speaking Latin and wake up speaking French. Words break up, combine with words mysteriously imported from other languages, play tricks upon their own components. In the twinkling of a closed eye a red rose becomes a red nose, a phoenix becomes a finish, a funeral becomes a funforall. Joyce insisted that he was working strictly in accordance with the laws of phonetics, the only difference being that he accomplished in one fictional night what might take hundreds of years to occur through gradual linguistic change. He commented to a friend,

Jacques Mercanton, "I reconstruct the life of the night the way the Demiurge goes about his creation, on the basis of a mental scenario that never varies. The only difference is that I obey laws I have not chosen. And he?" (He did not continue.) When people complained that the puns he was obliged by his scenario to use were trivial he made the famous retort, "Yes, some of my means are trivial, and some are quadrivial." When they said his puns were childish, he accepted the supposed blame with alacrity. He prided himself on not having grown up. His voice, he said, had never changed in adolscence. "It's because I've not developed. If I had matured, I wouldn't be so committed to the *folie* of writing *Work in Progress*." Keeping the child in the man gave him access to the universe which adults repressed.

In these ways Joyce radicalized literature, so that it would never recover. He reconstructed narrative, both external and internal; he changed our conception of daytime consciousness and of nighttime unconsciousness. He made us reconsider language as the product and prompter of unconscious imaginings. These did not come to him as experiments or as innovations; he did not regard himself as an experimenter. Rather they were solutions to the literary and intellectual problems he set himself.

Yet though his determination to change the way we think about ourselves and others as well as the way we read required the most elaborate methods, Joyce always insisted that his means were one thing, his meaning another. Complication was not in itself a good. "Can you not see the simplicity which is at the back of all my disguises?" he asked his wife before they eloped together. He objected to slavishness and ignobility; he thought they were fostered by conventional notions of heroism, which turned men and women into effigies. He wished them to know themselves as they really were, not as they were taught by church and state to consider themselves to be. He gave dignity to the common life that we all share. As he wrote to his brother, "Anyway my opinion is that if I put down a bucket into my own soul's well, sexual department, I draw up Griffith's and Ibsen's and Skeffington's and Bernard Vaughan's and St. Aloysius' and Shelley's and Renan's water along with my own. And I am going to do that in my novel (inter alia) and plank the bucket down before the shades and substances above mentioned to see how they like it: and if they don't like it I can't help them." Yet he was not impervious to those other qualities people also held in common, moments of exaltation and lyricism as important as they were infrequent.

He made no personal claims. "A man of small virtue, inclined to extravagance and alcoholism" was how he described himself to the psychologist Jung. He disclaimed genius, disclaimed imagination, only asserted that when he was writing his mind was as nearly normal as possible (November 10, 1907). He wished to give his contemporaries, especially his Irish ones, a good look at themselves in his polished looking glass—as he said—but not to destroy them. They must known themselves in order to become freer and more alive. Shear away adhesion to conventions and shibboleths, and what have we left?

More, I think, than Lear's forked animal. We have the language-making and using capacity, we have affections and disaffections, we have also humor, through which we tumble to our likeness to others. That likeness is seen in sad as well as joyful moments. The function of literature, as Joyce and his hero Stephen Dedalus both define it with unaccustomed fervor, is the eternal affirmation of the spirit of man, suffering and rollicking. We can shed what he called "laughtears" as his writings confront us with this spectacle.

The Fiction of James Joyce

Denis Donoghue

In the fourth chapter of Joyce's *Portrait of the Artist as a Young Man,* the young man Stephen Dedalus is walking along the wooden bridge down the Bull Wall. 'He drew forth,' Joyce reports, 'a phrase from his treasure and spoke it softly to himself:

—A day of dappled seaborne clouds.
   The phrase and the day and the scene harmonised in a chord. Words. Was it their colours? He allowed them to glow and fade, hue after hue: sunrise gold, the russet and green of apple orchards, azure of waves, the grey-fringed fleece of clouds. No, it was not their colours: it was the poise and balance of the period itself. Did he then love the rhythmic rise and fall of words better than their associations of legend and colour? Or was it that, being as weak of sight as he was shy of mind, he drew less pleasure from the reflection of the glowing sensible world through the prism of a language many-coloured and richly storied than from the contemplation of an inner world of individual emotions mirrored perfectly in a lucid supple periodic prose?'[1]

The part of his treasure from which Stephen has drawn the phrase—a day of dappled seaborne clouds—is a book by a minor early nineteenth-century American writer, Hugh Miller, called *The Testimony of the Rocks; or, Geology in its Bearings on the Two Theologies, Natural and Revealed;* it was published in 1857. The book is an attempt to reconcile the biblical account of creation with the new arguments from geology. At one point far out in the book, Miller imagines Satan contemplating the divine creation but unable to comprehend it; least of all to comprehend that God has created the universe as a home, Miller says, for 'higher and higher forms of existence'. How must Satan have felt, he says, 'when looking back upon myriads of ages, and when calling up in

From *The Genius of Irish Prose,* ed. Augustine Martin (Dublin and Cork: The Mercier Press, Ltd., 1985), 76–88. Copyright 1984 by Denis Donoghue. Reprinted by permission of Denis Donoghue and The Mercier Press, Ltd.

[1]The best text of Joyce's *Portrait of the Artist as a Young Man* is the Viking Press edition (1964), prepared by Chester G. Anderson, with Richard Ellmann; it is conveniently reprinted in *The Portable James Joyce,* edited by Harry Levin (Penguin, 1976), from which I quote here (p. 428).

memory what once had been, the features of the earth seemed scarce more fixed to his view than the features of the sky in a day of dappled, breeze-borne clouds. . . .'[2]

You'll notice that Stephen has not recalled the phrase quite accurately: 'breeze-borne' has become 'sea-borne'. But no matter. What is more to the point is that the phrase has floated free from its context and lodged in his mind as an independent particle of language, as if it were a phrase in music, which in a sense it is. Stephen is not averse to satanic contemplation, but it is the phrase as such that has occurred to him, not even the sentence in which it has participated.

When Stephen starts questioning himself about his relation to words, he comes upon several possibilities, but mostly to dispose of them. The colours of words: it was a standard speculation, especially in nineteenth-century French poetry and poetics, that syllables might be related to one another as in the relation of colours, shades, and tones; that the syllables of a word might stir into action the several senses, and not merely the mind intent on replacing the word by its meaning. Stephen puts aside the notion, at least for the moment, and he thinks of his preference for the rhythmic rise and fall of words rather than 'their associations of legend and colour'. I have always interpreted that phrase as pointing to the early Yeats, and to his cult of what Ezra Pound called 'the associations that hang near words'. If so, Stephen's preference is an occasion, one of many, on which Joyce distanced himself from a Yeatsian aesthetic which he had to guard himself against, as against an exotic temptation.

The third possibility Stephen considers is the most telling one; that he derives less pleasure from 'the glowing sensible world' reflected in language than from 'an inner world of individual emotions mirrored perfectly in a lucid supple periodic prose'. It is itself a glowing preference, but a curious one. The sensible world glows and is sensible only to a mind interested in seeing it in that character; interested to the point of seeing it 'through the prism of a language many-coloured and richly storied. There is no question of merely seeing the world as in itself, severely, it really is. We are free to think that Stephen, short-sighted or not, sees the glow of the world enough to be afraid of seeing it too keenly; as if he were afraid that the 'inner world' of his purely individual emotions might have to take a secondary place in his sensibility. So he moves from the colours of language, its glows and associations, to whatever quality is enacted in 'a lucid supple periodic prose'.

It sounds as if he means a style chiefly characterised by its syntax, and means to praise the flexibility of its performances; which is very odd, since the phrase which started the whole speculation has no syntax at all and is all poetic diction. But I think Stephen is urging himself to move beyond the rich

[2]Hugh Miller, *The Testimony of the Rocks: or, Geology in its Bearings on the Two Theologies, Natural and Revealed* Boston, 1857, p. 277.

adhering words of a poetic diction—to escape from his lyric prison, to a life of decision and action, much as Yeats had to put behind him the entrancing associations that hang near words before he could write the far more resilient poems of his middle books.

How much Stephen has to urge himself to leave the lyric prison is shown on the next page, his mind still occupied by Miller's phrase, 'Disheartened, he raised his eyes towards the slow-drifting clouds, dappled and seaborne. They were voyaging across the deserts of the sky, a host of nomads on the march, voyaging high over Ireland, westward bound. The Europe they had come from lay out there beyond the Irish Sea, Europe of strange tongues and valleyed and woodbegirt and citadelled and of entrenched and marshalled races.'[3]

That is not a style in which a writer goes forth to do anything. Stephen's diction is drawn from literature, from anthologies of prose style, and diverse translations of Latin, Greek and German texts. But I would make much of his sense of Europe, which extends, a few pages later, into more particular affiliations; references to the plays of Gerhart Hauptmann, Newman's prose, 'the dark humour of Guido Cavalcanti', 'the spirit of Ibsen', and a line of poetry recalled from Ben Jonson.

I have gone into the episode in the *Portrait* mainly to emphasise that to Joyce, as to Stephen, language always seemed to offer itself as a counter-truth to the truth of reality. Of course, among his many senses of language he had a journeyman's sense, too. He was quite willing to treat sentences as useful instruments to disclose a reality not itself linguistic. One of the stories in *Dubliners* begins: 'Mrs Mooney was a butcher's daughter. She was a woman who was quite able to keep things to herself: a determined woman.'[4] These sentences are not as straightforward as they sound. They tell us not necessarily the truth about Mrs Mooney or what God or the world thinks of her, but what she thinks of herself. It is her accent we hear, the precise degree of assertiveness her voice would deliver. But the sentences are still predicated on the assumption that there is a world which language merely negotiates: dappled seaborne clouds would persist even if the English language did not.

Granted. But Joyce was deeply susceptible to the opposite notion, too, that words as such far surpass the character by which they usefully refer to things and help us to administer them. It was Samuel Beckett and not Joyce who wrote: 'Words have been my only loves, not many'. But Joyce might have written it, for the sentiment that finds words purer and richer than anything they merely denote. Some of his styles acknowledge, like Mrs Mooney, a world more or less given; its reality can be manipulated but not, in the end, transformed. But he has other styles which testify not to worlds and realities as given but to another world sustained only by the desire of it. In Joyce's

[3]*The Portable James Joyce*, p. 429.
[4]'The Boarding House' in ibid., p. 71.

early poems and in the *Portrait*, this world that exists only in the desire of it is represented by poetry, or by phrases of it, remembered and fondled. Sometimes the beauty of the phrase depends upon Stephen's removing it from its context, as if from every mere historical condition, as at one point he removes Luigi Galvani's phrase, 'the enchantment of the heart', and lets it dominate his sentences: 'An enchantment of the heart! The night had been enchanted. In a dream or vision he had known the ecstasy of seraphic life. Was it an instant of enchantment only or long hours and days and years and ages?'

If the world is, according to Wittgenstein, 'everything that is the case', then in reading Joyce we have to assume also a second world, everything that is not the case but is so intensely desired that, so far as the imagination of desire is in question, it amounts to its own case. The two worlds are not, indeed, totally separate; they couldn't be. The first world, even in a life like Joyce's of much grief, is likely to give forth a few consolations, appeasing some old wounds. The second world, so far as it takes a linguistic form, has to admit many echoes from the world it otherwise repudiates. But if there are writers who accept the given world to the extent of annotating it and finding their satisfaction in doing little more, Joyce is not one of them. He is intransigent in desiring a world that never was, or that was only in the poetic fragments that would replace it.

But I have to qualify this report, if only to take account of such a scene as the one in *Ulysses,* the second chapter, where Stephen helps the boy Cyril Sargent with his sums: 'Ugly and futile: lean neck and tangled hair and a stain of ink, a snail's bed. Yet someone had loved him, borne him in her arms and in her heart. But for her the race of the world would have trampled him under foot, a squashed boneless snail.'[5] Richard Blackmur, I recall, once quoted that passage, and distinguished between Stephen Dedalus and Leopold Bloom largely on the strength of it, saying that the passage shows Stephen at his most tender. 'He transcends his intransigence, and comes on the conditions of life—which is where Bloom is all the time.' There again we have the two worlds, and only a different vocabulary for them. Leopold Bloom accepts the conditions of his life and wants only to succeed in forgetting their most painful embodiments—his father's suicide, his son's death, fears for his daughter, and at four o'clock the certainty that Molly is taking Blazes Boylan to her bed. Still, Bloom remains in his conditions and makes the middling best of them. But Stephen resents every condition, and would accept life only if it were another life; except for rare lapses into a more general acknowledgement.

The question is: what form does desire take, in this intransigent sense, when it comes into language and disdains the chore of annotation?

I want to come upon an answer to this a little roundabout. Several years

---

[5]*Ulysses*. London; *Ulysses: The Corrected Text*. London & New York: Viking-Penguin, 1986, p. 23; 2–139.

ago the critic Kenneth Burke proposed a certain pattern in the development of a writer. His notion is that most writers start off by writing of themselves and giving every privilege to their own feelings. The ideal form of this phase is the short lyric poem, or the lyrical fiction which is hardly fiction at all. Some writers never escape from this phase. But the major writer escapes at least far enough to acknowledge the existence of other people and to let them live their own lives. Better still if he can imagine other lives, and best of all if these lives are vigorously distinct from his own. If the chronology could be bent a little, we might take Joyce as a case in point. Starting out with early fragile poems, the first version of the *Portrait*, the *Portrait* itself, and the luridly imagined episode that took the form of the play *Exiles*. Then the crucial development in his career would be the diversion of privileged interest from Stephen, the hero of lyrical experience, to Leopold Bloom, who sustains the middling perfection of putting up with things. But *Dubliners* breaks the symmetry of his development, a very early work largely written in 1905 from jottings earlier still. So we have to say that there were at least early stirrings, even in the lyrical or self-expressive phase, of the recognitions that issued fully in *Ulysses*. But the pattern has further to go. It sometimes happens, even in a book which takes communication as its morality, that a writer in the process of imagining lives other than his own will come upon possibilities purely internal to his medium, possibilities which surpass the morality of communication. Some writers may glimpse these possibilities and decide to leave them alone, presumably because they find security in the bond of communication and would not want to be released from it. But there are other writers who, coming upon those possibilities, will insist on exploiting them as if 'to the end of the line'. To those writers, if something is glimpsed as possible, it becomes an aesthetic necessity; it must be done.

You see already how the pattern might be called upon to explain Joyce's development in his later work. In *Ulysses*, for the most part, he accepts the bond of communication. At least in the first half of the book he rarely affronts his readers, or confounds them. But it is clear that as the book proceeded Joyce indeed came upon purely internal possibilities, which offered themselves as a pun might offer itself to someone in a conversation, and in some of the late chapters of the book, tentatively, he explores those possibilities. Several years later he develops them with full panache in *Finnegans Wake*, where he sees a possibility and never looks back.

In *Ulysses* the two worlds I have referred to—we can now call them the world of conditions and the world of desire—are generously projected. Every reader of the book warms to its presentation of the sights, sounds, and smells of Dublin, the noise of its streets, the lore and gossip, both eloquent to the pitch of exorbitance. If you want an example of reality which gives the impression that it hadn't to be imagined at all but only transcribed, think of Paddy Dignam's funeral, and the man in the macintosh who turns up in Glasnevin. Bloom wonders who he is: 'Now who is that lankylooking galoot

over there in the macintosh? Now who is he I'd like to know? Now, I'd give a
trifle to know who he is. Always someone turns up you never dreamt of.'[6]
Bloom counts the mourners at the graveside, and makes the man in the
macintosh number thirteen. The reporter Hynes is listing the mourners, and
after a misunderstanding with Bloom he puts the stranger down as Mr
M'Intosh. And so on. The stranger turns up again, indeed several times, later
in the book; or at least he enters into Bloom's meanderings. So he can readily
stand for the supreme condition of their being life at all, a life that has to be
lived rather than imagined.

Now the world of desire is so pervasive in *Ulysses* that there is no point in
giving an example of it; it is incorrigible. It is there in every daydream, every
swoon of apprehension, every poetic phrase which surpasses whatever it
denotes. It is there whenever an event at large is seen and pondered and
fondled in someone's mind to the point at which it is no longer merely an
external event but has become an internal event of still richer account in that
character. The Marxist critic Fredric Jameson[7] has gone so far as to say that
the fundamental device of *Ulysses* is a technique by which events in an
alienated world are converted into inwardness, where they are reconciled by
the tone in which they are received. Jameson resents the technique, for
obvious reasons. As a Marxist, he wants to change the world of conditions. He
does not want to further the possibility of leaving the world as it is by having
its conditions end up, accepted for the most part, in Bloom's meandering
mind. If everything that crosses Bloom's path can be transposed into himself,
converted into inwardness, there is no urgent reason to change the world. It
is for this reason that a Marxist resents the stratagems of consciousness, the
techniques of inwardness by which a reconciling tone displaces every political
incitement.

The particular possibility Joyce came upon in writing the later chapters of
Ulysses was that of dissolving the barrier between one world and another, a
procedure which might correspond to dissolving the distinction between the
conscious and the unconscious phases of the mind. Language is not responsive
to transitions, states of feeling which melt or merge in one another beyond
rational discrimination. The reason is that words in conventional forms are
separated from one another, and tend to divide states of feeling into particles
which do not correspond to the history of the feeling it denotes. Music was
the most fascinating art to writers in the last years of the nineteenth century
because it is good at transitions. Think of the 'natural history' of feelings as we
hear them in Wagner and Debussy; there are no fractures, no clear demarcation between one feeling and another. The deficiency of words is not the
indeterminacy which is said to afflict them but the abrupt demarcation

6Ibid., p. 9.
7Fredric Jameson, *Fables of Aggression*. Berkeley and Los Angeles: University of California
Press, 1979, p. 57.

between one word and the next, which corresponds to nothing in anyone's experience.

Suppose you wanted to write a book, a kind of dream-play, in which the conscious and unconscious phases of the mind would be blurred beyond rational redemption, in which the conventional distinctions on which we rely would be dissolved—distinctions between past and present, the dead and the living, one person and another, history and myth, animal and human. When Joyce walked through the British Museum and looked at the Assyrian and Egyptian monuments, he felt, as he told Arthur Power, that 'the Assyrians and Egyptians understood better than we do the mystery of animal life, a mystery which Christianity has almost ignored. Since the advent of Christianity', he said, 'we seem to have lost our sense of proportion, for too great stress is laid on man.'[8] Scholars have argued that it was the Egyptian *Book of the Dead* which most inspired Joyce to write a book in which such conventionally useful distinctions would be dissolved. The *Book* tells of the journey of the dead to achieve eternal justification and resurrection in Amenti, the Elysian fields. The deceased assumed the power of the gods, and above all identified himself with Osiris, the type of death and resurrection. Osiris and his sister-wife each played many roles, their personalities constantly dissolving and forming again, as in a dream of being. The material Joyce read in Sir E. A. Wallis Budge's *Gods of the Egyptians*,[9] and several other similar books, gave him the motif of death and resurrection in a tradition far removed from the Christian one, and therefore free of the historical complication in a doctrine too familiar for his purposes.

Finnegans Wake is still a book in English, of a sort. Or rather, the structure of such divisions as it allows, whether we call them sentences or not, is recognisably English. But the words are confounded by taking to themselves diverse linguistic affiliations and echoes from a dozen languages. Some parts of it are more speakable than others, notably the famous section we can still hear in Joyce's recording of it, the scene in which washerwomen gossip as they do their chores on the banks of the Liffey.

But by and large, the book remains a private place for scholars.

That situation may change. *Ulysses* was many years in the world before anyone but a professional student thought of reading it. Now it is widely read, and not merely studied. The history of Radio Telefís Éireann will document as a notable exploit the reading of the entire book, an act sure to gain entry to the *Guinness Book of Records* not only for its length but for its bravado. *Finnegans Wake*, too, may have such a future, though many of its sequences seem to defeat the speaking voice. But I doubt if the *Wake* will ever be

[8]Arthur Power, *Conversations with James Joyce*, edited by Clive Hart. London: Millington, 1974, p. 48.

[9]E. A. Wallis Budge, *The Gods of the Egyptians; or, Studies in Egyptian Mythology.* London: Methuen, 1904.

readable unless we extend our notion of language to accommodate its procedures. Instead of receiving words as tokens of reference and vehicles of a
meaning separable from the words, we would have to think of words as what
the *Wake* once calls them, 'words of silent power', for which the required
authority is not the dictionary but the history of magical practice. And if we
want a motto from the *Wake* itself, there is one on page 570, a reference to
Thoth, the god of speech, magic, and writing, secretary to the gods, and, as
Mark Troy has pointed out, responsible for the writing of the *Book of the
Dead*.[10] So we read on page 570: '. . . Well but remind to think, you were
yestoday Ys Morganas war and that it is always to-morrow in toth's tother's
place. Amen.'[11]

I have mentioned 'words of silent power' for a more available reason. A
well-known episode in the *Portrait of the Artist* has Stephen engaged in a
little struggle of words with the English Dean of Studies in the university, a
struggle on the respective provenance of the words 'funnel' and 'tundish'.
Stephen wins the occasion, for what it is worth, but then he starts thinking of
the English language, and of the Dean's possession of it. He felt, we read:
'with a smart of dejection that the man to whom he was speaking was a
countryman of Ben Jonson.' He thought 'the language in which we are
speaking is his before it is mine. How different are the words *home, Christ,
ale, master,* on his lips and on mine! I cannot speak or write these words
without unrest of spirit. His language, so familiar and so foreign, will always
be for me an acquired speech. I have not made or accepted its words. My
voice holds them at bay. My soul frets in the shadow of his language.'[12]

I have quoted that passage mainly to remark upon the edginess of Joyce's
own relation to the English language. It is not precisely the edginess of those
Irish writers in our own day who feel that they must retain contact, in some
way, with the Irish language, either by writing in it, as several poets do and as
Michael Hartnett has given up writing in English to do; or by translating it, as
Thomas Kinsella, Seamus Heaney, and other poets have done, into an English
mindful of the language it has displaced. I cannot hear in Joyce any such
misgiving. I don't recognise any evidence that he ever wanted to write in Irish
or to pay his tribute to a dispossessed language and its culture. But I think he
needed, as Stephen did, the sentiment of being homeless, at odds with
whatever offered itself to him as his condition.

There are some artists who need restlessness as others need peace: as
Goldsmith said of someone, 'he only frets to keep himself employed'. Joyce
did not say, as Stephen did, 'My soul frets in the shadow of his language', but
Joyce, too, cultivated a fretting if not a fretful relation to the English

[10]Mark L. Troy, *Mummeries of Resurrection.* Uppsala: University of Uppsala Publications,
1976.
[11]*Finnegans Wake.* London: Faber and Faber, 1975, reprint, p. 570.
[12]*The Portable James Joyce,* p. 453.

language, and, I think, because he needed the conditions which could only be met by an exertion of will and power. He needed to refuse the 'mother tongue', as Stephen needed to refuse his mother's death-bed request.

Joyce's exercise of will and power is clear in several aspects of his career. He wrote in an English which he thought of as something to be mastered. He did not think of his work in that language as a work of collaboration with the great writers in the English tradition, or with the values that tradition embodied. F. R. Leavis often maintained that William Blake's genius was most fully manifested in his sense of being an English poet, a poet, that is, engaged in 'a continuous creative collaboration' with and within the English language. There is nothing of such a sentiment in Joyce's relation to English. How could there be, given that he was an Irishman whether he liked that fate or not?

But he also exercised his power nearer home and homelessness. If he had been willing to subdue his pride, he could have aligned himself with the aims of the Irish Literary Revival, a movement, after all, hospitable to the extremely diverse purposes reflected in George Moore, Yeats, Douglas Hyde, Lady Gregory and J. M. Synge. But he was never willing to subdue his pride for such a cause. Indeed, while his work is full of Yeatsian echoes and allusions, he took Yeats as his chief antagonist. There is a current theory of literary history, best recommended by the critic Harold Bloom, that a strong writer turns his strength to account by choosing a great precursor, a major writer different in the kind of his genius and incorrigible in its degree; by choosing him and engaging him in a struggle as if to the death. In that sense, Yeats is Joyce's chosen and fated precursor. Joyce had to swerve from Yeats's way of being a genius, and disown its forms to accomplish his own.

So it was almost inevitable that Joyce would choose not any of the Irish ways of being a genius, but the European way. I have never felt much inclined to lose sleep over Joyce's exile, or the conditions which allegedly drove him from Ireland. The truth is that he was not driven, unless we mean that he was driven by a fretting and chafing sense of any conditions offered him. The collusion of chance and choice made Joyce the kind of artist he became; chance, by making him an Irishman and keeping him in that condition; choice, by which I mean his choosing to become an artist of European scope and grandeur, blood-brother to Dante, Shakespeare, Swift, Flaubert, Pater and Ibsen.

A European, in that sense, is something you choose to become. You cannot be born to it. You are not a European merely by being born in France or Germany. Yeats chose Plato and Plotinus for friends, but the choice was merely opportunistic, not a matter of principle. Joyce's choice of Europe was indeed a matter of principle. I think he wanted to live in such a spirit as to make home whatever he chose to remember, and thereafter to have a chiefly nomadic relation to life. This suggests that he wanted the unsettled conditions from which the artistic detachment which we associate with Flaubert would emerge. But I have been persuaded by William Empson to emphasise rather the example of Ibsen. Empson has argued that Joyce's belief 'that in Ibsen Europe was going ahead with its own large development was what prevented him from being an Irish Nationalist.'[13] There's much to be said for that view, and a good deal of biographical evidence in its favour, starting with Joyce's learning enough Norwegian as a young man to read Ibsen in the original, and publishing a high-flying article in the *Fortnightly Review* in 1900 to praise Ibsen and, I think, to tell the world where his own artistic eyes were turning.

But in any case Joyce gave definitive form, starting with the last pages of the *Portrait*, to the desire which begins in Ireland and defines itself in Europe, seeking not its fortune but its providential form. In his domestic life he spoke more Italian than French, more French than English. *Finnegans Wake* is Irish of necessity, European in its diction, and Egyptian in its major mythology. That should be enough to be going on with, if an art of European scale is in question.

As an Irishman by necessity, Joyce set astir a fiction, as in Flann O'Brien's *At Swim-Two-Birds* and *The Third Policeman*, of comic ingenuity, the words on the page in blatant disproportion to any use they might be turned to. As a European on principle, he set a pattern for the disinterested occupation of space. Its chief exponent since Joyce has been Samuel Beckett, a writer as different from Joyce as he could reasonably be, given so many similarities. But as soon as you start naming names to denote such consequences and consanguinities, there is no end to it.

Meanwhile we proceed. *Finnegans Wake* is clearly the next item, after forty-four years in which most of us have left it well alone. Is it an example of language secreting itself from resources as promiscuous as Europe itself? Or, beneath every surface, is it a story not much different from any other? The most recent suggestion I have seen is Hugh Kenner's, that the book started out from some sense of Erskine Childers' execution in 1922 and became a story about a family in Chapelizod, ending in the dormant mind of the mother, widowed now, the morning after, 'trying not to awaken to awareness that her husband lies beside her no longer'.[14] We could do worse than begin with that end.

---

[13]William Empson, 'The Theme of *Ulysses*' in *The Kenyon Review*, Vol. XVIII, Winter 1956, pp. 26–52.
[14]Hugh Kenner, *A Colder Eye*. New York: Knopf, 1983, pp. 230, 231.

Language of/as Gesture in Joyce

David Hayman

Gesture is the means through and by which we express without saying. According to Julia Kristeva, "Avant et derriére la *voix* et la *graphie* il y a *l'anaphore*: le geste qui *indique*, instaure des *relations* et élimine les entités."[1] If we put aside its role in sign language and emphasize its more universal functions, gesture is both pre- and post-verbal, both silent and spoken, both conscious and subliminal. In the verbal arts it is largely a function of rhythms and attitudes, of relationship, of timing and nuance. A treatment of this question in relation to Joyce, the theorist, and Joyce, the practitioner, divides itself naturally into two competing and interpenetrating halves: an account of the evolution and piecemeal evocation of a preoccupation interlocks with the study of gesture as a theme in and an attribute of his works. The latter study, though it can hardly be more than tentative and fragmentary, should confirm and support the former upon which it "tootoologically" hangs as pendant and pointer.

Joyce's lifelong interest in what may be called a semiotics of the minimal expressive act must date back very far indeed. We may trace it, if not to his early study of etymology or to his interest in Vico and mythography, at least to the Paris epoque during which he finished formulating his aesthetics. From the start gesture (physical, oral, and verbal) was a large topic, associated with the question of rhythm, by which Joyce meant a structural attribute. Thus, he could speak of the "individuating rhythm" of a life in his early essay "A Portrait of the Artist,"[2] or later of a "rhythm of beauty" which induces, maintains, and finally dissolves the ideal "aesthetic stasis." In his more specific statements Joyce went further, attempting to define the art of gesture, or the gestural quality, of a special sort of word, and the means by which gestures are conveyed.

From *"Ulysses: Cinquante ans après,"* ed. Louis Bonnerot (Paris: Didier, 1974), 209–21. Copyright 1974 by Didier. Reprinted by permission of David Hayman and the publisher.

[1]"Le Geste, pratique ou communication?" in Σημειωτιχὴ, *Recherches pour une sémanalyse*, Paris, Seuil, 1969.

[2]R. Scholes and Richard M. Kain, *The Workshop of Daedalus*. Evanston, Ill., Northwestern University Press, 1965, pp. 60–68.

We note four *états* of Joyce's theory, three literary, one biographical, all suggestive enough to give the reader pause. In *Stephen Hero*, Stephen shares with a sceptical Cranly the following thoughts which must be quoted at length if they are to be understood in our context:

> —There should be an art of gesture. . . . Of course I don't mean art of gesture in the sense that the elocution professor understands the word. For him gesture is an emphasis. I mean a rhythm. You know the song 'Come unto these yellow sands'? . . . This is it, said the youth making a graceful anapaestic gesture with each arm. That's the rhythm. . . . Do you believe that one line of verse can immortalize a man?
> —Why not one word?
> —*Sitio* is a classical cry. Try to improve on it.
> —Do you think that Jesus when he hung on the cross appreciated what you call the rhythm of that remark? Do you think Shakespeare when he wrote a song went out into the street to make gestures for the people?
> —It is evident that Jesus was unable to illustrate his remark by a correspondingly magnificent gesture but I do not imagine he uttered it in a matter-of-fact tone. . . . I don't believe [Shakespeare] wanted to go out into the street but I am sure he appreciated his own music. I don't believe that beauty is fortuitous. (*SH* 188)[3]

Here it is language that gestures, both oral language which may be accompanied by gestures, or may by intonation constitute a sort of gesture, and written language which implies and thus embodies gestures. Stephen is not speaking here of the primacy of gesture, of wordless physical gestures or of sounds as gestures, but even these dimensions are available to the reader of *Stephen Hero*. After having explored the roots of linguistic experience and experimented with contemporary language, Stephen

> doubled backwards into the past of humanity and caught glimpses of emergent art as one might have a vision of the plesiosauros emerging from his ocean of slime. He seemed almost to hear the simple cries of fear and joy and wonder which are antecedent to all song, the savage rhythms of men pulling at the oar, to see the rude scrawls and the portable gods of men whose legacy Leonardo and Michelangelo inherit. (*SH* 37–38)

As a view of the gestural basis of art, the citation is consistent with later theories and practice. That is, all art, all expression, has its origins in the primitive need to express simple emotions, in gestures which adhere as hieroglyphs even to the sophisticated work.

In the light of his study of etymology he sees words as repositories of gesture:

> It was not only in Skeat that he found words for his treasure-house, he found them also at haphazard in the shops, on advertisements, in the mouths of the plodding

[3]*Stephen Hero*, edited with an introduction by Theodore Spencer. Revised edition with a foreword by John J. Slocum and Herbert Cahoon, London, Jonathan Cape, 1956.

public. He kept repeating them to himself till they lost all instantaneous meaning for him and became wonderful vocables. (*SH* 36)

This is more than a puerile infatuation with sound. In the manner of Rimbaud, Stephen is seeking, by reducing language to its primitive status, to find a fresh and efficacious medium:

> He sought in his verses to fix the most elusive of his moods and he put his lines together not word by word but letter by letter. He read Blake and Rimbaud on the values of letters and even permuted and combined the five vowels to construct cries for primitive emotions. (*SH* 37)

Unsystematic, yes, ironically presented as well, but surely these citations form a basis for the no less ironically presented but increasingly significant theories to come.

The exchange with Cranly and most but not all of the other relevant materials were omitted from *A Portrait of the Artist as a Young Man* along with the famous epiphany theory. They reappear transmuted (seachanged) in *Ulysses.* Aristotelean gravity gives way to Aristophanean play as we enter Nighttown in "Circe." In what at first seems either a purely symbolic action, a burlesque of priestly behavior, or simply drunken maundering, Stephen chants the paschal *introit*. Indeed, given the context, we may even read his behavior as an aspect of the hallucination. But since the chant is accompanied by both physical and phonic gestures[4] and since Lynch asks, "so that," we are aware that Stephen is in the act of illustrating his theory of gesture. What he has been demonstrating is the gestural aspect of speech itself, or at least of chant, its power to express through intonation and emphasis. What he now shows, though not to Lynch's satisfaction, is the capacity of physical gesture to express a complex idea: "the loaf and jug . . . of Omar" (*U* 1961:433; *U* 1986: 353; 15–117):

> (*Stephen thrusts the ashplant on him and slowly holds out his hands, his head going back till both hands are a span from his breast, down turned in planes intersecting, the fingers about to part, the left being higher.*) (*U* 1961:433; *U* 1986:353; 15–124)

The image is one of drinking and holding, but in itself it is less important than the idea Stephen is illustrating for his whetstone: that "gesture . . . would be a universal language, rendering visible not the lay sense but the first entelechy, the structural rhythm" (*U* 1961:432; *U* 1986:353; 15–105). The structural rhythm is significant quite apart from any "sense" the event may have. Through it we perceive the aesthetic and spiritual sense. "Circe" is devoted to disclosing mental states through the description and enactment of real and

---

4Stephen flourishes the ash-plant, "*with joy,*' and mimes the lamp-shattering while his chant is described by the notations "*Altius aliquantulum*" and "*Triumphaliter*" (*U* 1961:431; *U* 1986:353; 15–99).

imagined gestures. By its hallucinations and its pantomime effects it supports a reading of gesture as a physical phenomenon, but Stephen on the threshhold of Nighttown refers directly to qualities of delivery, and indirectly to language or words as gesture, in short to aspects of the theory revealed in *Stephen Hero*.

It was Mary Colum who first underscored Joyce's keen interest in the work of the Jesuit Abbé Marcel Jousse, whose views concerning the development of language out of gesture and the permanent primacy of gesture, and whose methods curiously parallel Stephen's. Joyce having attended at least one, perhaps several of Jousse's demonstrations, asked Mary Colum to accompany him to a session. To judge by her account, Joyce found in Jousse's approach a genuine echo of his own theory and practice:

> [Jousse] was a noted propounder of a theory that Joyce gave adherence to. . . . "In the beginning was the rhythmic gesture," Joyce often said. . . . [Jousse's] lecture [given] in a small hall . . . took the form of a little play, based on the Gospels. Around the lecturer was a group of girls, who addressed him as "Rabbi Jesus" . . . what was shown was that the word was shaped by the gesture. Joyce was full of the subject and talked to me about the lecture as we went along to the cafe. . . .[5]

The view that language was derived from and still conceals gesture, a view backed up by considerable contemporary speculation, was bound to interest Joyce at a time when he was trying to reconstruct and convey by articulate indirection the total human experience. Ample evidence of that interest is available in the notebooks for *Finnegans Wake*[6] and in the *Wake* itself. Both contain references not only to Jousse but to the Joussian terminology, references which suggest that besides attending the demonstrations Joyce also read Jousse's curious book *Le style oral rhythmique chez les Verbo-moteurs*.[7] In the *Wake* there are at least six references to Jousse and his theory and six related references to terms used by Jousse in his book.[8]

---

[5]Mary and Padraic Colum, *Our Friend James Joyce*. N.Y., Doubleday, 1958, pp. 130–131. Add to this account a comment delivered to me orally some years before the Colums wrote their book. Mrs Colum then quoted Joyce as saying, "If you understand that you know what I am trying to do." (David Hayman, *Joyce et Mallarmé*, vol. I, Paris, Les Lettres Modernes, 1956, pp. 160–161.) Clearly, Joyce was not discovering so much as rediscovering through Jousse the principles reflected in his own work.

[6]Now in the library of the University of Buffalo.

[7]Paris, Gabriel Beauchesne, 1925.

[8]See the lists in James Atherton, *The Books at the Wake* (N.Y.: Viking, 1960), pp. 54, 177, 259; Adaline Glasheen, *A Second Census of Finnegans Wake* (Evanston, Ill.: Northwestern University Press, 1963), and Stephen Heath, "Ambiviolences (2)" in *Tel Quel* 51 (automne 1972), pp. 68-70. The following list of Jousse-related references is the most complete to date. I include it as a measure of Joyce's interest and awareness: FW 36:8–10; FW 56:23; FW 441:24–28; FW 465:12; FW 467:32–468:8. This list by no means exhausts references to gesture. The term *mimographic* is probably from Jousse, referring to the mimetic qualities of primitive hieroglyphics. "Recitandas" suggests Jousse's view on the origins of recitation and his method of demonstration. The whole Dancekerl passage of Chapter III (FW 429:15–468:19) is relevant to linguistics and the theory and practice of gesture. At FW 568:4–10 ("The annamation of evabusies . . . Britus and Gothius shall no more joustle for that sonneplace . . .) the gestural quality of *annamation* (Jousse's word *annonination*) and the Jousse in *joustle* seems clear.

Of even more direct interest are certain passages which allude to or describe in some detail patterns of gesture. The earliest version of "The Mime of Mick, Nick and the Maggies" (chapter II) contains a bit of heliotropical naughtiness reminiscent of the jug and loaf gesture in *Ulysses*: "Clap your lingua to your pallet, drop your jowl with a jolt, tambourine until your breath slides, pet a pout and it's out."[9] In this pantomime context the production of sound becomes a hieroglyphic for the word (heliotrope). By contrast, the print-oriented "studies" chapter (II,ii), contains a whole mimodrama in a context relating to the study of language which includes a reference to I. A. Richard's *The Meaning of Meaning*:

> O june of eves the jenniest, thou who fleeest flicklesome the fond fervid frondeur to thickly thyself attach with thine efteased ensuer, ondrawer of our *unconscionable*, flickerflapper fore our unterdrugged. . . . Mimosa *Multimimetica*, the *maymeaminning of maimoomeining!* . . . Whence followeup with *endspeaking nots for yestures*. . . . Belisha beacon, *beckon* bright! . . . *Where flash becomes word and silents selfloud.* (FW 266–267)

The italicized words speak (or gesture) for themselves and the passage with its multiplication of visual and audible effects constitutes a demonstration of Joyce's use of gesturing language as well as a statement about language as kinesis and gesture as basic expression.

Putting this evidence together, we can begin to see where Joyce's speculation took him. His interest in gesture derived naturally from a desire to discover the sources of expression. If his original impulse was descriptive, he gradually rethought the problem and turned to the question of how gesture can be translated into words and how words approximate gesture (see his intense and continuing interest in etymology). Perhaps by *A Portrait*, certainly by *Ulysses*, and most emphatically in *Finnegans Wake*, he began to make words serve as gestures, mining language for its expressive potential. The prime question by the time we reach the *Wake* is "how do words *act*." Jousse, Richards and perhaps Saussure may have helped him clarify his ideas on language in its two natures (synchronic and diachronic) and thus on language as a figure both for mankind's stability and for historical change.

At the same time that he was rarefying and broadening his view of the gestural quality of language (of language *as* rather than *of* gesture) and putting his ideas into practice throughout *Ulysses* and *Finnegans Wake*, Joyce maintained his interest in the physical gesture, in gesture as an art (in mime and pantomime), and in dance (and chant) as primal gesture. Certain aspects of this interest are best illustrated by the descriptive vignettes he called epiphanies, verbal snapshots dating from the period when he was framing his aesthetic theories. The essence of the social epiphanies is a capacity to convey

---

[9] David Hayman, ed., *A First-Draft Version of Finnegans Wake*, Austin; University of Texas Press, 1963, p. 138. *Finnegans Wake*, p. 248.

directly a complex of revealing motions. Here for example is part of epiphany 21:

> Two mourners push on through the crowd. The girl, one hand catching the woman's skirt, runs in advance. . . . The girl, her mouth distorted, looks up at the woman to see if it is time to cry; the woman, settling a flat bonnet, hurries on towards the mortuary chapel.[10]

We note that this is a dumb show with strong dramatic overtones. The whole existence of these people is in the sparse gestures of the girl and her mother. The power of the description is in the quality of language as well, in expressions like "push on through," in the clear diction, the unqualified nouns, the active verbs and participles, all contributing to a mimesis of action, of mindless haste and a false show of emotion. Joyce reworked this moment for inclusion in *Ulysses* (page 101; 6–518), where the perception is Bloom's, as he did the following account of a race meeting used in "Nestor" and "Circe" (*U* 1961:32, 572, 573; *U* 1986:27, 467; 2–309; 17–3964) and perhaps in *A Portrait* (*P* 137–138), where the reflection is Stephen's:

> The human crowd swarms in the enclosure, moving through the slush. A fat woman passes, her dress lifted boldly, her face nozzling in an orange. . . . Bookies are bawling out names and prices; one of them screams with the voice of a child— "Bonny Boy!" "Bonny Boy!" . . . Human creatures are swarming in the enclosure, moving backwards and forwards through the thick ooze. Some ask if the race is going on; they are answered "Yes" and "No". . . .[11]

Quite apart from the speaking gestures of the bold woman, we sense that this account condenses gestural qualities of a festival which might belong to any time and virtually any place. Gestures of grotesque surplus derive from the disjunct catalogue and from words like "swarms" applied to a "human crowd" or the vaguely animal and infernal evocation of "creatures . . . swarming in the enclosure, moving . . . through the thick ooze." Then too there is the evocation of pointless but baffled activity: see "swarming in the enclosure," "moving backwards and forwards," and the repetition of the initial image. Joyce is not so much describing an event as reenacting it through a combination of sounds, rhythms and attitudes. The eerie quality results partly from the significant omission of facts that would orient us in relation to a speaker-observer and a location, partly from the quality of language which minimizes coherence, while creating a universe of signs. We note that this crowd scene, painted in its particularity, is the inverse of the scene at the cemetery, which isolates one couple to convey character. Here it is atmosphere that counts, in the manner of photo-montage, atmosphere conveyed through the evocation of significant detail in motion.

[10]Scholes and Kain, *op. cit.*, p. 31.
[11]*Ibid.*, p. 42. *A Portrait of the Artist as a Young Man*, edited by Chester G. Anderson, N.Y., Viking, 1968.

As for the pantomime, we may point first to the gestural component of the "Cyclops" chapter with its play of shifting-conflicting scenes and voices, its profusion of the sort of detail which, without moving, conveys movement (see the catalogue of trees, the congeries of notables at the execution). Quite apart from these extravagant effects, the expressive jargon of the dun conveys with startling directness a rich vocabulary of gestures, physical and rhetorical:

> That's an almanac picture for you. Mark for a softnosed bullet. Old lardyface standing up to the business end of a gun. Gob, he'd adorn a sweepingbrush, so he would, if he only had a nurse's apron on him. And then he collapses all of a sudden, twisting around all the opposite, as limp as a wet rag. (*U* 1961: 333; *U* 1986: 273; 12–1476)

With the aid of his visual imagination, pointed up by his racy language, the speaker first presents Bloom through two brutal caricatures: as soft soldier and as transvestite, both conceived in the broadest pantomime tradition. Then, with remarkable felicity, he uses three parallel images to convey Bloom's sudden movement of despair. It seems paradoxical that this highly original voice speaks largely in clichés and that commonplaces of pub talk function for the reader as counterfeit gestures. But then we tend to forget that at base the cliché or formula is a social convention on the order of (and accepted as) gesture. We may add that the verbal ornamentation, the exclamations and dialectical interjections, serves a similar function in relation to the action of telling: speech as performance. It is to a degree the total context that refreshes this talk, vitalizes it so that, as readers of *Ulysses*, we perceive and experience the gestural component which would be lost on listeners accustomed to pub rhetoric. But what is striking for the informed reader is the way Joyce manages, while avoiding Laforgue's trick of twisting the cliché, to "make it new," how he conveys the uncommon expressive value of the commonplace.[12] Unnecessary on the level of description, since it repeats the first clause, the tired simile: "limp as a wet rag" functions superficially as reenforcement, for emphasis. But, coming as it does after a string of obvious but more dramatic and less blatantly metaphorical clichés, it acquires startling freshness. What should be anticlimatic is in fact vivid, serving as a natural and effective climax for the action.[13]

[12]By way of contrast we may point to the proliferation of tired language and false elegance (another form of cliché) in "Eumaeus," where language functions as a prolonged and complex gesture of avoidance.

[13]More light is thrown on Joyce's sense of the gestural component of the cliché by his practice first in his notes and then in the text of *Finnegans Wake*. These notes abound in commonplaces which are either slightly twisted in the manner of Laforgue or simply susceptible to interesting literal readings. In the *Wake*, where we are accustomed to the expression which explodes into a variety of contradictory readings, clichés like "I could eat you up," the parent-ogre's expression of endearment, assume their emotive force as a gesture of ritual-real love-hate: "We could ate you, par Buccas, and imbabe through you, reassuranced in the wild lac of gotliness." (*FW*, 378/2-4) Of course the cliché is only one of many devices capable of activating words, of *returning* them to gesture. Take the word plague as it is used in the following evocation of pleasure in pain: "The playgue will soon be over, rats!" (378/20).

On a very different level, Joyce frequently associates gesture with the dance as a primitive form of expressive language. In both the "Dave the Dancekerl" passage from III,ii of *Finnegans Wake* (which contains most of the Jousse allusions) and "Circe," he verbalizes the rhythmic or systematic gesture, describing and imitating it through sounds or syntax. Significantly, the notes for "Circe" are rich in dance images and references, in catalogues of gestures, and in shorthand accounts of gestural codes (see fanplay). There is also one reference to the "art of gestures."[14] In the following passage we experience the effects of a wild drunken dizzying dance both on the observer and on the dancer:

> Stephen with hat ashplant frogsplits in middle highkicks with skykicking mouth shut hand clasp part under thigh, with clang tinkle boomhammer tallyho hornblower blue green yellow flashes. Toft's cumbersome turns with hobbyhorse riders from gilded snakes dangled, bowels fandango leaping spurn soil foot and fall again. (*U* 1961: 578; *U* 1986:472; 15–4123)

This passage combines three sorts of material: description of physical gestures in relation to decor, rhetorical evocation of that gesture as sensation, and metaphorical (hallucinated) projection of action. The actual physical dance with its splits and kicks, its hand-under-thigh gesture, the turn, leap and fall mingles with the associative movement which includes the detail of the hunt riding across the wallpaper while the piano clangs and tinkles. Graphically, the splits and kicks and other bifurcating actions are present in double words like "frogsplits," "highkicks" and "skykicking," which set sharp cutting syllables against soft ones. The disjunct arrangement of words and sounds makes enunciation of the lines difficult, an action in itself, altering pacing to conform with the events. Beyond this are the onomatopoeia, assonances, and alliteration.

Consistent with Joyce's method, this chapter is at once the funniest and the most serious. It is also the most overtly mimetic in that it not only describes but recreates "real" actions which mingle with enactments of suppressed impulses (the unconscious life of Bloom and Stephen) within a babel of dramatic contexts. Thus, for example, Stephen's mad joy prefigures his insane vision of the rotting mother whom he has failed to abandon. In the description of the dance, while inverting the tame jug-and-loaf gesture executed for Lynch earlier in the chapter, Joyce's creative persona has made Stephen's point for him: he has "rendered visible not the lay sense but the first entelechy, the structural rhythm" of Stephen's experience. That is, he has disclosed directly, without having recourse to significance, the basic shape of a moment. To accomplish this Joyce has been obliged to wrench language out of shape prefiguring his practice in the *Wake*. The passage illustrates an extreme

---

[14]See Philip F. Herring, ed., *Joyce's Ulysses Notesheets in the British Museum*, University of Virginia Press, Charlottesville, 1972, pp. 288, 299 and *passim*.

form of expression, perhaps too extreme to show how subtle Joyce's anaphoric use of language in *Ulysses* can be.

To conclude this tentative study, therefore, we will reverse our field, choosing an example from the morning rather than the night of the book, from calm rather than frenzy. "Telemachus" opens upon an outdoor stage set and a dramatic action, though without the benefit of a *dramatis personae* or scenic indications. As usual in Joyce's fiction, we must find our way about a scene, adjust to the conventions which constitute so important a part of the action.

> Stately, plump Buck Mulligan came from the stairhead, bearing a bowl of lather on which a mirror and a razor lay crossed. A yellow dressinggown, ungirdled, was sustained gently behind him by the mild morning air. He held the bowl aloft and intoned:
>
> —*Introibo ad altare Dei.*
>
> Halted, he peered down the dark winding stairs and called out coarsely.
>
> —Come up, Kinch. Come up, you fearful jesuit.
>
> Solemnly he came forward and mounted the round gunrest. He faced about and blessed gravely thrice the tower, the surrounding country and the awaking mountains. Then, catching sight of Stephen Dedalus, he bent towards him and made rapid crosses in the air, gurgling in his throat and shaking his head. Stephen Dedalus, displeased and sleepy, leaned his arms on the top of the staircase and looked coldly at the shaking gurgling face that blessed him, equine in its length, and at the light untonsured hair, grained and hued like pale oak. (*U* 1961:3; *U* 1986:1; 1–16)

This is an extraordinary opening. Like the persona it projects, it is a marvel of whimsy, characterized by incessant shifts in tone and attitude. Like the book, it manifests from the start attitudes spanning the extremes of irreverence and awe, captivating the reader with movements of which he is hardly aware or, if aware, he can hardly control. Rather than say that Mulligan is a patch-harlequin, Joyce uses mumming language to project the figure of joyous (if disturbing) disruption, a figure at base depressingly conventional.

How then does Joyce's language *move* in the half-figurative, half-literal sense alluded to above? Or better how does it indicate attitudes; how does it translate action? Take, for example, the opening phrase: "Stately, plump Buck Mulligan came from the stairhead. . . ." The processional quality, the quality of motion one associates with the priest at a mass, is *in* the metrical emphasis of "Stately, plump Buck . . . came from the stairhead." Even the verb "came," which is only minimally descriptive of the action, contributes to this aspect of the total effect. But the statement encloses its own ironic counterstatement. The words "plump Buck" do double duty, contributing to an anti-processional motion focussed by the name Mulligan. By contrast with the long vowel sounds in "Stately," "came" and "stair," the short vowel in these three words convey a light, almost a jigging, motion. Mulligan's stateliness is belied by his plumpness and by his goatish roisterer's nickname and, yes, even by the "tripping" "dactyl" in "Mulligan." The word "plump" with its overtones of jollity and pleasantness carries with it lump-dump-clump. Through such words our Buck makes a little skip on his way to the mock altar, a gunrest.[15] How different the impact would be were we to read "Portly" for "Stately." By adding an alliteration without altering either meaning or meter, this substitution eliminates the dual perspective: grave-mockery or clowning solemnity.

The second sentence, continuing the processional movement and raising the rhetorical level, metrically echoes the first. Here too, there is a play of contraries.' The gurgling g's in "dressinggown, ungirdled" are in phonic opposition to the soft sounds and gentle lilt of what follows, especially of "mild morning air," an expression suggestive of Joyce's own lyrics in *Chamber Music*. Like the "bowl of lather" with its prosaic cargo, the "dressinggown" seems an ironic object for such airy treatment, such floating language. There is a further play of tone against content in "Halted, he peered down the dark winding stairs and called out coarsely." The discrepancy is both between the tonality of "peered down the dark" and "called out coarsely" and between the two acts themselves which contrast with the intoning of the Mass. We may also point to the adverbial development "Stately . . . gently . . . coarsely . . . Solemnly . . . gravely" which characterizes the somber side of Buck's deportment and aura. Significantly, a final adverb, "coldly" refers to Stephen's attitude (vs Mulligan's mask).

The examples can be multiplied of language acting and modifying action through its graphic, phonic and syntactic qualities as much as its semantic ones. But perhaps one last instance will suffice to show how Joyce reinforces his descriptive prose with effects perceived subliminally by the reader. The key word in the second sentence of our final paragraph is "thrice," suggestive in this context of ritual behavior. In the second and third sentences Joyce enacts thriceness twice over and even conveys the specificity of gestures. We may compare first the openings:

"He faced about/and blessed gravely . . ."
"Then, catching sight of Stephen Dedalus,/he bent towards him. . . ."

Here the two pairs of actions serve as preludes to the triple act. In the second sentence the double blends with the triple act. Still, it is the metronomic rhythm of what follows, consistent with the suggested redundancy, that enacts gesture, or rather reproduces gestural effects, increasingly broadly conceived as mocking counterfeits of serious behavior:

". . . thrice the tower, the surrounding country and the awaking mountains."
". . . made rapid crosses in the air, gurgling in his throat and shaking his head."
". . . leaned his arms on the top of the staircase and looked coldly at the shaking

---

[15]We may note in passing certain touches predictive of the black mass in "Circe" where "*Father Malachi O'Flynn, in a lace petticoat and reversed chasuble, his two left feet back to the front, celebrates camp mass.*" (*U* 1961:599; *U* 1986:489; 15–4693).

gurgling face that blessed him, equine in its length, and at the light untonsured hair, grained and hued like pale oak."

Each succeeding sentence further elaborates on the triune gesture, expanding its range and clouding its import. If the first sentence gives us three objects, two of which are qualified by adjectives of motion, the second gives us three distinct gestures of which the second and third (the up and down motion, conveyed by "gurgling in his throat," and the sideward motion of the head) reproduce the cross. The last sentence introduces Stephen as interference, slows the action, which has been clownishly frenzied in the central sentence, to convey the rhythm of reaction. Together, these sentences mime not only threeness, but also the behavior of Buck and the encounter of Buck and Stephen, with their contrasting moods and natures, the rhythms of their identities.

It is always best to be cautious when applying Joyce to Joyce. The various references and utterances do not after all constitute a clear and unambiguous statement about the role of gesture in written language. Rather, they leave us to puzzle out precisely how Joyce hoped to *activate* his prose and they move us to a closer inspection of the nonsignifying aspects of his prose and toward a theory of gesture in literature. If we can't prove that Joyce meant precisely this when he enunciated his theory, giving it thematic consequence in his works, the emphasis of delivery in *Stephen Hero,* the illustration or delivery in the Latin passage in "Circe" and the Joussian emphasis (a reaffirmation rather than a new departure) in *Finnegans Wake,* combine to justify our search for possible applications.[16] At the very least we may conclude that, led by the internal necessities of his self-imposed discipline and by a fascination with the origins and native power of words, Joyce accentuated the Pointing functions inherent in all language.

[16]To this we might add Joyce's interest in I. A. Richards, in Jacques Dalcroze, and Ernest Fenellosa, to say nothing of other theorists of language and gesture. On the subject of Fenellosa and Joyce see my remarks in "Tristram and Isolde in *Finnegans Wake:* a Study of the Sources and Evolution of a Theme," *Comparative Literature Studies,* I (1964), 93–112. See also Stephen Heath, *op. cit.*

Joyce's Misconducting Universe

Fritz Senn

Mistakes are everywhere and errors abound. Things have a way of going wrong. This is shown by Joyce and it happens *to* him. In almost any thumb-nail biography, or encyclopedia entry, chances are that some facts are misrepresented: Joyce is turned into a student of medicine, or married off in 1904, or made blind. Or remember the title of his last work as it generally finds its way into print, *Finnegan*-apostrophe-*s Wake*. The centenary is a great opportunity for new journalistic fumbles as the calendar seems to provoke erudite utter-ances. For many reasons then, errors seem to cluster around Joyce, more than other writers. It is annoying, and it is wholly appropriate.

The eighth International Symposium provides an instructive example. A transformation of a whole chapter of *Ulysses* into an unusual but relevant medium was staged—into a city walk within Dublin's labyrinthine surface. The chapter was naturally the one called, at Joyce's instigation and by critical near-consensus, "Wandering Rocks." It deals with 19 smallish sections at different places, its main feature, locomotion and juxtaposition and the inter-locking of various actions, offers itself for acting out and for visualization. The fictional characters, impersonated by actors (including some Joyce scholars with a newly found vocation) were walking the streets at the respective spots, according to the itineraries mapped out in the book and a time schedule worked out by Clive Hart—who fittingly initiated the performance as Father Conmee, S. J., from the presbytery steps in upper Gardiner Street, at five to three p.m.

Such a collective ambulatory-staging of one whole chapter (disconcertingly accompanied by a reading of the text as heard through transistor radios, the spoken text of course never matching the scene) made evident to its spectators some platitudes that we had become accustomed to. One is that reading a story can give us the impression of being where in actual fact we could never be, in different places simultaneously. The city reenactment demonstrated that no single observer was able to witness more than a small part of the entire procedures, whereas a reader moves effortlessly from one location to the next, almost imperceptibly and, oddly enough, without surprise. By

From *International Perspectives on James Joyce*, ed., Gottlieb Gaiser (Troy, N.Y.: Whitson Publishing Co., 1986), 161–71. Copyright 1986 by Gottlieb Gaiser. Reprinted by permission of Fritz Senn, Gottlieb Gaiser, and Whitston Publishing Company.

putting oneself into one section, one automatically excluded all the others, except those taking part in the vicinity. The mere necessity to choose one place of observation made it clear that linear language in what is called "story," or "tale," or even "narrative," can streamline spatial variety into one comfortable sequence that we take for granted. Which taught us the irony that a chapter that is also an extreme of surface realism poignantly falsifies its realities and tricks us into a multipresence impossible to experience in real life.

There were other displacements. The *Ulysses* characters were dressed up in colourful period costumes to make them distinct from the crowds of onlookers and the ordinary Dubliners who were, somewhat irreverently, using their city as though it were not the scene of a chapter in a fiction. This naturally amounted to a reversal of the novel's reality, for its characters, with a few well-marked exceptions, are rather drab and inconspicuous, in fact precisely not to be distinguished from the fellow-citizens, except of course through the author's singular attention to them. The medium, in other words, aiming for visibility, imposed its own rules which in turn warped the realism that the whole event was intended to document. And since the centre of Dublin 1982 is a more congested place than it was in 1904, the various characters could not proceed at their prescribed pace (the viceregal cavalcade even had to reroute itself completely to comply to traffic regulations) or were actually impeded by clusters of spectators. Leopold Bloom, remarkable in the book for being chiefly neglected and overlooked, drew the largest crowd, which occulted him most of the time—another paradox of congenial reenactment. And, inevitably, some pivotal meeting points were missed, which simply shows that urban navigation, logistics, surface interlinkings—major concerns of the chapter—are irreproducible.

My own chosen site was Crampton Court (in ruinous condition), from where Lenehan and M'Coy take their departure turning first south, then east, then north, then west and finally north again (section 9); this would bring me to Wellington quay and, ultimately, close to the Ormond Hotel in time for the final confluence. But the timing went wrong and the two characters arrived too late at Merchant's Arch to find Bloom inspecting the books. He had already left, and so there would have been no reason for Lenehan to boast of a minor adventure with Molly, or to comment on a "touch of the artist about old Bloom" (*U* 1961:235; *U* 1986:193; 10–582). So the book's tight cross-referential network was being minutely disrupted.

Moreover, the actor playing Lenehan did not, as the script demanded, pop into a bookmaker's shop (one good reason being that it no longer exists) to enquire about the betting odds of the Ascot Gold Cup race which is being run at, more or less, this moment in distant England and which seemed to involve practically every Dubliner of 1904. Not much of an oversight this, perhaps, but just the sort of thing a pedantic Joycean comma-hunter (in 1982) would pick out to cavil at.

Well, perhaps it is not just pedantry, for in his pursuit of betting information Lenehan in *Ulysses* is told that Bloom (who ought to be hovering nearby) has given out a tip on the rank outsider that will actually win the race. This is based, as we know, on a misunderstanding, but Lenehan will pass on the rumour and help create an envious notion that the sly stingy jew has won a sizeable amount of money and will not even stand a drink. The rumour is believed and will result in much verbal, and some physical, assault and co-determine much of the action of the "Cyclops" chapter. In other words, because of a wholly minor omission the whole subsequent mechanistic chain of events is disrupted. A later clashing scene would become pointless. The plot has been derailed. Causal links have been severed, the clockwork has become defective. If Lenehan was not misinformed, the rest of *Ulysses* would have become a different book.

Because of trivia like that, large later portions would be affected. Intertexture is in disarray, this in a chapter that highlights mechanistic causality and is designed like clockwork ("Very large and wonderful and keeps famous time," *U* 1961:242; *U* 1986:199; 10–828), or like a military campaign, with map and compasses. Did then the whole experiment—to turn a whole episode into concrete, mobile, interlocking actions—fail? It didn't, because derailment, deviation, dislocation, omissions, chance delays and collisions, accidents—failure itself—are part and parcel of the chapter's intrinsic malfunction. The points being missed add up to the point the chapter is trying to make, among others: places and times are out of joint. The centenary reincarnation of a Dublin miniature was out of gear, and this perversely proved it true. Joyce presents an erroneous universe on a local scale. It works, but never quite as expected or wanted. There are spanners in the works, the machinery is warped, and in bad repair.

Joyce found alternative ways of reminding us that the Universe itself resembles its Dublin microcosmos. As Genesis tells us, it got off on a bad start soon after its seventh day. Our ancestors did what they ought not to have done, they fell, and some remedial plans had to be substituted. Joyce, whose prose began with the mischance in a priest's life, put original sin which necessitated the divine undoing of that initial damage, into one of the energetic non-centres of *Finnegans Wake*. A *felix culpa* varies from a parochial transgression in a park, "O foenix culprit," to "felicitous culpability." It may become a psychologically "freudful mistake" or a "fatal slip," even a "foetal sleep," with other translations like an apparently Chinese "Fu Li's gulpa" thrown in. The felicitous original misconduct suffuses Christian faith and keeps the *Wake* shapes fumbling. So Lenehan's double failure to hit upon a non-truth is also exemplarily apt in a flawed cosmos.

Joyce's early terms for an imperfect world tended to be medical (or biological), "*paralysis*," or theological, "*simony*"; and they, together with an illustrative cue from geometry, "*gnomon*," have been perpetually used by us as significant levers for multiform human blunders. If things in our lives didn't go wrong, there would be no stories, neither of Father Flynn, nor Odysseus, nor Adam, nor Oedipus, nor HCE. Joyce exemplifies this with a broader than the customary spectrum. At the naturalistic end we have defective objects, a humpy tray, a chipped eggcup, a creaky and soiled funeral carriage, a "onehandled" statue, or a cup "held by nothandle." Bloom's latchkey is disturbingly absent. All of which may also reflect a domestic, and a national, and a cultural situation. The process of thinking itself is naturalistically rendered as chancey, haphazard beyond the reaches of our notions of correctness. In *Ulysses* Joyce had perfected his devices for evoking the imperfections of our mental gropings; they seem to go on very much in analogy to the actions narrated in "Wandering Rocks": a path is pursued, deviated from, interfered with. There are distractions, confusions, misdirections, illusions; hopes, fears, and escape techniques, repressions, odd coincidences. This must also affect language itself, neither words nor syntax remain untampered.

Strange to observe then how some scholarly, superior readers of *Ulysses* condescendingly tend to pass misguided judgments of "correctness." Leopold Bloom, in his private ramblings or instant speeches, does not get things immediately right—as though we ever did! He feels the warmth on his black clothes: "Black conducts, reflects (refracts is it?) the heat" (*U* 1961:57; *U* 1986:46; 4–80). Memories of physics linger, too many. From our leisurely distance we may correct him by recalling that it is light, radiated by the sun, that can be reflected, or refracted, but that heat is conducted, and what Bloom tries to remember is the optical term "absorb"; but the fumble is appropriate since colour, light, and heat all come into play. The scientifically correct term is occluded by similar Latin compounds. Bloom could only be wrong if he offered a conclusive choice in public, or signalled some complacency. Phases of consciousness are not posing as scholarly statements. Bloom has been blamed for erroneously claiming that there are no rhymes in Shakespeare. But not even in the intimacy of his own mind does he ever claim this. He merely modifies his own hasty generalisation that poets write in "similar sounds," typically checking himself: "But then Shakespeare has no rhymes: blank verse" (*U* 1961:152; *U* 1986:125; 8–64). As a cautious qualification this is correct and could be "wrong" only if isolated as a critical statement (and even then it would be acceptable in the sense that "no rhymes" is in fact what Shakespeare "has" in the vast majority of his passages). Joyce devised a defective shorthand for the often random, tentative processes of thinking. Once some of them have to be released into public speech, as it happens to Bloom in his more unguarded moments, they may become factually wrong: "Mercadante . . . was a jew" (*U* 1961:342; *U* 1986:280; 12–1804). And it seems to occur in all forms of communication. In the newspaper account of Dignam's funeral which puts Stephen, C. P. M'Coy and M'Intosh, to say nothing of L. Boom, among the mourners present at Glasnevin cemetery, we may learn what happens in reports. *Finnegans Wake* goes on to treat all events and reports, facts or fictions, history or myth, eyewitness accounts, rumours or legend, as hardly distinguishable. No utterance or document deserves trust any more. Language itself has given up all pretense to conform. What in Bloom's day still looks like a frequent exception has become a natural state of confusion in *Finnegans Wake*.

This might be in tune with the transition from the daylight that still illuminates an important first half of *Ulysses* into a nocturnal or even dream-like opaqueness. Noonday clarity or meaning have given way to a "nooning-less knockturn" (*FW* 64.15); and it is the knocks and turns that meanings take which interest us here. A glutted adverb like "nichthemerically" (*FW* 185.29) tantalizingly flashes suggestions of how either *Ulysses* or the *Wake* itself appears to have been produced. Less by day (as through Greek *hēmera*), than by not-(German *nicht*)-day (and a slight transposition from a Scottish looking "nicht" to "night" reinforces the nocturnal reading defectively). Or we may choose to approximate the whole conglomerate to a genuine Greek word for a night and a day, *nychthēmeron*. This is a trifle more than the temporal scope of *Ulysses*, but also a term that St. Paul, a latter-day, converted Odysseus, used to describe his being shipwrecked "a night and a day in the deep" (2 Cor. 11:25). *Ulysses*, depending on one's perspective, is either Homeric(al) or "nicht-Homerical"—if not downright nihilistic (German *Nichts* would fit this view). The heterographic chiaroscuro taunts such significations into spectral being: and by any normative standards it is simple to prove that none of them are present. We tend to shape graphic errors into plausible near-truths. *Ulysses*, in fact all the earlier works, have prepared us for teasing patterns out of textual disorder.

When things go amiss, language cannot remain unaffected according to standards of schoolmasters or proofreaders. Bloom, early on, takes his hat from the peg in the hall and reads its legend: "Plasto's high grade ha" (*U* 1961:56; *U* 1986:46; 4–69). This is primarily an instant of being faithful in recording what is there; the hatband, belying its "high grade" quality, no longer contains the terminal letter "-t," and it is not for the author to interfere and to mend matters. Sherlock Holmes, we may remember, was an ingenious student of objects like hats suffering wear and tear; like him, the reader of *Ulysses* can draw conclusions about its wearer. Bloom's defectively lettered hat keeps surfacing, and the missing *t* may have strange power over our reconstructive minds. Is a "Ba" similarly deficient (occurring three times in short succession, (*U* 1961:377–378; *U* 1986:309; 13–1117), a similarly trun-cated "Bat?" One will soon be flying around Bloom. Or is it some kind of stifled exclamation? Do we determine that by consulting the two "authorized" translations? The French team offers "Ahââh" (*Ulysse*, Paris, Gallimard, 1948); Georg Goyert settled for "Na." (*Ulysses*, Zürich: Rhein Verlag, 1956). The later Italian translation, benefiting from decades of scholarship, decided in favour of "Pip" as a particle of "Pipistrello probabilmente" (*Ulisse*, Milano: Mondadori, 1968, 510; "Bat probably"), and Bloom's high grade "ha" may well have been instrumental to this reading. But not even every "ha" in *Ulysses* need be an imperfect hat. A fourfold "Ha ha ha ha" in the Circe episode does not denote headgear but the derisive amusement of Zoe and Florry as they are watching Bloom watching (in one of the phantasies) Blazes Boylan vis-à-vis Molly (*U* 1961:565; *U* 1986:460; 15–3755). Even so it is intriguing that, just a few lines afterwards, Boylan hangs *his* "hat smartly on a peg of Bloom's antlered head." In the morning, when Bloom returned from the pork butcher's, it had been Boylan's letter (*U* 1961:61; *U* 1986:50; 4–244) that had made him forget what he did with his own de-lettered hat, as he later remembers (*U* 1961:68; *U* 1986:56; 4–486); it is equally odd that it was right after passing "Plasto's" shop, on the way to Glasnevin, that he first caught sight of Boylan (*U* 1961:92; *U* 1986:76; 6–191). Somehow the missing terminal letter seems to make us more aware of potential connections.

As readers in search of pertinence we may align Bloom's incomplete "ha" with his whole situation. Once we become alerted to a letter that is not there, especially when a terminal omission seems to be emphasized by an "*initialed . . .* overcoat" (*U* 1961:56; *U* 1986:46; 4–66), we notice it all the better when it is. "See blank tee what domestic animal?" is a puzzle whose answer rhymes with "hat." In such ways we learn, as readers, to pay attention to blanks, and to "See blank tee" (*U* 1961:283; *U* 1986:233; 11–1025), or to supplement "Tee dash ar." Simon Dedalus takes off—not a hat, but—Larry O'Rourke "to a tee" (*U* 1961:58; *U* 1986:47; 4–115), and one implication seems to be that a small difference may really matter. In another context the same letter may function as a merely opportune stratagem of transatlantic information: "T is viceregal lodge" (*U* 1961:136; *U* 1986:112; 7–661), a somewhat arbitrary assignment.

A letter missing in one place may be matched by one intruding somewhere else: "Do ptake some ptarmigan" (*U* 1961:175; *U* 1986:144; 8–887). This reminds us of the relation between sounds and letters, and the vagaries of English spelling. In Joyce's dystypographical universe we must not be misled by appearances. "See you in tea" (*U* 1961:497; *U* 1986:405; 15–1895) appears to announce a vision and a beverage, but naughtily reveals itself as a suggestive sequence of letters. And what then is to detain us from an analogous semantic faking and playing off Mulligan's making tea with Bloom's missing "t?" Mulligan's impersonation is conspicuous: "When I makes tea I makes tea, as old mother Grogan said. And when I makes water I makes water" (*U* 1961:12; *U* 1986:11; 1–358). Such conflation of liquids, along with its blasphemous escalation in "water . . . That I make when the wine becomes water again" (*U* 1961:19; *U* 1986:16; 1–592), seems to receive involitional clerical sanction by the mere name of "the Rev. T. Waters" present in a list of ecclesiastical dignitaries (*U* 1961:317; *U* 1986:260; 12–929). But Mulligan's quip has nothing whatever to do with Bloom's ha, nor does Mrs. Cahill's retort: "God send you don't make them in the one pot" (*U* 1961:12; *U* 1986:11; 1–362), except that Bloom, "nursing his hat" in a bench of the church of All Hallows, muses: "These pots we have to wear" (*U* 1961:80; *U* 1986:66; 5–355). Later on "teapot" will become a suggestive word in turn—a blank to

be filled—in a parlour game: "I confess I'm teapot with curiosity to find out
whether some person's something is a little teapot at present. . . . I'm simply
teapot all over me" (*U* 1961:445; *U* 1986:364; 15–465). Immediately afterwards
Bloom is wearing "a purple Napoleon hat."

All of which merely goes to say that an omission, an absence, may
reverberate considerably, and a letter that is not there may become very
officious and unsettling. Joyce makes *t*'s tease us into dubious semantification
long before *Finnegans Wake* spells O. U. T. as "oh you tease" (*FW* 461), or
warns us to "tot the ites like you corss the tees" (*FW* 542), when the decencies
of typographical norms are no longer observed. A little *t*—conspicuous,
absent or superfluous—can go a long way, from next to nothing to totality: "T"
may be an abbreviated Latin *totum*, which led to "teetotum": "As we there are
where are we are we there from tomtittot to teetootomtotalitarian. Tea tea too
oo" sets off the scholarly tenth chapter of the *Wake* (*FW* 260), but Molly
Bloom had already thought of Patrick Dignam as a "comical little teetotum" (*U*
1961:774; *U* 1986:636; 18–1281).

Instances of erratic *t*'s have been paraded here as equivalent substitutes for
the much better advertised odyssey of the letter L, which potently turns a
strong word into a cosmic "world" in Martha Clifford's letter or, inversely,
demotes Leopold ("—L, Mr. Bloom said. Leopold," (*U* 1961:111; *U* 1986:92;
6–882)) Bloom to "L. Boom" in irreverent print (*U* 1961:647; *U* 1986:529; 16–
1262). In Hebrew (Stephen's inattentive remark on the onomastic insult
contains "that first epistle to the hebrews," (*U* 1961:648; *U* 1986:529; 16–1268)
"*el*" can mean God ("El, yes," (*U* 1961:71; *U* 1986:58; 5–11)). Disorderly
shapes like "ha" or "Boom," at any rate invigorate or discompose precarious
textures. In the semantic ecology of Joyce's erroneous universe they can be
read as minor losses easily rectified, and multiple gains due to our corrective
urges and our tendency towards systematic completion. Mistakes, errors,
misprints, defacements and the like also behave as tangential new creations.
They generate new meanings or microcosmic sidespins.

By such inadvertence a budding artist named Stephen Dedalus contami-
nated something heard,

> O, the wild rose blossoms
> On the little geen place

into

> O, the geen wothe botheth. (p. 7)

("geen" is what Joyce wrote and meant, precisely noting infantile articulation;
it was the copyists who standardized the adjective to "green," in all editions,
dictionary norms prevailing over the empirical observation that children in
their first phonetic ventures usually have a hard time with the liquids).
Stephen's condensation of the two lines is, pardonably, inept and faulty. It is
also a variant creation. Two separate elements, a wild rose and a green place,

have been faultily amalgamated into something doubly non-existent, lexically and botanically. But a new shape has been offered as well, something that language—or the imagination—can produce much more effortlessly than even nature. A "geen wothe" is a fabrication (a Greek term would have been *poiēsis*) beyond the jurisdiction of biology (that the infantile and Joycean word "geen" chances to be a botanical term as well, also spelled "gean," a wild cherry, looks like the kind of gratuitous philology that we tend to utilize in *Finnegans Wake* when it suits our hermeneutical aims). Treated as a suggestive non-word in need of semantic supplementation, "geen" would be appropriate for *Finnegans Wake*, where in fact it does turn up: "As soon as we sale him geen we gates a sprise" (*FW* 606), yet awaiting plausible clarification.

Similarly "wothe botheth," a mere defect of articulation, consists of non-words, of which at least the second one seems oddly appropriate. For Stephen in his single botched line has indeed "bothed" the two lines of the original, he has similarly conflated two distinct items, the flower itself and its location. We are faced with *both* an erroneous imitation and, perhaps, the signalling of an artefact. We have, in other words, both *less* than reality (a linguistic and conceptual defect), and *more* than it, a reaching out into what we may call symbolic ramification or a provocation of interpretative projection. We can construe the mistakes into a foreshadowing of the artist. The ultimate development of such conflations is *Finnegans Wake*, a work characterized by significant *bothings* throughout, an animated jumble of either linguistic shortcomings or teeming plurabilities.

Our lives, the world we live in or that of the *Wake*, made up of "errears and erroriboose of combarative embottled history" (*FW* 140.32), Dublin of 1904, the Bloom ménage, are all like Home Without Plumtree's Potted Meat— Incomplete. This leaves us with the intriguing, fascinating, and ever frustrated task of completing, straightening, modifying, clarifying, improving, systematizing it, which we inevitably perform in our own idiosyncratic likeness, propelled by our own brand of curiosity and ignorance.

Station Island

Seamus Heaney

Like a convalescent, I took the hand
stretched down from the jetty, sensed again
an alien comfort as I stepped on ground

to find the helping hand still gripping mine,
fish-cold and bony, but whether to guide
or to be guided I could not be certain

for the tall man in step at my side
seemed blind, though he walked straight as a rush
upon his ash plant, his eyes fixed straight ahead.

Then I knew him in the flesh
out there on the tarmac among the cars,
wintered hard and sharp as a blackthorn bush.

His voice eddying with the vowels of all rivers
came back to me, though he did not speak yet,
a voice like a prosecutor's or a singer's,

cunning, narcotic, mimic, definite
as a steel nib's downstroke, quick and clean,
and suddenly he hit a litter basket

with his stick, saying, 'Your obligation
is not discharged by any common rite.
What you must do must be done on your own

so get back in harness. The main thing is to write
for the joy of it. Cultivate a work-lust
that imagines its haven like your hands at night

dreaming the sun in the sunspot of a breast.
You are fasted now, light-headed, dangerous.
Take off from here. And don't be so earnest,

let others wear the sackcloth and the ashes.
Let go, let fly, forget.
You've listened long enough. Now strike your note.'

It was as if I had stepped free into space
alone with nothing that I had not known
already. Raindrops blew in my face

as I came to. 'Old father, mother's son,
there is a moment in Stephen's diary
for April the thirteenth, a revelation

set among my stars—that one entry
has been a sort of password in my ears,
the collect of a new epiphany,

the Feast of the Holy Tundish.' 'Who cares,'
he jeered, 'any more? The English language
belongs to us. You are raking at dead fires,

a waste of time for somebody your age.
That subject people stuff is a cod's game,
infantile, like your peasant pilgrimage.

You lose more of yourself than you redeem
doing the decent thing. Keep at a tangent.
When they make the circle wide, it's time to swim

out on your own and fill the element
with signatures on your own frequency,
echo soundings, searches, probes, allurements,

elver-gleams in the dark of the whole sea.'
The shower broke in a cloudburst, the tarmac
fumed and sizzled. As he moved off quickly

the downpour loosed its screens round his straight walk.

Gender, Discourse, and Culture: *Exiles*

Bonnie Kime Scott

Did you note that worrid expressionism on his megalogue? A full octavium below
me! And did you hear his browrings rattle-making when he was preaching to
himself? And, whoa! do you twig the schamlooking leaf greeping ghastly down his
blousy-frock? Our national umbloom! Areesh! (FW 467:7–11)

James Joyce has been widely praised for re-creating a bourgeois, barely post-
Victorian Dublin world in the words of *Dubliners, A Portrait* and *Ulysses.* As
is appropriate to his original model, Joyce distributes men and women to
largely separate, but occasionally overlapping territories. If we apply the
anthropological feminist model of overlapping circles of male and female sub-
cultures, we find in Joyce a particularly rich recording of the discourse and
experience of all-male culture. We visit the male preserves of boys' schools,
pubs, political committee rooms, a businessmen's retreat, a funeral, the inner
sanctum of a library, a newspaper office, and a medical students' lounge in a
hospital. In sections of the *Dubliners* stories and *A Portrait,* and at the
beginning and end of Leopold Bloom's day in *Ulysses,* men enter a domestic
realm shared with women. But even in many scenes where women are
present, as in the formal dinner scenes of 'The Dead' and *A Portrait,* men
interact mainly with one another or are lost in their own performance and/or
thoughts. Family scenes tend to be presided over by a man. His rhetoric is
appropriate to a position of patriarchal power, even though that power may
already be undermined. Joyce's less known drama, *Exiles,* has a domestic
setting shared by men and women. But, as we shall see, it offers a meaningful
variant from Dublin culture. . . .

The play *Exiles* (published before *Ulysses,* in 1918) sets up a series of
encounters between mature men and women in a domestic setting where
freedom from patriarchal Irish marital norms has at least been attempted. A
nine-year stay on the Continent and Richard's denial of the institution of
marriage have made the Rowans' relationship daringly unconventional by
Dublin standards. *Exiles'* themes of freedom and love are far removed from

From *James Joyce*, Bonnie Kime Scott (Brighton: Harvester Press, and Atlantic Highlands, N.J.:
Humanities Press International Inc., 1987), pp. 46–47, 67–76. Copyright © 1987 by Bonnie Kime
Scott. Reprinted by kind permission of the author and publisher.

the discourse of the pub. . . .* Clearly the play is dominated by a male figure, Richard Rowan, who has male bonds, including the father–son liaison so typical in Joyce. Richard's relationship with Robert clearly resembles Birkin's love of Gerald Crich in D.H. Lawrence's *Women in Love*. Richard has overcome many of the limitations of the immature male protagonist in *Stephen Hero* and *A Portrait*. He achieves more conversation with his wife than Gabriel Conroy manages in 'The Dead'. Mr Duffy, another social non-conformist, had used his relationship with Mrs Sinico to sound off his own ideas, brutally rejecting her on the basis of her single, mild physical initiative in 'A Painful Case'. Her punishment with death fulfils the patriarchal, dys-phoric (as opposed to euphoric) ending of a heroine's text, as defined by Nancy Miller.[1]

Unlike the married woman of *Dubliners*, or Mrs Dedalus or Gerty Mac-Dowell, Bertha Rowan has a variety of positive interactions with characters of both genders. In his supplementary notes to the play, Joyce imagines what Bertha might have become, had she stayed behind as the wife of Robert Hand, Richard's more conventional friend and a successful Dublin journalist: 'Mrs Robert Hand (because he intended to do it decently) ordering carpets in Grafton Street, at Leopardstown races, provided with a seat on the platform at the unveiling of a statue, putting out the lights in the drawing room . . . , kneeling outside a confessional in the jesuit church' (*E* 151). In short she would have shared Annie Chandler's suspected materialism, E.C.'s suspected respectability, and the allegiance to the church of all the wives in *Dubliners* and *A Portrait*. She would have been trapped in the marriage that ends the no longer satisfactory plot of the romance.

Richard's greater maturity and his identity as a husband have a biographical counterpart in Joyce, who had lived with Nora Barnacle for eight years by 1912, the referential date of the play. Joyce felt his shift from Dedalus to Rowan was comparable to a new emphasis in Flaubert, itself a response to economic factors in the audience:

> Since the publication of the lost pages of *Madame Bovary* the centre of sympathy appears to have been esthetically shifted from the lover or fancyman to the husband or cuckold. This displacement is also rendered more stable by the gradual growth of a collective practical realism due to changed economic conditions in the mass of the people who are called to hear and feel a work of art relating to their lives. (*E* 151)

Joyce's responsiveness to the public's sense of their own lives matches the

---

*The reference is to Dublin pub conversation as Joyce presents it in the 12th chapter of *Ulysses* ("Cyclops"). Page references to *Exiles* are given in the parentheses: *Exiles*, "A Play in Three Acts," with the author's own notes and an introduction by Padraic Colum. New York and Harmondsworth: Penguin Books Ltd. Viking Press, 1951, Penguin Books, 1973, 1979.–*Editor's note*.

[1]Nancy K. Miller, *The Heroine's Text* (Columbia University Press, 1980), xi. [*Editor's note*: Miller's book discusses problems of female ambition in the work of women writers.]

gynocritic's response to women's interest in realistic rendering of experience. I find it odd, however, that Charles Bovary and not Mme Bovary should be considered a 'centre of sympathy'. Joyce's obsession with the 'cuckold' in *Ulysses* and *Exiles* still suggests a double standard.[2] Nevertheless, the movement to 'husband or cuckold' defines the male character by his relationship to a woman.

Richard Rowan admits the benefits of his association with Bertha, telling his bachelor friend, Hand, 'Many ideas strike a man who has lived nine years with a woman' (*E* 150). Bertha takes pride in the sense that she has done more for Richard than the Irish, 'What have I done for him? I made him a man. What are they in his life? No more than the dirt under his boots' (*E* 130) Whatever Richard says about having formed Bertha, it is important to realize that, in her own opinion, she has also formed him.

Exiles has an obvious, frequently mentioned debt to Ibsen. It takes up his favoured themes of the artist in his relation to female subjects and the problems of marriage—both of which Joyce had discussed in a review of Ibsen's *When We Dead Awaken* (1900). As in Ibsen, argumentative dialogues present issues openly, and women characters express their dissent. Joyce sets up different combinations in the dialogues between his four major characters, allowing for variation of gender and personality. The fourth character, Beatrice, is the cousin of Robert Hand and considered marrying him as a young woman; yet she has a stronger mental tie to Richard. She resembles Ibsen's intellectual women. Richard and Beatrice have corresponded for eight years and he has made her the subject of his 'sketches'. Beatrice is comparable to the female figure of *Giacomo Joyce*, a student who became the subject of Joyce's own 'sketches', finished in mid-1914, but not published in Joyce's lifetime (*GJ* xvi). The *Exiles* sketches lie outside the work, but it would be interesting to compare Richard's imaging of woman to Stephen's bird girl or Gabriel Conroy's symbolic rendering of Gretta on the stairs in 'The Dead', both questionable renderings suited to male desire and mastery and their silencing of the female.

Richard has been the major force in shaping the terms of his partnership with Bertha, though both Bertha and Robert question those terms, and Bertha seems to have got beyond the control of Richard and even Joyce in some instances. Robert proposes to set rumours afloat to counteract public disapproval of Richard's unwed exile. He does this, as Richard charges, 'for the sake of social conventions'. Robert adds, 'for the sake of . . . our friendship . . . also for the sake of—your present partner in life' (*E* 46). Robert is well aware of Richard's battle against conventions, including marriage. They had hoped that the house of revelry they formerly shared (the setting for Robert's seduction of Bertha in Act II), would become also 'the hearth of a new life'. But Robert has worried from the start about Bertha's place in

[2]Richard Brown discusses the vogue for works on adultery in *James Joyce and Sexuality*, 16–22.

Richard's life. He cautioned against her going abroad with Richard and still questions Richard's fairness and Bertha's freedom of choice. Richard responds, 'I played for her against all that you say or can say; and I won' (*E* 47). The response makes Bertha seem like the stakes at a male game or a prize quested by the brave hero. Nora Barnacle followed Joyce to the Continent on similar terms. Shortly before their elopement, Joyce wrote Nora, 'The fact that you can choose to stand beside me in this way in my hazardous life fills me with great pride and joy' (*L* II 53). But, speaking to Beatrice, Bertha (perhaps merely echoing social opinion) claims less value: 'He is able to do something. Me, no. I am nothing.' Beatrice consoles, 'You stand by his side', to which Bertha responds, 'Ah, nonsense, Miss Justice! I am only a thing he got entangled with . . .' (*E* 130).

Robert would construct a more solid, traditional social base for Bertha, and he worships her with flowers and talk of the moon, a romantic sentimentalism Richard discards, but that Joyce was capable of with women. Robert is in fact wooing Bertha and justifies himself with the modern code of 'free love'. In its favour, free love allows no double standard. Robert's 'Almighty' intended free love: 'You were made to give yourselves to many, freely. I wrote that law with My fingers on your hearts' (*E* 81). The dialogue which follows can be compared to discussions on purity that Stephen has with his feminist friend McCann in *Stephen Hero*. Like Stephen Dedalus, Richard finds problems with a single standard for both genders. He balks at the idea that women should give themselves to many and freely. Robert reinforces the notion: 'A woman, too, has the right to try with many men until she finds love', and he speaks of ' a woman who seemed to me to be doing that'. Richard would prefer not to have heard of this sort of woman and sits with head on hands when Robert reveals that he had known the woman's husband intimately. This information confirms Richard's expectation of betrayal by male friends, an expectation shared by Stephen in both *A Portrait* and *Ulysses*. . . .

Richard attempts to define his own code for Bertha. He states that 'I tried to give her a new life', but fears 'I have killed her', meaning the 'virginity of her soul' (*E* 84). This concept, and its effect on Bertha, is elaborated in Joyce's notes:

> The soul like the body may have a virginity. For the woman to yield it or for the man to take it is the act of love. Love (understood as the desire of good for another) is in fact so unnatural a phenomenon that it can scarcely repeat itself, the soul being unable to become virgin again and not having energy enough to cast itself out again into the ocean of another's soul. It is the repressed consciousness of this inability and lack of spiritual energy which explains Bertha's mental paralysis. (*E* 148)

There are many problems with this theo-psycho-philosophical explanation, some of them occasioned by the difficulty of adapting Aquinas' theories of soul and body to real, modern situations. 'Soul' had traditionally been assigned female gender in church writings. Bertha's soul has an added feature, a female's investment in love. Joyce also uses parenthetically the same general definition of love that reappears in *Ulysses* 'The desire of good for another'.[3] Bertha's 'act of love' as female outflow reverses the physical flow of heterosexual lovemaking, but suggests an economy Joyce continues to associate with the female, on through his evocation of ALP as outflowing river in *Finnegans Wake*. In Bertha's case, the female soul is an exhaustible, one-time force—a limitation with useful implications for the male. It suits his ego to have had this extraordinary gift, and it offers some security from her betrayal with another man. The paradigm also suggests a spiritual basis for the double standard, the female simply lacking the energy of soul for female free love, as envisioned by Robert. Joyce's later sense of female libidinal economy would be less limited and exclusive.

Richard suggests, furthermore, that the female needs contact with the male both to think and feel. He challenges Robert (who has wanted, more 'brutally', to 'possess' Bertha) with a more constructive aim: 'Have you the luminous certitude that yours is the brain in contact with which she must think and understand and that yours is the body in contact with which her body must feel?' (*E* 80). Implicitly, Robert agrees that Richard has been an essential contact for Bertha, that Richard has re-created her. Richard also claims to have expressed Beatrice's soul for her in his writing (*E* 19). Neither man admits to any need for female contact in order to think and feel. Richard's power to infuse himself into others, to re-create them, complicates the situation of love relationships. Robert may use Bertha as a means of loving Richard (the Richard in Bertha). Beatrice seems to have loved the reflection of Richard in Robert, a quality that faded after Richard's departure to the Continent. Richard's plan for re-creating Bertha now seems to demand the giving up of a second form of virginity, her fidelity. The notes say, 'To understand the chastity of her nature' Bertha must 'lose it in adultery' (*E* 153). Richard's motivations are more selfish, as the notes straightforwardly proclaim: 'Richard must not appear as a champion of woman's rights. . . . He is in fact fighting for his own hand, for his own emotional dignity and liberation in which Bertha, no less and no more than Beatrice or any other woman is coinvolved' (*E* 154).

Bertha seems well equipped to challenge Richard's plans and paradigms involving her. Whatever the notes say about paralysis (*E* 148), she emanates more energy than Richard, especially by the end of the play. Exhaustion is more directly associated with intellect than gender, since Beatrice shares Richard's fatigue in her chronic illness. Bertha works with an explanation of love as a process of giving and taking that is comparable to Richard's, but with significant differences. Perhaps her most interesting discovery (or charge) is that love exists between Richard and Beatrice. We may suspect Richard of a

---

[3]The 1984 edition restores Stephen's thoughts in Latin along these lines to the 'Scylla and Charybdis' episode: 'Love, yes. Word known to all men. *Amor vero aliquid alicui bonum vult unde et ea quae concupiscimus.*' He is summarizing Aquinas' *Summa contra Gentiles.*

high degree of interest in Beatrice at the start of the play, when he knows exactly how many days she has been away (*E* 16). Bertha feels that Richard's letters to Beatrice are his 'giving' of love. She also realizes that Beatrice falls into a different category of woman from herself. Beatrice is more capable of 'understanding' Richard than Bertha or Robert. Intellect, we might infer, is the quality offered in conjunction and exchange by Beatrice. But Bertha is also wary:

> You have given that woman very much, Dick. And she may be worthy of it. And she may understand it all, too. I know she is that kind. . . . But I believe you will get very little from her in return—or from any of her clan. . . . Because she is not generous and they are not generous. (*E* 68–69)

Bertha requires giving and generosity of both genders in a love relationship, making her concept of love more egalitarian than Richard's. She may overstate Richard's generosity to Beatrice. For one thing, his letters started only after a year of separation, a period of considerable suffering for Beatrice. Bertha is alienated from Beatrice by class considerations, Beatrice's 'clan', the respectable middle class, whose love was more sold than given. Beatrice's Protestantism may also be connected with giving and taking, the Protestants possessing the established church and controlling much of the commerce of Ireland. *Exiles* makes a more definite point of their 'gloom, seriousness, righteousness' (*E* 33). It is interesting that Richard refuses to 'take' Bertha's ideas on these matters (*E* 67). Bertha's 'soul' is fine for taking, but not her mind.

Although Richard's relationships are central in *Exiles*, Bertha provides a sense of female relationships and female community. Speaking of Beatrice to Richard she says, 'I feel for her more than you can because I am a woman' (*E* 68). In Act III, after first accusing Beatrice of sharing in public disapproval of her, Bertha asks Beatrice for her friendship. She reveals that she had long thought about her and always wanted to speak to her in this way (*E* 132). She also discloses to her the suffering she has endured for Richard, 'I gave up everything for him, religion, family, my own peace' (*E* 129). She finds beauty in Beatrice's long lashes and the sad expression of her eyes, turning her remark toward empathy for Beatrice's own suffering (*E* 130). Bertha, in turn, receives comfort from Brigid, the family servant. This older woman reassures her of Richard's regard, 'Sure he thinks the sun shines out of your face ma'am.' As a lower-class woman, Brigid is more accessible to Bertha, and has been similarly empathetic to Richard in the past. He had told Brigid, not his own mother, of his love: 'I can see him sitting on the kitchen table, swinging his legs and spinning out of him yards of talk about you and him and Ireland' (*E* 116).

Richard's mother offers an interesting case in gender definition. Brigid feels a certain triumph over her, disclosing another female division partially attributable to class. Mrs Rowan's hardness partakes of stereotypical maleness, while Richard's father was soft-hearted and he remembers him much more fondly. Both Beatrice and Bertha are concerned about Richard's poor relationship with his mother. Bertha accuses him of never having loved her (*E* 64). Beatrice does not like the way he describes her having 'died alone, not having forgiven me, fortified by the rites of the holy church'. (*E* 23) That the church, and not he, should have given her fortification troubles Richard. The notes to *Exiles* suggest that Beatrice's mind has comparable church associations: It is 'an abandoned cold temple . . . where now a doddering priest offers alone and hopelessly prayers to the Most High' (*E* 153). Here Joyce discloses his own distrust of woman's relationship to a hopeless institution (Protestantism being even more deprived of meaning for him than Catholicism). Beatrice perhaps suspects Richard of projecting his sense of his mother's attitudes upon her.

One of the worst effects of the partnership Richard has established with Bertha is its effect on her ability to relate to others, including males. She fears that Beatrice hates her (*E* 126). She worries that her detailed disclosures to Richard may turn Robert from her. Robert does accuse her of ruining the men's friendship with her revelations (*E* 97). Richard's leniency with their son Archie worries Bertha too. In comparison, she may seem hard-hearted, as Richard's mother had seemed to him (*E* 64–65). She summarizes these feelings to Richard, 'You try to turn everyone against me. All is to be for you. I am to appear false and cruel to everyone except you.' Richard realizes this statement takes 'courage' and says so 'violently' (*E* 65).

One phase of female experience and community gets into the notes, but not the body of *Exiles*. These notes prepare the way for Molly Bloom's reminiscences in *Ulysses*, and are based partially on the evidence of Joyce's mother's keepsakes, and largely upon Nora's girlhood in Galway. The notes offer a series of word associations to explore repressed memories of girlhood that are rich in female relationships. 'The blister reminds her of the burning of her hand as a girl. She sees her own amber hair and her mother's silver hair. This silver is the crown of age but also the stigma of care and grief which she and her lover have laid upon it' (*E* 153). Another series of associations 'holly and ivy, currant cake, lemonade' take her back to her grandmother's Christmas fare for her', and her dark friend, Emily Lyons, who had gone away, and for whom her grandmother consoles her (*E* 155). In this 'homesickness and regret for dead girlish days' (*E* 155), 'a faint glimmer of lesbianism irradiates this mind' (*E* 156). The relationships of girlish days are all female, descending from grandmother to mother to friend, and women are left with a sense of loss. By offering Beatrice tea in Act I and a kiss in Act III, Bertha revives these associations.

Exiles is a confusing play because of its effort to sort out themes of freedom and the creation of character where men and women are co-involved. Its love quadrangle might be compared to H.D.'s novel, *Bid Me to Live*, which explores a similar structure of relationships, but from a female centre. Richard suffers in part from his own contorted theories. In the end, after resisting his theories, but involving herself in them as well, Bertha sets about re-creating Richard. He has wounded his soul for her, he says, and is tired. She has the last word, a coda form Joyce would use again with Molly in *Ulysses* and ALP in *Finnegans Wake*. Bertha calls for selfless, mutual giving. 'Forget me, Dick. Forget me and love me again as you did the first time. I want my lover. To meet him, to go to him, to give myself to him. You, Dick. O my strange wild lover, come back to me again!' (*E* 147). Bertha is not merely nostalgic. That was the trait of Mrs Kernan of the *Dubliners* story, 'Grace', who recalls the surface delights of her wedding. . . . Bertha's recollections apply to a larger life principle. She would have Richard return to youth and wildness, as well as love.

Disappointingly, the other relationships recede for Bertha and Richard at the end of *Exiles*. Lost are the involvements with Beatrice, the intellectual woman, and Robert, the establishment man, who in a less exclusive arrangement might have transformed and facilitated transformation. There is a conservative reassertion of heterosexual monogamy, a theme also present at the end of *Ulysses*, which places both works in the tradition of the patriarchal, two-suitor narrative, where conventional morality demands the woman's choice. But desire has been redefined as selfless, and enunciated both in Richard's intellectual tones and Bertha's simple lyrical call. Richard has learned to doubt. The principle of 'incertitude' replacing authority moves Joyce toward new territory, narrative patterns and language that are more dependent upon the female and the unconscious, a direction we will pursue in his later writing, and with feminist strategies more attuned to the unconscious.

Dubliners: The Trials of Adolescence

Phillip F. Herring

Gnomon and the Rhetoric of Absence

Joyce's seemingly contradictory strategy of producing both ambiguous texts and the keys to interpreting them may have the effect of keeping professors busy, one of his stated purposes, but it also reveals a genuine skepticism about our ability to get at the truth except in fragments, to understand finally and completely the impressions that our senses bring us, to analyze and interpret experience with a high degree of certainty, and to express ourselves unambiguously in eel-slippery language.

In Joyce's earliest work, however, skepticism was often a less prominent concern than politics, for in *Dubliners* he wrote with great bitterness and in considerable fear a political indictment of his city using a hidden rhetoric of absence. Out of this strategy grew his uncertainty principle, but it was surely no coincidence that it flourished only when he felt safe enough to condemn directly the sources of oppression.

Joyce's rhetoric of absence made its initial appearance on the first page of *Dubliners*, where we find the three words in italics generally accepted as key words for interpretation. (Most critics have said that they are keys to the first story alone; I say they are relevant to the entire collection.) While *paralysis*, the first key word, has been widely discussed, *gnomon*, the second one, has remained murky. The *OED* tells us that it is both a parallelogram with a smaller parallelogram missing in one corner and the pillar of a sundial, which tells time by casting part of a circle into shadow.[1] One should give more

From *Joyce's Uncertainty Principle*, Phillip F. Herring (Princeton: Princeton University Press, 1987), pp. 3–17, 18, 203–7 incl. Copyright © 1987 by Princeton University Press. Reprinted by permission of Phillip Herring and Princeton University Press.

[1]See Euclid, in his *Elements* (Book II, Definition 2), on *gnomon*, and Thomas E. Connolly ("Joyce's 'The Sisters,' ":*College English* 27 [1965] 195), on the edition of Euclid that Joyce probably used. The most authoritative article on *gnomon*, and one to which I am indebted for several ideas, is by Gerhard Friedrich, "The Gnomonic Clue to James Joyce's *Dubliners*." He says that " 'paralysis' means literally a loosening or weakening at the side. . . . Parallelograms that are non-rectangular may be thought of as loosened at the side; and the Euclidean gnomon has moreover the appearance of an impaired, cutaway parallelogram . . ." ("The Gnomic Clue to Joyce's *Dubliners*," *Modern Language Notes* 72 [1957], 422). See also David Fabian, "Joyce's 'The Sisters': Gnomon, Gnomic, Gnome," *Studies in Short Fiction* 5 (1968), 187–89; Robert Adams Day, "Joyce's Gnomons, Lenehan, and the Persistence of an Image," *Novel* 14 (1980), 5–19; and B. L. Reid, "Gnomon and Order in Joyce's *Portrait*," *Sewanee Review* 94 (1984), 397–420. All

credence to Euclidian usage, since in the story the boy's understanding is probably restricted to that, but Joyce surely knew that in both definitions the missing part is what is important, either as a space that defines a geometric shape or as a shadow that indicates the time of day. *Gnomon* signaled his creation of absences that readers must make speak if they are to gain insight into character, structure, and narrative technique. In Greek, γνώμων means "judge" or "interpreter," which might provide a fanciful etymological link between the reader as interpreter in *Dubliners* and that which is to be discovered—significant but suppressed meaning. The richness of *gnomon* is precisely its vagueness.[2]

"Gnomonic" language may contain ellipses, hiatuses in meaning, significant silences, empty and ritualistic dialogue. We note the continual emphasis on emptiness, incompletion, solitude, loneliness, shadow, darkness, and failure, which so affect the lives of Joyce's Dubliners and allow subtle expression of his political views.

Joyce must have been well instructed in the dictionary meanings of *gnomon*, because the concept is relevant to most of the major concerns of *Dubliners*. It suggests that certain kinds of absence are typical of the whole of Dublin life at a significant *time* in its history. (Here the sundial meaning of the word is applicable.) In effect, a *gnomon* may be a key synecdoche of absence, part of a political rhetoric of silence within a larger framework of language. In general, it indicates how selective examples such as the characters of *Dubliners* define life in their city, how shades illuminate presences, even how abnormality can define the normal.

The third key word in the opening paragraph of "The Sisters" is *simony*, the buying and selling of ecclesiastical preferment. If *paralysis* describes the moral and physical condition of Dubliners, given their need for freedom, transcendence, and fulfillment, and *gnomon* reemphasizes these absences at a particular time in history, then *simony* points to corruption in high places and illegitimate ecclesiastical authority as the primary obstacles to people's fulfillment. The first two terms describe the condition, telling readers how to arrive at meanings deeper than the textual surface, while the word *simony* places the blame squarely where Joyce thought it belonged—on institutions and their representatives who barter sacred rights. Ambition, energy, free will, revolutionary zeal—these forces play no role and could not, Joyce thought, in a city and country where centuries of political and religious oppression had caused a general paralysis of mind and will. Transcendence came only through death or emigration.

John Fowles recently said in an interview that "academic critics seem often to me to be blind to a negative side of the novel: what it does not say, what is

references to Joyce's *Dubliners* (*D*) and *A Portrait of the Artist as a Young Man* (*P*) are to the Viking Critical Editions.

[2]For a discussion of the ideological implications of a text's silences or gaps, see Pierre Macherey's *A Theory of Literary Production*. See also Thomas F. Staley, "A Beginning: Signification, Story and Discourse in Joyce's 'The Sisters,' " in *Critical Essays on James Joyce*, ed. Bernard Benstock (Boston: G. K. Hall, 1985), 176–90.

left out.""[3] A major exception is Hugh Kenner, who has become well known in Joycean circles for his gnomonic perspectives in revealing important textual lacunae, which have sparked both wide interest and controversy.[4] His article "The Rhetoric of Silence" is the pioneering work in this area, and it has given me my chapter subtitle, but my emphasis is on absence rather than silence, and in *Dubliners* at least, politics as often as puzzles.

Bernard Benstock called Kenner "the man in the gap" ("The Kenner Conundrum": *JJQ* 13 [1976] 434) for, as Milton's angel Gabriel might have said, "busying his thoughts with matters hid," but Benstock also said that Kenner's

> speculations are important since they open up investigation into the missing sections of *Ulysses* and attempt to account for the events which must have taken place during the hours in which Joyce does not allow us to witness the progress of his characters. This exercise in gnomonic criticism focuses on the shadows conveniently overlooked by many readers of the novel, and regardless of Kenner's success as a detective of the unsubstantial, his efforts force attention about the neglected pockets of darkness. (ibid., 428)

Benstock points to three examples of gnomonic criticism in Kenner's work: (1) In *The Pound Era,* Kenner discusses a vital bit of information, not present in the story "Eveline," about the boat from the North Wall. Presumably Eveline freezes at dockside because she has been promised that the ship would take her and Frank to Buenos Aires, but she now sees that ships from the North Wall dock sail to Liverpool. I disagree with Kenner's interpretation, but the discovery of a vital missing detail, upon which any convincing interpretation of a story would depend, is a good example of gnomonic criticism. (2) Late in *Ulysses* Stephen complains of an injured hand, but there is scant evidence as to how this injury occurred. In his chapter on "Circe" in the Hart-Hayman book, Kenner recreates for us a missing scene at the end of "Oxen," where Stephen strikes Buck Mulligan at the Westland Row Station. (3) In "Molly's Masterstroke," Kenner sees importance in the fact that the furniture at 7 Eccles Street has been rearranged in Bloom's absence, causing him to bump his head (*U* 1961:690; *U* 1986:579; 17–1275). My view would be that the Greek generals returning from the Trojan War were often startled to find their homes rearranged; Bloom, an Odysseus figure, comes into contact with tangible evidence of this. Kenner imagines a scene in which Molly has Boylan rearrange the furniture in order to tire him out and thus guard her virtue. In any event, Kenner's attempts to recreate missing scenes on the basis of scattered evidence are gnomonic exercises that Joyce would have applauded.

Even Leopold Bloom plays a gnomonic game when at the end of "Nausi-

---

3In "An Interview with John Fowles," *Modern Fiction Studies* 31 (1985): 189.
4See Kenner, "Molly's Masterstroke," *JJQ* 10 (1972); and "The Rhetoric of Silence" *JJQ* 14 (1977); see also Wellington, Frederick V., "A Missing Conversation in *Ulysses.*" *JJQ* 14 (1977), 476–79.

caa" he writes with a stick in the sand "I.AM.A.," thus insuring future speculation about both his message and his identity as he sees it (*U* 1961:381; *U* 1986:312; 13:1258–64). The difficulty, of course, comes in knowing which "pockets of darkness" will yield up secrets and which will not, for along with the invitation to probe into absence we have abundant evidence of Joyce's love for trickery. It is finally he who manipulates Bloom's stick, beckoning us to look closer.

Why Joyce should wish to employ subterfuge in *Dubliners* rather than targeting his enemies directly as he did in later works is obvious when one contemplates what actually happened to the collection of stories. Irish publishers such as Grant Richards and George Roberts, with whom Joyce negotiated about publication, anticipated censorship and demanded changes in the text; Roberts's printer John Falconer eventually destroyed the proofsheets. All had good reason to fear litigation that could have landed them in prison. Joyce's broadside "Gas from a Burner" (*CW* 243) was written out of a deep indignation at his treatment by Irish publishers.

Cheryl Herr mentions the heavy-handed intervention of Church and State[5] in matters of publishing and clearly demonstrates by reference to "Aeolus" Joyce's "idea that art should not only circumvent the censor wherever possible but also eschew altogether the end-oriented rhetoric of politics even when the end sought is the alleviation of ideological oppression" (142 n.5). Such cunning Stephen Dedalus would vow to practice; *"per vias rectas"* was the motto of the reactionary Garrett Deasy of "Nestor," but Joyce knew from the beginning that straight ways were dangerous. In 1915 Joyce's bitterness over censorship would equal D. H. Lawrence's at the suppression of *The Rainbow*. The key words on the first page of *Dubliners* reveal Joyce's concern with, maybe even his prediction of, censorship and persecution.

As Dubliners seek to fly by nets erected to keep them down, one of the chief benefits of an uncertainty principle emerges: stories may achieve greater depth and complexity and yet seem simple enough to have broad, popular appeal. (They are hence invaluable for teaching close reading to students.) Adopting a gnomonic perspective helps us to see more clearly the nature of Joyce's embittered social commentary, the interplay of presence and absence from the viewpoint of a subversive artist with a social conscience. Readers alerted to the implications of the three key words from the first, "trained" to read the stories skeptically, could feel more deeply the political impact they contain. In theory the author then need not fear censorship because libelous thoughts are in the reader's mind, not in the text. *Gnomon* therefore has the effect of enlisting a reader as co-creator in the production of meanings that are in harmony with the author's political concerns. Joyce thus evoked the odor of corruption that hangs over his stories, pointed the finger at the forces of

[5]Cheryl Herr, "Irish Censorship and 'The Pleasure of The Text': The 'Aeolus' Episode of Joyce's *Ulysses*." In *Irish Renaissance Annual III*, ed. Dennis Jackson (Newark: University of Delaware Press, 1982), 141–79.

oppression, and hoped to evade the consequences.[6] "Heard melodies are sweet, but those unheard / Are sweeter," not to mention safer to sing.

About a third of my book [from which this reading is excerpted] concerns *Dubliners* because readers associate Joycean experimentalism with the later works, but seldom if ever see that the uncertainty principle that generated much of the obscurity was in his work from the beginning. Still, such an approach is not without problems. While gnomonic structures often have political implications in *Dubliners*, or at least foster skepticism, some stories obviously fit the pattern better than others. We begin with a story about uncertainty in interpretation from a boy's more mature perspective in later years, and end with the mystery surrounding Gabriel Conroy's fading identity, but in between the three key words were not always uppermost in Joyce's mind. (Of course there is no reason why he should have felt bound by consistency.) But the general neglect of *Dubliners* in theoretical matters of broader scope has prompted me to say something about all the stories, and to argue that gnomonic absence in its early form often has moral and political implications, as when what is missing is some vital human quality such as love or compassion or empathy, emotions consistently absent in *Dubliners*. In some stories absence has little to do with mystery or uncertainty, but everything to do with privation. If this strategy is a weak link in my conceptual chain, then at the least it provides two useful correctives: it emphasizes the radical politics of Joyce's youth, and it saves us from yet another series of discrete interpretations.

Structure and Meaning in "The Sisters"

On numerous occasions Joyce provided guideposts to interpretation (see Herring, *Joyce's Notes* 121–23), but it has not been generally accepted that "The Sisters" itself functions in that capacity. Still, the story is clearly about ambiguity, about the impossibility of reaching certainty. The reader encounters several barriers to understanding: the text is full of elliptical language filtered through the consciousness of a bewildered youth who broods over the deceased father Flynn and the meaning of their friendship. Readers are easily deceived into thinking that the boy is merely naive, and that greater maturity would be an advantage to him in wrestling with the holes in meaning, an illusion that should be dispelled at the story's end when we are denied access to the boy's final thoughts. His reaction to new and probably decisive information is cloaked in ellipses, while the reader is left to fill in the gaps. Both reader and boy are frustrated by an unsuccessful exercise in gnomonic interpretation.

---

[6]If this was Joyce's assumption, it turned out to be false. His publisher Grant Richards and the printer were to demand excisions of essential pieces that would mar his carefully uncompleted texts; i.e., their gnomonic strategy wasn't Joyce's.

The opening lines of the early version of the story, published in *The Irish Homestead* in 1904 (*D* 243) illustrate that the uncertainty principle was already present (italics mine):

> Three nights in succession I had found myself in Great Britain Street at that hour, as if by *providence*. Three nights I had raised my eyes to that lighted square of window and *speculated*. *I seemed to understand* that it would occur at night. But in spite of the providence which had led my feet and in spite of the reverent curiosity of my eyes *I had discovered nothing*.

This theme of uncertainty was reinforced in the story's final version with the addition of our three key words. Here the boy's interpretative difficulty, first attributed to fickle providence and human frailties, is now located in language itself: "Every night as I gazed up at the window I said softly to myself the word *paralysis*. It had always sounded strangely in my ears, like the word *gnomon* in the Euclid and the word *simony* in the Catechism" (*D* 9).

No logic binds these three italicized words together—only the strangeness of their sounds in the boy's ear. To him the meanings are private ones, perhaps only loosely connected, if at all, to dictionary definitions. The words seem to cast a spell over him and, at the same time, to point to many interpretative possibilities about which the sensitive reader may speculate. Father Flynn was a paralytic; what do *gnomon* and *simony* have to do with him? Can these terms be applied to anyone or anything else? Yet the reader, like the boy, is impelled to seek a truth he can never find: the three words provide no illumination, but neither are they meaningless. This is the dilemma of following the lead of the author-critic-tease who provides keys to understanding an ambiguous text. We shall see how it is possible to use one term—*gnomon*—as an instrument of interpretation within this curious epistemological framework.

Let us take a closer look at the key words. The narrator of *A Portrait* says of young Stephen Dedalus, "Words which he did not understand he said over and over to himself till he had learned them by heart: and through them he had glimpses of the real world about him" (*AP* 62). The comprehension of key concepts is also the primary means of orientation for the boy in "The Sisters," who, with the reader, may see that the magical word that has preoccupied him—*paralysis*—describes considerably more than Father Flynn's physical debility. In the final story of *Dubliners*, "The Dead," the word "dead"—that final paralysis—may refer not only to those faithful departed, but to their survivors; in this first story *paralysis* is applicable both to the priest (it has become his *rigor mortis*) and to those who mourn him, perhaps even his young friend in his interpretative dilemma, or even the reader. Upon reflection we are meant to see that it is epidemic in Ireland's capital (*D* 269; Joyce, *Letters* 1:55, 2:134).

Like most of Joyce's work, "The Sisters" is about transcendence, in this case how a young boy wishes to elude the authority of elders, who unwittingly inhibit the youth's spiritual and intellectual growth, who are instructive only as negative examples. His impatience indicates that his uncle and Mr. Cotter are antagonists, a class eventually to be joined by the sisters of Father Flynn and perhaps the priest himself. More than age, what distinguishes the boy from the others is a condition of mind: the boy knows he knows little and seeks to arrive at understanding through inquiry, while the others think they know and obviously do not, long ago having given up the search for meaning. He is open to learning and experience, they are not. A condition of mind such as the elders have could be called *paralysis*, though, ironically, the boy will approach no nearer the truth than they. Still, his struggle to interpret is more noble than their acquiescence.

Upon reflection, a reader might first be struck with the gnomonic nature of the story's language: it is elliptical, evasive, sometimes mysterious. A mystery is there to be uncovered, but boy and reader will be frustrated by language in their attempts to solve it. We do know that it concerns the priest's vocation, his apparently forced retirement due to the effects of paralysis (however that is defined), and the exact nature of his friendship with the boy, for whom all this is an area of experience cast in perpetual shadow. The boy seems totally dependent on his elders (who won't knowingly cooperate) for information, just as the reader is on the text. Candlelight on a darkened blind (a geometrical form partially cast in light) may tell the boy that the priest is dead, but that will hardly be an issue. Too many pieces are missing from the puzzle for him to see the picture clearly. Even when important pieces are filled in, such as the story's end, neither boy nor reader is party to any epiphany.

Gnomonic language works as follows: if the boy eschews dictionary meanings, unsympathetic characters in "The Sisters" misuse words and fracture sentence structure. Associated with their narrative style is the ellipsis, which presents hiatuses of meaning that can only be filled in by readers or listeners.[7] The tiresome, pipe-puffing Mr. Cotter, speaking of the dead priest, says, "There was something queer . . . there was something uncanny about him. I'll tell you my opinion . . ." (*D* 9-10), thus producing spaces in meaning while he hints at a clerical weakness that he cannot or will not articulate. Even the boy falters at one point when comparing the atmosphere of his mysterious dream to Persia. Like us, he is baffled by these holes in meaning: "I puzzled my head to extract meaning from his [Cotter's] unfinished sentences" (*D* 11). Ellipses frequently signify euphony, especially in the final section, and at the story's end they could theoretically prod the reader toward eventual illumination.

Questing characters in *Dubliners* are frequently assaulted by something I call a "tyranny of triteness," being vacuous language or malapropisms spoken by people who await them at their destinations. In "The Sisters," the boy hears misnomers like "the *Freeman's General*" for "the *Freeman's Journal*,"

---

[7]Ellipses are a prominent feature of the epiphanies collected in Scholes and Kain and in other *Dubliners* stories, where they often function merely as pauses in narration. See also Marilyn French, "Missing Pieces in Joyce's *Dubliners*," *Twentieth Century Literature* 24 (1978), 443–72.

"rheumatic" for "pneumatic" wheels, and ritual dialogue. These signs of defective language are appropriate to the conversation's subject—a defective priest. Father Flynn "was too scrupulous always," Eliza says. "The duties of the priesthood was too much for him. And then his life was, you might say, crossed." (These hollow phrases, pumped so long for meaning by the critics, are meant to evoke laughter in the reader as they must have in Joyce.) Speaking at cross purposes, the aunt says, "He was a disappointed man. You could see that" (D 17).

This exchange occurs as part of a ritual dialogue of condolence that Joyce must have heard at funerals or wakes.[8] It is the gesture that is important, for the ritual words themselves are not really vehicles for direct communication. The dialogue begins (D 15) with the aunt saying "Ah, well, he's gone to a better world." One expects to learn nothing, yet the shocker comes when the sisters deviate from traditional inanity to reveal information about their brother that the priest would have wished left unsaid. This the boy must try to evaluate, but the story's final ellipses prevent readers from gauging his success.

The first sentence of "The Sisters" describes the hopelessness of Father Flynn's physical condition by saying that his time is growing short: "It was the third stroke." Immediately thereafter we are told that the school term is over—"it was vacation time," which here denotes free time within a school calendar and may hint at the story's theme of freedom and bondage. In the night a rectangular window is lighted in the priest's house; if he is dead two candles will illuminate his head, while his feet are cast in relative darkness. If some words or silences are significant, clichés like *"I am not long for this world"* are thought "idle." All this play on light and shadow, presence and absence, is set forth in the first half page of "The Sisters."

As we read along, the word *gnomon* suggests additional possibilities: the boy lacks direction and guidance; he is told to box his corner as if his life had geometric shape; like the story his dream is open-ended; he usually sits in the corner of the priest's room. Father Flynn lacks a whole chalice, an intact vocation, muscular coordination, a confessor to absolve him, an appropriate vehicle in which to revisit the house of his youth. His mourners "gazed at the empty fireplace" in his room (D 15); the fallen chalice "contained nothing." An obsolete meaning of *gnomon* is "nose" (OED), the cavities of which Father Flynn attempts to fill with snuff, though the greater part falls on his vestments. Boy and priest are counterparts as failed clerics, a small corner in the geometric shape of the Church in Ireland, but one of real significance. Like their fellow Dubliners, they are gnomonic in their needs, gnomonic in their representativeness, and their story is gnomonic in that the precise description of their problems, and the remedies thereof, are left to the reader.

---

[8]On the decorum of wake visits, see pages 379–80 of the very thorough article by Florence Walzl, "Joyce's 'The Sisters': A Development," *JJQ* 10 (1973); 375–421.

Simony reinforces *gnomon* and *paralysis* as a thematic key for understanding the story's central problem—what the boy and priest meant to each other. The term may be a broad paintbrush for church walls in Ireland, but it also works on the individual level. Father Flynn's own indoctrination program could in part have had personal gain as its motive; having cracked a chalice and lost a vocation, whatever guilt he might suffer could possibly be expiated by providing a clerical replacement. Spiritually, says Thomas E. Connolly, Father Flynn "has become a 'remainder after something else is removed,' a gnomon" (Connolly, " 'The Sisters' "): 195). If, in addition, he is "not all there" mentally as well as physically incapable of coordination, this defective priest who is, after all, defined in terms of vocation, might from impure motives be capable of seeking a replacement for himself. The boy's preoccupation with *simony* might indicate an awareness that this trap has been evaded, but he too suffers from a kind of gnomonic vacancy in terms of vocation and experience.

The boy's dream of the priest trying to confess to him may be the beginning of the boy's awareness of impropriety. To hear the priest's confession is to accept the priestly vocation. Though this happens in a dream, he is aware of coercion and feels his "soul receding into some pleasant and vicious region" (*D* 11), where, unwanted, the priest follows. We cannot know whether or not the priest has committed the sin of simony, but his young friend is definitely suspicious that he has been coerced by an old teacher who at the least has charged a tuition in snuff.

Perhaps not fully aware of these conditions, the boy in "The Sisters" is nevertheless sufficiently repulsed by his world to seek spiritual guidance from an old priest whose physical debility would frighten most children. He has the disconcerting habit, for instance, of uncovering "big discoloured teeth" when he smiles, and draping his tongue over his lower lip (*D* 13). Though by no means homosexual or sado-masochistic, as some critics have suggested, their relationship has become symbiotic: the boy seeks escape and guidance through admission to a new and different world. A Persia of strange customs being unattainable except in dreams, he explores the mysteries, rituals, sacred lore of the Church. The priest, who no longer officially represents the Church in Ireland (critics have mostly said otherwise), takes a disciple as the main reason for his existence and a reliable source of snuff. Fellow Dubliners are convinced that he is defective both mentally and physically, but what life and mind he has left are dedicated to instructing a neophyte. (An early draft reads, "His life was so methodical and uneventful. I think he said more to me than to anyone else" [*D* 247]). Aware of this bond, the boy imagines his "heavy gray face, following him in a dream, desiring to confess something. What secrets he learns, if any, are appropriately unrevealed. Like the story, the dream is gnomonic, or open-ended. The central point, however, is the boy's awareness that he was meant to fill the paralytic's shoes.

The boy's singleminded desire in the story is to understand what this relationship meant—the death of the priest and the process of clarification representing the end of one kind of quest and the beginning of another that we suspect has something to do with language. Freed from the constraints of the classroom (it is vacation time), he will free himself from the effects of a more sinister form of indoctrination, yet will stay to contemplate this strange disease, to "look upon its deadly work" (*D* 9). He senses a mystery here—why does this paralysis suggest to him "some maleficent and sinful being" (*D* 9)? Do Mr. Cotter and his uncle think *any* tutorial relationship between a boy and a priest unnatural, or do they know something, do their ellipses hide unspoken meaning? Their opposition, plus the sinister dream and the boy's sense of newly won freedom prepare him (us) to interpret the concluding scene, where general awkwardness in verbal expression (a function of paralysis?) and a dominant quality of mind as shabby as the setting prepare for what promises to be a moment of illumination.

The structure of a number of the stories in *Dubliners* requires the protagonists to leave their familiar world on quests that end up shocking them into an awareness that life in their city is far uglier than they ever imagined it to be. In his "scrupulous meanness" (*D* 269) Joyce sends them to one destination to have them arrive at another. Epiphany, or clarification, if and when it comes, arrives suddenly and in the oddest circumstances, in the first three stories resulting in the protagonists' frustration with their previous naiveté and a noticeably more cynical attitude. This is the process of maturation for the boys in *Dubliners*.

"The Sisters" sets the stage for epiphany by the ironic fusion of ecclesiastical ritual and the decorum of wake visits. With the priest dead and coffined, the sisters are now in charge (thus the title), and in their benign ignorance they reveal secrets perhaps hinted at by Mr. Cotter and the uncle.

Understandably, the boy cannot pray. The sisters of the priest of the cracked chalice offer a communion of crackers and sherry, unconsecrated yet unmistakable. Ritual questions lead to revelation—to a new knowledge of Father Flynn's paralysis in both the physical and spiritual sense. Reluctant to traffic in secrets, the boy has tried to escape the priest's dream confession, but he has also sought clarification. Now it will come. In the final section, ritual questions about peaceful death, extreme unction, and resignation are followed by a shocking comment (the first in a series) about a woman brought in to wash the corpse, who comments on its beauty (*D* 15). Unwittingly, Eliza betrays her brother's memory as materialist imagery betrays all hope of transcendence. Her vulgarity offends the boy's sense of delicacy and prepares for what promises to be the final rejection of his defunct vocational model.

If "The Sisters" is seen as a geometric structure, then one part of it will always remain in shadow. Indeed, the elusive title suggests that meaning will be displaced. With an uncertainty principle in evidence, interpretation must thus involve speculation about textual meaning, and what follows is mine: If Father Flynn has sought to bind his novice, he has probably freed him instead; if he has wished to indoctrinate him, it is surely the example of what he became that made the more lasting impression. Whatever transcendence the youth has gained, it involves not religion, but a deeper knowledge of what it is to know. Like the boys in "An Encounter" and "Araby," or Little Chandler in "A Little Cloud," the price he pays for such rude instruction will be a sense of humiliation that will not soon fade. The protagonists in all of these stories have sought light, positive images, and have been taught by negatives, shadows, the incomplete geometric shape instead of the whole one. The last sentence of "The Sisters" described Father Flynn in the confession box; like the coffin that will contain him, it is a rectangular shape, now in shadow, now in light. The door is opened to reveal him laughing to himself, but what precisely causes this laughter, what it means, or what its consequences for his vocation will remain forever in doubt. The story's final ellipses do leave space for our minds to focus on unspoken implications, but the reader must supply the missing pieces for the puzzle to be complete.

Boy and reader in "The Sisters" seem to follow a parallel course in their struggle with meaning, but this is actually an illusion. The boy interprets the world as text, and the reader interprets the text as world. A sophisticated reader, recognizing the self-reflexive qualities of the story, can also read the text as text and consider its playfulness, but whereas there is no limit to the range of readers who may read the story, there is only one protagonist-narrator, and his level of sophistication can be established within a narrow compass. Though he narrates, he cannot read the text, nor can he be responsible for the range of possible meanings there. Though obliged to read the world as text, he cannot read the world as world, and denied a glimpse at that epiphanic moment, the reader cannot know at the story's end how much the boy has learned about his world or even what the more mature narrator knows. Even if both decipher, the nature of their ignorance differs because of a time gap and the struggle of narration, differing as well from that of any reader.

In the end, a potential advantage lies with the reader, for the words of the text, regardless of slippery etymologies, do not change, while the boy-narrator must deal with shifting impressions based on incomplete information about a forbidden subject. Consciously or unconsciously, the narrator provides the reader with signposts to meaning, even if nobody in the text's world seems willing to render the narrator a similar service. . . .

From early to late in Joyce's work one finds an uncertainty principle responsible for obfuscation; its effect is to make readers think harder, to question what is missing, and with absence in mind to interpret what is present in the text. In the process of interpretation we find that in important questions the evidence for decidability is usually ambiguous, of dubious veracity, or missing. I have not begun to exhaust the possibilities in this line of interpretation. My purpose, rather, has been to describe the origin and development of Joyce's principle in its earlier forms, providing appropriate examples, and to trace its effect on character and structure as it grew in complexity. Ultimately this principle became perhaps the central topic of *Finnegans Wake* (not to mention modern literary theory), which questions how validity is possible in the interpretation of world or text.

Gnomon, which in Euclid means an incomplete geometrical structure, in *Dubliners* was a heuristic concept designed to control perspectives so that a maximum of political and moral impact could be attained with a minimum risk of censorship. In creating gnomonic strategies, Joyce probably hoped readers would share his sense of pity or grief or outrage at inadequate human beings, largely self-condemned, who fail to understand the nature of power and oppression. *Gnomon* could also be seen as an early endorsement of a kind of reader response theory that assumes that readers will bring to the text a range of perspectives. The effect was somewhat more complicated, and to Joyce surely more exciting: readers brought their perspectives, but they confused mysteries with problems, mostly believing that mysteries were simply more complicated problems having real solutions. That careers have been made and bibliographies padded with arguments that purport to give us the final word on unsolvable problems or mysteries would not have bothered our mischievous Mr. Joyce, who welcomed attention in whatever form.

Occasionally cruces are actually solved, as with the meaning of the "word known to all men" (*U* 1961:581; *U* 1986:474; 15–4192. cf. *U* 1961:195; *U* 1986:161; 9–429); a motif in Stephen's thoughts which a hitherto unknown passage in the Garland edition of *Ulysses* now makes clear. Whether mysteries or problems, we are normally pleased to read arguments that are more convincing than others we have read, and that is as it should be. What has been troublesome in Joyce studies is our inability to identify cruces that were obviously designed to entrap us into gathering specious evidence in the service of unsolvable problems. There are cases no good lawyer would voluntarily accept; some Joyceans, forgetting Leopold Bloom's impossible attempt to square the circle, have been most enticed by the hopeless ones.

What is the nature of the mystery surrounding Father Flynn? Why is "An Encounter's" ending so elliptical? What is the subject of the bantering conversation near the end of "Araby," and why precisely does it disturb the boy? Why does Eveline not board the ship? Has the housemaid in "Two Gallants" stolen or earned the gold coin? Has there possibly been no sexual intercourse between Bob Doran and Polly Mooney in "The Boarding House"? We are told that during Bob's confession, "the priest had drawn out every ridiculous detail of the affair and in the end had so magnified his sin . . ." (*D* 65). How is the sin of fornication magnified? What precisely is happening to Gabriel Conroy during the conclusion of 'The Dead"? Convincing evidence that would lead us to certainty in the above cases is missing.

"Missing pieces" itself is the subject of "The Sisters," "Clay," and "Ivy Day in the Committee Room," stories in which a boy fails to reach certainty in interpretation, a series of missing items defines the nature of a romantic middle-aged woman, and a missing political leader, whose memory is being celebrated, defines the moral poverty of certain political flunkeys.

Has Bertha of *Exiles* been to bed with Robert Hand? This ought to be *the* central question of the play, certainly for Bertha's husband Richard, yet the evidence has been arranged so that we cannot know the answer. As spectators we are carefully absented during the evening hours when consummation would have taken place. On the morning after, the conversation between Bertha, Robert, and Richard is tantalizingly ambiguous throughout.

In *A Portrait* we see the uncertainty principle at work in characterization: we witness the growth of a young man who is defined in terms of his presumed vocation. Paradoxically, though, Stephen Dedalus seems not to be becoming what he is destined to become, given the book title *A Portrait of the Artist as a Young Man*. He may be the first of a series of Joycean characters who somehow cannot be what they are, whose essence is ultimately indeterminate. A major reason for this in Stephen's case may be that he is blocked in the apprentice stage by an experimental forebear he cannot go beyond.

The focal point of vocation has revealed another paradox in Stephen's character. If he is trapped in the tradition of Rimbaud and the decadents of the 1890s, sinking ever deeper into interior realms that lead away from the social conscience that sparked Joyce's own career, his path diverges from his autobiographical model. Joyce's own social conscience was very active at Stephen's age; it surely prompted the writing of *Dubliners*, a work that Stephen would seem incapable of writing.

We have seen that other major characters of *Ulysses* also contain paradoxes at the center. Molly is a Dublin woman (very Irish-Catholic indeed) who is having a love affair but secretly prefers her husband; but she is also a woman of Gibraltar, legally Jewish according to Jewish law, who was raised in a garrison (highly uncustomary) until she left for Dublin at the age of sixteen. She knows little Spanish, seems unaware of what became of her mother or that her mother's family was in Gibraltar during her girlhood. An excellent example of indeterminate character, Molly cannot be what she is, being of sociologically mismatched parts. One is hardly surprised to find her married to an indeterminate husband, who loves her and shares her, a Protestant-Catholic Jew who suffers from anti-Semitism, even though at birth he was probably not legally Jewish.

Small wonder, then, that minor mysteries of character have been so troublesome to interpreters of Joyce: from those like the Man in the Macintosh, whose identity was never meant to be discovered, to characters who seem to be somebody other than who they say they are, we have seen that Joyce's texts are peopled with identities that seem to pose questions for which there are no reliable answers.

Joyce's uncertainty principle poses difficulties, proliferates error, so that these concepts have required redefinition in the Joycean context. We often say that some sections of his work are more difficult than others, but what, precisely, makes them so? What happens to authority in interpretation when there is an authorial intent to promote perspectivism? Is it possible to find a defensible middle ground between the naive tolerance of all interpretations and the dogmatic insistence upon one "true," perhaps authorially sanctioned, reading of any given passage?

We have looked at intentional error in Joyce's works and have found that error itself is a subject. Mistakes are nearly always a source of comedy there, but it is quite a serious matter when, as in Stephen's case, a character chooses to fall into error. We saw that in most Joycean contexts the word *error* means *sin*. Sin and opposition to authority have a paralyzing effect upon Stephen, who seems self-condemned in this world and the next.

If the uncertainty principle affects character, it also affects structure, ... Joyce is famous for his circular endings, one kind of structural indeterminacy, but from the enigmatic endings of the *Dubliners* stories, which return us to the text for clarification, to *Finnegans Wake*, where the last sentence flows into the first, we also find an implicit theory of closure.

In *Finnegans Wake* we have seen that the uncertainty principle produced Joyce's most radical experimentation in language, character, plot, structure— in short, every traditional aspect of the novel becomes indeterminate. In the *Wake*, Joyce discusses his principle most openly and directly, especially in those sections where ALP's letter appears in defense of her husband. There we arrived again at *gnomon* and absence: although snippets of the letter's content appear in the *Wake*, the letter in its most genuine form does not. Though it generates much controversy, and large parts of it are scattered through Book Four, its content is least unadulterated in manuscript form. Even in his last work we saw Joyce teasing his readers with absence and presence, using the letter to address most directly, though with heavy irony, the problems he foresaw readers having with literature's most radical experiment.

The Sermon as Massproduct: "Grace" and *A Portrait*

Cheryl Herr

The Sermon in Song, the Sermon as Stump Speech

Nothing revealed the conventionality of the church in the popular mind more clearly than parodies of religious doctrine and of the sermon form itself. Joyce's sermons in fact mirror the popular use of the form for subversive purposes. Principally, parodic sermonizing showed up or was referred to in the London music halls, as an article in the August 1874 *Dublin University Magazine* mentions:

> There is now a character popular at the Music Halls, personated by more than one vocalist, announced in countless advertisements, and celebrated on street hoardings, by the title of the "D———d Scamp!". . . . This personage, who is dressed in a manner denoting apparent or superficial respectability, is furnished with a string of verses set to a "catching" air, wherein he proceeds to accuse himself of a series of the most despicable rogueries (of which preaching a street sermon against intemperance, and getting drunk on the proceeds, may serve as an example. . .).

The author laments the evil influence of such a song on "all the street boys in London," who currently sang it.[1] The vocalist in question was, of course, the Irish performer G. H. Macdermott, who appeared at Dan Lowrey's in 1882, 1884, 1885 and 1889,[2] thus insuring that the Dublin audience, too, was more than familiar with "The Scamp" and his outrageous lyrics.

But songs were not the only vehicles for allusion to sermons, street variety or more formal. *The Leader* for 1 September 1900 deplores the fact that at the Lyric Music Hall in Dublin such songs, although overshadowed by even more disturbing references to religion, were allowed. The writer mentions a comedian whose song described "how he collected in church and went off with the proceeds." Another turn involved "living statuary," of which the writer comments that "better taste would have been displayed if they kept them on such

From *Joyce's Anatomy of Culture*, Cheryl Herr (Champaign: University of Illinois Press, 1986), 236–55. Copyright © 1986 by the Board of Trustees of the University of Illinois. Reprinted by permission of Cheryl Herr and the University of Illinois Press.

[1]"Our Popular Amusements." *Dublin University Magazine* 85 (1875), 233–44, p. 234.

[2]Eugene Watters and Matthew Murtagh, *Infinite Variety: Dan Lowrey's Music Hall 1879–97* (Dublin: Gill and Macmillan, 1975), pp. 58–59, 71–72, 75–76, 110–11.

subjects as 'Mars and Venus,' for dragging in 'The Rock of Ages,' a young girl clinging to the Cross, and 'The Angelus' into such a moral atmosphere was a disgusting example of British hypocrisy, if not indeed flat blasphemy." A further act during the same evening at the Lyric—indeed, the star performer's turn—included a song which the writer found marked by "vulgar grossness" even though the vocalist had described it as "the prettiest little hymn you ever heard in your life."[3] But the act that most offended was the appearance of an artiste who, "dressed up as a sort of lay preacher, and no doubt intended to personify Religion, managed to get a large amount of indecent suggestion into his mock sermonising about the danger of mixed bathing and like matters."[4] Given that these references to religion allegedly occurred within a single evening's entertainment in a Dublin hall, it seems clear that the music hall as a whole took on the ecclesiastical institutions of its day as fully as it did the swell, the boss, and the mother-in-law—those perennial comic representatives of oppression. The music-hall sermon spoke for social discomfort over the church's position of power, and provides historical evidence of the conflicts which religious institutions generated in the popular mind.

Such satire was not sophisticated; it operated mainly by inversion in that it celebrated behavior deplored by the churches. The message of the halls was that one could have more fun when stealing tithes than when contributing them. In addition, only the "unique" lion comiques and seriocomics could get away with such behavior. They seemed to be freer and more authentic individuals for their picaresque undermining of conventions and bohemian disregard for middle-class mores. Of course, performers such as Macdermott and Marie Lloyd were not so much unique as they were epitomes of a style. As has been indicated, the halls immediately standardized any successful act and generated from it endless spin-offs. But that conventionalizing seems to have remained secondary in the popular mind to the primary impact of enhanced freedom and singularity which antiestablishment turns celebrated. *The Leader,* for all of its efforts to free Ireland from British control, remained insensitive to the halls' lauding of the individual at the expense of the institution and to the proletarian's need to attack the social forces that confined him or her. On some level, the worker recognized what for the middle classes was masked—the power links among church, economy, and all other organs of cultural control to which the lower orders were abandoned.

To this point, I have argued that the theology of Joyce's era was conventionalized on a mass scale, especially in sermon books, and that the doctrinal rigidity suggested by this fact found responses on the stage and in the pulpit

[3]The star in whom *The Leader* found such fault was Madge Ellis. According to the *Irish Times* for 1 September 1900, she appeared on a bill at the Lyric which included the famous Percy Honri; the August 20 advertisement in the *Times* (p. 4, col. 2) for her engagement in Dublin called her "Dublin's Favourite," "America's Star," and "London's Sensation."

[4]*The Leader*, 1 September 1900, pp. 2–3.

in several ways. The stage priest of the melodrama sometimes lived the doctrine of acceptance, peace, and love without questioning it; other priestly dramatis personae were revolutionaries. The often theatrical preachers of Joyce's day were similarly divided. Clearly, the institutional acts of the church did not satisfy all of the clergy's or the society's desires for social change. In addition, music hall parodies of sermons signify the questioning which took place throughout the culture (but perhaps especially in the disfranchised classes) of religious authority over social relations. The rest of this chapter examines the social impact of the sermon in "Grace" and *Portrait*; it demonstrates that in Joyce's work, the sermon signifies the economic matrix in which Irish culture operated, a matrix responsible for the divided images of the church that popular culture presented.

"Grace"

"Grace" stands as one of Joyce's most direct indictments of the financial enterprise of the church and of its accommodation of theology to secular demands, specifically to the attitudes represented by the backsliding businessmen pictured in the sketch. When Martin Cunningham silences the men in Tom Kernan's bedroom with stories of the church, it is power that he evokes, a power which plays over those gathered and persuades even the comically reprehensible tea taster to affiliate himself, quite apart from belief, with an institution that wields clout. Their awe over the doctrine of papal infallibility provides evidence of their cultural conditioning in that they respond to the image of a potent church more or less independently of their knowledge, inadequate as it is, of theology. The story as a whole attacks this automatic response to the sacred, especially when the briefly presented sermon speaks its content more directly than was often true in conventional published sermons. Openly asserting his modestly matter-of-fact aim for the retreat, the priest actually defuses the men's expectation of conversion. Far from being too challenging, the church reflects the society's everyday behavior while it benefits from the shared desire for personal change. Joyce's cultural anatomy operates here as always to undermine our sense of individual value and development as something other than a complex by-product of social forms and cultural operations. Really to change Tom Kernan would require alteration of the institutions that shape him.

As Joyce's story presents it, the church is not distinct from any secular institution: it defines behavior according to binary codes that appear to be fixed; it seeks to enlarge its membership and to preempt other institutions in the struggle for social control. The conversion of the individual has become a function of hegemonic maneuvers in that the church teaches its members to become better businesspeople and to help themselves to a bigger piece of the financial pie. Joyce's using as a model for Father Purdon the Jesuit Bernard

Vaughan enhances our recognition of the church's intimate ties to the economic system from which it often attempted to distance itself in the public mind.

Like Purdon, Vaughan followed and even exaggerated the contemporary popularizing of theology for the masses. Part of this effort centered on offering specialized retreats for people in different walks of life. Vaughan conducted many such retreats; he also published an address given to a group of businessmen and entitled "The Uses of Advertisement." The preacher argues that he is "a member of the oldest advertising firm in religion on this planet." Asserting that "expediency" is more important than "taste" where religion is concerned, Vaughan defends himself against those "superior-minded people" who "object to modern methods of advertisement" and who believe that the preacher should not "turn the House of God into a sort of theatre." He responds that such a stance makes religion "the only . . . tabooed" subject "in the modern world." About advertising itself, Vaughan speaks with great regard. He calls it both an art and a science that requires a knowledge of human psychology and the means of "arresting attention." He adds, "I do not say that advertising is free from abuse. Cheap and nasty things which nobody needs are forced upon our attention unblushingly and boldly. But what good thing is there in the world which is not equally misused? The honest advertiser of an honest article has my approbation all the time, and the attitude of those who condemn him is little short of hypocritical."[5]

It seems unlikely that Joyce was aware of this speech—one which suggests that Bernard Vaughan and Leopold Bloom could easily have talked shop—but Joyce did know of similar clerical presentations. As is well known, Stanislaus reports that a "retreat for business men" was held by a Jesuit in Gardiner Street Church and that John Joyce had been persuaded to attend. "Out of sarcastic curiosity," Stanislaus continues, "I followed them to the church on the last evening of the retreat to listen to the sermon and watch my father fumbling shamefacedly with his lighted candle. The sermon was a man-to-man talk in a chatty tone. I came out into the fresh air before the end." Stanislaus also mentions that his brother had attended a sermon on the subject of grace "and had come away angry and disgusted at the inadequacy of the exposition. He said the preacher had not even tried to know what he was talking about, but assumed that anything was good enough for his listeners. It angered him that such shoddy stuff should pass for spiritual guidance."[6] Drawn from both

---

[5]Rev. Bernard Vaughan, *What of To-Day?* (London: Cassell, 1914), pp. 350, 349, 348. This collection of addresses was first published in 1914, but it includes no information about the original delivery date of the sermon on advertising. Martindale says that it is "the transcript, I think, of an address given to those whose business advertising was." Martindale also states of Vaughan that "in Manchester, he willingly used trade expressions—he liked to say that he belonged 'to the firm that defied all competition,' and was for ever talking about 'delivering the goods' . . ." (Martindale, pp. 230, 56–57).

[6]S. Joyce, *My Brother's Keeper*, ed. Richard Ellmann (London: Faber & Faber, 1958), pp. 223, 224–25. See also pp. 104–6 in *The Complete Dublin Diary*, ed. George H. Healey (Ithaca, N.Y.:

experiences and from the media image of Vaughan, Father Purdon in part represents the oversimplification, inaccuracy, and reliance on showmanship that characterized many popular sermons. In contrast, consider Stephen's attendance at the Capuchin church, where he finds that "the sermons of the priests were grateful to him inasmuch as the speakers did not seem inclined to make much use of their rhetorical and elocutionary training nor anxious to reveal themselves in theory, at least, men of the world" (*SH* 177).

One other acclaimed preacher drew Joyce's attention in "Grace." Kernan and his friends all agree that Father Tom Burke was one of the greatest preachers of their day. Drawing "crowds of Protestants" along with Catholics, Burke was known for his "style" and "voice" (*D* 165), and yet he is questioned, even by the likes of Kernan and his cohorts, for theological imprecision:

—And yet they say he wasn't much of a theologian, said Mr Cunningham.
—Is that so? said Mr M'Coy.
—O, of course, nothing wrong, you know. Only sometimes, they say, he didn't preach what was quite orthodox. (*D* 165)

Given this comment, it is of interest that Burke's 1872 volume of lectures does have the imprimatur, yet in his preface, Burke (who was perhaps aware of such criticisms) remarks, "If . . . there be anything in them contrary to the teachings of the Catholic Church, that, I am the first to condemn and repudiate."[7]

In that both the style and the content of popularized sermons seem to have irritated Joyce, both informal delivery and uninformed preacher receive attention in "Grace." Skepticism over the doctrine aside, he appears to have objected to any job poorly done and especially to sermons that reflected only the lowest state of the art. This ineffectuality is linked explicitly in the story with sermons that do not differentiate theological doctrine from sound financial methods, for "Grace" shows us the harmony of the business world with the religious teachings available for popular consumption.

From the outset of the story we are led to see that religious conversion is not the answer to the Kernans' problems. Proud of being a tea taster and commercial traveler, the once-successful protagonist has been destroyed not so much by drink as by changes in the economic environment: "Modern business methods had spared him only so far as to allow him a little office in Crowe Street on the window blind of which was written the name of his firm with the address—London, E.C." (*D* 154). Like an out-of-date Jehovah, Mr. Kernan passes judgment, spitting teas into the grate. Directly following the description of Kernan's background and job, the narrative introduces the aptly named Mr. Power, the "much younger man" who rescued Tom when he drunkenly fell down the stairs and who is employed, like Martin Cun-

Cornell University Press, 1962), where Stanislaus dates the retreat attended by his father around 1902. He says that the presiding priest was Father Vernon, which the editor emends to Father John T. Verdon—a name close to Purdon.
[7]Rev. Thomas Burke, *Lectures and Sermons* (New York: Haverty, 1872), p. [5].

ningham, in Dublin Castle. That the "arc of his social rise intersected the arc of his friend's decline" (*D* 154) is significant because those two trajectories describe both the access to power provided by political employment and the inevitable failure of those who have not made the economic choices necessary for survival in the modern business world, even in the seemingly casual way in which that world established itself in early twentieth-century Dublin. Not religion but economics has defined Mr. Kernan's obsolescence and his family's rude poverty.

The relationship of the church to social change is playfully suggested at the story's opening by several uses of the word "curate." This slang term for bartender appears to have amused Joyce (compare the playbill in *Finnegans Wake* in which Saunderson is described as a "spoilcurate" [*FW* 221.10]) and implies the church's role in a modernizing world, for the curates first set up Tom Kernan for his fall by serving him liquor and then cover up the evidence of the fall ("a curate set about removing the traces of blood from the floor"—*D* 153). Like Father Purdon, whose discourse on grace ignores the doctrine of original sin, these secular curates efface the signs of Kernan's decline. What they have to offer addresses the causes and cures of Kernan's woes as poorly as Father Purdon does.

The economic relationships that define the state of affairs in the story surface in many details. For instance, we are led to believe that Mrs. Kernan is kept from thinking the emblematic Mr. Power responsible for her husband's dismal state by "remembering Mr Power's good offices during domestic quarrels as well as many small, but opportune loans" (*D* 155). Mr. Fogarty, the grocer whom Kernan owes money, has already "failed in business in a licensed house in the city because his financial condition had constrained him to tie himself to second-class distillers and brewers" (*D* 166). Mr. M'Coy is mildly ostracized because he mooches off his friends, and Mr. Harford the financier is quietly censured because he charges usurious rates to lend money to the workers and failing businesspeople of Dublin. Similarly, the very Jesuits who offer the retreat are presented as not just "an educated order" but also as "the boyos [that] have influence"; as Mr. M'Coy crassly notes, "The Jesuits cater for the upper classes," and Power agrees, "Of course" (*D* 163–64). Such references to the dominating socioeconomic relations are too insistent to be ignored. In this Dublin, money talks, while poverty is both powerless and quietly resentful.

The retreat itself turns out to be a microcosm of the culture. Mr. Harford attends along with politicians, a pawnbroker, a pressman, and, no doubt, more than one "commercial figure" on the way down (*D* 173). Father Purdon, who is "powerful-looking" but too bulky to get into the pulpit with grace, is the perfect speaker for them. Mimicking the theatrical media priest of his day, he pauses before speaking to roll "back each wide sleeve of his surplice with an elaborate large gesture" (*D* 173). The priest, far from being there for a "terrifying" or "extravagant" purpose, came "as a man of the world," a "spiritual accountant" (*D* 174). The priest is not the only one who does not expect much from religious experience. Of Mrs. Kernan we are told that "Her beliefs were not extravagant. She believed steadily in the Sacred Heart as the most generally useful of all Catholic devotions and approved of the sacraments. Her faith was bounded by her kitchen but, if she was put to it, she could believe also in the banshee and in the Holy Ghost" (*D* 158). Like her husband and even the wise Martin Cunningham, Mrs. Kernan owns to beliefs that are liberally mixed with superstition or misinformation, but she does not attribute any extraordinary power to religion itself.

The preacher's focus is the parable of the unjust steward, which most critics of "Grace" have discussed.[8] The text quoted by Father Purdon is, of course, taken out of context. He intones: *"For the children of this world are wiser in their generation than the children of light. Wherefore make unto yourselves friends out of the mammon of iniquity so that when you die they may receive you into everlasting dwellings"* (*D* 173). From this unsettling and perhaps permanently murky quotation, Purdon arrives at the unlikely point that Christ would have businessmen set the pattern of behavior for the world, that their living "to a certain extent, for the world" is perfectly all right as long as they have balanced the books of their "spiritual life" (*D* 174).[9] On several counts, Father Purdon deviates from even the most generously conceived Christian doctrine.[10] For one thing, he validates a worldly orientation toward economic gain even though those who are involved with "the mammon of iniquity" are not merely friends of the rich but are also allies of those who have gained wealth through wickedness. (The OED entry on "mammon" emphasizes the diabolic connotations of the word.) The cloak of religiosity seemingly typical of the comrades of mammon appears to be asserted when the *Wake* sums up the writers of the gospels as "Mammon Lujius" (*FW* 13.20). For another thing, Purdon portrays a Christ who always condones failings as long as one is "straight and manly with God" (*D* 174): to be courteous and "never to peach

[8]See especially Robert Sumner Jackson's elaborate reading of Joyce's use of this parable, "A Parabolic Reading of James Joyce's 'Grace,' " *Modern Language Notes* 76 (1961), 719–24.

[9]Eugene R. August comments that "part of his [Joyce's] point about the Irish Jesuits is precisely that they have sold their religious heritage in order to make friends with the mammon of iniquity. . . . In 'Grace' Joyce lets the passage from Luke 16: 8–9 comment ironically upon the worldly Jesuit and his well fed order." See "Father Arnall's Use of Scripture in *A Portrait*," *James Joyce Quarterly* 4 (1967), 275.

[10]Cf. Fritz Senn, "A Rhetorical Account of James Joyce's 'Grace,' " *Moderna Språk* 74 (1980), 121–28. Similarly, much has been made of the errors in the *Portrait* sermons. Bernard Duyfhuizen, " 'Words [Mis]taken': The Opening Sentence of the Retreat Sermons," *James Joyce Quarterly* 16 (1979), discusses a "mistaken reference to Ecclesiastes" (p. 489), and August deals with both this reference and ones in Isaiah and Psalms which reveal Father Arnall's willful distortion of the scriptures to suit his own rhetorical ends (pp. 275–78). . . . But compare J. Mitchell Morse, *The Sympathetic Alien: James Joyce and Catholicism* (Washington Square: New York University Press, 1959), who discusses the relationship of Purdon's accommodating doctrine and St. Ignatius' *Spiritual Exercises*: "The whole burden of his friendly talk is that Jesus Christ is not a hard taskmaster but only wants them to correct any errors there may be in their accounts. This is straight out of the *Spiritual Exercises*" (pp. 74–76).

on a fellow" (*P* 9) turn out to be, as Simon Dedalus counseled his son, a sufficient moral code after all. Further, the priest misleadingly allots the burden and indeed the power of achieving grace to the individual rather than to God. By this logic, the businessman can say either "I find all well" or "I find this wrong and this wrong. But, with God's grace, I will rectify this and this. I will set right my accounts" (*D* 174). Divine grace enters this audit in the form of a casual expression rather than a theological concept, in a qualifying phrase set off between commas, while the repeated "I" controls the spiritual inquiry. At the very least, the priest's portrayal of the mechanisms of contrition and absolution would leave his auditors not only unredeemed but also egotistical. The myth of selfhood which "Circe" attacks subsumes Purdon's theology.

Further, the thrust of the sermon is that newness of spirit ("We'll make a new man of him," says Mr. Power) may be achieved by following Purdon's advice. Such distortion of doctrine emerges from Purdon's twisting of the biblical text itself. Although the parable is extremely ambiguous, it is perhaps most readily interpreted as a displacement of spiritual terms by mundane ones. Hence, the steward's fixing of his master's books, which would ordinarily be seen as a corrupt action, may be compared to the laying up of treasure in heaven.[11] This substitution is ignored by Purdon, whose businesslike outlook reinforces the implications of his name. Not just a gibe at the church because of the connection of prostitution to Purdon Street, "Purdon" also signals the brand of simony that prostitution represents. The trading of sex for money makes the body a site of economic exchange. The priest would have his auditors enact his bogus and socially damaging system of "spiritual" accountancy.

Robert Jackson suggests the prevailing critical opinion of Purdon's brand of religion when he says that Joyce "condemns . . . the church which supports the set of values by which Kernan is obliged to repent."[12] Similarly, Howard Lachtman finds the story implicitly deploring the fact that in "his betrayal of spiritual values, Father Purdon is another perverse paradigm of what is wrong in Joyce's Dublin. Religion has gone mad, departed, or become, as here, the bastard of business." He adds that the story "has a dark undercurrent of complaint about a faith which has become a social league and a business proposition."[13] Both of these commentators seem to have accepted as definitive Stanislaus's lead in interpreting the story. That his brother found Joyce angry at the befuddled theology he heard from the pulpit does not guarantee, however, that "Grace" became the vehicle for that anger in its initial form. Joyce's personal values might have included many traditional humanistic and

---

[11]Of course, as Jackson argues, the steward never does achieve worthiness of salvation; he is rather granted grace by God. Hence, the lord in the parable commends the steward despite the latter's persistent unworthiness (Jackson, p. 721).

[12]Jackson, p. 723.

[13]Howard Lachtman, "The Magic-Lantern Business: James Joyce's Ecclesiastical Satire in *Dubliners*," *James Joyce Quarterly* 7 (1970), 89.

Christian qualities, but there is nothing in his writings to suggest that any church can or should be the means by which the modern man or woman achieves any kind of grace. Readers who find here primarily a critique of the church rather than an anatomy of its cultural function attribute to Joyce an underlying belief in religion as the vessel of truth; they ignore his identification of the church as an economic institution. In effect, much of what "Grace" does is to provide evidence of this status.

Certainly, the commercial forces in Joyce's society could do nothing with traditional religious values except use them to further hegemonic ends in a society utterly lacking the possibility for sustained application of such ideals. In addition, the efforts of Dubliners to live by a religious code perpetuate their willed blindness to the economic and political conditions which guarantee the poor quality of their lives. Even Martin Cunningham, who suffers long and is kind to his drunken wife and his comical friends, spends most of his days serving mammon at Dublin Castle. That Bernard Vaughan, the best-known preacher of his day, stands as a likely model for Purdon and provides a definite analogue for his brand of preaching indicates Joyce's assessment of the popular sermon as the means by which not only bogus theology but also economic ideology was transmitted to the mass mind. What looks like Purdon's intentionally deceptive equation of spiritual values with shrewd financial dealing turns out to be merely a clue to the economic underpinnings of religious doctrine in the prevailing capitalistic recoding of scriptural ideas. As "Grace" presents it, the church is undeniably among the powers responsible for the "paralysis" of Dubliners. That state is not just a result of personal ineptitude: Tom Kernan has fallen from social grace not simply because he is not up on the latest business methods but also because he is controlled by institutions that respond to an oppressive economic system. Kernan goes to church to remedy the ills wrought in him by the business world and discovers in the chapel more of the same. Purdon does not so much deviate from doctrine as he reveals its practical impact.

The Sermon in Portrait

In extension of this revelation, the sermon presented in *Finnegans Wake* III, ii both adumbrates and actively preaches economic motivations. In this light, the fragment of Alexander J. Dowie's preaching that shows up in "Oxen of the Sun" documents the continuity of Catholic and Protestant theology in accommodating social exigencies. Dowie parodies the theatrical salespitch of a Vaughan and targets the ease with which the language of popular religion coalesces with an economic vocabulary:[14] "The Deity aint no nickel dime bumshow. I put it to you that He's on the square and a corking fine business

---

[14]Duyfhuizen calls Father Arnall in *Portrait* "nothing more than an old huckster trying to sell genuine rattlesnake oil in a wild west medicine show" (p. 490).

proposition. . . . He's got a coughmixture with a punch in it for you, my friend, in his back pocket. Just you try it on" (*U* 1961:428; *U* 1986:349; 14–1585). When this evangelistic huckster performs in "Circe" as Elijah, he continues his merchandising: "Rush your order and you play a slick ace. . . . Bumboosers, save your stamps" (*U* 1961:507; *U* 1986:414; 15–2207). But in *Portrait*, not the sermon's language but the impact of the sermon on the individual is the mechanism for revealing the church's power interests.

Part of the mechanism for the religious conditioning of Dubliners was the sermon to children (in *Portrait* and in *Finnegans Wake* the sermons are delivered to schoolchildren). Many readers of Joyce have regarded the *Portrait* sermons as his anguished recreation of his own pious childhood. Whether or not the motive for composition was therapeutic, the conventionality of Father Arnall's retreat addresses is perhaps their most important characteristic. More than the church itself, it is the power of institutionalized cultural convention that Stephen learns to recognize and resist through his spiritual bout with the church. By the end of chapter iv of *Portrait*, Stephen has turned not just from the religious life but toward what he sees as the wild, the free, the uninhibited—all the things symbolized for him by the bird-girl on the strand. She defies convention by the twisted height of her skirts and bareness of her thighs as well as by her direct gaze, which Stephen interprets as neither seductive nor shrinkingly virginal. Many critics have argued that the girl combines for Stephen the sacred and the secular, but she also represents a cultural quantity not immediately categorized into one stereotyped realm or the other. In fact, the representation of Stephen's vision of her as birdlike signifies a willing fusion of the two categories—the animal or bestial and the human—that Father Arnall's sermons set in opposition.[15] The priest's assertion that the "lower nature" (*P* 123) tends always toward the "gross and beastlike" (*P* 127) takes on a personal shape in Stephen's dream of "Goatish creatures with human faces" (*P* 137); yet that visionary concretion of Father Arnall's metaphoric language may be viewed, too, as the dark side of an imaginative desire to transform cultural dichotomies into continuities. The bright side of this creative impulse determines Stephen's complex vision of the avian girl. Certainly, the girl signifies the mortal danger of conventional ideas and the power of the ambiguous to remake an outlook founded on religious absolutism.

Power is indeed one of the most important terms in chapters iii and iv of *Portrait*, for it is power that Stephen craves and the church's cultural ascendancy that excites him to repentance and to temporary religious amendment of his life. When the rector recalls to the boys' attention the story of St. Francis Xavier, he labels him "A saint who has great power in heaven, remember: power to intercede for us in our grief, power to obtain whatever we pray for if

---

[15]I am indebted to Tim Ireland, a student of mine at Swarthmore College in the fall of 1984, for his valuable discussion of the destabilized distinction in Chapter 3 of *Portrait* of body and soul, beast and human being.

it be for the good of our souls, power above all to obtain for us the grace to repent if we be in sin" (*P* 108). Similarly, the sermon on death and judgment calls forth more than any other image that of "God Omnipotent" (*P* 113), no longer meekly forgiving but judging and punishing. In the face of such power, "the jeweleyed harlots" that Stephen has sinned with both imaginatively and actually are replaced by fear, and the evoked potency of God wins the place in Stephen's soul previously held by "his presumptuous peace" and arrogant independence (*P* 115).

Once the physical and spiritual torments of hell have been graphically presented by Father Arnall, Stephen's personal hell begins in earnest. The effect of the sermons is such that he has trouble entering his room for fear of devils and is able to go into the shadows only after praying "that the fiends that inhabit darkness might not be given power over him" (*P* 136). Stephen's intellect directly assaults itself when his curiously auditory hallucinations speak to him: "We knew perfectly well of course that although it was bound to come to the light he would find considerable difficulty in endeavouring to try to induce himself to try to endeavour to ascertain the spiritual plenipotentiary and so we knew of course perfectly well—." At the moment, Stephen needs to locate a priest to hear his confession because only a priest is empowered by the church to help him, but Stephen lacks the strength that confession will require of him. So forceful is the sermon's rhetoric that he is weakened by it before he is strengthened in the faith. Fearfully, he tells himself "that those words had absolutely no sense which had seemed to rise murmurously from the dark" (*P* 136), but at least one word—"plenipotentiary"—resonates with the issue at the heart of Stephen's trial and the church's institutional efforts. In its mythic role as all-powerful, the church offers its potency only to those who follow its directives, who surrender individual control to institutional ends. Hence, to continue the process of redemption, in his postnausea prayer Stephen identifies himself with Christ: "*So He came Himself in weakness not in power . . .*" (*P* 138).

Although Stephen eventually humbles himself to enter Church Street chapel and make his confession in the company of laborers, chapter iv finds him characteristically trying to obtain and wield the might of the institution that has educated him. He works to accrue for souls in purgatory "fabulous ages of canonical penances" (*P* 147). He monitors his every sensation and thought so that all seemed to "revibrate radiantly in heaven: and at times his sense of such immediate repercussion was so lively that he seemed to feel his soul in devotion pressing like fingers the keyboard of a great cash register and to see the amount of his purchase start forth immediately in heaven" (*P* 148). The economic metaphor attributed to Stephen underscores Joyce's usual connection of religion and the commercial enterprises that ruled his Dublin. Further, Stephen assumes various attitudes of devotion so that the "world for all its solid substance and complexity no longer existed for his soul save as a theorem of divine power and love and universality" (*P* 150).

It is finally the sense of his own strength that pushes Stephen into doubt: "It gave him an intense sense of power to know that he could by a single act of consent, in a moment of thought, undo all that he had done." Each time he resists temptation, he feels "a new thrill of power and satisfaction" (*P* 152). This theme of individual and institutional power comes to a head when the director, who has summoned Stephen to discuss a vocation for the priesthood, pridefully enlarges on the benefits of being a priest:

> —To receive that call, Stephen, said the priest, is the greatest honour that the Almighty God can bestow upon a man. No king or emperor on this earth has the power of the priest of God. No angel or archangel in heaven, no saint, not even the Blessed Virgin herself has the power of a priest of God: the power of the keys, the power to bind and to loose from sin, the power of exorcism, the power to cast out from the creatures of God the evil spirits that have power over them, the power, the authority, to make the great God of Heaven come down upon the altar and take the form of bread and wine. What an awful power, Stephen! (*P* 158)

The concentrated repetition of "power" makes inescapable the fact that in this final bid for his allegiance, the church plays on Stephen's most vulnerable spot—his intense desire for a mastery and for a social validation that will enable his personal talents to find an outlet.

What follows in the narrative provides for us one reason that Joyce included in the novel the transcript or narrative record of Father Arnall's introductory address and three long sermons. Stephen responds to an "instinct" that is "stronger than education or piety," to the "pride of his spirit which had always made him conceive himself as a being apart in every order." The sovereignty of the church that had educated him falls away, its "hold" over him "frail" despite "years of order and obedience" (*P* 161). Although the conditioning is in place (he recalls the "voice of the director urging upon him the proud claims of the church and the mystery and power of the priestly office"), Stephen elects "to be elusive of social or religious orders" (*P* 162); he chooses the "freedom and power of his soul" (*P* 170) over the omnipotence of the Deity as presented in the accumulated traditions of hundreds of years. The retreat sermons thus mark for Stephen not the beginning or renewal of piety but the inception of his awareness of the church as a cultural institution. Even though the very terms used to define his individual goals have been appropriated from the institution he wants to elude, Stephen begins to anatomize the church which Joyce presents as a creature of convention and social function.

The material that Joyce used as an immediate source for Father Arnall's lectures helps the reader to that same realization. In separate articles, James R. Thrane, Elizabeth F. Boyd, and James Doherty have together argued that the sermons on hell derived from an 1889 edition of an English translation of the seventeenth-century Jesuit Giovanni Pietro Pinamonti's devotional volume *L'Inferno aperto (Hell Opened to Christians)*. They also explain that Joyce and Pinamonti alike drew on a long tradition of writing about hell which had its own conventions about the landscape and conditions of the Christian Hades. Doherty comments, "Almost any nineteenth-century Catholic sermon book has a sermon for the Fifth Sunday after Epiphany that sounds quite a bit like Pinamonti."[16] Although I believe that assessment to be exaggerated, a perusal of the Rev. Charles J. Callan's section on hell in his *Illustrations for Sermons and Instructions* quickly reveals that the *Portrait* sermons represent virtually a compendium of folklore about such topics as the remorse and self-accusation of the damned, the fire of hell, and eternal punishment.[17] Such matters as the stench of hell, and eternity expressed through the image of a bird's carrying away grains from a mountain of sand were ready topoi in nineteenth-century Catholic preaching.[18] In defense of Joyce's "plagiarism," Boyd observes, "He probably wanted his borrowing to be recognized, for it is a kind of silent comment on the unyielding traditions of the type of Catholicism he grew up with, toward which he maintained all his life the ambivalent attitude of admiration and rejection."[19]

Partly by being more fiery than most sermons typical of the era, Joyce's text announces its desire to be compared with this tradition of conventions that so often substituted in the popular mind for the established doctrine of the church. That tradition had the power not just to move the heart but also, owing to constant repetition, to hold the mind. For Stephen, these conventions constitute much of the church's power and define a relationship that his will alone cannot sever. The issue of plagiarism becomes ludicrous in the light of this recognition, for quotation and allusion are for Joyce always the way toward dissection of culture and exposure of institutional control of the individual.

Joyce's attention to the church's place in the social network in fact eludes the formulations of much criticism of *Portrait*. For instance, one writer states: "Through the sermons of Father Arnall during the Belvedere school retreat, Joyce bodies forth the Irish church in all its narrowness and perversion. In

---

[16]James Doherty, "Joyce and *Hell Opened to Christians:* The Edition He Used for His Sermons," *Modern Philology* 61 (1963), 119. Boyd, "James Joyce's Hell-Fire Sermons," *Modern Language Notes* 75 (1960), 563, Doherty (pp. 111–18), and Thrane, "Joyce's Sermon on Hell: Its Sources and Backgrounds," *Modern Philology* 57 (1960), 189, discuss Joyce's condensation and intensification of Pinamonti's meditations.

[17]Rev. Charles J. Callan, O.P., ed., *Illustrations for Sermons and Instructions* (New York: Wagner, 1916), pp. 93–99. On conventions of doctrine about hell, see also Bruce Bradley, S.J., *James Joyce's Schooldays* (New York: St. Martin's Press, 1982), pp. 125–28. Sullivan points to the parallels between Father Arnall's statements and *The Sodality Manual or a Collection of Prayers and Spiritual Exercises for Members of the Sodality of the Blessed Virgin Mary*, compiled by Fr. James A. Cullen, S.J. But Sullivan asserts the presence of the sermon's dominant ideas in devotional materials written over "hundreds of years" (Kevin Sullivan, *Joyce Among the Jesuits* [New York: Columbia University Press, 1958], pp. 138–41).

[18]Once Bernard Vaughan stayed the night with a man who felt himself pursued by the devil; afterwards, Vaughan "insisted that the stench of evil made itself perceptible to the very nostrils, and he would explain what he meant by that, leaving little enough to the imagination" (Cyril C. Martindale, *Bernard Vaughn, S.J.* [London: Longmans Green, 1923], pp. 53–54).

[19]Elizabeth F. Boyd, "James Joyce's Hell-Fire Sermons," *Modern Language Notes* 75 (1960), 561–71, at 571.

these sermons Stephen comes face to face with that virulent form of Irish Catholicism he must escape if he is to be free."[20] Scholars have also noted the presence in the sermons of errors in biblical reference and have charted the rhetorical role of those errors. However, the "deception" practiced on Stephen involves not only misquotation and distortion but also, and more important, a censoring of context that Stephen chooses not to sustain. A retreat is, after all, an isolation from all cultural influences but one ("A retreat, my dear boys, signifies a withdrawal for a while from the cares of our life . . ." [*P* 109]). The terms in which the church presents its power force a choice between adherence to a single code of conduct in isolation from all others and what Stephen sees as "freedom"—a recognition of the many aspects (though, to be sure, most are institutional) of experience. Predisposed to act first and discriminate later, Stephen prefers to test institutional practices and reject that which would cut him off from all others.

A major irony of *Portrait* is that what Stephen chooses and finds cannot be the freedom he seeks. The cultural operations that Joyce's texts adumbrate more than document the illusoriness of that state. To be truly free, the artist would have to exist absolutely apart from society, but if it were possible for him to move beyond the nets of culture, Stephen would cease to be even an incipient artist; he would have no conceptual codes with which to accomplish the artist's work of transformation. Instead, *Portrait* places the church at the heart of the culture's predilection for binarisms such as good/evil, human/animal, saved/damned, and liberated/entrapped. In doing so, Joyce's narrative portrays the community's belief that the moral and spiritual dichotomies of religious doctrine provide intellectual power over existential ambiguities. Just as the church offers Tom Kernan and his friends what appears to be a measure of personal control over the ravages of socioeconomic conditions, so the church entices Stephen with a vision of his future command over the incertitudes of life, sexual identity, and death. But Stephen rejects this offer and the isolation of the priesthood to plunge into the contradictions of cultural experience. His decision to "forge . . . the uncreated conscience of . . . [his] race" (*P* 253) suggests that in some sense Stephen has learned that personal salvation cannot occur apart from communal change.

But Stephen does not choose only a bogus freedom; he chooses also the three tools of "silence, exile, and cunning." Announcing as much, Stephen elicits Cranly's amusement: "Cunning indeed!" (*P* 247). To be sure, the third term poses the biggest obstacle to Stephen's success; whereas silence and exile suggest a movement out of the linguistically communicated ideology that Stephen finds constraining, cunning brings Stephen back into language. The Middle English "conning," from which "cunning" derives, means both knowing and reading. Further, through what *The American Heritage Dictionary of the English Language* asserts to be the term's Indo-European root (*-gno*),

[20]Eugene R. August, "Father Arnall's Use of Scripture in *A Portrait*," *James Joyce Quarterly* 4 (1967), 275–79, at 275.

cunning shares its linguistic soil with the word "narrate." For Stephen—as for anyone in his society—reading, knowing, and narrating depend on access to the cultural matrix from which Stephen would exile himself; the unreachable outside of culture may be construed as silence, but it is the constraining interior which provides the artist's words.

Irish culture as Joyce knew it revealed not only the power of traditional Catholic theology but also the tensions with the church that grew from its role in history. The popularity of stage priests and of media priests demonstrated the centrality of the church as a social presence and of the sermon as a significant cultural voice. But despite the modern publications of the church's received conventions and the standardized preaching that resulted, the Catholic establishment was riven by political and other differences. The theatrical presence of the priest and of parodic sermons in the music halls argues for the culture's awareness of what Joyce explicitly defines—the status of the church not as spiritual guide but as socioeconomic institution—a fact that Stephen Dedalus recognizes even though Tom Kernan remains trapped by powers in which he does not even believe.

"O, an Impossible Person!"

Hugh Kenner

What the first readers of *Ulysses* were meant to know of its author may be gathered from *A Portrait of the Artist as a Young Man*, in which a youth named Stephen from a moneyless Irish Catholic home undergoes a Jesuit education, opts against the priesthood and for what he calls 'Life'—which connotes living somewhere else—develops a subtle dogmatism about aesthetics, defines the terms of a struggle in which 'silence, exile, and cunning' will be his weapons, and on the last page is poised to fly abroad, 'to encounter for the millionth time the reality of experience and to forge in the smithy of my soul the uncreated conscience of my race'.

We learn all this, at any rate, about Stephen, and to some extent we know it of Joyce, too. To what extent? While there can be no doubt that the book mirrors James Joyce's childhood and adolescence, we cannot feel confident that the mirroring is steady and whole. The book's method is insidious; told in the third person until the last few pages, where a transcription from Stephen's diary supervenes, it mimics a tranquil narrative detachment while in fact confining us to Stephen's view of everything.

For decades there have been readers aplenty to accept Stephen's view, and it is reasonable to ask if the *Portrait* provides sanctions for doing anything else. The question is of more than biographical interest, since Stephen, grown a year or two older, is a principal character in *Ulysses*, too, and what we are to make of him there depends a good deal on whether he has the author's complete indulgence. Stephen's way of experiencing and judging may seem so thoroughly to pervade the *Portrait* that there is no way he can be appraised: whatever he says or does seems utterly reasonable.

A written style, however: that is something to appraise, once we become aware of it; and the *Portrait* makes us highly aware of style by the unusual device, much extended and complicated in *Ulysses*, of changing the style continually, from the Stein-like sub-style of the first pages to the wrought periods of the last.

Every reader perceives that as Stephen's experience increases the prose grows more resourceful. At first we find short words and paratactic sentences:

Extract taken from *Ulysses*, rev. ed., by Hugh Kenner (Baltimore: The Johns Hopkins University Press, 1987), pp. 6–18. Copyright © 1980 by George Allen & Unwin, Ltd. Reproduced by kind permission of Unwin Hyman, Ltd., The Johns Hopkins University Press, and Hugh Kenner.

To remember that and the white look of the lavatory made him feel cold and then hot. There were two cocks that you turned and water came out: cold and hot. He felt cold and then a little hot: and he could see the names printed on the cocks. That was a very queer thing. (*P* 11)

And here, from a late page, is the cry of circling birds:

He listened to the cries: like the shriek of mice behind the wainscot: a shrill twofold note. But the notes were long and shrill and whirring, unlike the cry of vermin, falling a third or a fourth and trilled as the flying beaks clove the air. Their cry was shrill and clear and fine and falling like threads of silken light unwound from whirring spools. (*P* 224)

The difference is a measure of Stephen's increased adeptness: for the language, without our being quite told so, is really his, and we are to understand that the simile of whirring spools originates in his mind. The canons of imitative form would be satisfied were the style simply to mature as the subject ages. But in the *Portrait*, equivocally, intermittently, we are to think of Stephen as *responsible* for the style: certainly at moments of perceptual intensity, when it tends to exhibit effects we can sense him admiring.

Though he outgrows admirations, they circumscribe him while they are indulged. Thus shortly before he enters the University he has a period of conspicuous indulgence in *chiasmus*: 'The towels with which they smacked their bodies were heavy with cold seawater: and drenched with cold brine was their matted hair' (*P* 168). Subject$_1$ was [predicate]: and [similar predicate] was likewise Subject$_2$.

In celebrating its rituals of finality, *chiasmus* leaves after-vibrations of sententiousness by which the young man does not seem to be troubled. 'There's English for you,' part of his mind is saying, and his fondness, at this period, for this figure—'The clouds were drifting above him silently and silently the seatangle was drifting below him'—as well as for variations on it— 'An ecstasy of flight made radiant his eyes and wild his breath and tremulous and wild and radiant his windswept limbs'—affects his very perceptions with a certain staginess, something to bear in mind when we come to the celebrated paragraph in which a girl standing in a tidal stream becomes the apparition of a wild angel, 'the angel of mortal youth and beauty, an envoy from the fair courts of life'. For the paragraph that describes her, and studiously half-turns her into a bird, is written with ostentatious deliberation and brings itself to climax with a *chiasmus*: 'But her long fair hair was girlish: and girlish, and touched with the wonder of mortal beauty, her face.' *Chiasmus* is not conspicuous again in the book.

This girl, encountered near the end of the fourth chapter, embodies the future of multiform possibility on which Stephen has staked everything. He accords her so much significance because he is already excited; afflatus is sustaining paragraph after paragraph; now we hear of 'the holy silence of his ecstasy'. It is a silence induced by the following:

A girl stood before him in midstream, alone and still, gazing out to sea. She seemed like one whom magic had changed into the likeness of a strange and beautiful seabird. Her long slender bare legs were delicate as a crane's and pure save where an emerald trail of seaweed had fastened itself as a sign upon the flesh. Her thighs, fuller and softhued as ivory, were bared almost to the hips where the white fringes of her drawers were like featherings of soft white down. Her slateblue skirts were kilted boldly about her waist and dovetailed behind her. Her bosom was as a bird's soft and slight, slight and soft as the breast of some darkplumaged dove. But her long fair hair was girlish: and girlish, and touched with the wonder of mortal beauty, her face. (*P* 171)

Assenting to Stephen's joy, we may let this prose work on us as it seems to want to, and later think it bad and overdone, Joyce trapped by the need, or the will, to make more of the experience than it will yield. But these are thoughtless readings. We ought to be asking what the passage *is*. And once the *chiasmus,* or some other sign, has prompted us to scan it curiously it comes to seem a young man's copybook page: not exactly an experience we are to share with Stephen, but something like a piece he might have written out afterwards, practising his new vocation.

'Her bosom was as a bird's soft and slight, slight and soft as the breast of some darkplumaged dove.' We may note the chiasmic detailing, also the omitted comma which makes the first clause say 'soft and slight as a bird's', not 'as a bird's in being soft and slight', but say the simpler thing the more portentously. We should reflect that Stephen would have been 16,[1] and would be working from the kind of preliminary outline in which his Jesuit masters had drilled him. So a topic sentence proposes the optical fact, a girl, and a second sentence rolls up its sleeves to state what the paragraph will elucidate, that she seems changed by magic into the likeness of a seabird. Four more sentences deal with this statement as though it were a proposition to be demonstrated; each, beginning with 'Her', affirms something birdlike of a separate part of her body, the scan proceeding upward, her legs, her thighs, her waist, her bosom. Then an orderly 'But', when we come to hair and face, affirms the unvanquished categories of girlishness, with the solemnly cadenced *chiasmus* to achieve finality.

This passage, like the narrative sequence of which it is an element, is as nicely calculated as the poem on Parnell which a journalist named Hynes recites at the end of Joyce's story 'Ivy Day in the Committee Room'. The rightness of the poem as Joyce concocted it has been justly celebrated ever since Padraic Colum drew attention to the way real feeling breaks through its hand-me-down idiom.[2]

---

[1]Joyce (born 2 February 1882) was 16 in the summer that preceded his matriculation into the University. Not that Joyce's calendar is always a safe guide to Stephen's.

[2]In his preface to the Modern Library *Dubliners,* dated October 1926. 'It is an amateurish and conventional piece of rhetoric, and yet, amazingly enough, a real grief and a real loyalty break through the hand-me-down verse. . . . He must have entered into Hynes's mind before he could recreate the verses that have just the exact heat, just the exact flourishes that a passionate and

He lies slain by the coward hounds
   He raised to glory from the mire;
And Erin's hopes and Erin's dreams
   Perish upon her monarch's pyre.

No one has ever surpassed James Joyce's skill at contriving plausible limits for expressive competence, and like Hynes's poem Stephen's paragraph careers near the brink of parody without detriment to our awareness that something enchanting has happened.

What happened next was that the girl turned her head toward Stephen and discovered that he was looking at her; after a long exchange of stares she then lowered her eyes and commenced paddling about with her foot, and blushed. This is re-created as follows:

> She was alone and still, gazing out to sea; and when she felt his presence and the worship of his eyes her eyes turned to him in quiet sufferance of his gaze, without shame or wantonness. Long, long she suffered his gaze and then quietly withdrew her eyes from his and bent them towards the stream, gently stirring the water with her foot hither and thither. The first faint noise of gently moving water broke the silence, low and faint and whispering, faint as the bells of sleep; hither and thither, hither and thither; and a faint flame trembled on her cheek.

We should recall that the year is about 1898, and that she is posed like a naughty beauty on a cigarette card of that period; her skirts tucked up and her bare legs on show. Pictorially considered, this apparition is thoroughly conventional *Kitsch*. Socially considered, she is a very cool young woman indeed for those times; there are hints in *Ulysses* that a girl at leisure on the beach may even be of dubious virtue. (Leopold Bloom sees three girls on Sandymount strand, and two of them, or their namesakes, later turn up in Nighttown.)

Symbolically, she is easier to assimilate; she combines a conventional late-nineteenth-century emblem, Woman Epitome of the Ennobling, with the bird-motif that twines its way through the *Portrait*, from the vengeful eagles of the opening sequence to the birds of augury watched outside the library and the emblematic kinsmen who shake 'the wings of their exultant and terrible youth' in the antepenultimate entry in Stephen's diary. A charming awkwardness, even, may inhere in his effort to combine these emblems, bird and girl, so soon after finding a prophetic force in his own strange surname, which is Dedalus.

> Now, at the name of the fabulous artificer, he seemed to hear the noise of dim waves and to see a winged form flying above the waves and slowly climbing the air. What did it mean? Was it a quaint device opening a page of some medieval book of prophecies and symbols, a hawklike man flying sunward above the sea, a prophecy of the end he had been born to serve and had been following through the mists of

semi-literate man would give to his subject according to the literary convention which he knew.'
James Joyce, *Dubliners* (New York: Random House, Modern Library, 1926, 1954).

childhood and boyhood, a symbol of the artist forging anew in his workshop out of the sluggish matter of the earth a new soaring impalpable imperishable being? (*P* 169)

We may say that the *Portrait* is unified by Stephen's twenty years' effort to substitute one father for another. In the first sentence his father, of the 'hairy face', is telling him a story about a moocow. That father descends—'. . . a small landlord, a small investor, a drinker, a good fellow, a storyteller, somebody's secretary, something in a distillery, a taxgatherer, a bankrupt and at present a praiser of his own past' (*P* 241)—and in the book's last sentence the word 'father' points past him, aloft: 'Old father, old artificer, stand me now and ever in good stead.' Now Stephen is praying, as it were, to his name-saint, the pagan Dedalus, a father whose example represents liberty from the father who has gone down so far in the world. Appealing from father to father was a habit formed early. In the first chapter, after Father Dolan beats him, Father Conmee promises him safety. In the third chapter Father Arnall's sermons scare him witless and a nameless Father grants him absolution. As these priestly examples indicate, fatherhood is rather a role than an estate; to shift fathers is for the son, too, to shift roles, to be no longer the son of a drunken bankrupt but heir to the vocation of the fabulous artificer.

In Chapter IV a different possibility is dangled before him: he may think of becoming the Reverend Stephen Dedalus, SJ. He would owe allegiance to the Holy Father, and be himself Father Dedalus. But no sooner does the Director of Studies formulate this possibility than Stephen knows it is unreal, and he finds himself wondering at 'the remoteness of his soul from what he had hitherto imagined her sanctuary, at the faint hold which so many years of order and obedience had on him when once a definite and irrevocable act of his threatened to end forever, in time and eternity, his freedom' (*P* 161). And as he picks his way homeward through the slum where the Dedaluses live now he smiles 'to think that it was this disorder, the misrule and confusion of his father's house and the stagnation of vegetable life, which was to win the day in his soul' (*P* 162).

We learn from these important sentences that Stephen has for a long time vaguely assumed that the priesthood lay ahead.[3] Now that he knows he will never be a priest, the alternative appears to be his father's 'misrule and confusion'.

It is in the final part of Chapter IV that a new alternative to 'misrule and confusion' presents itself. His schooldays are behind him; entry to the University has been arranged; he feels an elated freedom; his soul (he soon phrases it) has 'arisen from the grave of boyhood'. And the revelation comes: 'Yes! Yes! Yes! He would create proudly out of the freedom and power of his

---

[3]Cf. 'All through his boyhood he had mused upon that which he had so often thought to be his destiny and when the moment had come for him to obey the call he had turned aside, obeying a wayward instinct' (*P* 165).

soul, as the great artificer whose name he bore, a living thing, new and soaring and beautiful, impalpable, imperishable' (*P* 170).

It is then that he sees the girl, and almost smothers whatever it was he saw beneath an appliqué of bird-phrases. If this written-out bird-girl is an instance of the 'new and soaring and beautiful', the artificer is off to a doubtful start. Still, the life of an excited 16-year-old seems to have acquired a momentum.

What he writes in the fifth chapter isn't better: a Swinburnian villanelle, very much of the nineties, to a Temptress who might have been painted by Gustave Moreau—

And still you hold our longing gaze
With languorous look and lavish limb! (*P* 223)

—'lure of the fallen seraphim', in fact, to whom go up 'smoke of praise', a world-wide 'eucharistic hymn', and an uplifted 'chalice flowing to the brim' in which beneath the trappings of studio satanism we can just discern a naughty nineties wine-glass: wine and woman and song, no less. The account of the poem's composition permits us the dry observation that Stephen is writing, still in bed of a morning, in the afterglow of a wet dream. In France the Symbolist Movement, villanelle-makers at its fringes, was staffed by lapsed Catholics in quest of efficacious words of power, and Stephen, too, thinks of himself as 'a priest of eternal imagination, transmuting the daily bread of experience into the radiant body of everliving life' (*P* 221). So the old destiny and the new have fused.

Stephen's other achievements in this final chapter include the outlines of a theory of the beautiful and an extended prose style which still courts Newman and Pater but can make do tellingly with the short sentence. 'Talked rapidly of myself and my plans. In the midst of it I unluckily made a sudden gesture of a revolutionary nature. I must have looked like a fellow throwing a handful of peas into the air. People began to look at us. She shook hands a moment after and, in going away, said she hoped I would do what I said.' That is from Stephen's diary entry for 15 April, and if it has a little fun with her hope that he would do what he said it has fun with the figure he was cutting, too. 'Welcome, O Life,' he writes on the 26th, and the prayer to the Old Father is dated the 27th. Stephen's departure from Ireland is surely imminent and, if it is 1902, Ascension Day is eleven days off.[4]

Had James Joyce died in mid-1914, leaving the *Portrait* for posthumous publication, it would no doubt be the kind of minor masterpiece, like Alain-

[4]Again, *if* it is 1902, as Joyce seems to have once intended. Appendix 1 explains why he changed to 1903, though the revisions were never quite completed. To let Stephen commence his flight on Ascension Day of whatever year would have been heavy-handed, but the connection asked to be made and while he was considering 1902 'eleven' would have seemed a good way to make it. Eleven is a recurrent Joyce-number. Bloom's son in *Ulysses* lived 11 days and would be in his eleventh year if he were alive on Bloomsday. The last phrase in *Finnegans Wake* has 11 words, and the text encodes variations on 11 throughout. By one gloss, 11 signifies renewal by inaugurating a new decade, and Joyce may have noticed that 1881, the year of his conception, is divisible by 11.

Fournier's *Le Grand Meaulnes*, that is accorded enthusiastic rediscovery from time to time without ever quite commanding attention. Fitting it to the Joyce canon would present no problems, since the rest of the canon would consist only of the thirty-six poems of *Chamber Music* which it is easy to imagine Stephen writing, and the fifteen stories of *Dubliners* which are perfectly compatible with the *Portrait* in presenting Dublin as a city to get out of. Some reader of all three books might occasionally ponder the fact that the careful documentary prose of the stories predates the bird-girl rhapsody.

> Mrs. Mooney was a butcher's daughter. She was a woman who was quite able to keep things to herself: a determined woman. She had married her father's foreman and opened a butcher's shop near Spring Gardens. But as soon as his father-in-law was dead Mr. Mooney began to go to the devil. He drank, plundered the till, ran headlong into debt. It was no use making him take the pledge: he was sure to break out again a few days after. By fighting his wife in the presence of customers and by buying bad meat he ruined the business. One night he went for his wife with the cleaver and she had to sleep in a neighbour's house. (D 61)

That compresses much character, incident and observation into a few lines, and why the man who had written it in 1905 should eight or nine years later be writing of a bosom 'as a bird's soft and slight, slight and soft as the breast of some darkplumaged dove' is a question we can imagine being answered in several ways, supposing this comparatively minor author seemed worth the speculation. There might not even seem to be a question; such a reader, in his nearly Joyce-less library, might actually prefer the darkplumaged prose and imagine a Joyce who before his unlucky death at 32 had evolved from mean little sentences all the way to a rhetoric of some amplitude. But we have the advantage over that reader that we have learned to prize a tautness and economy of little words and cunning syntax as a consequence of the revolution of taste at the centre of which stands *Ulysses*, and it is now as impossible to imagine a twentieth-century literature without *Ulysses* as to imagine a twentieth-century physics without Relativity.

It is *Ulysses* that compels the attention the rest of the canon routinely receives: that has trained the readers who can see how much is achieved in *Dubliners*, or are willing to venture amid the lianas and mocking mirrors of the *Wake*. And, in being a book in which Stephen figures again, *Ulysses* reacts with the *Portrait* in complex ways. Is his being back in Dublin a grim joke of fortune? Or is he to find only here the Life to which he bade welcome? At any rate, he has tumbled from aloft into a very different sort of book, one he cannot dominate as he dominated the *Portrait*. He walks out of it near the end, as if out of the universe.

The *Portrait* is a book of vignettes and inner symmetries, so compliant to the fluid play of Stephen's memory that the reader must exert attention, against the suasions of the text, to keep even some rudimentary grasp on chronology. A publisher rejected it in 1916 for being 'discursive, formless, unrestrained' and needing to be 'pulled into shape'.[5] It had cost Joyce years of effort to pull it out of the shape in which the unfinished first version, *Stephen Hero*, had implicated it, and if a first-time reader is unlikely to perceive that in Chapter I everything between the first row of asterisks and the second, from 'The wide playgrounds . . .' to '. . . the water's edge', takes place in a twenty-four-hour span, or if the cunning with which the three episodes and diary of Chapter V reverse the overture and three episodes of Chapter I went unnoticed for sixty years,[6] Joyce had achieved what he thought the book required, a fluidity with a rigour deep beneath it. Time and place are equally understressed. It is only the death of Parnell that establishes what part of the nineteenth century we are in, and Dublin, when the Dedalus family moves there from Bray, is presented with no special vividness: a large squalid commercial city with some local history like all cities.

But the calculated vagueness of the *Portrait* answers the imperatives of a nearly solipsistic novel. In *Dubliners* (written 1904–7) Joyce had specified times, places, idioms so stubbornly the book's publication was delayed for years while publishers fretted over single words that registered quiddities of dialogue ('. . . if any fellow tried that sort of a game on with his sister he'd bloody well put his teeth down his throat, so he would') or designated actual pubs by name ('Nosey Flynn was sitting up in his usual corner of Davy Byrne's'). Joyce declined to delete this one 'bloody' from 'The Boarding House', though elsewhere in the book there were other 'bloody's' he would sacrifice 'with infinite regret', because 'the word, the exact expression I have used, is in my opinion the one expression in the English language which can create on the reader the effect which I wish to create', and he declined to delete mention of Davy Byrne's and several other pubs from 'Counterparts', though in other stories he had used fictitious pub-names, because they served as ports of call in a rain-soaked Odyssey: 'the names are real because the persons walked from place to place',[7] and to alter them, he implied, would be like inventing fictitious substitutes for Genoa, Istanbul, Marseilles. In fiction certain things at least had to be *so*, and in *Ulysses* the list of what could not be altered grew enormously longer. Some time after *Ulysses* was published Joyce told Arthur Power:

> In realism you are down to facts on which the world is based: that sudden reality which smashes romanticism into a pulp. What makes most people's lives unhappy is some disappointed romanticism, some unrealizable or misconceived ideal. In fact you may say that idealism is the ruin of man, and if we lived down to fact, as

[5]Richard Ellmann, *James Joyce* (New York: Oxford University Press, 1959), 416–7; revised edition 1982, 403–4. The reader was Edward Garnett.
[6]It was Hans Walter Gabler who spotted this chiasmatic structure. See his essay in Thomas F. Staley and Bernard Benstock, *Approaches to James Joyce's 'Portrait'* (Pittsburgh: University of Pittsburgh Press, 1976), 25–60.
[7]*Letters*, II, 136, and II, 312.

primitive man had to do, we would be better off. That is what we were made for. Nature is quite unromantic. It is we who put romance into her, which is a false attitude, an egotism, absurd like all egotisms. In *Ulysses* I tried to keep close to fact.[8]

In *Ulysses*, clocks and church-bells keep us aware of the hour, a stenographer's typewriter clicks out day, month and year ('16 June 1904'), newspapers specify local and world events, and feet move on clearly named streets past clearly named houses and places of business, several hundred with specified and verifiable addresses.

All this has an immediate effect on our sense of Stephen Dedalus, whose mind in the old way can transport us instantly from Sandymount strand to Paris, but whose body, now subject to the necessity of getting some six miles from Dalkey (10.30 a.m.) to the strand (11.05 a.m.), would have been borne on the Dalkey tram from Castle Street, Dalkey, to Haddington Road, thence on the Sandymount line to Tritonville Road. Though the book does not particularise this journey it permits us to work it out, and the Stephen who must take the new electric trams[9] to be in definite places at definite times is no longer in command of the new book the way his psyche was in command of the *Portrait*.

A worked example may be in order. Stephen is free to leave his post at Mr Deasy's school early because it is Thursday, a half-day, and the latter half of the half-day is for hockey, starting 'at ten' (*U* 1961:26; *U* 1986:22; 2–92). After the boys file out he spends a few minutes with a boy named Sargent, and rather longer with his headmaster Deasy, who types in his presence the final sentences of a letter. The two conversations and the business with the typewriter delay him till perhaps 10.30. He is next seen near Watery Lane (*U* 1961:88; *U* 1986:73; 6–39) from the carriage of a funeral procession which was to start at eleven (*U* 1961:73; *U* 1986:60; 5–95) and has been under way perhaps five minutes; he would then be walking from the tram-stop in Tritonville Road to the beach. So he has come from Dalkey (six miles) in about half an hour; the logistic details can be deduced from a tram-map.[10]

Though no reader need feel obliged to perform such researches, anyone can welcome their corroboration of the sureness we feel underlying each page of the book. Joyce obeyed a principle Hemingway later enunciated, that a writer's omissions will show only when he omits things because he doesn't

---

[8]Arthur Power, *Conversations with James Joyce* (London: Barnes and Noble, 1974), 98.

[9]The tram of an idyllic scene in the second chapter of the *Portrait* (69–70) is horse-drawn, but by 1904 Dublin had the most advanced electric tram system in Europe.

[10]Expertise in the space–time continuum of *Ulysses* characterises some of the best recent Joyce scholarship. The analysis above is paraphrased from Clive Hart and Leo Knuth's *Topographical Guide to James Joyce's 'Ulysses'* (Colchester: Wake Newsletter Press, 1975), 24. See also Clive Hart's essay and chart in the Clive Hart and David Hayman *James Joyce's 'Ulysses'* (Berkeley, London: University of California Press, 1974), 181–216, where minute by minute the movements of some thirty characters in the sixty-five-minute 'Wandering Rocks' episode are accounted for.

know them, and he worked out elaborate *schemata* so as to be able to suppress them. Except for the funeral cortège, with which we ride swaying and rattling clear across the city with frequent indications of time and place ('Are we late?' asks Martin Cunningham; Paddy Dignam has an appointment with the grave), Joyce nowhere takes us aboard the wheeled conveyances his characters use so freely. An abrupt cessation of action here, an abrupt resumption there—such is his staccato notation: the cut, not the dissolve. The effect, for a reader trained on the *Portrait*'s suave transitions (where cuts signify the passage of days, or years) is one of calculated disorientation: Where are we now? How did we get here?

We see Stephen Dedalus leave Deasy's school in Dalkey; the eye traversing a narrow white space on the page next picks him up on the strand framing sentences about ineluctable modalities (*U* 1961:37; *U* 1986:31; 3–1). Especially when we reflect that he must have just alighted from a tram, we can guess why he should be musing on entrapment in a space–time continuum, moving 'a very short space of time through very short times of space' the interstices of which Joyce plotted with such rigorous care it is possible to account for the entire day, 8 a.m. to midnight, of a secondary character, Buck Mulligan, whose onstage appearances are only four in number and widely separated.[11]

Deasy's typewriter, two telephones, the brand-new electric trams, some talk of motorcars—these epitomise a Dublin that has changed since Stephen walked its streets in the *Portrait*. Machinery is interpenetrating the ancient, stagnant city. More important, gadgetry epitomises a shift of emphasis between the two books. In *Ulysses*, as Joyce's friend and one of his best commentators, the late Frank Budgen, shrewdly observes, people have 'just that social time sense that is part of the general social mentality of the period, and no more. This arises out of the necessity for coordinating their daily social movements. . . . James Watt invented the steam engine, and the steam engine begat the locomotive, and the locomotive begat the timetable, forcing people to . . . think in minutes where their great-grandfathers thought in hours. . . . The discoveries of the astronomer and the mathematician have less immediate effect on [social time-sense] than the electrification of the suburban lines.'[12]

Now, all this was true, if less egregiously true, of the Dublin of the *Portrait*, the last chapter of which precedes the action of *Ulysses* by no more than a couple of years. Joyce opened that chapter, though, by explicitly stressing Stephen's indifference to the space–time grid.

—How much is the clock fast now?

His mother straightened the battered alarmclock that was lying on its side in

---

[11]See Hart and Knuth, 35–6.

[12]Frank Budgen, *James Joyce and the Making of Ulysses* (London: Grayson, 1934), 131–2. Reprinted with additional material (London: Oxford University Press, 1972).

the middle of the mantelpiece until its dial showed a quarter to twelve and then laid it once more on its side.

—An hour and twentyfive minutes, she said. The right time now is twenty past ten. The dear knows you might try to be in time for your lectures. (*P* 174)

Lost in his thoughts, he sets out on a walk of over two miles to the University, and has not gone halfway when a clock beats 'eleven strokes in swift precision'.

Eleven! Then he was late for that lecture too. What day of the week was it? He stopped at a newsagent's to read the headline of a placard. Thursday. Ten to eleven, English: eleven to twelve, French; twelve to one, physics. (*P* 177)

He sees almost nothing of the city's busy morning life. His passage past Trinity and along the awninged and thronged bustle of Grafton Street—a route Bloom traces in *Ulysses,* on pages (*U* 1961:162; *U* 1986:137; 8–614) thronged with sensuous particulars—is obliterated by much revery and reminiscence from which a flower-seller's hand on his arm arouses him. He arrives too late for the English class, or the French. As if in anticipation of the norms of *Ulysses,* the only class Stephen can attend that day is physics, where on borrowed paper he copies 'spectrelike symbols of force and velocity', and hears words about an ellipsoidal ball and about the currents that induce magnetism in coils.

Ulysses lets us know that its doings are transacted in a designated zone on the surface of the magnetic ellipsoidal earthball, near the intersection of its 53rd parallel of latitude, north, and its sixth meridian of longitude, west (*U* 1961:736; *U* 1986:606; 17–2304). It is 1904, 16 June (*U* 1961:229; *U* 1986:188; 10–379). The sun rose at 3.33 a.m. local time, will set at 8.27 p.m. The action of the book begins at 8 a.m. atop the Martello tower at Sandycove. And the book is no more than a few pages old when we commence to divine that Stephen, returned from Paris, has become a drinker like his father Simon.

He has not changed fathers after all; and, no longer sustained by the myth of sonship to the fabulous artificer, he is becoming another improvident Dublin character. People notice his resemblance to his father, the voice, the eyes; and he and Si Dedalus, pursuing their separate ways the length of the book, pursue them in parallel, never meeting, drinking, drinking. 'Chip off the old block!' (*U* 1961:144; *U* 1986:118; 7–899) cries one of the company when Stephen suggests a pub. He uses up about a pound, drinking and treating, in a day when stout was twopence a pint and one could live on less than a pound a week. One time when father and son almost meet there is a suggestive parallelism of behaviour. Stephen's persistent sister Dilly extracts from her father 14*d* to feed the family (*U* 1961:237; *U* 1986:195; 10–678). Just a few pages later (*U* 1961:243; *U* 1986:200; 10–867) Stephen encounters her at a book-cart. Her intellectual cravings shadow his; she has spent a penny on Chardenal's French primer. He has at that moment over three pounds in his pocket (*U* 1961:391; *U* 1986:320; 14–286). He indulges in eloquent unspoken words, pitying them both, but does not offer her a penny.

In neighbouring chapters we even see father and son performing: Si Dedalus in the Ormond bar (*U* 1961:273; *U* 1986:225; 11–667) in glorious song at the insistence of cronies, Stephen in the National Library (*U* 1961:188; *U* 1986:154; 9–130 *ff*) fortified by three whiskeys (*U* 1961:199; *U* 1986:163; 9–533) and performing with no less virtuosity his lengthy *Hamlet* turn, earlier scheduled for a pub. The Stephen of this book would appear to be headed toward as predictable a future as any of the young men in *Dubliners*, several of whom turn up in *Ulysses* as if to verify the sure workings of destiny. Corley is still the sponger of 'Two Gallants', Lenehan still the agile leech, while being son-in-law to Mrs Mooney of 'The Boarding House' as we might have expected drives Bob Doran to periodic benders. A great dreary stagnant mechanism, locked in space, locked in time, the city slowly turns its cogs and millwheels; men down their pints and emit their witticisms on schedule, and a married woman who isn't busy with children is very lonely.

But the air is bright, colours sparkle, the city has a carnival glitter, and in a long book free of the drizzle and cold that dominated so much of *Dubliners* we shall be spending many hours with a prudent citizen, a non-toper, a non-idler, who observes everything that goes on and has no quarrel with clock and tram necessities. He is Leopold Bloom. *Ulysses* is his book (he is 'Ulysses'), he dominates it, and Stephen is now a secondary character. And if the *Portrait* may be summarised as Stephen's effort to substitute one father for another, *Ulysses* may be (most imperfectly) summarised as the story of Bloom's futile effort to treat Stephen as a son. Stephen in *Ulysses* is no longer in search of a father, as he was in the *Portrait*. He is obsessed by a dead mother, and as for fathers, living or mythic, elected or adoptive, his present instinct is to get clear of them.

The Genre of *Ulysses*

A. Walton Litz

Standing at the confluence of so many literary traditions and genres, Joyce's *Ulysses* has become the supreme challenge for the theoretical critic of fiction. At one time or another *Ulysses* has been presented as a stark naturalistic drama, a symbolist poem, a comic epic in prose, even a conventional novel of character and situation. The problem I shall consider in this essay is easily stated: what are the rewards, and dangers, of reading *Ulysses* with a particular view of the novel *as a form* constantly in mind? If we go beyond the convenient shorthand of calling *Ulysses* a novel because it is a large and various prose work which rests heavily in the hand, and try to process it into a general theory of the novel—does this approach really yield a more delicate understanding of *Ulysses*, or does it, like so many critical strategies, produce more mischief than clarification?

We might remind ourselves at the outset that Joyce put little store in the traditional classifications of literature by type and genre. His early aesthetic, in so far as we can reconstruct it from the notebooks and *Stephen Hero*, was aggressively psychological and affective, concerned with the work's relationship to its maker and its audience. Joyce abandoned the conventional definitions of kinds derived from structure and subject matter. Instead, he defined the major "conditions" of art in terms of the artist's relationship to his creation, as in this passage from the Paris notebook:

> There are three conditions of art: the lyrical, the epical and the dramatic. That art is lyrical whereby the artist sets forth the image in immediate relation to himself; that art is epical whereby the artist sets forth the image in immediate relation to himself and to others; that art is dramatic whereby the artist sets forth the image in immediate relation to others. . . . (6 March 1903)

Over against these broad categories, which apply to every kind of art, Joyce set the qualities of the beautiful work, borrowing his tags from Aquinas and defining "the beautiful" in relation to the act of apprehension: wholeness, harmony, and radiance are primarily phases in the mind of the audience. Similarly, tragedy and comedy are defined not in terms of structure or action, but in terms of the reader's psychology. "Stasis" is Joyce's *fin de siècle*

From *The Theory of the Novel: New Essays*, ed. John Halperin (Oxford and New York: Oxford University Press, 1974), 109–120. Copyright © 1974 by Oxford University Press, Inc. Reprinted by permission of A. Walton Litz and Oxford University Press.

modification of the Aristotelian catharsis, applying as in Aristotle to both tragedy and comedy; but unlike Aristotle, Joyce has nothing to say about the particular forms of comedy or tragedy, nor about the various species of literature. His early critical system is essentially a psychology of the artist and the artistic experience. The kinds of art are determined by the relationship between the artist and the image; beauty is defined through analysis of the act of apprehension. In the void between lies the work of art itself, with all its formal qualities. Like so many aesthetic theories, Joyce's is weakest where it touches the practical problems of formal criticism.

Joyce's subsequent reading of Croce (c. 1911) would have confirmed his early disregard for generic criticism, and it should not be surprising that he finally abandoned the world "novel" as a descriptive term for *Ulysses*. He seldom if ever referred to *Ulysses* as a "novel" after mid-1918, a point in time which coincides almost exactly with that moment in the process of composition when *Ulysses* ceased to resemble a conventional novel of internal-external reality and Joyce began to pour his creative energy into the various expressive techniques of his *schema*. As Joyce gradually realized his full-scale plan of symbolic resemblances and correspondences, often reworking the earlier episodes to harmonize them with the total design, he abandoned the term "novel" and began to describe his work-in-progress as a museum of different literary kinds. A letter to Carlo Linati of September 1920, which accompanied a first version of the *schema*, is typical of this new attitude:

> It [*Ulysses*] is an epic of two races (Israelite-Irish) and at the same time the cycle of the human body as well as a little story of a day (life). . . . It is also a sort of encyclopaedia. My intention is to transpose the myth *sub specie temporis nostri*.

If Joyce felt that he had left any definite conception of the "novel" far behind by the time he finished *Ulysses*, so did the most perceptive of the early readers and reviewers. Ezra Pound saw *Ulysses*, like Flaubert's *Bouvard et Pécuchet*, as a work which "does not continue the tradition of the novel or the short story." In fact, Pound assigned *Ulysses* to the sonata form and the paternity theme, thereby taking it out of the parochial tradition of the English novel and aligning it with a whole series of continental archetypes. And T. S. Eliot, in a seldom-quoted part of his much-quoted review, "*Ulysses*, Order, and Myth," described *Ulysses* as a departure from the novel-form, not a continuation of it.

> I am not begging the question in calling *Ulysses* a "novel"; and if you call it an epic it will not matter. If it is not a novel, that is simply because the novel is a form which will no longer serve; it is because the novel, instead of being a form, was simply the expression of an age which had not sufficiently lost all form to feel the need of something stricter. Mr. Joyce has written one novel—the *Portrait*; Mr. Wyndham Lewis has written one novel—*Tarr*. I do not suppose that either of them will ever write another "novel." The novel ended with Flaubert and with James. It is, I think, because Mr. Joyce and Mr. Lewis, being "in advance" of their time, felt

a conscious or probably unconscious dissatisfaction with the form, that their novels are more formless than those of a dozen clever writers who are unaware of its obsolescence.

So neither Joyce, nor the most acute of his early readers, were much concerned with defining the genre of *Ulysses*. To them the significance of the work lay in its disintegration and reorganization of traditional forms, and Eliot's review has more to say about the "individual talent," about Joyce's innovations, than it has to say about "tradition." This same willingness to accept *Ulysses* as a more or less unique form, although belonging to a large family of traditional forms, marked most of the important criticism from the 1920's to the 1950's, and although *Ulysses* was constantly referred to as a "novel" there was little effort to place the work in a theoretical view of the history of fiction, or to make real critical use of generic distinctions. However, since the publication of Northrop Frye's *Anatomy of Criticism* in 1957, *Ulysses* has become a crucial testing-ground for new theories of fiction and new methods of generic criticism. This essay will review some of these attempts to define the genre of *Ulysses*, with an eye toward discovering how much—and in what ways—they enhance our understanding of Joyce's masterpiece.

Let us begin with two terms loosely adapted from E. D. Hirsch's study, *Validity in Interpretation* (1967). An *extrinsic* genre is some *a priori* notion, such as the notion of what a "novel" should be, that one brings to the work of art as a fixed frame-of-reference; an *intrinsic* genre is our sense of the work's total form, which emerges from a process of re-reading and re-adjustment. Clearly, most of the recent attempts to read *Ulysses* as a "novel" have made use of some extrinsic notion of what the form should be, the most obvious and valuable example being S. L. Goldberg's *The Classical Temper* (1961). Approaching *Ulysses* with a restrictive—typically English—model of the "novel" as a dramatic and realistic form, Goldberg seeks to reconstruct the novel which was botched or obscured by Joyce's persistent intellectualism and his willful parade of symbolic correspondences. Goldberg is absolutely explicit about the "model" which governs his reading of *Ulysses*.

> *Ulysses* is [not] a case requiring special methods of interpretation or special assumptions about Symbols or Myths or Art in general. What meaning is truly realized in it, what value it has, lies in its *dramatic* presentation and ordering of human experience, and nowhere else. In short, it is not "Romance," not a joke, not a spiritual guide, not even an encyclopaedia of social disintegration or a re-creation of Myth or a symbolist poem; it is a novel, and what is of permanent interest about it is what always interests us with the novel: its imaginative illumination of the moral—and ultimately, spiritual—experience of representative human beings. And though it is an unusual novel, and complicated with extraordinary elements, its importance is founded, in the last analysis, on that fact. (p. 30)

. . . .

> The common assumption that *Ulysses* is a complex, symbolic poem, to which the ordinary interests and techniques of the novel are irrelevant, is justifiable only so

long as we do not forget that it is also—and rather more obviously—a representational novel, and much, if not most, of its meaning is expressed in and through its representational mode. It contains "probable" and significant characters, in a "probable" and significant setting, doing and saying "probable" and significant things, so that it inevitably calls into play those expectations and assumptions we bring to the novel (as to each literary form) and which control the way we seek its meaning. (p. 107)

When reading *The Classical Temper* I am always reminded of Henry James's amusing and highly illuminating attempt to disengage a Jamesian novel from Browning's *The Ring and the Book*. In his 1912 lecture honoring the centenary of Browning's birth, James confessed that he had always longed to turn *The Ring and the Book* into a novel of the "historic type."

> From far back, from my first reading of these volumes, which took place at the time of their disclosure to the world, when I was a fairly young person, the sense, almost the pang, of the novel they might have constituted sprang sharply from them; so that I was to go on through the years almost irreverently, all but quite profanely if you will, thinking of the great loose and uncontrolled composition, the great heavy-hanging cluster of related but unreconciled parts, as a fiction of the so-called historic type, that is as a suggested study of the manners and conditions from which our own have more or less traceably issued, just tragically spoiled—or as a work of art, in other words, smothered in the producing ("The Novel in *The Ring and the Book*").

Just as James brought to Browning's poem a fixed notion of what "historic fiction" should be, so Goldberg brought to *Ulysses* a narrowly conceived view of the novel as a genre, but with one important difference: James is heuristic and almost playful, whereas Goldberg has the missionary purpose of saving Joyce from himself and the modern world. I find Goldberg's book one of the most useful critical studies of *Ulysses*, since it brings to the foreground several neglected aspects of the work and serves as a healthy counteragent to the more extravagant symbolic readings of the 1950's; but the "novel" Goldberg delivers is a sad diminution of Joyce's achievement. The real problem in Goldberg's critical approach is his exclusively "English" view of the novel's properties, one which slights the diversity and elasticity of the form: it is a narrowly conceived view which demands that the novel attain some kind of realism through probable dramatic action. I do not think it accidental that Goldberg's study was received with much greater enthusiasm in England than in America or on the Continent. The persistent strains of Romance and fantasy in American and Continental fiction have always made Joyce's reception easier outside of England. In the English reviews of *The Classical Temper* there was a clear feeling that Joyce had been saved for the English novel and at the same time put firmly in his place.

The Classical Temper exhibits all the virtues of a sharply defined, *extrinsic* critical approach: it is a method which extracts and clarifies the representational dimensions of *Ulysses*. But at the same time it leaves out most of the structures and harmonies that give the work a special form and special impact. Goldberg quotes approvingly as his epigraph the remark by D. H. Lawrence that "most books that live, live in spite of the author's laying it on thick." But the life of *Ulysses* resides in the thickness of the narrative, and it seems clear that midway in the writing of the book Joyce's fictional ideals ceased to have any vital relationship to those of Professor Goldberg. To insist that *Ulysses* is a traditional English novel is to corrupt it back into its origins, and to allow Joyce no significant development beyond the world of the *Portrait*. It is one thing to *evaluate* the course of Joyce's later artistic development, and I share many of Professor Goldberg's doubts and reservations. But it is quite another thing to adopt a generic frame which will allow for no sympathetic under-standing of Joyce's mature art. As Arnold Goldman pointed out in a review of *The Classical Temper*, Stephen Dedalus may have chosen the "classical temper" but Joyce himself—in his 1902 essay on James Clarence Mangan—called both the romantic and classical tempers "constant states of mind." The young Joyce saw the "unrest" between classicism and romanticism as "the condition of all achievement": and the quick of *Ulysses* lies precisely in a creative "unrest" between classical representation and romantic correspon-dences.

At the opposite extreme from Goldberg's tendentious and at times moralis-tic use of generic definitions stand the works of those theorists who would construct an archetype for the novel out of the actual diversity of prose fiction. Because of the extraordinary diversity in the origins and evolution of narrative fiction, generic criticism is always falling toward one of two ex-tremes: either a single strain—Romance, the picaresque, epic, "myth"—is selected as the norm (this would be Goldberg's method in his choice of the English realistic novel as model); or a category is invented which is so comprehensive that it can encompass all the diverse strains. Typical of the latter method would be Northrop Frye's division of fiction, the genre of the written word, into four dominant modes: Novel, Confession, Anatomy, and Romance. In Frye's system, *Ulysses* becomes the archetypal work of fiction, the "complete prose epic with all four forms employed in it, all of practically equal importance, and all essential to one another, so that the book is a unity and not an aggregate." Frye's description of *Ulysses* is much more satisfactory than Goldberg's, since it reaches out to embrace all the diverse aspects of the work; it is, like most of the *Anatomy*, elegant, comprehensive, and of limited value to the practical critic. Frye's system is infinitely stimulating because it is a work of imagination in itself, and because it brings *Ulysses* into startling alignment with many other works of literature. In effect, Frye's method breaks through the restrictions of conventional notions about literary "influ-ence" and enables us to see *Ulysses* in relation to works which are apparently quite dissimilar. But when it comes to dealing with the local effects and internal symmetries of *Ulysses*, Frye's theories have little to offer. It would seem that we are confronted with a stubborn paradox: the more limited extrinsic concepts of genre, such as Goldberg's model of the representational novel, can be highly effective tools for practical criticism, with sharp cutting edges; while the comprehensive extrinsic genres, such as Frye's anatomy of fiction, are almost useless to the practical critic even though they may provide convincing theoretical models. The trouble with Goldberg's method is that it willfully disregards some of the most obvious achievements in *Ulysses*; the trouble with Frye's method is its purity, which cannot accommodate the shifting mixtures of forms and kinds that we encounter in the actual process of reading. *Ulysses* is a book which talks constantly about itself, and one of the things it talks about is the diversity of prose fiction. No extrinsic notion of what the novel or fiction should be can be taken as an ideal model, and we must allow the work to establish its own *intrinsic* genre as we read it.

It would be equally foolish to approach *Ulysses* without any preconceptions about its genre (always an impossibility anyway) and to approach it with a fixed generic concept in mind. The ideal reading of the work should correspond to the ideal scanning of a picture described by E. H. Gombrich in *Art and Illusion*. We bring to *Ulysses* all the schemata available to us, both from Joyce's earlier works and from the literary tradition, since we know that without such schemata we cannot begin to see or understand; but we should also be prepared to modify and rearrange our preconceptions as we go along. Since *Ulysses* demands that we understand it both spatially and temporally— by which I mean that we should have, as we read it, a simultaneous sense of the book as a timeless image, like the city it imitates, and of the book developing through time—the intrinsic genre of *Ulysses* is our total image of the work, which is recreated and modified each time we re-read it.

Whatever *stemma* or family tree one postulates for prose narrative (that presented by Robert Scholes and Robert Kellogg in *The Nature of Narrative* will serve very well), *Ulysses* can be viewed as a synthesis of the myriad forms which went into the making of modern fiction. It was Joyce's intention to disintegrate the well-made "novel" into its origins, and then to perform a prodigious act of re-integration. Most of our difficulties with the genre of *Ulysses* fall away when we cease to fret about a single "model" for the work and concentrate upon the experience of reading, which involves the constant use of familiar genres and types. At the outset of *Ulysses*, the title, the opening lines, and even the physical shape of the book raise certain expectations about narrative, mythic, and epic forms. The opening chapters, in their renderings of inner and outer reality, depend upon conventions and generic distinctions already familiar to the accomplished reader of the *Portrait* or the modern novel in general. But beginning roughly with "Aeolus" and "Lestrygonians" (episodes 7 and 8), the conventional models of a "novel" begin to show their inadequacies, and in the second half of *Ulysses* ("Wandering Rocks" onward) we are constantly shifting our schemes of expectation as Joyce rings his changes on a number of genres and conventions, conducting us through the rich repertoire of epic, satiric, and dramatic forms. *Ulysses* may be viewed as a two-part performance in which the modern novel is built up and then disintengrated into its original components. By the time we reach "Ithaca" the two extremes of historical fact and mythical fiction have been so separated that they begin to resemble each other, fact taking on a mythic dimension through Joyce's sheer encyclopedism: in effect, the schoolroom catechism of "Ithaca" provides us with the raw materials for a novelistic ending, which the actual narrative tails away into the farthest reaches of factual catalogue and mythopoetic allegory.

So *Ulysses* raises in acute form the central problem of generic criticism. As E. D. Hirsch has pointed out, the generic critic is always plagued by "a version of the hermeneutic circle, which in its classical formulation has been described as the interdependence of part and whole: the whole can be understood only through its parts, but the parts can be understood only through the whole." We are faced with a vexing question:

> Is there really a stable generic concept, constitutive of meaning, which lies somewhere between the vague, heuristic genre idea with which an interpreter always starts and the individual, determinate meaning with which he ends? At first glance the answer seems to be no, since apparently the interpreter's idea of the whole becomes continuously more explicit until the genre idea at last fades imperceptibly into a particularized and individual meaning. If this is so, and if the intrinsic genre is defined as a conception shared by the speaker and the interpreter, it would seem that what I have called the "intrinsic genre" is neither more nor less than the meaning of the utterance as a whole. Obviously, it is a useless tautology to assert that the interpreter must understand the speaker's meaning in order to understand the speaker's meaning. That is a circularity no more helpful than the paradox of the hermeneutic circle as promulgated by Heidegger. If we cannot preserve a distinction between the particular *type* of meaning expressed and the particular meaning itself, then the intrinsic genre becomes simply the meaning as a whole. Nothing but confusion is achieved by calling a particular meaning a "genre". (Hirsch, p. 81)[1]

We begin *Ulysses* with a scheme of expectations, differing from reader to reader, based on our experience of Joyce's earlier work and of literature as a whole. We respond to various signals, refining and enlarging our sense of the work as Joyce plays upon our various generic expectations. But finally, when we have read *Ulysses* several times and have settled into some sense of its total meaning, does the work remain representative of a type or kind of fiction; or has its intrinsic genre gradually become identical with its unique meaning? The prime value of some generic frame lies in the temporal nature of language. As Hirsch comments:

> One basis for the distinction between genres and particular meanings can be sought in a consideration that necessitated the genre concept in the first place—the temporal character of speaking and understanding. Because words follow one

[1]E. D. Hirsch, *Validity in Interpretation* (New Haven: Yale University Press, 1967).

another sequentially, and because the words that will come later are not present to consciousness along with the words experienced here and now, the speaker or listener must have an anticipated sense of the whole by virtue of which the presently experienced words are understood in their capacity as parts functioning in a whole. (p. 82)

But is this conventional argument relevant in a work such as *Ulysses,* one of the aims of which is to surmount or circumvent the "temporality" of language? If *Ulysses* cannot be read, only re-read, as Joseph Frank argued years ago, then ultimately we have our total, spatial understanding of the work to use in place of any preconceived generic expectations, and we re-read the book against our previous experience of it as well as against our models of prose fiction.

What I am saying is that *Ulysses,* at its deepest reaches, denies the validity of genres and seeks to be wholly itself. One could argue that all successful works of literature ultimately undergo such a transformation, but I do not believe that to be true; the phenomenon strikes me as distinctly modern, and peculiar to Joyce's aims. The title and opening lines of *Paradise Lost,* to adapt an example from Hirsch, announce a subject and generic expectations that are never fundamentally altered, no matter how profound our experience of the poem becomes. To understand the opening of *Paradise Lost,* and indeed the whole poem, the sensitive reader must know the genre, and if he does not then no amount of reading and re-reading will completely reveal the poem. On the other hand, a well-trained reader who knew the genre could tell you a great deal about *Paradise Lost* without reading beyond the first pages.

The case with *Ulysses* is much more compromised. The generic signals are all there, in greater profusion perhaps than in any other work of English literature, but the ultimate schema is something every reader must construct for himself. Inevitably, therefore, readings of *Ulysses* will be more various and more indeterminate than those of *Paradise Lost.* To try to reduce this indeterminacy and "openness," as Professor Goldberg does, is to go against the nature of *Ulysses,* since the collapse of the genres is one of its subjects. One important aspect of *Ulysses* is its self-conscious commentary on literary theory, most obvious in the course of the Library episode where Stephen's view of Shakespeare's plays—like the aesthetic of the young James Joyce—is uncompromisingly anti-generic. Joyce wished to re-create the ideals of Classical art under the conditions of modern life and his own personality; but he believed that it is the "classical temper," not Classicism with its trappings of types and kinds, that lead to "the sane and joyful spirit."

Recent attempts to incorporate *Ulysses* into various theories of the novel have simply reinforced my respect for Joyce's earliest readers, and my appreciation for his youthful aesthetic. Just as the best Shakespearean criticism often begins with a generic model—revenge tragedy, Romance, historical allegory—but then goes beyond this model to talk of the total experience of the plays, so the best criticism of *Ulysses* must be a statement of the total and unique experience which the work delivers to a sensitive reader. This is the final norm against which we test, with each re-reading, the consistency of the different parts. In fact, the three stages of artistic apprehension as described in Joyce's early notebooks and fictions make a fair model for our gradual apprehension of *Ulysses*. The sequence—*integritas, consonantia, claritas*—is a movement from cognition to recognition to satisfaction. First we must understand the integrity and symmetry of the work, which involves seeing it in relation to other works and tracing the relationship of part to part: it is here that our knowledge and experience of the various traditional genres comes into play. But finally, when our experience of the different parts and their relationship is fused into a single image, the unique meaning of the work stands forth in individual clarity. Joyce's methods and intentions would seem to demand a Crocean aesthetic, where "the particular throbs with the life of the whole intuition, and the whole exists in the life of the particular. Every pure artistic image is at one and the same time itself and the universe, the universe in this individual form and this individual form equivalent to the universe" (*New Essays on Aesthetic*).

So we are led to a process of understanding *Ulysses* very like Gombrich's notion of "perceptual trial and error." As Gombrich discovered from his own experience and the experiments of modern psychologists, we cannot begin to perceive without a framework of illusions, of provisional hypotheses, and in the case of *Ulysses* these hypotheses are provided by our experience of the genres. They shape our expectations, but unless we are willing to modify them we place the work in a strait-jacket. Joyce demands a lot of the reader: like Gombrich's ideal viewer of an Impressionist painting, Joyce's ideal reader must read across the brushstrokes as well as with them, supplying provisional forms to support the artist's impressions. This process of perceptual trial and error may seem obvious, but it is worth belaboring because the present trend toward theoretical criticism of fiction contains a potential threat to a work such as *Ulysses*, which lends itself easily to categories and classifications that give so little in return. Indeed, the current trends in generic criticism may pose a threat to the whole pluralistic world in which the masterpieces of modern art developed, smoothing away the irregular achievements of Joyce's generation. One of the essential characteristics of *Ulysses* is that it resembles many other works of literature, but other works do not resemble it: the balance-of-trade is mainly one way, not reciprocal as in a world of genres and decorum. We have a double sense of *Ulysses*: a sense of how we came to understand it, through a series of perceptual adjustments; and a sense of the whole work as a timeless image. *Ulysses* lives in our minds as both process and product, always evolving and yet always the same, and any theory which threatens this double sense, whether it be put forward in the cause of the "novel" or some other genre, is ultimately self-defeating. The term "heuristic," which was invented by the nineteenth century to describe its new awareness of indeterminacy and openness, should be the motto for any sympathetic reading of *Ulysses*.

Ulysses: The Narrative Norm

Karen Lawrence

The first three chapters of *Ulysses* pay homage to both the personal tradition Joyce had created in his previous works of fiction and to the traditional novel. In its dominant narrative voice and interest in the character of the artist, the "Telemachiad" resembles *A Portrait* in particular, and even the reader of *Ulysses* who fails to recognize this continuity will experience a sense of security from the presence of this narrative voice. The staples of the novel—third-person narration, dialogue, and dramatization of a scene—also promise narrative security to the reader who begins *Ulysses:* they act as signposts promising him familiar terrain on the subsequent pages. No matter what we may know about the structural apparatus and levels of allegory in the work after reading Joyce's notesheets, letters, and tips to Stuart Gilbert, what we experience when beginning *Ulysses* is a novel that promises a story, a narrator, and a plot. "Stately, plump Buck Mulligan came from the stairhead" (*U* 1961:2–3; *U* 1986:3; 1–1) is a plausible beginning for any novel. *Ulysses* begins like a narrative with confidence in the adequacy of the novel form.

It is important to underscore the initial narrative promises to the reader made in the novel not only because they will be broken later on but also because they provide an interesting contrast to the change in Joyce's basic conceptions of plot and significance in fiction, a change that must have antedated, at least in part, the beginning of the novel. *Ulysses* offers, in a sense, a "rewriting" of *Dubliners*: it presents another portrait of Dublin designed to reveal the soul of the city and its citizens. But in arriving at the basic conception of *Ulysses*—the condensing of the wanderings of Odysseus to one day in the life of certain Dublin citizens—Joyce radically altered his conception of what a portrait of Dublin should be.

In the initial conception of *Ulysses*, Joyce departed from the aesthetic of economy and scrupulous choice that had directed the writing of *Dubliners* in favor of an aesthetic of comprehensiveness and minute representation. This aesthetic is implied in Joyce's statement to Budgen about his desire to give so complete a picture of Dublin in *Ulysses* that if the city were to disappear it could be reconstructed from the book.[1] Although the "story" of *Ulysses* takes place during one day only, this day is infinitely expansible by being infinitely divisible—the rendering of the complete "details" of life almost obscure the sense of story. Unlike *Dubliners*, which promises to end the narrative as soon as the "soul" of a character is revealed, *Ulysses* offers no clear principle of completeness. The frustration critics felt at what they thought of as Joyce's infidelity to the minimal requirements of a story is reflected in Edmund Wilson's comment in *Axel's Castle:* "It is almost as if he had elaborated [the story] so much and worked over it so long that he had forgotten . . . the drama which he had originally intended to stage."[2]

Ulysses also offers no clear principle of emphasis or proportion. In the stories of *Dubliners*, the right "trivial" incident in the life of a character epiphanizes the meaning of the life; in *Ulysses*, no one particular incident in a life is considered to be of supreme importance. Because the characters carry within them the same problems, desires, and past, no matter when we see them, no day is essentially different from any other. If *Dubliners* focuses on a particularly significant day in the lives of its characters, *Ulysses* focuses on any day in Dublin's diary, and the day happens to be June 16, 1904. It is as if an entry in the diary of Dublin, rather than in a personal diary such as the one that ends *A Portrait*, was blown up in a great, Brobdingnagian gesture; in the world of *Ulysses*, as in Brobdingnag, a molehill can indeed become a mountain. The slight rise in the plot that the theory of epiphany suggests is almost completely eliminated in the narrative of *Ulysses*. What is important here is not the transition between a "short story" and the long story of development told in a traditional novel but the transition from fiction interested in plot to fiction in which plot becomes synonymous with digression.

The stream-of-consciousness technique in the "Telemachiad" does alert the reader to some of these changes in overall conception. In using this technique increasingly until it almost dominates the narrative in Chapter Three ("Proteus"), Joyce offered his third-person narrator less and less to do. The retrospective narrative voice of a conventional novel is replaced almost entirely, so that "plot" changes from a form of narrative memory to a rendering of "the very process in which meaning is apprehended in life."[3]

But in the first three chapters of the novel (even in "Proteus"), the third-person narrator exists and serves some important narrative functions. The dominant narrative voice in the "Telemachiad" provides the narrative norm for the novel (and continues in subsequent chapters), and it is the voice that, for a long time, was ignored in critical discussions of *Ulysses*. Although some

---

[1]Frank Budgen, *James Joyce and the Making of Ulysses* (1934; reprint ed., Bloomington: Indiana University Press, 1960), pp. 67-68.

[2]Edmund Wilson, *Axel's Castle: A Study in the Imaginative Literature of 1870–1930* (New York: Charles Scribner's Sons, 1959), p. 217.

[3]S. L. Goldberg, *The Classical Temper: A Study of James Joyce's Ulysses* (London: Chatto and Windus, 1961), p. 92.

critics have described the quality of this voice,[4] many recent critics have tended to pass over this narrative norm on the way to discussions of narrative distortions that occur primarily in the latter half of the book.[5] But the primary reason for this omission is the importance that decades of critics have placed on the stream-of-consciousness technique in the early chapters: in focusing on the "innovativeness" of this technique, they have tended to underestimate the importance of the narrative norm.

The narrative conventions established in the early chapters of *Ulysses* include the presence of an identifiable and relatively consistent style of narration that persists in the first eleven chapters of the book and the tendency of the narrative to borrow the pace and diction of the characters' language. In other words, the conventions include *both* the continued presence of a particular style *and* the adaptability of style to character. Critics who focus on the stream-of-consciousness emphasize the importance of the character's mind and treat the third-person narration as an adjunct of character.[6] This is only partly correct, since it fails to acknowledge the recognizable, idiosyncratic narrative voice that does exist.

For example, the following sentences, the first from "Telemachus," the second from "Proteus," display the characteristic Joycean qualities seen in *A Portrait* and now heightened in *Ulysses*: "Two shafts of soft daylight fell across the flagged floor from the high barbicans: and at the meeting of their rays a cloud of coalsmoke and fumes of fried grease floated, turning" (*U* 1961:11; *U* 1986:10; 1–317); and "The cry brought him skulking back to his master and a blunt bootless kick sent him unscathed across a spit of sand, crouched in flight" (*U* 1961:46; *U* 1986:39; 3–355). The denotative style in *A Portrait* is evident here, with greater syntactic dislocation and more unusual diction. The extreme concern with the sounds of words—that is, the alliteration ("flagged floor," "blunt bootless," "spit of sand") and what Anthony Burgess has called the "clotted" effect of the double and triple consonants[7]—and the strange placement of the modifying adverb ("fried grease floated, turning") produce a sentence that, as Burgess says, reveals "a distinctive approach to what might

---

[4]See David Hayman's *Ulysses: The Mechanics of Meaning* (Englewood Cliffs, N.J.: Prentice-Hall, Inc., 1970), especially pp. 75-79, and Anthony Burgess's *Joysprick: An Introduction to the Language of James Joyce* (London: André Deutsch, 1973) for two of the earliest and best discussions of this narrative norm. Recently, discussions of the narrative norm have become more common. See, for example, Hugh Kenner's *Joyce's Voices* (Berkeley: University of California Press, 1978), and Marilyn French's *The Book as World: James Joyce's Ulysses* (Cambridge, Mass.: Harvard University Press, 1976).

[5]See, for example, Wolfgang Iser, *The Implied Reader: Patterns of Communication in Prose Fiction from Bunyan to Beckett* (Baltimore: The Johns Hopkins University Press, 1974), pp. 179-233, and Ben D. Kimpel, "The Voices of *Ulysses*," *Style* 9 (Summer 1975): 283-319.

[6]See, for example, Erwin R. Steinberg's *The Stream of Consciousness and Beyond in Ulysses* (Pittsburgh: University of Pittsburgh Press, 1973) for the most extensive treatment of Joyce's use of the stream-of-consciousness technique.

[7]Burgess, *Joysprick*, p. 68.

be termed literary engineering."[8] This is prose that is competently, indeed masterfully crafted, precisely and poetically written.

Especially in the "Telemachiad," this literate, formal, poetic language is associated with the character of Stephen Dedalus. In the first three chapters, we perceive the world largely through the eyes of an aspiring artist, and, as in *A Portrait,* the linguistic "sympathy" between character and narrative voice blurs the distinctions between them. "Wood shadows floated silently by through the morning peace from the stairhead seaward where he gazed" (*U* 1961:9; *U* 1986:8; 1–243) is a narrative statement that "borrows" Stephen's lyricism. Throughout the chapter, the narration will often present Stephen's poetic and melancholy perceptions of things in language appropriate to his sensibility.

But despite the close connection between the style and the mind of Stephen in the "Telemachiad," the style exists independently in subsequent chapters, as is evident from the following examples:

> The caretaker hung his thumbs in the loops of his gold watch chain and spoke in a discreet tone to their vacant smiles. ("Hades," *U* 1961:107; *U* 1986:88; 6–72)

> It passed stately up the staircase steered by an umbrella, a solemn beardframed face. ("Aeolus," *U* 1961:117; *U* 1986:97; 7–46)

> The young woman with slow care detached from her light skirt a clinging twig. ("Wandering Rocks," *U* 1961:231; *U* 1986:190; 10–441)

> Miss Douce's brave eyes, unregarded, turned from the crossblind, smitten by sunlight. ("Sirens," *U* 1961:268; *U* 1986:220)

In the first eleven chapters of *Ulysses,* this narrative style establishes the empirical world of the novel; it provides stability and continuity. The persistence of this type of narrative sentence provides a sign of the original narrative authority amidst the increasingly bizarre narrative developments of the later chapters, until it disappears in "Cyclops." . . . It is a style that orients the reader and offers him a certain security by establishing the sense of the solidity of external reality.

It seems to me that this type of narrative sentence, along with the other staples of the narrative mode of the early chapters—interior monologue, free indirect discourse, and dialogue—functions as the "rock of Ithaca," "the initial style" to which Joyce alluded in a letter to Harriet Weaver in 1919: "I understand that you may begin to regard the various styles of the episodes with dismay and prefer the initial style much as the wanderer did who longed for the rock of Ithaca."[9] This is the nonparodic style that establishes the decorum of the novel. When it disappears later on in the text, we realize that

---

[8]Ibid., p. 74.

[9]Letter, 6 August 1919, *Letters of James Joyce,* Vol. 1, ed. Stuart Gilbert (New York: The Viking Press, 1957), p. 129. However, when I refer to the "initial style" henceforth, I mean specifically the prose style of the third-person narration.

it too was a choice among many possibilities, a mode of presentation. But in its seeming fidelity to the details of both the thoughts and actions of the characters it provides us with a sense of the real world of the novel. With all its precision and fastidiousness, it functions for us as a narrative norm.[10]

However, while the decorum of the novel is established, the presence of another narrative strand in the first chapter slyly questions the assumptions about language upon which the normative style is based. The effect of this narrative strand is subtle, nothing like the radical disruptions of narrative stability in the later chapters. And yet this narrative fluctuation in the first chapter of the book serves as a warning to the reader of the strange narrative distortions to come. The following passage illustrates the intertwining of the narrative strands in the first chapter:

> He [Mulligan] shaved evenly and with care, in silence, seriously.
>   Stephen, an elbow rested on the jagged granite, leaned his palm against his brow and gazed at the fraying edge of his shiny black coat-sleeve. Pain, that was not yet the pain of love, fretted his heart. (U 1961:5; U 1986:5; 1–102)

The second sentence is an example of the denotative narrative norm. The past participle "rested," surprising the reader prepared to encounter the present participle "resting," is a characteristic kind of dislocation. The third sentence, "Pain, that was not yet the pain of love, fretted his heart," is a clear example of free indirect discourse. But the first sentence is puzzling—the number of adverbs and adverbial phrases surprises us. There is a naive quality to this writing that separates parts of speech as if they were about to be diagrammed.

In fact, the first chapter of Ulysses provides numerous examples of this naive narrative quality. This strand of the narration reveals itself in the repeated use of certain formulaic narrative constructions of which no student of creative writing, however inexperienced, would be proud. The proliferation of the following phrases in the early pages of the novel suggests that something strange is taking place in the narrative: "he said sternly," "he cried briskly," "he said gaily" (U 1961:3; U 1986:3; 1–19, 29, 34); and "He laid the brush aside and, laughing with delight, cried," "Stephen said quietly," "he said frankly," "Stephen said with energy and growing fear," "he cried thickly" (U 1961:4; U 1986:4; 1–66). What kind of narrative world is created by these

---

[10]Hugh Kenner's ingenuity and prolificacy illustrate the possibilities for characterizing the early narrative style of Ulysses. In The Stoic Comedians: Flaubert, Joyce, and Beckett (Berkeley: University of California Press, 1962), the following narrative sentence is cited as an example of Joyce's characteristic manipulation of language and his "resolute artistry": "Two shafts of soft daylight fell across the flagged floor from the high barbicans: and at the meeting of their rays a cloud of coalsmoke and fumes of fried grease floated, turning" (pp. 30-31). In Joyce's Voices, the same marked precision is said to exemplify the "fussiness of setting and decor" of "Edwardian novelese" (pp. 68-69). Both descriptions are intriguing, the second moving us, as it does, further away from a view of the early style as normative and nonparodic. The style becomes just another example of a particular kind of rhetoric, despite its temporal primacy in the text. Although the sentence does exhibit stylistic idiosyncrasies, I favor Kenner's first description of it as an example of Joyce's characteristic style, more normative at this point than parodic.

descriptions and what purpose could Joyce have had in using this type of prose in the beginning of the novel?

Joyce called the technique of this chapter "narrative young," and this description, while it probably refers to Stephen to some extent, also applies to the quality of narration: it is appropriate to the self-conscious, naive literary style exemplified above. Unlike the naiveté of the narrator in stories like "Clay" in *Dubliners,* stories in which through free indirect discourse the narrator ostensibly accepts his protagonist's assessment of the world, the naiveté of the narrative in "Telemachus" is literary as well as psychological. We notice an innocence concerning the very act of telling a story, an innocence that is a quality of the narrative itself rather than a property of a particular character.

What we are provided with in the early pages of *Ulysses,* disturbing the basically serious and authoritative narrative voice that creates a world we can believe in, is a different narrative strand that parodies the process of creation. Prose like "he cried thickly" and "he said contentedly" is the unsophisticated prose of fourth-rate fiction; a novel that begins this way parodies its own ability to tell a story. Even in the first chapter of the novel, Joyce begins to turn novelistic convention into novelistic cliché, and it is here that the reader glimpses language beginning to quote itself, its characteristic activity in the latter half of the book. While making use of the conventional tools of the novel, Joyce uses one strand of the narrative to upset the stability created by these conventions and to point to their inadequacy. As the normative style asserts its ability to capture reality in language, this narrative voice advertises its own incompetence. The world in which Buck Mulligan wears a "tolerant smile" and laughs "with delight" or in which Stephen says something "with energy and growing fear" is about as far from Henry James's world of "delicate adjustments" and "exquisite chemistry"[11] as a novelist can get. The sentences of this naive narrative point to the falsification and oversimplification that language wreaks on emotions by organizing them in discrete grammatical parts.

This narrative strand in Chapter One provides the first example of narrative performance and stylistic bravado in *Ulysses,* different from that in later chapters like "Cyclops" and "Ithaca," but stylistic exhibition nonetheless. There is a comic excess of labor in evidence in the narration: the narrator seems to wrestle with the discrete parts of speech available to him only to pin down the most commonplace of descriptions. The subtle nuances captured in sentences of the "initial style" elude the narrator's grasp. The excess of labor here is the antithesis of the coolness of scrupulous meanness in *Dubliners—*

[11]See James's Preface to *The Tragic Muse,* reprinted in *The Art of The Novel: Critical Prefaces* by Henry James (New York: Charles Scribner's Sons, 1962), p. 87: "To put all that is possible of one's idea into a form and compass that will contain and express it only by delicate adjustments and an exquisite chemistry . . . every artist will remember how often that sort of necessity has carried with it its particular inspiration."

the production of meaning seems to be a Herculean task.[12] But there is an air of safety that surrounds the "risks" the narrator seems to take. He is like a clown walking a tightrope only one foot above the ground. What is suppressed here is not so much a narrator as a grin.

It is possible to explain this adverbial mania in "Telemachus" in relation to the characters described. Hugh Kenner, for example, has discussed the presence of these adverbs in regard to the role playing of Stephen and Buck Mulligan.[13] While the thematic connection between the adverbial style and the role playing of the characters makes sense, it limits the significance of the strange verbal tic by giving it so exclusively a character-based explanation. The adverbial style tells us something about the kinds of utterances we find in certain types of narratives, as well as something about the characters in this one. The presence of the naive literary style suggests that the text as well as the character is trying on a costume. In Chapter One, we get a brief glimpse of the kind of narrative mimicry that dominates the later chapters of the book—the mimicry of a type of text rather than a particular character. What I find most interesting about the naive narrative strand in Chapter One is the beginning of an interest in language apart from character, language that calls attention to its own clichéd nature without providing the vehicle for the ironic exposure of a character. Instead of parodying the linguistic idiosyncrasies of a type of character, the narrator dons a stylistic mask of innocence to parody the very enterprise of telling a story. Parody is cut loose from the concerns of character and becomes an aspect of narrative.

Thus, Steinberg and other critics interested in the early chapters of *Ulysses* seem to me to have erred in assuming that if the narrator is not an *unreliable character* in the story (like the lawyer in Melville's "Bartleby, the Scrivener," for example, or the narrator in Ford's *The Good Soldier*), then the narrative can be trusted. Frank Kermode writes in an essay entitled "Novels: Recognition and Deception" that "we have bothered too much about the authority of the narrator and too little about that of the narrative,"[14] and this distinction between the authority of the narrator and the narrative is an extremely important one for the reading of *Ulysses*.

The tone of the opening chapter of *Ulysses*, then, seems to oscillate: in certain parts of the narrative *Ulysses* announces itself as a comedy, but for the most part it is dominated by the rather bitter and serious Stephen Dedalus. The copresence of the naive aspect of the narrative and the well-written, precise narrative norm makes it difficult for the reader to form a clear perception of a unified narrator.

---

[12]This sense of the excess of labor in the writing appears again in subsequent chapters like "Sirens," "Eumaeus," and "Ithaca," even though different styles are used in each case.

[13]See Kenner, *Joyce's Voices*, pp. 69-70.

[14]Frank Kermode, "Novels: Recognition and Deception," *Critical Inquiry* 1 (Sept. 1974): 117. Kermode's comment, made in reference to Ford's *The Good Soldier*, seems to me to apply much more appropriately to *Ulysses*.

And yet, this one narrative strand found in the first chapter of the novel is quickly overshadowed by the narrative norm and the stream-of-consciousness technique in the rest of the "Telemachiad." The mimicry of a type of text rather than a character will resurface in later chapters—most obviously in "Cyclops" and "Oxen of the Sun." But after Chapter One, this naive parodic style vanishes. Despite Joyce's developing interest in representing the inadequacies of language, despite the warning about the enterprise of novel writing in the first chapter, it is character, not narration, that is the most important subject of the first six chapters of the novel. Simultaneous with Joyce's perceptions of the limitations of both the conventional novel and his own previous fiction was an interest in further developing a method with which to present the workings of consciousness. The "Proteus" chapter is, as critics have suggested, the culmination of the "Telemachiad," not only chronologically, but stylistically as well; here the stream-of-consciousness technique reaches its peak in transcribing an educated, artistic mind. The use of stream-of-consciousness was experimental for Joyce when he wrote the "Telemachiad"—it carried further the "direct" representation of the mind of the artist begun in *A Portrait*. It is the drama of the character's mind, rather than the drama of novel writing, that is still paramount. As S. L. Goldberg has pointed out, the paragraph is still a dramatic unit of consciousness, the "artistic medium of a particular *act* of understanding."[15]

In the next three chapters of *Ulysses*, devoted to Leopold Bloom, this interest in character is still paramount. In these chapters, the reader finds the same texture of narration as in the "Telemachiad": a combination of third-person narration, dialogue, free indirect discourse, and the stream-of-consciousness of the character. The denotative norm of the "Telemachiad" persists in these chapters: "By lorries along Sir John Rogerson's Quay Mr Bloom walked soberly, past Windmill Lane, Leask's the linseed crusher's, the postal telegraph office" (U 1961:71; U 1986:58; 5–2, "Lotus-Eaters"); "The metal wheels ground the gravel with a sharp grating cry and the pack of blunt boots followed the barrow along a lane of sepulchres" (U 1961:104; U 1986:86; 6–639, "Hades"). The denotative norm continues to establish our sense of external reality and our sense of a narrative presence by assuring us that despite the introduction of a new character who sees the world differently from Stephen Dedalus, the world is the same. This second triad of chapters continues to build up our sense of what the world of Dublin and the world of the novel are like. The symmetry of this second triad with the "Telemachiad" and the persistence of the same basic rules of narration encourage us to group the first six chapters together as providing the norm of the book.

As in the "Telemachiad," one finds in these chapters a sympathy between

---

[15]S. L. Goldberg, *Joyce* (Edinburgh, 1962; reprint ed., New York: Capricorn Books, 1972), p. 90.

narrator and character that again involves the borrowing of linguistic habits. To turn the page from the heraldic image of Stephen Dedalus "rere regardant" and to encounter Leopold Bloom eating "with relish the inner organs of beasts and fowls" is to sense a difference in mood that depends in part on a change in style. The language associated with Bloom (both his stream-of-consciousness and some third-person narration) is more simple syntactically, more colloquial, and more redundant than Stephen's. (See, for example, the prose of the opening of the chapter.)

What is most interesting about the "sympathy" between narrator and character in Bloom's chapters, however, is its occasional comic manipulation. Although the exchange between character and narrator in these chapters follows the rules set in the "Telemachiad," at times this exchange seems to pick up speed. In the following passage from "Hades," for example, Bloom and the narrator carry on a rapid and weird exchange of images:

> The whitesmocked priest came after him tidying his stole with one hand, balancing with the other a little book against his toad's belly. Who'll read the book? I, said the rook.
> They halted by the bier and the priest began to read out of his book with a fluent croak. (*U* 1961:103; *U* 1986:85; 6–594)

The narrator describes the priest's belly as "his toad's belly"; then it is Bloom presumably who thinks "Who'll read the book? I, said the rook." Again, the third-person narration resumes in what seems like the initial style, except for the presence of the word "croak." Soon after this passage, Bloom looks at the priest and thinks "Eyes of a toad too," and the word "too" must refer to the "toad's belly" mentioned in the narrator's statement. There is a strange kind of play between narrator and character, almost a parodic form of sympathy between the two. This is a kind of "sympathy" that reduces the distance between the telling of the story and the story itself, a distance that will be manipulated in increasingly bizarre ways as the book progresses. This passage in "Hades" looks forward to the exchanges between narrator and speaker in "Scylla and Charybdis":

> —Yes, Mr Best said youngly, I feel Hamlet quite young. (*U* 1961:194; *U* 1986:160; 9–387)

> —Bosh! Stephen said rudely. A man of genius makes no mistakes. His errors are volitional and are the portals of discovery.
> Portals of discovery opened to let in the quaker librarian, softcreakfooted, bald, eared and assiduous. (*U* 1961:190; *U* 1986:156; 9–231)

Recently, Hugh Kenner has pointed out another anomaly of the second triad of chapters that emphasizes the artifice of the text. In his article, "The Rhetoric of Silence," Kenner cites several omissions in the text, some of which are highly significant to the plot. Chief among these gaps is a missing scene between Molly and Bloom, in which she tells him when Boylan is coming to

Eccles Street ("At four"), and Bloom tells her he will attend the Gaiety Theatre (the cue she needs to assure her Bloom will not be home at four). Based upon Bloom's later recollection of Molly's words ("At four, she said" [*U* 1961:260; *U* 1986:214; 11–188]) and Molly's recollection of Bloom's statement that he would be dining out ("he said I'm dining out and going to the Gaiety" [*U* 1961:740; *U* 1986:610; 18–82]), Kenner deduces that the painful scene between the two is omitted or repressed in the narrative. Since we cannot locate this conversation among the exchanges between Molly and Bloom that are recorded, Kenner concludes that they must have occurred offstage, like Molly's adultery or Bloom's visit to the insurance office on behalf of Paddy Dignam's widow.[16] Although this particular gap in the conversation can be recognized only retrospectively, when the missing lines are recollected, this playfulness in the selection of dramatized details puts into question our initial assumption that the narrative is recording all significant action. But, as Kenner says, we can reconstruct the scene in our minds, based on our knowledge of the characters and our sense of the empirical world that Joyce goes to such lengths to depict.[17] As Stephen discovers in "Proteus," the world is "there all the time without you. . . world without end" (*U* 1961:37; *U* 1986:31; 3–28). Narrative selection rather than empirical reality is questioned; the concept of omission presupposes that something in particular is being omitted.

In the second triad of chapters, we move closer to the comic play to come. In fact, I would argue that the mind of Leopold Bloom and the more comic and parodic tone of his chapters predict the direction of the rest of the narrative. It is Bloom's rather than Stephen's sensibility that dominates the *kind* of book *Ulysses* will become. The opening of the book to the subliterary as well as the literary and the movement from statement to cliché are predicted by the movement from Stephen Dedalus to Leopold Bloom. In some ways, the general tone and feeling of the book and some of the narrative strategies of the later chapters are also predicted in the book's first half.

By the end of "Hades," we have been introduced to the two main characters in a thorough way. In the stream-of-consciousness of each character, in each private memory emerges a particular way of making sense of the world and the self. In "reading" the world, the characters rely on different tools of interpretation: Bloom on clichés and bits of popular information, Stephen on abstruse allusion and esoteric philosophy. Both characters, however, are concerned with making sense of their pasts, not by an act of retrospection, as can be found in the novels of James or Proust, but in random associations that surface while they live their lives. "It is the 'stream of consciousness' which serves to clarify or render intelligible both the element of duration in time and the aspect of an enduring self. The technique is designed to give some

---

[16]Hugh Kenner, "The Rhetoric of Silence," *James Joyce Quarterly* 14 (Summer 1977): 382–394.
[17]Ibid., p. 383.

kind of visible, sensible impression of how it is meaningful and intelligible to think of the self as a continuing unit despite the most perplexing and chaotic manifold of immediate experience."[18] Amidst the sense of the "immediate experience" of life that we get in the first six chapters of *Ulysses* is the faith in character not as a "construct" seen from the outside but, nevertheless, as a "self" that is constant.

Thus, in the early chapters of *Ulysses* the characters carry the main burden of interpreting the world. "Proteus" is the culmination of Stephen's attempt to interpret his surroundings. In fact, his portentous announcement, "Signatures of all things I am here to read," is one of the most explicit declarations of character as interpreter in literature. As Fredric Jameson has said of psychological novels in general (and this applies to the early chapters of *Ulysses*), the character "from within the book, reflecting on the meaning of his experiences, does the actual work of exegesis for us before our own eyes."[19] In subsequent chapters, the reader and the writer participate more strenuously in the hermeneutic process. But in the beginning of the book, the major "burden" of interpretation is placed on the characters.

By providing a norm in its first six chapters that later would be subverted, the novel encompasses its author's changing interests; it can thus be said that the book, as well as Joyce, the author, changes its mind. When he wrote the first six chapters, Joyce did not yet fully realize the direction the second half of the novel would take. But his decision to leave the first chapters substantially intact was made after writing the entire novel. The opening section of the book was left as a kind of testimony to an older order, a norm for the reader at the same time as it is an anachronism in terms of the book as a whole. Consequently, the opening of the novel does not prepare the reader for what follows. A novel usually offers its reader built-in strategies for interpreting the world it presents. The concept of development in most novels insures that the early parts of the work in some way prepare the reader for what is to come (Henry James's *Prefaces* devote considerable space to this idea of preparation). But the first six chapters of *Ulysses* lead the reader to have certain unfulfilled expectations, that is, they make a certain contract that is subverted (for instance, that the normative voice will be sustained throughout the novel, that character will be the major concern). Although Joyce, unlike Kierkegaard, never openly confessed to this kind of "deception,"[20] *Ulysses* begins by deliberately establishing narrative rules that are bent and finally broken later on.

[18]Hans Meyerhoff, *Time in Literature* (Berkeley: University of California Press, 1955), p. 37.
[19]Fredric Jameson, "Metacommentary," *PMLA* 86 (Jan. 1971): 13.
[20]See Søren Kierkegaard, *The Point of View for My Work as an Author: A Report to History and Related Writings*, trans. Walter Lowrie; ed. Benjamin Nelson (New York: Harper & Brothers, 1962). The work announces that for the purpose of arriving at "truth," Kierkegaard had lulled his unsuspecting readers into a sense of narrative security in his aesthetic writings, only to subvert this security later in the religious writings.

In *Ulysses*, Joyce leaves the "tracks" of his artistic journey. Throughout his career Joyce transformed and developed his materials, but in the process he tended to outgrow a specific form and move on to another. Before writing *Ulysses* he had abandoned poetry for the short story and the short story for the extended narrative record of the growth of the artist's mind in *A Portrait*. Then, as S. L. Goldberg has observed, discovering that the record of the growth of the artist's mind was severely limited by the artist's awareness,[21] he began *Ulysses*. Realizing that Stephen had "a shape that [couldn't] be changed,"[22] he became more interested in Leopold Bloom. And, finally, finding obsolete the idea of a narrative norm that tells a story, with "Aeolus" as a clue and with "Wandering Rocks" and "Sirens" as the new formal beginning, he went beyond the novel to something else. In each case, the changes in form and style reflect the shedding of an artistic belief no longer sufficient to his vision.

[21]See Goldberg, *Joyce*, p. 63.
[22]Quoted in Budgen, *James Joyce and the Making of Ulysses*, p. 105.

Mockery in *Ulysses*

James H. Maddox

When Little Chandler goes to meet Ignatius Gallaher at Corless's in "A Little Cloud," their conversation at once becomes a struggle for dominance, and Little Chandler never has a chance. "And is [Paris] really so beautiful as they say?" he asks; and, a little later, "is it true that Paris is so . . . immoral as they say?" In his answer to the first question, Gallaher shows that "beautiful" is an inoperative word in the vocabulary of a bon vivant such as himself, and in his answer to the second he magisterially transforms "immoral" into "spicy" (*D*, 76, 77). Chandler, who is dependent upon hearsay in the first place (". . . as they say"), is quelled by this man who dictates with such authority the meanings and efficacy of words.

Gallaher's discourse has mastered Chandler's—not a particularly grand feat, since Chandler habitually thinks of himself in the terms described by the discourses of others. (He can imagine his future success as a poet only by imagining the words the English critics might evolve to describe his Celtic-twilight poetry.) But Gallaher too has a discourse that the story presents as being easily mastered. Here, for example, mediated through Joyce's free indirect style, is Gallaher's description of life abroad:

> Ignatius Gallaher puffed thoughtfully at his cigar and then, in a calm historian's tone, he proceeded to sketch for his friend some pictures of the corruption which was rife abroad. He summarised the vices of many capitals and seemed inclined to award the palm to Berlin. Some things he could not vouch for (his friends had told him), but of others he had had personal experience. He spared neither rank nor caste. He revealed many of the secrets of religious houses on the Continent and described some of the practices which were fashionable in high society and ended by telling, with details, a story about an English duchess—a story which he knew to be true. Little Chandler was astonished. (*D*, 78)

The thoughtful puff at the cigar (compare the dramatic striking of the match in Aeolus, which takes place in the newspaper office that is Gallaher's old stamping grounds); the denomination of the "corruption" as "rife"; the cosmopolitan pause before the journalistic "awarding the palm" to Berlin; the soft-porn stories of nuns and duchessess—every cliché reinforces the sense of

From *Joyce's Ulysses and the Assault upon Character*, James H. Maddox, Jr. (New Brunswick, N.J.: Rutgers University Press, 1978), pp. 141–154. Copyright © 1978 by Rutgers, The State University of New Jersey. Reprinted by permission of James Maddox and Rutgers University Press.

Gallaher's vulgar parade of noblesse oblige. The passage is humorous because it mocks by imitation, and mockery is so aggressive and effective a form of humor because it seems to reduce another's discourse to a relatively simple and knowable code.

Free indirect style in *Dubliners* reveals the limitations of a character's discourse while showing at the same time the character's blithe comfort within that discourse. The technique works in many of these stories to create a war between discourses, in which one character seeks to dominate another by demonstrating a superior description—hence knowledge—of the world. "An Encounter" is about the relationship between the two discourses we can hear in the following sentence: "Mahony said it would be right skit to run away to sea on one of those big ships and even I, looking at the high masts, saw, or imagined, the geography which had been scantily dosed to me at school gradually taking substance under my eyes" (*D*, 23). Both Farrington and Alleyne in "Counterparts" sneeringly mimic the speech and accent of the other; they know that to mimic is to reduce and to control. Most complexly of all, Gabriel Conroy labors all evening to demonstrate his superiority to and facility with various forms of discourse, none of which he quite succeeds in mastering: noblesse oblige (every Dubliner's dream) with Lily, banter with Molly Ivors, assumed dongiovannism with his wife. None of these ploys quite works, and it turns out that Gabriel has no confident voice of his own. His dilemma is to be taken up by other characters later in *Ulysses*.

Stephen Dedalus in the *Portrait* experiences, exactly, the obverse of this discovery of one's voicelessness. The chapter-by-chapter progression of this novel shows Stephen mastering more and more complex forms of speech; every new realm of experience presents itself as a new language to be acquired; even a prostitute's lips pressed upon his own seem to him "the vehicle of a vague speech" (*P*, 101). Moreover, the book is celebratory of Stephen's ability not only to master but then to escape limiting discourses. In one passage, which has always seemed to me the least distanced paragraph in *Portrait*, the passage in which one feels authorial "authority" backing Stephen more than anywhere else in the book, Joyce gives us a Stephen who has successfully resisted "the constant voices of his father and of his masters, urging him to be a gentleman above all things and urging him to be a good catholic above all things" as well as other voices, one of which bids him "be true to his country and help to raise up her fallen language and tradition" (*P*, 83–84). We later see in a more fully dramatized form this escape from the discourse of others when Stephen stands aside from competition with the discourses of MacCann and Davin in the final chapter. At the end, Stephen finds his own voice in the journal that constitutes the closing pages of the novel. He feels himself controlled only by that large discourse of the English language (*home, Christ, ale, master*), in whose shadow his soul frets. This is all before Paris and before Buck Mulligan.

Ulysses brings together the hero of *Portrait* and the dramatis personae of *Dubliners*, and it plunges Stephen Dedalus into an acute form of the battle of discourses to be found in the short stories. Paris has had its effect upon Stephen, in part simply by encouraging that predilection for the polyglot which was already becoming clear in him near the end of *Portrait*. Paris has created the Frenchified Stephen of *Ulysses*, with his Latin quarter hat, but it also seems to have released all his polylingual powers as well as an anxiety at what Bakhtin has called polyglossia, the polyglot's awareness of the inadequacy and relativity of any single language-system.[1] Post-Paris Stephen, with his *naturlich*, his *oinopa ponton*, his *maestro di color che sanno*, his *frate porcospino*, as well as his *Lui, c'est moi*, is lost in a welter of discourses and wishing he had land under his feet. And now Stephen finds himself living with a man who seems to need no land under his feet, who in fact is a powerful swimmer, and who is a tirelessly inventive and protean talker. We need only read Mulligan's conversation over breakfast with Stephen and Haines to understand why Stephen feels such panic and hatred in his presence. Mulligan is Stephen's Gallaher, not because he is in control of one dominant discourse, but because he seems capable of mastering *so many* discourses (he absolutely preempts the aesthetic Swinburne-Nietzsche line), and the intimidating insouciance of Mulligan's manner effectively silences Stephen. Mulligan has confidence, presence, and, to Stephen's knuckle-gnawing grief, authority. He can parody and trivialize Stephen's Shakespeare-theory and have Haines believe him: he has this kind of authority. And, much more importantly, Mulligan has immense authority within Stephen's own mind, where his strong, taunting voice echoes all day.

Mulligan wields such almost magical power because he is the catalyst that has brought to completion the destabilizing process begun in Stephen by his experience of Paris and the death of his mother. It took Mulligan to complete the process because Mulligan himself is a destabilized play of voices, offering, with a cynical Cheshire-cat smile, the principle that no voice or discourse is really important. For Mulligan, all that is real is the mocking smile itself, left suspended derisively in the air. And the truth is that Stephen must come to

---

[1]The great relevance of Bakhtin's "dialogism" to Joyce's narratives, especially *Ulysses* and *Finnegans Wake*, has not yet received the major attention it deserves. Let it suffice here to mention how Bakhtin's description of the mentality that produced a "novelistic" consciousness among Roman writers aware of literary Greek is remarkably like Joyce's depiction of an Irishman's attitude toward literary English. . . . (Mikhail M. Bakhtin, "From the Prehistory of Novelistic Discourse," in *The Dialogic Imagination*, ed. Michael Holquist, trans. Caryl Emerson and Michael Holquist [Austin and London: University of Texas Press, 1981], 61, 62–63).

Other formulations of Bakhtin's—for example, that the novel appears when the epic can no longer be looked upon without humor—make him a critic potentially invaluable for an analysis of Joyce's work. Interestingly, however, Bakhtin seems to have had little use for that work itself; in *Problems of Dostoevsky's Poetics* (ed. and trans. Caryl Emerson [Minneapolis: University of Minnesota Press, 1984]), his Marxism is uncharacteristically reductive and predictable as he approvingly quotes another critic's description of "the degenerate decadent psychologism of Proust or Joyce" (37).

agree that Mulligan is in some way right, even as he rejects Mulligan's solution of mockery. That is why, in one of the most important Homeric details of the book, Mulligan is the equivalent of Scyllá, the danger Stephen-Ulysses has to steer toward and then escape.

In the following few lines from Proteus, Stephen remembers three phrases of Mulligan's from earlier in the day, and they initiate a monologue—a dialogue, rather, or even a mini-drama—in which Stephen talks back and forth to himself and effectively finds it impossible to grant faith to any stance, any single voice that exists in his head:

> My Latin quarter hat. God, we simply must dress the character. I want puce gloves. You were a student, weren't you? Of what in the other devil's name? Paysayenn, P. C. N., you know: *physiques, chimiques et naturelles.* Aha. Eating your groatsworth of *mou en civet,* fleshpots of Egypt, elbowed by belching cabmen. Just say in the most natural tone: when I was in Paris, *boul' Mich',* I used to. (*U* 1961:41; *U* 1986:9; 3–174)

A quality that recent critics have found in the text of *Ulysses* is here grounded in the mind of Stephen Dedalus. Stephen can find no "meta-language" within his own consciousness. He is aware of the fragility of every statement he makes and the tenuousness of every stance he assumes because of the reflection that his own internalized Mulligan shows him in a mocking mirror.[2]

"The mockery of it," says Mulligan on the first full page of *Ulysses:* he opens the book with a mock mass, and he performs a fair mock-Synge and mock-Yeats in the library scene. And that particularly aggressive form of mockery, the mockery of the jeer and jibe, extends far beyond Mulligan in *Ulysses* and is indeed something of a Dublin tic: think of Martin Cunningham and (the report of) Paddy Leonard taking off Tom Kernan or Simon Dedalus doing the Goulding family or (in Bloom's memory) doing Larry O'Rourke. Think of the newsboys taking off Bloom's walk and the boots in Ormond responding to Miss Douce: "Imperthnthn thnthnthn" (*U* 1961:258; *U* 1986:212; 11–100). Mockery in all these cases is an act of aggression, an effort to make ridicule manifest. Compulsive mockery—and foremost among the book's compulsive mockers is Mulligan—is the signature of the frustrated and impotent and seems, in Joyce's work, the terrible Scylla for all the Irish. The compulsive mocker is still chained to the object of his scorn: there is something servile in this mockery. (Recall the linkage between these qualities in the description of Lenehan in "Two Gallants": "A shade of mockery relieved the servility of his manner" [*D* 52].) This insight of Joyce's accounts in part for the peculiar treatment of politics in *Ulysses.* The major form of political feeling exposed in the book is, precisely, the Citizen's luxuriating in his impotent mockery which is a form of bondage to the object of his hatred. And Joyce's perception also explains why Mulligan looms so large as Stephen's

[2]See in particular Colin MacCabe, *James Joyce and the Revolution of the Word* (New York: Barnes & Noble, 1979), chap. 2.

bogeyman. Not only does Mulligan mock Haines even as he envies his Oxford manner; vis-a-vis Stephen, Mulligan is envious of artistic power and therefore composes ditties and pastiches to trivialize art and bring it low. Ah, the mockery of it.[3]

It is worth remembering that Yeats was meditating upon the Irish penchant for mockery during the time that Joyce was bringing *Ulysses* to a close. Thoughts upon the uses of mockery (and, secondarily, upon his own fear of mockery)—thoughts never very far from Yeats's poems—are absolutely central to the magnificent "Nineteen Hundred and Nineteen," which presents a Yeatsian version of Stephen's dilemma. The bitter ironies following upon failed idealism; the desire for some cold-eyed knowledge beyond irony, some transcendent desolate heaven; the collapse of that superhuman effort into the malice of all-too-human mockery; the perception of mockery itself as an inauthentic superiority, a superiority of bad faith—the poem offers up a cold-heaven, bleak version of the polyphony of voices and attitudes in Stephen's head. And both Stephen and Joyce, though in different ways, devise an idea of voice or discourse that is a radical extension of the polyphonic form of the poems that Yeats was writing and would gather together in *The Tower:* for Yeats, for Stephen and for Joyce, the work of art comes to be conceived of as a panoply of discourses arrayed beneath a hypothetical ultimate discourse— "hypothetical" because it is unattainable. For Yeats, that ultimate discourse, which could master all other discourses, had a metaphysical reality undiscoverable in life because it was the knowledge of Byzantium, the knowledge of the afterlife, disdaining all mere complexities. To understand Joyce's rejection of an ultimate discourse (except perhaps as a hypothetical construct), we must first look at the still-evolving thought of Stephen Dedalus, who has not yet reached that point.

In *Ulysses*, Stephen thinks several times of the notion of the Great Memory, the great universal storehouse where all that has been thought and said is recorded and remembered. Recalling the pathos of his mother's

---

[3]It is interesting to find this ambivalence between mockery and artistic aspiration in the work of Gogarty himself. A fascinating instance is "Leda and the Swan," a poem Gogarty first published in *Selected Poems* (1933). The poem is a jeu d'esprit . . . (even though Gogarty apparently claimed that his poem was written before Yeats's), and there is something like an echoing of Yeats in Gogarty's closing stanza, which ends— as Yeats's sonnet ends—with a musing rhetorical question:

> When the hyacinthine
>   Eggs were in the basket,—
> Blue as at the whiteness
>   Where a cloud begins:
> Who would dream there lay there
>   All that Trojan brightness;
> Agamemnon murdered.
>   And the mighty twins?

The poem careens between facetiousness and "seriousness."

souvenirs of her youth, her tasseled dancecards and her memories of old Royce in *Turko The Terrible,* he muses that all those tokens of her past are now "Folded away in the memory of nature" (*U* 1961:10; *U* 1986:9; 1–265). Later, amid the rhetorics of Aeolus, he thinks of O'Connell's speeches for repeal of the union in the 1840s and of the mystical place where O'Connell's wind-scattered words still exist: "Akasic records of all that ever anywhere wherever was" (*U* 1961:143; *U* 1986:118; 7–882). Stephen recalls the Great Memory, not because he has a Yeatsian belief in the *Spiritus Mundi* but because the Great Memory is an image of his remembering soul, the form of forms, the form that contains the forms of all that he has perceived and experienced. And the soul (in Stephen's Aristotelian terminology) is capable not only of receiving the forms of the things it experiences but, in its ultimate act, of comprehending those forms in one act of understanding which is an act of self-understanding. That is the endpoint of Stephen's striving: "Thought is the thought of thought. Tranquil brightness. The soul is in a manner all that is: the soul is form of forms. Tranquility sudden, vast, candescent: form of forms" (*U* 1961:26; *U* 1986:21; 2–74).

And here, we realize, we are in the presence of Stephen's idea of an ultimate discourse. Stephen posits a future Stephen who will one day know the Truth, who will have arrived at some attitude of equanimity toward himself of which he is still, today, incapable. (It is the dream of the young. We may recall Lily Briscoe's dismay in *To the Lighthouse* that at age forty the muddle still has not disappeared. But we really need not go outside *Ulysses,* of course: the example of Bloom is an ample reminder that young kinesis never gives way completely to mature stasis.) His anticipation of such a future all-knowing self is especially evident in Scylla and Charybdis, where he virtually predicts the composition of the book we are reading: "So in the future, the sister of the past, I may see myself as I sit here now but by reflection from that which then I shall be" (*U* 1961:194; *U* 1986:160; 9–383).

Elsewhere in the same chapter, as he listens to discussion of a volume of young poets' verse that will not include the poems of Stephen Dedalus, he dictates to himself: "See this. Remember" (*U* 1961:192; *U* 1986:158; 9–294). Another scene has been stored away in the Great Memory, to be selected out and used years later. Thus, perhaps with some vagueness, Stephen characterizes his own future knowledge as understanding and transcending his present experience of anxiety. That future, superior understanding will itself be the ultimate discourse, a magical set of terms we might call maturity, that will clarify and redeem his life.

It is tempting to conjecture that Joyce himself began *Ulysses* with an idea about discourses rather like Stephen's. In the opening chapters of *Ulysses,* the interior monologues of Stephen and Bloom and the dozens of other competing discourses are set against the supple, meticulous "initial style," which in the opening chapters seems to function as the book's ultimate discourse. This third-person attendant to the characters' interior monologues and dialogue is extraordinarily, famously adept at conveying narrative information in free indirect discourse. In Calypso it can do this:

> His hand accepted the moist tender gland and slid it into a sidepocket. Then it fetched up three coins from his trousers' pocket and laid them on the rubber prickles. They lay, were read quickly and quickly slid, disc by disc, into the till. (*U* 1961:60; *U* 1986:49; 4–181)

And, as late as Wandering Rocks, it can do this:

> A tiny yawn opened the mouth of the wife of the gentleman with the glasses. She raised her small gloved fist, yawned ever so gently, tiptapping her small gloved fist on her opening mouth and smiled tinily, sweetly. (*U* 1961:222; *U* 1986:183; 10–125).

The great authority of this style derives from its slightly obtrusive elegance, the precision of its notation of gesture, and, as is especially clear in the second passage, its effortless absorption of the tonalities of the characters within its immediate vicinity.[4] It is even more tempting to see this entirely confident because entirely adequate initial style as the very voice that Stephen desires for himself; for Stephen represents the will toward Olympian authorial power, and the initial style impresses with how much it *knows*, how much it has observed: again and again, it records gestures we have never before seen set down on paper. The Stephen who posits the nail-paring God-like author of the *Portrait* is, after all, still alive in *Ulysses*, seeking some place to stand and imaginatively rule over experience. But just when we have begun to formulate the theory that this style is something like the telos toward which Stephen is headed, Joyce alters the rules of the game: just when Stephen finishes his Shakespeare-theory, the book undergoes a profound change.

In his examination of Joyce's composition of *Ulysses*, Michael Groden helps us see how crucial to Joyce was the completion of Scylla and Charybdis. Joyce at one time hoped to finish *Ulysses* in 1918, but by the end of that year he had finished only half the book's chapters and far less than half the completed book's pages. Nevertheless, he had completed *something*. As Groden tells us, "On the last page of 'Scylla and Charybdis' he wrote 'End of First Part of "Ulysses"' and the date, 'New Year's Eve 1918'. . ., as if to indicate that one

---

[4]The initial style has been the subject of intense scrutiny in recent years. See in particular Hugh Kenner's *Joyce's Voices* (Berkeley and Los Angeles: University of California Press, 1978), in the second chapter of which he proposes his famous Uncle Charles Principle (which is in reality free indirect style): his *Ulysses* (London: Allen and Unwin, 1980), in which he impressively extends the argument of the previous book; chap. 2 of Colin MacCabe's work already cited; Shari Benstock's "Who Killed Cock Robin? The Sources of Free Indirect Style in *Ulysses*," *Style* 14 (1980): 259–73; chap. 1 and 2 of Karen Lawrence's *The Odyssey of Style in* Ulysses (Princeton: Princeton University Press, 1981); and the long section on *Ulysses* in John Paul Riquelme's *Teller and Tale in Joyce's Fiction: Oscillating Perspectives* (Baltimore: Johns Hopkins University Press, 1983). MacCabe, Benstock, and Riquelme are especially interested in demonstrating that the diffusion of authorial presence, so obvious late in the book, has already taken place within the initial free indirect style itself.

phase of *Ulysses* was ending and something new was about to begin"[5] What was finished in 1918 was the great effort of the initial style, the style that seems to imply an author something like a mature Stephen-Shakespeare. Then, all changes, and, after the entr'acte of "Wandering Rocks," the radical chapter-by-chapter metamorphoses of style usurp the narration of the novel.[6]

That usurpation is the most notable formal characteristic of *Ulysses,* and it constitutes the most momentous change that ever took place in Joyce's conception of his art: after these new styles take over, the composition of *Finnegans Wake* seems to become virtually an inevitability. There is no doubt that the change in conception took place as a result of a long meditation of Joyce's upon the nature of language and narrative authority—a meditation that seems implicit in Joyce's work from "The Sisters" through *Finnegans Wake.* I wish now to propose that Joyce reached the critical point in this meditation and changed the stylistic nature of *Ulysses,* not simply because that meditation, of its own forward momentum, reached a great crisis in 1918 or 1919, but because the very subject-matter and dramatis personae of *Ulysses* brought him to that point. I wish to propose, in short, that the two things *Ulysses* is "about"— its novelistic concern with character and plot on one hand and its metanovelistic concern with narrative authority on the other—have more to do with one another than we have lately thought. If the initial style is the projected ultimate discourse of Stephen Dedalus, the multiple styles of the second half of the book are extrapolations from Joyce's discovery of the character of Leopold Bloom.[7]

Stephen desperately wants an assured voice of his own because he is so acutely aware of the voices of others crowding out everything else in his consciousness. He fears the mockery and intimidation of those other voices, he is uneasy that his gestures are only imitations of the gestures of others, and he seems to dread that his very life is a sort of plagiarism of other lives already lived. "Whom were you trying to walk like?" he asks himself on the beach, and a few minutes later he admonishes himself, "That is Kevin Egan's movement I made . . ." (*U* 1961:41, 49; *U* 1986:33, 41; 3–184, 438). He can hear (and other characters hear this too) that he speaks with his father's voice, and he doesn't like that. It is not surprising that when this young man writes a poem he plagiarizes from Douglas Hyde, or that when he expounds his

[5]Michael Groden, Ulysses *in Progress* (Princeton: Princeton University Press, 1977), 17.

[6]Obviously, the shift from the initial style to the various styles in the latter half of the book is immensely more involved than I express it as being here. Both Groden and Lawrence have written entire books tracing that shift.

[7]See the related argument of William B. Warner, "The Play of Fictions and Succession of Styles in *Ulysses,*" *James Joyce Quarterly* 15, 1 (1977): 18–35. Warner writes: "Bloom's play with fictions and use of language in the first half of *Ulysses* prepare for the more exotic gyrations of language in the last nine episodes" (20). See also Robert Storey's "The Argument of *Ulysses,* Reconsidered," *Modern Language Quarterly* 40 (1979): 175–95. Storey writes: "*Ulysses* is the vehicle that effected this imaginative transference of psychic sympathies [from Stephen to Bloom] for Joyce; I want to argue, in fact, that to a large extent that transference is what *Ulysses* is 'about' " (182).

Shakespeare-theory, his "voice" is a tissue of quotations. Stephen's desire to make a voice, to hammer out an authoritative, persuasive personal discourse, is intense.

Such a desire is very weak in Bloom, who, as Fritz Senn has been the most skillful at showing, is unlike most Joycean male Dubliners in having no strong, characteristic spoken idiom.[8] His interior monologues have the indelible Bloomian imprint but when he comes to speech he is something of a muff. Bloom is not really a member of the male tribe that creates the brilliant Dublin argot, nor does he have the necessary brassiness for speaking it. Probably the best of many examples of his relative incapacity is his funny, lame attempt to tell the story of Reuben J. and the son in Hades, when Martin Cunningham rudely—but, for the sake of the story, mercifully— intrudes to give the narration a much-needed oiling. Martin steals most of the story from Bloom, and when Bloom tries to reinsert himself into the narration at the end, Simon steals the whole show by proffering the punchline:

—Isn't it awfully good, Mr. Bloom said eagerly.
—One and eightpence too much, Mr. Dedalus said drily. (U 1961:95; U 1986:78; 6– 290)

Imagine Stephen's reaction to having his story stolen by one listener and capped by another: "Hast thou found me, O mine enemy?" would not even begin to express his exasperation. Imagine that, and then notice how Bloom responds a couple of hours later, when he remembers Simon's capping remark: "One and eightpence too much. Hhhhm. It's the droll way he comes out with the things. Knows how to tell a story too" (U 1961:152; U 1986:125; 8–53).

Without even trying to describe the powers that so often enable Bloom to escape rancor and resentment ("a good man," Joyce called him) let us simply note for the moment Bloom's unruffled ability to admire a turn of phrase and a narrative method.

Bloom's attitude—curious, diffident, appreciative—toward the discourse of others is especially clear in his many acts of reading during the day, acts in which he is strikingly aware of the textuality of what he is reading. (He is far more aware of the textuality of written language than Stephen on this particular day. The comparison of course is skewed by the fact that Stephen reads so little on 16 June: his glasses, remember, are broken. When he does read, at the bookcart in "Wandering Rocks," he characteristically reflects that even reading itself is somehow a repetition, a plagiarism: "Thumbed pages: read and read. Who has passed here before me?" (U 1961:242; U 1986:199; 10–845). When Bloom reads, he moves constantly into and out of the text, regarding it alternately as a transparent window opening onto a world of

[8]Fritz Senn, "Bloom among the Orators: The Why and the Wherefore and All the Codology," *Irish Renaissance Annual* 1 (1980): 168–90.

content and as an opaque object, a textual medium interesting to consider in itself. This tendency is no doubt heightened by his being a newspaper man and an ad man, but it seems deeply embedded in his temperament anyway. In Dlugacz's, reading the planting company prospectus, he is aware of the transparent language, the accompanying picture, the paper itself: "He held the page from him: interesting: read it nearer, the title, the blurred cropping cattle, the page rustling" (*U* 1961:59; *U* 1986:48; 4–157).

Later, in the funeral-carriage, he will be alternately aware of a list of names on the obituary page and of "Inked characters fast fading on the frayed breaking paper" (*U* 1961:91; *U* 1986:75; 6–160). His attention to textuality is reinforced by a very strong habit he has when a printed or written page is before him: he is a great re-reader. He usually scans first and then reads more closely (as with the planting company prospectus or Martha's letter); in the early chapters his eyes move over *Matcham's Masterstroke* three times, and he reads Milly's letter four times. Bloom re-reads, not simply in order to be certain that he has absorbed information but just as often to adjust himself to the reading and to appraise it as a text. (He is drawn to texts in something like the same way he is drawn to the clothed bodies of women: he alternates between the naive surrender to desire and an equally pleasurable musing over the media that solicit and engage his attention—words, or details of clothing. Reading newspapers or women, Bloom enjoys the pleasures of fetishism.) Here is Bloom the critic in the jakes:

> It did not move or touch him but it was something quick and neat. . . . Smart. He glanced back through what he had read and, while feeling his water flow quietly, he envied kindly Mr. Beaufoy who had written it and received payment of three pounds, thirteen and six (*U* 1961:69; *U* 1986:56; 4–511).

Kind envy: not bad as a description of Bloom's response to other Dubliners who draw profit (laughter; three pounds, thirteen and six) from their more capable and more public ways with words. Bloom does not hanker after an ultimate discourse; he has instead a wry, curious, observant play of mind that is attentive to discourse and is usually unthreatened when the discourse is superior to his own.

What happens, though, when those other forms of discourse become more openly antagonistic toward Bloom? How do his mental habits enable him to cope with mockery? There are mocking discourses aplenty in Cyclops: aggressive, snarling, competitive discourses are at once the subject-matter and the procedure of the whole chapter. There is something of Dublin in excelsis here as Joyce presents a confrontation between city and hero; it is rather as if Gabriel Conroy's after-dinner speech were to be answered by hoots and catcalls all up and down the table. To the non-Irish reader—to *this* non-Irish reader at any rate—Cyclops is the most Irish chapter in the book or, rather, virtually a parody of what Joyce usually presents as "Irish," in its competition of voices, each voice brilliantly and violently imposing a point of view—very often through mockery—and each voice also fretting under the consciousness of being itself the target of other mockers. The virulent power of the Citizen's rhetoric is the sign of a subjection that the rhetoric itself seeks to deny but only intensifies, for the whole chapter is about the complicitous nature of mocking hatred, which only rivets more securely the hater to the hated object. And, over the heads of the characters, the "gigantic" narrator, a sort of impassive parody-producing machine, constantly destabilizes the scene by offering mocking echoes of the characters' "sincere" statements. Everyone in the scene is in *the* paradigmatic Joycean dilemma: each character stands, with his own discourse, in the presence of another, mocking discourse.

How does Bloom respond? He is of course the target of multiple mockeries; he is being Ignatius Gallaher'd from all sides—outside his awareness by the two narrators, in his presence by the Citizen and company, and within his own consciousness by Boylan (". . . hated and persecuted. Also now. This very moment. This very instant"). He for awhile keeps his distance from the Citizen's conversation with his cronies by treating the conversation as a discourse to be mused over and tested by reason. Rower's heart, the natural phenomenon of a hanged man's erection, the universality of military discipline—those are some of Herr Professor Luitpold Blumenduft's well-observed but of course howlingly inappropriate footnotes added to the conversation in the bar. There, although on edge, is your usual Bloom, skeptical, curious, two-eyed. But, finally, only so many of the Citizen's increasingly barbed innuendos can be endured.

There is nothing more well-observed in Joyce's sharp-eyed fiction than his treatment of a character's being drawn into the competition of argument: think of Simon and Mr. Casey feigning to ignore Dante's remarks at the Christmas dinner-table or think yet one more time of Chandler for awhile refraining from responding to Gallaher's patronizing remarks. Then the pose of indifference becomes insupportable, and the character turns upon his heckler and becomes locked in dialectical combat. Something rather different from this happens to Bloom in Cyclops.

> —Those are nice things, says the citizen, coming over here to Ireland filling the country with bugs.
> So Bloom lets on he heard nothing. . . . (*U* 1961:323; *U* 1986:265; 12–1141)

Thus is a taunt launched forth into the obscure murk of Barney Kiernan's. Bloom at first seems to refuse a response, but he can't fully resist. More than two pages after the original taunt, he replies, with the same pretense as the Citizen's, that he is addressing absolutely no one in particular:

> —Some people, says Bloom, can see the mote in others' eyes but they can't see the beam in their own.
> —*Raimeis*, says the citizen. There's no-one as blind as the fellow that won't see, if you know what that means. (*U* 1961:326; *U* 1986:267; 12–1237)

Does Bloom know he is quoting Christ? Very probably, for he has had some time to consider an answer, and it is likely that, for once, he has come up with a felicitous phrase to speak. In Aeolus he fumbled for some time over what he should have said to Menton at the cemetery (*U* 1961:120; *U* 1986:100; 7–171).

In this moment of Cyclops, he seems to wait until the happy phrase comes. (Could even Bloom, with this much time to think, mistake the source of the phrase with that striking, unique "mote/beam" locution?) Bloom does not respond directly to the Citizen; he tries instead to fracture the basic vocabulary of the Citizen's discourse by responding to the Christian anti-Semite in the words of Christ. And that remains his strategy for the rest of the scene, as he first speaks, gamely if lamely, in defense of love and then in parting tries to unsettle the Citizen's anti-Semitic discourse completely with reminders of Christ's origins in Judaism. (By now, verbal felicity is quite out the window, as Bloom tries to bring in Christ's uncle.)

Bloom engages in argument with the Citizen by refusing to engage, by refusing to accept the Citizen's terms of discourse—by, in short, refusing to grant him authority. Bloom is not of Hungarian descent for nothing: this refusal to acknowledge unjust authority *is* exactly the "Hungarian system" Martin Cunningham speaks of in Cyclops.[9] The Citizen is so painfully stung, not because Bloom has argued with him (the Citizen deeply, almost erotically *desires* an argument and Bloom will not oblige him), but because Bloom's blurted-out "Christ was a jew like me" destroys the opposition upon which the Citizen's whole discourse is based. Moreover, later in the day, when Bloom in a retrospective arrangement looks back upon this scene, he dissolves the Citizen's dialectic of hatred even further: "Look at it other way round. Not so bad then. Perhaps not to hurt he meant. Three cheers for Israel. Three cheers for the sister-in-law he hawked about, three fangs in her mouth" (*U* 1961:380; *U* 1986:311; 13–1219). Bloom's dislike of the Citizen is clearly there in that final phrase of *Schadenfreude*, but it is counterbalanced by curiosity about the Citizen, even by a faint attempt to apologize for him. Here we are close to a central component of Bloom that could be fully clarified only if we were approaching him from a more purely psychological perspective: his readiness to identify with his enemies and his mockers.[10] For my purposes, I want to stress only the peculiarly liberating effects

[9]The question of whether Bloom could have been the source of Arthur Griffith's knowledge of "the Hungarian system" has its own rather acrimonious critical history. See Dominic Manganiello's résumé of the dispute in *Joyce's Politics* (London: Routledge and Kegan Paul, 1980), 121. The important point is . . . the Bloom-Hungary analogy the whole issue raises. Bloom follows a Hungarian policy in refusing to acknowledge the Citizen's authority, and he follows it again when he stays away from home all evening (as the Hungarian representatives stayed away from Vienna) and thereby piques Molly's curiosity. It is of interest to remember that the founding of the Dail Eireann in Dublin in 1919 could be described as an act according to the Hungarian system.

[10]Bloom's feelings toward Boylan obviously constitute the clearest example of this identification with the enemy. His most overt identification with Boylan takes place in the unanxious post-orgasmic pages of Nausicaa (not long after his reconsideration of the Citizen that I have quoted), following his thoughts of the sexual allure of women's clothing: "Us too: the tie he wore, his lovely socks and turnedup trousers" (*U* 1961:368; *U* 1986:302; 13–800).

of that identification, as it operates to break down the circuit of antagonism. The play of mind that allows Bloom a curious and detached critical attention to discourse makes him skeptical of any authority—even his own—and so releases him from the deadly, closed dialectic of mockery.

Just a few pages before Bloom's bemused reconsideration of the Citizen in Nausicaa (where his post-orgasmic languor no doubt encourages this relatively anxiety-free identification with the Other), he has a similar moment as he reflects upon a stroller on the beach: "Walk after him now make him awkward like those newsboys me today. Still you learn something. See ourselves as others see us" (U 1961:375–6; U 1986:307; 13–1056). This last phrase, from Burns, is evidently something of a favorite of Bloom's, since he has quoted it earlier (U 1961:169; U 1986:139; 8–662). It is the motto of a consciousness that frees itself from mockery precisely by giving partial assent to the mocker's point of view. The occupational hazard of this form of consciousness is a certain want of confidence and self-esteem, a want of faith in its own authority because it constantly experiences the relativity of personal authority by projecting itself into the attitudes of others. One of the strengths of this consciousness is that it alone of the consciousnesses registered in *Ulysses* seems capable of thinking, as everyone stands silent around the grave into which Paddy Dignam's coffin has just been lowered: "If we were all suddenly somebody else" (U 1961:110; U 1986:91; 6–836).

Bloom's mind contains an attitude toward discourse that, extrapolated, gives rise to the second half of *Ulysses,* and I would even guess that the extraordinary experience of creating Bloom (think of making Bloom up!) led Joyce to the discovery of how his book would continue. Stephen, as I have proposed, imagines something for himself very like the book's initial style. He wants a future knowledge that will set today's events in the lucid, all-revealing light of pure understanding. In such an effort as his "Parable of the Plums" he seems intent upon finding some language to be the stylistic equivalent of that knowledge (and he is at least in part successful). Even his conversation often strives for a marmoreal, aphoristic quality: "You behold in me, Stephen said with grim displeasure, a horrible example of free thought" (U 1961:20; U 1986:175; 1–625); "I fear those big words, Stephen said, which make us so unhappy" (U 1961:31; U 1986:17; 2–264). These are sentences every word of which has been rung on a mental counter; these words are pre-tested to be mockery-proof. (Do we not imagine them to have been stored up, as Stephen stores up his "disappointed bridge" for Haines?) Ah, how sensitive this young man is to mockery, and how he longs to transcend it.

It is possible that Joyce originally set out to show his own style transcending all mockery, as if free indirect style could mimic and yet through its very purity escape the antagonism that consistently hovers around mimicry. If all the novel had been written in that style, *Ulysses* would be the greatest Flaubertian novel ever written, its style claiming for itself an Olympian calm, but its implied aesthetic rationale would reveal that the novel itself was still caught up in a battle of mockeries. When Joyce gave his first novel a title that called attention to its autobiographical nature, the very last words—"Dublin 1904/Trieste 1914"—had the implication that those ten years account for the gap between the still-callow young hero and the mature, understanding artist: by living through those ten years, the author now comprehends and controls the past. *Ulysses* up through Scylla and Charybdis (and especially *in* Scylla and Charybdis) seems to be following the same plan. But all is changed by Joyce's deeper, more searching portrayal of mockery in *Ulysses*. The *Portrait* at one point asks us to accept that Stephen "bore no malice now to those who had tormented him. . . . Even that night as he stumbled homewards along Jones's Road he had felt that some power was divesting him of that suddenwoven anger as easily as a fruit is divested of its soft ripe peel" (*P*, 82). This is more a description of what an angry person wants his enemies to feel than it is a convincing presentation of an overcoming of rancor.[11] *Ulysses* makes Stephen morbidly sensitive to mockery and denies him the ease of that earlier immunity to anger and resentment as it places him at once in the presence of Buck Mulligan. The admirably honest opening of *Ulysses* at once makes Mulligan's mockery a central problem—in a way altogether different from the too-easily transcended taunts of the *Portrait*. Were *Ulysses* to continue with its initial style to the end, its own strategy of mockery and revenge would lie revealed: the young man in the novel who anticipates the novel we are reading may have been reviled and scorned in 1904 ("Ten years, he said, chewing and laughing. He is going to write something in ten years" [*U* 1961:249; *U* 1986:205; 10–1089)]), but see how he has turned the light of understanding back upon those persecutors in 1922! This much could be inferred from the text itself, quite without our ever knowing of Gogarty, say, or of Messrs. Rumbold, Bennett, Compton, and Carr. The novel would then be what indeed, to a lesser degree, it still is: an attempt to play the final card in the game of mockery, as the book achieves its superiority by mastering all the subsidiary discourses of Dublin.

The full discovery of Bloom at least helped to alleviate Joyce's dilemma. Bloom saves Joyce from Stephen not only because of the evident attractive-

---

[11]I am not necessarily assigning an inadequate psychological sense to Joyce here. It can very well be argued that these words do not show Stephen's actual superiority to anger, but are signs of that chilly affectlessness that begins to grow upon him as he enters adolescence. . . . In *Ulysses* the death of May Dedalus has released in Stephen powerful feelings, formerly repressed, of love and hate that the *Portrait* did not record for the simple reason that they were unavailable to Stephen's consciousness. This sort of back-reading is an instance of a principle very perceptively formulated by Mark Shechner: "What *Ulysses* does it make manifest the subtle thread of irony that is latent in so much of Joyce's previous work, liberating it and giving it a voice of its own" (*Joyce in Nighttown: A Psychoanalytic Inquiry into* Ulysses [Berkeley and Los Angeles: University of California Press, 1974], 186).

ness and variety of Bloom, but also because Bloom is content not to win, content not to have the one last word. The second half of *Ulysses* thus shows Joyce letting go of one sort of power: the book gives up its initial style and fiddles with new ways of writing, as if it were setting out to explore that Bloomian musing at the cemetery, "If we were all suddenly somebody else." The book deprives us of the lucidity it at first seemed to proffer as it places us in a competition of discourses, with no hope of our ever regaining even the semblance of an ultimate discourse. Bloom ousts Mulligan, not only by taking Stephen's arm in Eumaeus as Mulligan took it in Telemachus, but also by suggesting through his example a replacement of Stephen's fear of mockery with some actual acceptance of mockery and a curious-minded attraction to the discourses of others.

That is my main contention, but I must admit it needs a final qualifier. This cannot be the total view of *Ulysses;* this view is a little too sweet. Joyce creates Bloom and in creating him discovers a new attitude toward discourse, but Bloom is finally put back into the service of Stephen Dedalus. (This is one thing that the meeting of Stephen and Bloom *means.*) When, late in Oxen of the Sun, the Carlylean voice addresses Theodore Purefoy, it calls him "the remarkablest progenitor barring none in this chaffering allincluding most farraginous chronicle" (*U* 1961:423; *U* 1986:345; 14–1411). This voice makes the claim that the book containing it is "allincluding," as if *Ulysses* actually *were* equivalent to the akasic records holding *all* the discourses of Dublin. The artistic will to power of Stephen Dedalus and the wry humility of Bloom constitute the inescapable dialectic of Joyce's art in *Ulysses.* In his great novel Joyce sought some way out of competition and the battle for mastery; nevertheless, he could not resist showing that he was the master of more discourses than all the other Dubliners put together.

Ulysses in History

Fredric R. Jameson

One does not read Joyce today, let alone write about him, without remembering the struggle for freedom of the people of Northern Ireland; the following essay, then, for whatever it is worth, must necessarily be dedicated to them.

It would be surprising indeed if we were unable to invent newer and fresher ways of reading Joyce; on the other hand, the traditional interpretations I am about to mention have become so sedimented into our text—*Ulysses* being one of those books which is 'always-already-read,' always seen and interpreted by other people before you begin—that it is hard to see it afresh and impossible to read it as though those interpretations had never existed.

Perhaps some new way in may be afforded by the more arid places in the novel; those interminable stretches—such as the scene in the cabman's shelter and the catechism—which seem to have evaded the most capacious hermeneutic traditions. The boredom Eumaeus and Ithaca seem so often to have inspired may itself furnish a guiding thread, if it is so that boredom is sometimes a blockage and a repression, rather than a natural reaction that needs no further explanation in its own right: in that case, there may well be a productive use of boredom that has something interesting to tell us about ourselves and our reactions, fully as much as it does about the canonical text.

A somewhat different fatigue may cling, in full postmodernism, to the once standard readings and interpretive frames through which Joyce's text was assimilated to the canons of high modernism. These frameworks are largely threefold, and I will call them the mythical, the psychoanalytical, and the ethical readings respectively. These are, in other words, the readings of *Ulysses*, first in terms of the Odyssey parallel; second, in terms of the father-son relationship; and third, in terms of some possible happy end according to which this day, Bloomsday, will have changed everything, and will in particular have modified Mr Bloom's position in the home and relationship to his wife.

Let me take this last reading first. I will have little to say here about Molly's monologue, and only want now to ask not merely why we are so attached to the project of making something decisive happen during this representative day, transforming it in other words into an Event; but also and

From *James Joyce and Modern Literature*, ed. W. J. McCormack and Alistair Stead (London and New York: Routledge, Kegan Paul, 1982), 126–41. Copyright © 1982 by Routledge, Kegan Paul. Reprinted by permission of Fredric Jameson and Routledge, Chapman and Hall.

above all to ask why we should be committed to this particular kind of event, in which Mr Bloom is seen as reasserting his authority in what can therefore presumably once again become a vital family unit. (You will recall that he has asked Molly to bring him breakfast in bed the next day—the triumph over the suitors!) In this day and age, in which the whole thrust of a militant feminism has been against the nuclear and the patriarchal family, is it really appropriate to recast *Ulysses* along the lines of marriage counselling and anxiously to interrogate its characters and their destinies with a view towards saving this marriage and restoring this family? Has our whole experience of Mr Bloom's Dublin reduced itself to this, the quest for a 'happy ending' in which the hapless protagonist is to virilise himself and become a more successful realisation of the dominant, patriarchal, authoritarian male?

Still, it will be said that this particular reading is part of the more general attempt to fit *Ulysses* back into the Odyssey parallel. As for the mythical interpretation—the Odyssey parallel undoubtedly underscored for us by the text itself as well as by generations of slavish interpreters—here too it would be desirable to think of something else. We are today, one would hope, well beyond that moment of classical modernism and its ideologies in which, as Sartre said somewhere, there was a 'myth of myth', in which the very notion of some mythic unity and reconciliation was used in a mythical, or as I would prefer to say, a fetishised way. The bankruptcy of the ideology of the mythic is only one feature of the bankruptcy of the ideology of modernism in general; yet it is a most interesting one, on which (had we more time) it might have been instructive to dwell. Why is it that, in the depthlessness of consumer society, the essential surface logic of our world of simulacra—why is it that the mythic ideal of some kind of depth integration is no longer attractive and no longer presents itself as a possible or workable solution? There is a kinship here, surely, between this waning of the mythic ideal or mirage and the disappearance of another cherished theme and experience of classical or high modernism, namely that of temporality, 'durée', lived time, the passage of time. But perhaps the easiest way to dramatise the breakdown of myth and myth criticism is simply to suggest that we suddenly, with anthropologists like Lévi-Strauss, discovered that myths were not what we thought they were in the first place: not the place of some deep Jungian integration of the psyche, but quite the opposite, a space preceding the very construction of the psyche or the subject itself, the ego, personality identity and the like: a space of the pre-individualistic, of the collective, which could scarcely be appealed to offer the consolations that myth criticism had promised us.

On the other hand, as I stated previously, we can scarcely hope to read *Ulysses* as though it were called something else. I would suggest, then, that we displace the act or the operation of interpretation itself. The Odyssey parallel can then be seen as one of the organisational frameworks of the narrative text: but it is not itself the interpretation of that narrative, as the ideologues of myth have thought. Rather it is itself—qua organisational framework—what remains to be interpreted. In itself, the *Odyssey* parallel—like so much of that whole tradition of the classical pastiche from Cocteau or even from 'La Belle Hélène' all the way to Giraudoux or Sartre or even John Updike—functions as wit: a matching operation is demanded of us as readers, in which the fit of the modern detail to its classical overtext is admired for its elegance and economy, as when, in *Ulysses*, Odysseus' long separation from Penelope is evoked in terms of a ten-year period of coitus interruptus or anal intercourse between the partners of the Bloom household. You will agree, however, that the establishment of the parallel is scarcely a matter of interpretation—that is, no fresh meaning is conferred either on the classical Homeric text, or on the practices of contemporary birth control, by the matching of these two things.

Genuine interpretation is something other than this, and involves the radical historisation of the form itself: what is to be interpreted is then the historical necessity for this very peculiar and complex textual structure or reading operation in the first place. We can make a beginning on this, I think, by evoking the philosophical concept, but also the existential experience, called *contingency*. Something seems to have happened at a certain point in modern times to the old unproblematic meaning of things, or to what we could call the content of experience; and this particular event is as so often first most tangibly detectable and visible on the aesthetic level. There is something like a crisis of detail, in which we may, in the course of our narrative, need a house for our characters to sleep in, a room in which they may converse, but nothing is there any longer to justify our choice of this particular house rather than that other, or this particular room, furniture, view, and the like. It is a very peculiar dilemma, which Barthes described as well as anyone else, when he accounted for the fundamental experience of the modern or of modernity in terms of something like a dissociation between meaning and existence:

> The pure and simple *representation* of the *real*, the naked account of *what is* (or what has been), thus proves to resist meaning; such resistance reconfirms the great mythic opposition between the *vécu* [that is, the experiential or what the existentialists called 'lived experience'] and the intelligible; we have only to recall how, in the ideology of our time, the obsessional evocation of the 'concrete' (in what we rhetorically demand of the human sciences, of literature, of social practices) is always staged as an aggressive arm against meaning, as though, by some *de jure* exclusion, what lives is structurally incapable of carrying a meaning—and vice versa.[1]

One would only want to correct this account by adding that the living, life, vitalism, is also an ideology, as it is appropriate to observe for Joyce himself more generally; but on the whole Barthes's opposition between what exists

---

[1]Roland Barthes, 'L'Effet de réel,' *Communications*, No. 11 (1968), p. 87.

and what means allows us to make sense of a whole range of formal strategies within what we call the high modernisms; these range clearly all the way from the dematerialisation of the work of art (Virginia Woolf's attack on naturalism, Gide's omission of the description of people and things, the emergence of an ideal of the 'pure' novel, on the order of 'pure poetry') to the practice of symbolism itself, which involves the illicit transformation of existing things into so many visible or tangible meanings. I believe that today, whatever our own aesthetic faults or blinkers, we have learned this particular lesson fairly well: and that for us, any art which practices symbolism is already discredited and worthless before the fact. A long experience of the classical modernisms has finally taught us the bankruptcy of the symbolic in literature; we demand something more from artists than this facile affirmation that the existent also means, that things are also symbols. But this is very precisely why I am anxious to rescue Joyce from the exceedingly doubtful merit of being called a symbolic writer.

Yet before I try to describe what is really going on in the text of *Ulysses*, let me do something Barthes did not care to do, in the passage I quoted, and designate the historical reasons for that modernist crisis, that dissociation of the existent and the meaningful, that intense experience of contingency in question here. We must explain this experience historically because it is not at all evident, and particularly not in the ideologic perspective—existential or Nietzchean—which is that of Roland Barthes, among many others, and for which the discovery of the absurd and of the radical contingency and meaninglessness of our object world is simply the result of the increasing lucidity and self-consciousness of human beings in a post-religious, secular, scientific age.

But in previous societies (or modes of production) it was Nature that was meaningless or anti-human. What is paradoxical about the historical experience of modernism is that it designates very precisely that period in which Nature—or the in- or anti-human—is everywhere in the process of being displaced or destroyed, expunged, eliminated, by the achievements of human praxis and human production. The great modernist literature—from Baudelaire and Flaubert to *Ulysses* and beyond—is a city literature: its object is therefore the anti-natural, the humanised, par excellence, a landscape which is everywhere the result of human labour, in which everything—including the formerly natural, grass, trees, our own bodies—is finally produced by human beings. This is then the historical paradox with which the experience of contingency confronts us (along with its ideologies—existentialism and nihilism—and its aesthetics—modernism): how can the city be meaningless? How can human production be felt to be absurd or contingent, when in another sense one would think it was only human labour which created genuine meaning in the first place?

Yet it is equally obvious that the experience of contingency is a real or 'objective' one, and not merely a matter of illusion or false consciousness (although it is that too). The missing step here—the gap between the fact of the human production of reality in modern times and the experience of the results or products of that production as meaningless—this essential mediation is surely to be located in the work process itself, whose organisation does not allow the producers to grasp their relationship to the final product; as well as in the market system, which does not allow the consumer to grasp the product's origins in collective production. I am assuming, rightly or wrongly, that I do not have to insert a general lecture on alienation and reification, on the dynamics of capital and the nature of exchange value, at this point: I do want to dwell at somewhat greater length on one of the basic forms taken by reification as a process, and that is what can be called the analytical fragmentation of older organic or at least 'naturwüchsige' or traditional processes.[2] Such fragmentation can be seen on any number of levels: on that of the labour process first of all, where the older unities of handicraft production are broken up and 'taylorised' into the meaningless yet efficient segments of mass industrial production; on that of the psyche or psychological subject, now broken up into a host of radically different mental functions, some of which— those of measurement and rational calculation—are privileged and others— the perceptual senses and aesthetic generally—are marginalised; on that of time, experience, and storytelling, all of which are inexorably atomised and broken down into their most minimal unities, into that well-known 'heap of fragments where the sun beats'; the fragmentation, finally, of the older hierarchical communities, neighbourhoods, and organic groups themselves, which, with the penetration of the money and market system, are systematically dissolved into relations of equivalent individuals, 'free but equal' monads, isolated subjects equally free to sell their labour power, yet living side by side in a merely additive way within those great agglomerations which are the modern cities. It is incidentally this final form of reification which accounts, be it said in passing, for the inadequacy of that third conventional interpretation of *Ulysses* mentioned above, namely the fetishisation of the text in terms of 'archetypal' patterns of father-son relationships, the quest for the ideal father or for the lost son, and so forth. But surely today, after so much prolonged scrutiny of the nuclear family, it has become apparent that the obsession with these relationships and the privileging of such impoverished interpersonal schemas drawn from the nuclear family itself are to be read as break-down products and as defence mechanisms against the loss of the knowable community. The efforts of Edward Said and others to demonstrate the omnipresence of such familial schemes in modern narrative should surely not be taken as an affirmation of the ultimate primacy of such relationships, but rather exactly the reverse, as sociopathology and as diagnosis of the

[2]See, for a more detailed account of reification, my *The Political Unconscious: Narrative as a Socially Symbolic Act*. London: Methuen; Ithaca: Cornell University Press, 1981, esp. pp. 62–64, 225–37, 249–52.

impoverishment of human relations which results from the destruction of the older forms of the collective.[3] The father-son relationships in *Ulysses* are all miserable failures, above all others the mythical ultimate 'meeting' between Bloom and Stephen; and if more is wanted on this particular theme, one might read into the record here the diatribes against the very notion of an Oedipus complex developed in Deleuze and Guattari's 'Anti-Oedipus', which I do not necessarily endorse but which should surely be enough to put an end to this particular interpretive temptation.

But the psychoanalytic or Oedipal interpretation was itself only a sub-set of the *Odyssey* parallel or mythological temptation, to which, after this digression, I promised to return. What I wanted to suggest about the kind of reading determined by the *Odyssey* parallel in *Ulysses* is that this parallelism, and the kind of matching it encourages between the two levels of written and over-text, functions as something like an empty form. Like the classical unities, it offers a useful but wholly extrinsic set of limits against which the writer works, and which serve as a purely mechanical check on what risks otherwise becoming an infinite proliferation of detail.[4] The point is that, as we suggested a moment ago, the older traditional narrative unities have disappeared, been destroyed in the process of universal fragmentation: the organic unity of the narrative can thus no longer serve as a symbol for the unity of experience, nor as a formal limit on the production of narrative sentences: the single day—that overarching formal unity of *Ulysses*—is a meaningful unit neither in human experience nor in narrative itself. But at that point, if what used to be experience, human destiny and the like, is shattered into such components as taking a walk at lunchtime from your place of business to a restaurant, buying a cake of soap, or having a drink, or visiting a patient in a hospital—each of these components being then in itself infinitely subdivisible—then there is absolutely no guarantee that the transformation of these segments into narrative sentences might not be infinitely extended and indeed last forever. The *Odyssey* parallel helps avoid this unwelcome development and sets just such external limits, which ultimately become those of Joyce's minimal units of composition—the individual chapters themselves.

But what I wanted to show you was that alongside the type of reading encouraged by the mythic parallels—which I have called a matching up— there is a rather different form of reading which resists that one in all kinds of ways, and ends up subverting it. This is a type of reading which interrupts the other, consecutive kind, and moves forward and backwards across the text in a cumulative search for the previous mention or the reference to come: as Kenner and others have pointed out, it is a type of reading, a mental operation, peculiarly inconceivable before printing, before numbered pages,

---

[3]Edward Said, *Beginnings*. New York: Basic Books, 1975, pp. 137–52.
[4]For further remarks on the proliferation of sentences, see my *Fables of Aggression: Wyndham Lewis, the Modernist as Fascist*. Berkeley: University of California Press, 1979.

and more particularly before the institutionalisation of those unusual objects called dictionaries or encyclopedias.[5] Now one is tempted to assimilate this kind of reading to the more customary thematic or thematising kind, where we compile lists of recurrent motifs, such as types of imagery, obsessive words or terms, peculiar gestures or emotional reactions; but this is not at all what happens in *Ulysses*, where the object of the cross-referencing activity is always an event: taking old Mrs Riordan for a walk, the borrowed pair of tight trousers worn by Ben Dollard at a memorable concert, or the assassination in Pheonix Park twenty-three years before. This is to say that these seemingly thematic motifs are here always referential: for they designate content beyond the text, beyond indeed the capacity of any of the given textual variants to express or exhaust them. In such cross-referencing, indeed, one can say that the referent itself is produced, as something which transcends every conceivable textualisation of it. The appropriate analogy might be with the return of characters in Balzac's *Comédie humaine*, where the varying status of a given character—the hero in one novel, a character actor in a second, a mere extra in a third and part of an enumeration of names in a fourth—tends effectively to destabilise each of the narrative forms in question, and to endow them all with a transcendental dimension on which they open so many relative perspectives.

What I want to suggest is that the analogous recurrence of events and characters throughout *Ulysses* can equally be understood as a process whereby the text itself is unsettled and undermined, a process whereby the universal tendency of its terms, narrative tokens, representations, to solidify into an achieved and codified symbolic order as well as a massive narrative surface, is perpetually suspended. I will call this process 'dereification', and I first want to describe its operation in terms of the city itself. The classical city is not a collection of buildings, nor even a collection of people living on top of one another; nor is it even mainly or primarily a collection of pathways, of the trajectories of people through those buildings or that urban space, although that gets us a little closer to it. No, the classical city, one would think—it always being understood that we are now talking about something virtually extinct, in the age of the suburb or megalopolis or the private car—the classical city is defined essentially by the nodal points at which all those pathways and trajectories meet, or which they traverse: points of totalisation, we may call them, which make shared experience possible, and also the storage of experience and information, which are in short something like a synthesis of the object (place) and the subject (population), focal points not unlike those possibilities of unifying perspectives and images which Kevin Lynch has identified as the signs and emblems of the successful, the non-alienating city.[6]

---

[5]See Hugh Kenner, *Flaubert, Joyce, Beckett: The Stoic Comedians*. Boston: Beacon, 1962. Also the work of MacLuhan and Walter Ong.

[6]Kevin Lynch, *The Image of the City*. Cambridge, Mass.: Harvard University Press, 1960.

But to talk about the city in this way, spatially, by identifying the collective transit points and roundabouts of temple and agora, pub and post office, park and cemetery, is not yet to identify the mediation whereby these spatial forms are at one with collective experience. Unsurprisingly that mediation will have to be linguistic, yet it will have to define a kind of speech which is neither uniquely private nor forbiddingly standardised in an impersonal public form, a type of discourse in which the same, in which repetition, is transmitted again and again through a host of eventful variations, each of which has its own value. That discourse is called gossip: and from the upper limits of city life—the world of patronage, machine politics, and the rise and fall of ward leaders—all the way down to the most minute aberrations of private life, it is by means of gossip and through the form of the anecdote that the dimensions of the city are maintained within humane limits and that the unity of city life is affirmed and celebrated. This is already the case with that ur-form of the city which is the village itself, as John Berger tell us in *Pig Earth*:

> The function of this gossip which, in fact, is close, oral, daily history, is to allow the whole village to define itself. . . . The village . . . is a living portrait of itself: a communal portrait, in that everybody is portrayed and everybody portrays. As with the carvings on the capitals in a Romanesque church, there is an identity of spirit between what is shown and how it is shown—as if the portrayed were also the carvers. Every village's portrait of itself is constructed, however, not out of stone, but out of words, spoken and remembered: out of opinions, stories, eye-witness reports, legends, comments and hearsay. And it is a continuous portrait: work on it never stops. Until very recently the only material available to a village and its peasants for defining themselves was their own spoken words. . . . Without such a portrait—and the gossip which is its raw material—the village would have been forced to doubt its own existence.[7]

So in that great village which is Joyce's Dublin, Parnell is still an anecdote about a hat knocked off, picked up and returned, not yet a television image nor even a name in a newspaper; and by the same token, as in the peasant village itself, the ostensibly private or personal—Molly's infidelities, or Mr Bloom's urge to discover how far the Greek sculptors went in portraying the female anatomy—all these things are public too, and the material for endless gossip and anecdotal transmission.

Now for a certain conservative thought, and for that heroic fascism of the 1920s for which the so-called 'masses' and their standardised city life had become the very symbol of everything degraded about modern life, gossip—Heidegger will call it 'das Gerede'—is stigmatised as the very language of inauthenticity, of that empty and stereotypical talking *pour rien dire* to which these ideologues oppose the supremely private and individual speech of the death anxiety or the heroic choice. But Joyce—a radical neither in the left-

---

7John Berger, *Pig Earth*. New York: Pantheon, 1981, p. 9.

wing nor the reactionary sense—was at least a populist and a plebeian. 'I don't know why the communists don't like me,' he complained once, 'I've never written about anything but common people.' Indeed, from the class perspective, Joyce had no more talent for or interest in the representation of aristocrats than Dickens; and no more experience with working-class people or with peasants than Balzac. (Beckett is indeed a far sounder guide to the Irish countryside or rural slum than the essentially urban Joyce.) In class terms, then, Joyce's characters are all resolutely petty-bourgeois: what gives this apparent limitation its representative value and its strength is the colonial situation itself. Whatever his hostility to Irish cultural nationalism, Joyce's is the epic of the metropolis under imperialism, in which the development of bourgeoisie and proletariat alike is stunted to the benefit of a national petty-bourgeoisie: indeed, precisely these rigid constraints imposed by imperialism on the development of human energies account for the symbolic displacement and flowering of the latter in eloquence, rhetoric and oratorical language of all kinds; symbolic practices not particularly essential either to businessmen or to working classes, but highly prized in precapitalist societies and preserved, as in a time capsule, in *Ulysses* itself. And this is the moment to rectify our previous account of the city and to observe that if *Ulysses* is also for us the classical, the supreme representation something like the Platonic idea of city life, this is also partly due to the fact that Dublin is not exactly the full-blown capitalist metropolis, but like the Paris of Flaubert, still regressive, still distantly akin to the village, still un- or under-developed enough to be representable, thanks to the domination of its foreign masters.

Now it is time to say what part gossip plays in the process of what I have called dereification, or indeed in that peculiar network of cross-references which causes us to read *Ulysses* backwards and forwards like a handbook. Gossip is indeed the very element in which reference—or, if you prefer, the 'referent' itself—expands and contracts, ceaselessly transformed from a mere token, a notation, a short-hand object, back into a full-dress narrative. People as well as things are the reified markers of such potential story-telling: and what for a high realism was the substantiality of character, of the individual ego, is here equally swept away into a flux of anecdotes—proper names on the one hand, an intermittent store of gossip on the other. But the process is to be sure more tangible and more dramatic when we see it at work on physical things: the statues, the commodities in the shopwindows, the clanking trolleylines that link Dublin to its suburbs (which dissolve, by way of Mr Deasy's anxieties about foot-and-mouth disease, into Mr Bloom's fantasy projects for tramlines to move cattle to the docks); or the three-master whose silent grace and respectability as an image is at length dissolved into the disreputable reality of its garrulous and yarn-spinning crewman; or, to take a final example, that file of sandwichmen whose letters troop unevenly through the text, seeming to move towards that ultimate visual reification fantasised by Mr Bloom virtually in analogue to Mallarmé's 'Livre':

Of some one sole unique advertisement to cause passers to stop in wonder, a poster
novelty, with all extraneous accretions excluded, reduced to its simplest and most
efficient terms not exceeding the span of casual vision and congruous with the
velocity of modern life. (*U* 1961:705; *U* 1986:592; 17–1770)

The visual, the spatially visible, the image, is, as has been observed, the final
form of the commodity itself, the ultimate terminus of reification. Yet even so
strikingly reified a datum as the sandwichboard ad is once again effortlessly
dereified and dissolved when, on his way to the cabman's shelter, Stephen
hears a down-and-out friend observe: 'I'd carry a sandwichboard only the girl
in the office told me they're full up for the next three weeks, man. God
you've to book ahead!' (*U* 1961:602; *U* 1986:505; 16–200). Suddenly the exotic
picture-postcard vision of a tourist Dublin is transformed back into the dreary
familiar reality of jobs and contracts and the next meal: yet this is not
necessarily a dreary prospect; rather it opens up a perspective in which, at
some ideal outside limit, everything seemingly material and solid in Dublin
itself can presumably be dissolved back into the underlying reality of human
relations and human praxis.

Yet the ambulatory letters of the sandwichmen are also the very emblem of
textuality itself, and this is the moment to say the price *Ulysses* must pay for
the seemingly limitless power of its play of reification and dereification; the
moment, in other words, to come to terms with Joyce's modernism. Stated
baldly, that price is radical depersonalisation, or in other words, Joyce's
completion of Flaubert's programme of removing the author from the text—a
programme which also removes the reader, and finally that unifying and
organising mirage or aftermirage of both author and reader which is the
'character', or better still, 'point of view'. What happens at that point can
perhaps oversimply be described this way: such essentially idealistic (or ideal,
or imaginary) categories formerly served as the supports for the unity of the
work or the unity of the process. Now that they have been withdrawn, only a
form of material unity is left, namely the printed book itself, and its material
unity as a bound set of pages within which the cross-references mentioned
above are contained. One of the classic definitions of modernism is of course
the increasing sense of the materiality of the medium itself (whether in
instrumental timbre or oil painting), the emergent foregrounding of the
medium in its materiality. It is paradoxical, of course, to evoke the materiality
of language; and as for the materiality of print or script, that particular
material medium is surely a good deal less satisfying or gratifying in a sensory,
perceptual way than the materials of oil paint or of orchestral coloration; none
the less, the role of the book itself is functionally analogous, in Joyce, to the
materialist dynamics of the other arts.

Now in one sense textualisation may be seen as a form or subset of
reification itself: but if so, it is a unique type of reification, which unbinds
fully as much as it fixes or crystallises. They may, indeed, offer the most
appropriate contemporary way of dealing with the phenomena Joseph Frank

described in his now classical essay as 'spatial form'. I am thinking, for instance, of the moment in which a remarkable and ingenious method for cabling news of the Phoenix Park murders across the Atlantic is described: the reporter takes an ad (Mr Bloom's 'one sole unique advertisement') and uses its spatial features to convey the trajectory of the gunmen and the map of the assassination (U 1961:136; U 1986:112; 7–661). This is to institute a peculiarly fluid relationship between the visually reified and the historically eventful, since here these categories pass ceaselessly back and forth into one another.

The climax of this development is in many ways reached in the Nighttown section, itself a prolongation of that comparable movement and outer limit reached by Flaubert in *La Tentation de Saint Antoine*. Indeed, had we more time, it would have been pleasant to discuss the peculiar representational space generated by these two 'reading plays', these two seeming eruptions and intrusions of a properly theatrical space in that very different space—no matter how experimental—of narrative or novelistic representation. I think we would have been able to show that this new space, with its ostensibly theatrical form (scenic indications, character attributions, printed speeches, notations of expression), has nothing to do with the closure of traditional theatrical representation; far more to do, indeed, with that space of hallucination in terms of which Flaubert often described his own creative processes, and which, in *Saint Antoine*, he represents as follows:

> And suddenly there move across the empty air first a puddle of water, then a prostitute, the edge of a temple, a soldier's face, a chariot drawn by two white horses rearing. These images arrive abruptly, jerkily, detached against the night like scarlet paintings on ebony. Their movement grows more rapid. They follow each other at a dizzying rate. At other times, they come to a halt and gradually waning, melt away; or else they fly off, and others take their place at once.[8]

Hallucinatory experience of this kind can be described, in the language of Gestalt psychology, as the perception of forms without background, forms or figures sundered from their ground or context, and passing discontinuously across the field of vision in a lateral movement, as though somehow on this side and nearer than the objects of the visible world. The instability of space or experience of this kind lies in the failure of the discrete or isolated image to generate any background or depth, any worldness in which it can take root. On the printed page, this essentially means that the ground, the anticipatory-retrospective texture, of narrative—what Greimas calls its isotopies, its ana- and cata-phoric relationships—is ruptured: it therefore falls to the typographic and material mechanisms of theatrical and scenic directions to bind (or rebind) these discontinuous images together. Typography thus becomes an event within the text among others. Or, if you prefer, since it is the reified sense of the visual which has here been solicited and stimulated, this sense

---

[8] Gustave Flaubert, *La Tentation de Saint Antoine*. Paris: La Pleiade, 1951, Vol. I, p. 69.

will now begin to function as it were in the void, taking as its object the
material signifiers, the printed words themselves, and no longer the latter's
signifieds or representations or meanings.

At any rate, this peculiar climax of *Ulysses* in the seeming immediacy of a
theatrical representation which is in reality the unmediated experience of the
printed book will now help us to understand two kinds of things: the
peculiarly anticlimactic nature of the chapters that follow it (I'm getting to
them, at last!), and the ground on which the depersonalised textualisation of
the narrative of *Ulysses* takes place, what one is tempted to call a kind of
'autistic textualization', the production of sentences in a void, moments in
which the book begins to elaborate its own text, under its own momentum,
with no further need of characters, point of view, author or perhaps even
reader:

> Mr Bloom reached Essex bridge. Yes, Mr Bloom crossed bridge of Yessex. (*U*
> 1961:261; *U* 1986:215; 11–229)

> Love loves to love love. Nurse loves the new chemist. Constable 14A loves Mary
> Kelly. Gerty MacDowell loves the boy that has the bicycle. M.B. loves a fair
> gentleman. Li Chi Han lovey up kissy Cha Pu Chow. Jumbo, the elephant, loves
> Alice, the elephant. Old Mr Verschoyle with the ear trumpet loves old Mrs
> Verschoyle with the turnedin eye. . . . You love a certain person. And this person
> loves that other person because everybody loves somebody but God loves every-
> body. (*U* 1961:333; *U* 1986:273; 12–1493)

The point I want to make about passages like these, and they are everywhere
in *Ulysses*, is that 'point of view' theory does not *take* on them, nor any
conceivable notion of the Implied Author, unless the I. A. is an imbecile or a
schizophrenic. No one is speaking these words or thinking them: they are
simply, one would want to say, printed sentences.

And this will be my transition to the two most boring chapters of *Ulysses*,
and thence to a close. Because what happens in the Eumaeus chapter is that,
so to speak, Joyce lapses back into more traditional narrative 'point of view':
that is, for the first time in *Ulysses* we once again get the 'he thought/she
thought' form of indirect discourse, what I will call the third person indistinct,
and a henceforth conventional belief in that central reflective consciousness
which is both appropriate and ironic in the chapter in which Bloom and
Stephen are finally able to sit down together, two closed or solipsistic monads
projecting that most boring theme of our own time, namely 'lack of communication'. Indeed, I am tempted to say, judging from the sentence structure, the
elaborate periphrases, the use of occasional foreign expressions as well as
cautiously isolated 'colloquial' ones, that this chapter really constitutes Joyce's
attempt at a parody or pastiche of a writer he had no particular sympathy or
respect for, namely Henry James. (If so, it is not a very good pastiche, and
only our supreme belief in Joyce's power of mimicry, in his ability to do
anything stylistically, has prevented us from noticing it.) Or better still, this

chapter deploys the stylistic mannerisms of Henry James in order to record a social and psychological content characteristic, rather, of James's enemy brother and archetypal rival, H. G. Wells—that is, an essentially petty-bourgeois content whose comfortable fit with the Jamesian narrative apparatus is somehow humiliating for both of them and sends both off back to back, as though their well-known differences on the form and function of the novel were less the taking of incompatible positions than—to use a more contemporary expression—mere variants within a single problematic, the problematic of the centred subject, of the closed monad, of the isolated or privatised subjectivity. The theory and practice of narrative 'point of view', as we associate it with Henry James, is not simply the result of a metaphysical option, a personal obsession, nor even a technical development in the history of form (although it is obviously also all those things): point of view is rather the quasi-material expression of a fundamental social development itself, namely the increasing social fragmentation and monadisation of late capitalist society, the intensifying privatisation and isolation of its subjects.

We have already touched on one aspect of this development—reification—which can now be characterised in another way, as the increasing separation, under capitalism, between the private and the public, between the personal and the political, between leisure and work, psychology and science, poetry and prose, or to put it all in a nutshell, between the subject and the object. The centred but psychologised subject and the reified object are indeed the respective orientations of these two concluding chapters, Eumaeus and Ithaca: and it is as though Joyce meant here to force us to work through in detail everything that is intolerable about this opposition. What we have been calling boredom is not Joyce's failure, then, but rather his success, and is the signal whereby we ourselves as organisms register a situation but also forms that are finally stifling for us.

This is perhaps a little easier to show in the Ithaca or catechism sequence: the format—question and answer—is not really, I think, a return to the experimentation—better still, the textualisation—of the earlier chapters. It is rather that quite different thing—the construction of a form of discourse from which the subject—sender or receiver—is radically excluded: a form of discourse, in other words, that would be somehow radically objective, if that were really possible. And if it is observed that even this seemingly sterilised alternation of question and answer turns increasingly, towards the end of the chapter, around Mr Bloom's private thoughts and fantasies, in other words, around the subjective rather than the objective, then I will reply by noting the degree to which those fantasies, Mr Bloom's 'bovarysme' (tactfully called 'ambition' by Joyce), are henceforth inextricably bound up with objects, in the best consumer society tradition. These are falsely subjective fantasies: here, in reality, commodities are dreaming about themselves through us.

These two final Bloom chapters, then, pose uncomfortable problems, and not least about narrative itself: the subjective or point-of-view chapter,

Eumaeus, asks us why we should be interested in stories about private individuals any longer, given the extraordinary relativisation of all individual experience, and the transformation of its contents into so many purely psychological reactions. Meanwhile, the objective chapter, Ithaca, completes an infinite subdivision of the objective contents of narrative, breaking 'events' into their smallest material components and asking whether, in that form, they still have any interest whatsoever. Two men have a discussion over cocoa, and that may be interesting in a pinch: but what about the act of putting the kettle on to boil—that is a part of the same vent, but is it still interesting? The elaborate anatomy of the process of boiling water (U 1961:670; U 1986:548; 17–164) is boring in three senses of the word: (1) it is essentially non-narrative; (2) it is inauthentic, in the sense in which these mass-produced material instruments (unlike Homer's spears and shields) cannot be said to be organic parts of their users' destinies; finally, (3) these objects are contingent and meaningless in their instrumental form, they are recuperable for literature only at the price of being transformed into symbols. Such passages thus ask three questions:

1. Why do we need narrative anyway? What are stories and what is our existential relation to them? Is a non-narrative relationship to the world and to Being possible?
2. What kind of lives are we leading and what kind of world are we living them in, if the objects that surround us are all somehow external, extrinsic, alienated from us? (It is a question about the simulacra of industrial society, essentially a question about the city, but in this form at least as old as the interrogation of the 'wholeness' of Greek culture by German romanticism.)
3. (A question I have already raised but which remains seemingly unanswered, namely) How can the products of human labour have come to be felt as meaningless or contingent?

Yet to this last question at least, Joyce's form has a kind of answer, and it is to be found in that great movement of dereification I have already invoked, in which the whole dead grid of the object world of greater Dublin is, in the catechism chapter, finally, disalienated and by the most subterranean detours traced back . . . less to its origins in Nature, than to the transformation of Nature by human and collective praxis deconcealed. So to the vitalist ideology of Molly's better known final affirmation, I tend rather to prefer this one:

> What did Bloom do at the range?
> He removed the saucepan to the left hob, rose and carried the iron kettle to the sink in order to tap the current by turning the faucet to let it flow.
> Did it flow?
> Yes. From Roundwood reservoir in county Wicklow of a cubic capacity of 2,400 million gallons, percolating through a subterranean aqueduct of filter mains of single and double pipeage constructed at an initial plant cost of £5 per linear yard. . . . (U 1961:670; U 1986:548; 17–160)

To Sing or to Sign

Maud Ellmann

"Par it's Greek: parallel, parallax," muses Bloom in "Lestrygonians." "Sirens" parallels "Proteus," and provides it with a kind of parallaxative. Like "Proteus," "Sirens" sets the audible against the visible, time against space, voice against writing: but Bloom's fart escapes both of the modalities which these two chapters pose as ineluctable.

As magicians of the voice, the Sirens stand for the enchantments of the audible. To resist them, Bloom must discover a new lure, and open an alternative modality. While the ear surrenders to the blandishments of voice, the roving Odyssean eye pursues the letter, and it is through writing that Bloom begins to make his getaway. What the ear hears, the eye reads; and in particular, the eye reads names and signatures. "Signatures of all things I am here to read" (*U* 1961:37; *U* 1986:31; 3–2), thinks Stephen, while in "Sirens," "Bloowhose dark eye read Aaron Figatner's name" (*U* 1961:259; *U* 1986:213; 11–149). As well as reading signatures, Bloom's task in "Sirens" is to write his name to Martha Clifford. Here he must summon all his polytropic cunning. For while he signs the letter, he must still preserve the incognito he imposes on himself, the law that Nosey Flynn nosed out in "Lestrygonians":

> O, Bloom has his good points. But there's one thing he'll never do.
> His hand scrawled a dry pen signature beside his grog.
> —I know, Davy Byrne said.
> —Nothing in black and white, Nosey Flynn said. (*U* 1961:178; *U* 1986:146; 8–984)

So Bloom must find a pseudo-signature: and more than that, a countersign (for Molly's countersign, see R. Ellmann, *Ulysses on the Liffey* 162). This mark enables him to face the music with unstopped ears, but it also gives him the guts to shun its charms. Because it sneaks *between* modalities, this autograph will open forth a heresy. The Greek root of "heresy" implies a middle voice, a middle way. "Heresy" resembles "odyssey," for both pursue a middle course of action or of thought, between antitheses or rocks and whirlpools. By eluding binarism, both condemn themselves to endless errancy.

"Proteus" and "Sirens" meditate the heresies couched in "contransmagnifi-

From *James Joyce: The Centennial Symposium*, eds. Morris Beja, Phillip Herring, Maurice Harmon, and David Norris (Champaign: University of Illinois Press, 1986), 66–9. Copyright © 1986 by The Board of Trustees of the University of Illinois. Reprinted by permission of Maud Ellmann and the Board of Trustees of the University of Illinois.

candjewbangstantiality." In "Sirens," song and signature compete for the annunciation of the Virgin. Ben Dollard would take her with his voice: "Sure, you'd burst the tympanum of her ear, man, Mr. Dedalus said through smoke aroma, with an organ like yours" (*U* 1961:270; *U* 1986:222; 11–536). Bloom foregoes the penetrations of the voice, but he would ravish with his writing. "Blank face," he thinks. "Virgin should say: or fingered only. Write something on it: page" (*U* 1961:285; *U* 1986:234; 11–1086). This image harks back to "Proteus," where Stephen envisions Eve's unnaveled flesh as a "buckler of taut vellum," an unwritten page (*U* 1961:38; *U* 1986:32; 3–42). The writing that blemishes this vellum is the navel, which undersigns the strandentwining cable of maternity. Because he would deny maternity, and beget a father for his name, Stephen must erase the navel from the page. But his own logic means that he can never write. If writing is the scar upon the belly where the mother's namelessness engraves itself upon the flesh in mockery of Stephen's name and patrimony, to write is to unname and to unman. This is why Bloom can only write his name in womantalk, the language of flowers, the language "they" like because "no-one can hear" (*U* 1961:78; *U* 1986:64; 5–261). He foregoes his father's name to write "an anemone's letter," and to disseminate maternal countersigns (*FW* 563).

How is Bloom to write umbiliform? An answer may be found in Plutarch's essay "On the E at Delphi," for the letter *E* was carved into the navel of the world, the stone of the Delphic oracle (*Plutarch's Morals* 173–96). When he countersigns his pseudo-signature with two "Greek ees," Bloom commemorates this ancient graffito, and hollows out an omphalos within his name. The difference between a Greek *E* and a Roman *E* cannot be enunciated; nor can it pierce the tympan of the ear. Only the eye can see the *E*. Through this navel strategy, our latter-day Odysseus eludes the Sirens and the perilous pleasures of the voice, as Homer's Noman once escaped the eyeless Cyclops.

So far, so good. Bloom supplants the phallus with the omphalos. He escapes the myth of vocal penetration by writing Greek *E*'s on the virgin page. The voice does not deflower Henry Flower, for the silent *E* subverts its whole modality. If, as Bloom says, "time makes the tune" (*U* 1961:278; *U* 1986:228; 11–841), it would seem that space and writing had outdone the Siren time, the Siren music. But the etymology of heresy involves the notion of a middle course, and Odysseus is one who steers *between* antitheses. Besides, Stephen indicates that the father governs *both* modalities. "The man with my voice and my eyes," he says (*U* 1961:38; *U* 1986:32, 3–46), the man who orders all the audible and visible. Bloom, the new womanly man, must uncover a new language which eludes both voice and eyes, both music and writing: a language which evades antithesis itself, as Penelope will add a dangerous supplement to the binary order of paternity.

The Greek *E* belongs to this new discourse, for it does not confine itself to one modality. Indeed, it crosses both and double-crosses their duality. Bloom's "kakography" is such a consummate escape that it escapes the text itself, and we only read the *E* in its transliterated form: "ee" (*U* 1961:279; *U* 1986:229; 11–865; also see *FW* 180). Besides, Bloom listens for the *E* as well as reading it and writing it. "There's music everywhere," he thinks. "Rutt-ledge's door: ee creaking" (*U* 1961:282; *U* 1986:281; 11–965). He hears ees cracking, he sees ees Greeking: and while the *E* enjoys the charms of both modalities, it also opens a defect in both, an unvoiced, unseen residue. Is it possible that we have missed a *third* modality? Bloom seems to think so when he muses, "Words? Music? No, it's what's behind" (*U* 1961:274; *U* 1986:226; 11–614). What's behind is Bloom's behind, and it is Bloom's behind that enunciates the missing ee. "Pwee! A wee little wind piped eeee. In Bloom's little wee" (*U* 1961:288; *U* 1986:237; 11–1203). This is an *E* that Bloom neither sings nor signs. He farts it. This ee outdoes Odysseus himself, the very principle of slippage and escape, for the fart escapes its own escaper. A new voice, its eeee belongs to music, but it also seeps into the written word, to vex the opposite modality. The fart explodes in the very letters of the word "written" which constitutes Bloom's epitaph: "My eppripfftaph. Be pfwritt" (*U* 1961:257; *U* 1986:211; 11–61). As writing, the fart cajoles the eye: as voice, it saturates the ear. But there is a third organ which can detect the fart when it is neither audible nor visible.

This organ may be found at the end of "Sirens" and of "Proteus," for these two endings mirror one another. In "Sirens," Bloom makes sure there is "No-one behind" (*U* 1961:291; *U* 1986:239; 11–1289), before he lets his behind utter its last word. Stephen mimes this gesture in "Proteus," turning his eyes "over a shoulder, rere regardant" (*U* 1961:51; *U* 1986:41; 3–503), before he dares to pick his nose. Later, Bloom appropriates his words in "Circe," when he stammers "rerererepugnant," guiltily (*U* 1961:538; *U* 1986:439; 15–3057). If this is a coincidence, Bloom twice indicates in "Sirens" that coincidence is the order of the day (*U* 1961:263, 275; *U* 1986:217, 226; 11–303, 713). How do Bloom's and Stephen's stealthy gestures coincide? Is there some link between the nose and rear, between the nose and what's behind?

If Bloom's fart escapes the father's ear, the father's eye, it leaves its "eppripfftaph" for the nose alone. It is in the nose that heresy has found its middle course, for the art of the fart could find no greater connoisseur. Similarly, when Stephen deposits his dry snot in "Proteus," he countersigns his carefully constructed patriarchal universe. Snot has become a matriarchal signifier, since the "grey sweet mother" is the "snot-green sea." For Bloom, the nose outdoes the phallus, and in the end defeats the suitors in "Penelope." While Molly broods of Boylan and "that tremendous big red brute of a thing," she wonders that "his nose is not so big" (*U* 1961:742; *U* 1986:611; 18–144). "Married to the greasy nose" (*U* 1961:260; *U* 1986:214; 11–173), she, too, has left the ear and eye behind in a voyage towards a new olfactory modality.

Why should the nose be greasy? It would be far-fetched to turn to Freud, and to the famous fetish of the shine on the nose that marked and masked the loss of the maternal phallus ("Fetishism," *Complete Works* 147–57). (Freud also argued that civilization with all its discontents came into being when the eye took over from the nose [*Civilization* 99n, 106n].) It is perhaps more pertinent that "grease" is slang for "unction," or that it eases entries and odyssean exits. Moreover, the Greek *E* whispers in greasy (Greece-ee), so that Bloom's nose may glisten with his secret signature. In "Sirens," nose becomes "knows" (*U* 1961:260; *U* 1986:214; 11–177), and since the word "knows" derives from "gnosis," it is as if knowledge itself were rooted in the wayward odysseys of heresy. By writing Greek "ees" where Roman "ees" should be, Bloom supplants the Roman Church with a nosey gnostic jewgreek heresy. What the ear hears, and the eye sees, give way to what the nose knows.

Works Cited

Ellman, Richard. *Ulysses on the Liffey.* New York: Oxford University Press, 1982.

Freud, Sigmund. *Civilization and its Discontents.* Standard Ed. 21. London: Hogarth Press, 1953–54.

———. "Fetishism." In *The Complete Psychological Works.* Standard Ed. Tr. James Strachey, 21. London: Hogarth Press, 1953–54.

Plutarch's Morals: Theosophical Essays. Tr. Charles William King. London: George Bell, 1882.

Finnegans Wake: The Critical Method

Margot Norris

Structure and Language

Thanks to the patient toil of its dedicated explicators, the major contours of Joyce's *Finnegans Wake* have gradually come into focus in the [fifty] years since its publication. Yet while more allusions, motifs, and linguistic details are continually coming to light, the intellectual orientation of the work remains largely obscure.

The attempt to assess the teleology of *Finnegans Wake* has always presented critics with a dilemma: the choice between a radical and a conversative interpretation of the book. A radical interpretation would maintain that *Finnegans Wake* subverts not only the literary status quo but the most cherished intellectual preconceptions of Western culture as well—a position most clearly maintained in the pioneer studies of the work. Yet in these early studies, such as *Our Exagmination*,[1] the weakness of the radical interpretation also becomes apparent. While proclaiming the revolutionary nature of *Work in Progress*, the writers lack scholarly pegs on which to hang their theories and finally resort to ad hoc analogies to support their theses. In contrast, the conservative critics, who have dominated *Wake* criticism for the last thirty years, possess a small but scholarly arsenal: the stylistic and thematic conservatism of the early manuscript drafts, the inclusion of traditional, even arcane, literary material in the work, Joyce's admission that the work's structural and philosophical models are derived from a sixteenth-century metaphysician and an eighteenth-century philosopher, and finally, Joyce's own decidedly reactionary tastes. Even . . . *A Conceptual Guide to "Finnegans Wake,"*[2] which aims at a comprehensive study of the work, embraces this conservative tradition by approaching the work as a novel: "along with the problem for the

From Introduction to *The Decentered Universe of "Finnegans Wake"*, Margot Norris (Baltimore: The Johns Hopkins University Press, 1976), 1–9. Copyright © 1976 by The Johns Hopkins University Press. Reprinted by permission of Margot Norris and The Johns Hopkins University Press.

[1]Samuel Beckett et al., *Our Exagmination Round His Factification for Incamination of Work in Progress* (New York: New Directions Books, 1962).
[2]Michael H. Begnal and Fritz Senn, eds., *A Conceptual Guide to "Finnegans Wake"* (University Park: Pennsylvania State University Press, 1974), p. x.

reader of deciphering Joyce's language goes the stumbling block of figuring out the narrative or the plot."

Joyce is himself partly responsible for this unsettled state of affairs. Throughout the progress of his writing, he sent friends and disciples scurrying to reference books that would unlock the secret of a phrase or passage, while his comments on the overall purpose and construction of the book remained enigmatic and vague—often phrased in negative terms that suggest what *Finnegans Wake* is not, rather than what it is. "I might easily have written this story in the traditional manner. . . . Every novelist knows the recipe. . . . It is not very difficult to follow a simple, chronological scheme which the critics will understand. . . . But I, after all, am trying to tell the story of this Chapelizod family in a new way. . . ."[3] We are left to wonder about the nature of this new way of telling the story. Joyce's sanction and supervision of *Our Exagmination* was clearly an effort to answer this question. Yet while approving his disciples' defense of his work on radical grounds, he failed to supply them with a theoretical base other than his references to Bruno and Vico.

Since the time of these pioneer *Wake* critics, an enormous amount of detailed explication of the text has become available, and new tools for critical investigation have emerged that make it possible to examine more thoroughly those aspects of the work that resist novelistic analysis. With these advantages, I hope to resume the radical viewpoints of the early critics and demonstrate the extent of the challenge that Joyce offered not only to conventional literary modes but also to many of the epistemological presuppositions of our culture. My argument will be based on the assumption that Joyce did not mount this challenge in a vacuum, but that knowingly or unknowingly he participated in those intellectual currents of early-twentieth-century Europe, whose destructive impact depended on a profound revision of the understanding of language. Eugene Jolas, a close personal friend and colleague of Joyce's, was extraordinarily sensitive to these currents. "The real metaphysical problem today is the word," he writes in *Our Exagmination*. "The new artist of the word has recognized the autonomy of language."[4] Jolas also connected Joyce with the literary experimentalists of the day.

> Léon-Paul Fargue, one of the great French poets of our age, has created astonishing neologisms in his prose poems. . . . The revolution of the surrealists, who destroyed completely the old relationships between words and thought, remains of immense significance. . . . André Breton, demoralizing the old psychic processes by the destruction of logic, has discovered a world of magic in the study of dream via the Freudian explorations. . . . Miss Gertrude Stein attempts to find a mysticism of the word by the process of thought thinking itself.[5]

---

[3] Eugene Jolas, "My Friend James Joyce," in Seon Givens, ed., *James Joyce: Two Decades of Criticism* (New York: Vanguard, Press, 1963), p. 11.

[4] Eugene Jolas, "The Revolution of Language and James Joyce," in Beckett et al., p. 79.

[5] Ibid., pp. 84–85.

At the time Jolas proclaimed "the revolution of the word," modern theoretical linguistics was in its infancy.[6] Ferdinand de Saussure's *Course in General Linguistics* was published in Paris in 1910 but appears to have gone unnoticed by contemporary writers. And yet we find in *Finnegans Wake* that intellectual shift which locates meaning in relationships and structure rather than in content—a shift formalized by Saussure's recognition of the arbitrary nature of the linguistic sign and his focus on the synchronic laws of language.

Among the many shocks administered to the Victorian mentality during the early twentieth century, the power and scope of the unconscious in human life was perhaps the least sensational but the most enduring. Freud's discovery of the extent to which man's psychic and emotional life is controlled by his unconscious adumbrated the complex role that language plays in that process. Psychoanalyst Jacques Lacan has recently restored this aspect of Freud's theory to prominence.[7] But those marvelously complicated workings of the unconscious that give us language were not truly recognized until Noam Chomsky's devastating refutation of behaviorist linguistic theory in the 1950s. Further evidence of man's lack of self-knowledge and impaired understanding of his condition ultimately served to raise criticism to the status of a highly self-conscious, creative act. In recent times this brand of self-reflexive criticism has expanded to many disciplines in a movement known broadly as structuralism. The theoretical roots of the structuralist method lie in linguistics, but its application ranges across the diverse human sciences, with particularly interesting developments in anthropology, psychoanalysis, and philosophy.

Structuralism presupposes that the organization of psychic and social life is based on similar unconscious laws and that the structures that underlie various human activities—language, family relationships, religious worship, social communications, for example—are therefore isomorphic. Consequently, relationships rather than substances, structures rather than contents, provide significant sources of meaning in human institutions and systems of communication.

---

[6]The available evidence indicates that Joyce attended a lecture on experimental linguistics by Père Marcel Jousse in 1931, although its effects on *Finnegan's Wake* are uncertain. See Richard Ellmann, *James Joyce* (New York: Oxford University Press, 1965), p. 647. Joyce's personal library contained virtually no works on linguistic theory per se. Thomas Connolly in *The Personal Library of James Joyce*, does list H. L. Mencken's *The American Language* and texts on auxiliary languages, Charles Kay Ogden's *Basic English and Debabelization*, "with a Survey of Contemporary Opinion on the Problem of Universal Language." Other language books in the personal library include foreign language dictionaries of slang, as well as texts on usage and etiquette: Basil Hargrave's *Origins and Meanings of Popular Phrases and Names Including Those Which Came into Use during the Great War*, also *English as She is Spoke: Or a Jest in Sober Earnest*, and Ogden's *Brighter Basic: Examples of Basic English for Young Persons of Taste and Feeling*. See Thomas E. Connolly, *The Personal Library of James Joyce: A Descriptive Bibliography* (Buffalo: The University of Buffalo Bookstore, 1957); Ronald Buckalew, "Night Lessons on Language," in Begnal and Senn, pp. 93–115, also contains a helpful discussion of Joyce's linguistic background.

[7]Jacques Lacan, "The Function of Language in Psychoanalysis," in Anthony Wilden, *The Language of the Self* (Baltimore: The Johns Hopkins University Press, 1968).

Structuralist theory is stubbornly at variance with those prevailing political and social philosophies that exhibit a distinct behaviorist bias, an underlying faith that man is shaped by the external forces of his environment and that human betterment depends on the improvement of that environment. Yet it is precisely this conflict that helps to illustrate the suitability of the structuralist approach to Joyce's work. In their grim depiction of the spiritual "paralysis" that Dublin visits on its citizens, *Dubliners* and *A Portrait of the Artist as a Young Man* (hereafter cited as *Portrait*) affirm the oppression of the individual by society and its institutions. But while Joyce is unconcerned with melioration in these works, his theme of exile does promise hope of escape. The local use of mythic patterns in *Portrait* expands in *Ulysses* to a massive mythic structure that ascribes the condition of the individual not merely to accidents of environment but to certain constant predispositions in his own nature and in the order of things as well. For example, the "brutal" fathers in *Dubliners*, Farrington and Little Chandler, are so crushed by their environments that they take their anger and frustration out on their small sons. But father-son relationships in *Ulysses* have become symbolic and complex. Stephen's *Hamlet* theory and numerous mythic analogues isolate recurrent difficulties that plague the hierarchical systems in which men relate to each other and to their gods. In *Finnegans Wake* the notion of an "environment"—which depends on an empirical belief in the separation of inner and outer, subjective and objective, mental and physical—completely disintegrates. Characters are fluid and interchangeable, melting easily into their landscapes to become river and land, tree and stone, Howth Castle and Environs, or HCE. We find in the *Wake* not characters as such but ciphers, in formal relationship to each other.

For all his reticence on the subject, Joyce did provide a single helpful clue to orient our approach to his new universe. Preceded by a theory of correspondences that he derived from Hermes Trismegistus and Swedenborg (cf. *P* 244), his last work employed the thought of Giordano Bruno, which he summarized as follows: "His philosophy is a kind of dualism—every power in nature must evolve an opposite in order to realise itself and opposition brings reunion etc etc."[8] Besides its resemblance to Hegelian dialectic, Bruno's philosophical dualism adumbrates the binary opposition of phonemes, which provided a central insight into the nature of linguistic meaning: meaning inheres not in sounds themselves—"d" and "t," for example—but in the contrast or difference between them, so that we can distinguish "dime" and "time." The concept of binary opposition is a cornerstone of the structuralist method. "But when, as in structuralism, substance is replaced by relationship, then the noun, the object, even the individual ego itself, becomes nothing but a locus of cross-references: not things, but differential perceptions, that is to say, a sense of the *identity* of a given element which derives solely from our

[8]James Joyce, *Letters of James Joyce*, ed. Stuart Gilbert (New York: Viking Press, 1966), 1:226. From a letter to Harriet Shaw Weaver dated 27 January 1925.

awareness of its *difference* from other elements, and ultimately from an implicit comparison of it with its own opposite."[9] I will try to use this method in a central, integrated approach to the entire work, its narrative structure, its themes, the nature of the discourse (point of view), and the technical and aesthetic aspects of the language.

Dream Theory

For all its stylistic innovations, *Ulysses* ceased to bedazzle critics and readers and started to "make sense" once the plot and story line were discovered and understood. Similar attempts to transcend the pryrotechnics of *Finnegans Wake* have more or less failed. Story lines and plots have had to be plugged with hallucinations and dreams within dreams. Yet annoying questions concerning the nature of the figures, events, and language have persisted all the same. I have tried to approach *Finnegans Wake* with an abiding trust in Joyce's artistry and professional experience and a modicum of trust in my own good sense as a reader and critic. I have resisted the promptings of armchair psychology to chalk up the puzzling and confusing nature of the work to Joyce's mischief, malice, or megalomania. And after much study, thought, and irritation, I have come to the conclusion that the key to the puzzle is the puzzle. In other words, expecting the work to "make sense" in the way *Portrait, Ulysses,* or traditional novels "make sense" implies a conceptual framework and epistemology that Joyce strongly intimated he wanted to undermine. *Finnegans Wake* is a puzzle because dreams are puzzles—elaborate, brilliant, purposeful puzzles, which constitute a universe quite unlike any we know or experience in waking life.

Although Freud's influence on Joyce is argued convincingly by Frederick J. Hoffman in his early essay[10] and endorsed by Atherton,[11] Clive Hart's preference for the *Upanishads* as the source of Joyce's dream theory[12] makes some restatement necessary. Joyce's reference to Freud's *The Interpretation of Dreams* in *Finnegans Wake* (FW 338.29) is supported by ample evidence that he read the book with care and applied the techniques of dream-work to the *Wake.* Virtually every one of the "typical dreams" described by Freud[13] constitutes a major theme in *Finnegans Wake.* "Embarrassing Dreams of Being Naked," which often find the subject naked before strangers, are

---

[9]Frederic Jameson, "Metacommentary," *PMLA* 86, no. 1 (January 1971):14.

[10]Frederic J. Hoffman, "Infroyce," in Seon Givens, *James Joyce: Two Decades of Criticism* (New York: Vanguard Press, 1948; Augmented edition 1963), pp. 390–435.

[11]James S. Atherton, *The Books at the Wake* (New York: Viking Press, 1960), pp. 37–39.

[12]Clive Hart, *Structure and Motif in "Finnegans Wake"* (London: Faber and Faber, 1962), Chapter 3.

[13]Sigmund Freud, "The Interpretation of Dreams," in *The Standard Edition of the Complete Psychological Works of Sigmund Freud,* trans. James Strachey (London: The Hogarth Press, 1953–74), 4:241–76.

reflected in the voyeurism of the three anonymous soldiers in the Phoenix Park incident. Freud points out that frequently the strangers in such dreams represent familiar persons: the *Wake's* soldiers represent HCE's sons, who view their father much as the sons of Noah viewed their father. Explaining dreams about the death of beloved persons, Freud discusses both sibling rivalry and the simultaneous incestuous and murderous feelings between parents and children. All of these taboos are at issue in the mysterious sin in *Finnegans Wake*. In fact, Freud reports a dream that contains a cluster of the elements found in the Phoenix Park incident. It shows "two boys struggling," like the *Wake's* enemy twins, with one of them fleeing for protection to a maternal woman, like ALP hiding the "lipoleums" under her skirt hoop to "sheltershock" (*FW* 8.30) them. Freud interprets the woman as representing both an incestuous and a voyeuristic object for the boy. "The dream combined two opportunities he had had as a little boy of seeing little girls' genitals: When they were *thrown down* and when they were *micturating*. And from the other part of the context it emerged that he had a recollection of being *chastised* or threatened by his father for the sexual curiosity he had evinced on these occasions."[14] Freud's dream resembles the homework chapter, II.2, where the boys examine their mother's genitals and one boy strikes the other in punishment. The merging of the boy with the threatening father in Freud's dream also recurs frequently in a merger of father and son in the *Wake*. Furthermore, the notion of voyeuristically watching girls urinate is a repeated Phoenix Park/Waterloo image. Freud discusses both children's games and examinations or academic tests as bearing sexual significance in typical dreams, a concept manifested in Chapters II.1 and II.2 of *Finnegans Wake*.

The dream universe is structured differently from the mental universe of conscious life because meanings are located in different places. One explanation for the encyclopedic nature of *Finnegans Wake* is that the dreaming psyche attaches items of knowledge or information from the waking consciousness and invests them with totally different meanings. The key to the new meanings is hidden in the connection between the two thoughts. For example, "Waterloo" means a famous Napoleonic battle to the waking mind. In the Wakean dream world it also means a place for urinating. If "Waterloo" reminds the dreamer of a juvenile chastisement for watching girls urinate, then the sexual and historical references to the place become linked by the common theme of humiliating defeat. Because meanings are dislocated—hidden in unexpected places, multiplied and split, given over to ambiguity, plurality, and uncertainty—the dream represents a decentered universe. Since this dream universe is so unlike waking life, the critical techniques designed to explore the traditional novel are unsuitable to the study of a dream-work. To examine various aspects of this decentered world, I have borrowed the ideas and tools of theoreticians in a variety of fields who share an interest in the structures of the systems they study.

14Ibid, p. 201.

The narrative structure of *Finnegans Wake* . . . appears more intelligible in the light of the modern myth theories of anthropologist Claude Lévi-Strauss than it did through attempts at finding correspondences to the Gilbert scheme for *Ulysses*. Lévi-Strauss's myth theory suggests a plausible reason for Joyce's "new way" of telling a story by collocating versions of the same event rather than developing a chronological plot. Furthermore, Lévi-Strauss's concept of the homology of myth and dream suggests a way of relating individual and social experience in *Finnegans Wake* without recourse to the Jungian concept of a "collective unconscious." While Lévi-Strauss argues that myths and dreams are governed by the same unconscious structures and that the meaning of myths and dreams resides in the relationships between their elements, Jungian theory posits the significance and persistence of the nature of types and images in the personal and racial memory.

The relationships between Wakean figures have such complex functions that a series of interlocking approaches [is] required . . . to describe them adequately. Insofar as these relationships are power relationships, they constitute a destructive and repetitive system that is reflected in the theories of Vico, Freud, and Hegel. Vico's socioreligious history is based on endless cycles produced by mankind's progress from one age to another as power relationships change. The sexual dynamic of the Freudian family is based on unconscious power relationships that were operative in establishing primitive society. The power relationships implicit in Hegel's Master-slave dialectic relate the concept of the fight to the emergence of human consciousness—a notion elaborated on at the psychoanalytic level by Jacques Lacan. The paradoxical nature of society as simultaneously lawful and repressive is reversed by the anarchic Oedipal drives in the *Wake*, which create a decentered dream world that is without law, but free.

The dream permits the dreamer's relationship to himself to assume dramatic form as he uses the disguises and defenses provided by the dream mechanism to communicate to himself about himself. Philosopher Martin Heidegger's theory of inauthentic being helps to explore the ontological condition of the dreamer through his comportment toward guilt, truth, and death.

. . . [D]ream language can be explored as poetic language, using Lacan's theories of language, repression, and poetry. It is the function of a dream to simultaneously conceal and reveal the nature of the "true" or unconscious self, a task accomplished through the structural operations described by Freud. Such techniques of dream-work as displacement, condensation, and distortion, correspond to the tropes that create the dense, ambiguous, polyvalent language of the work. The tension in the language, which bars semantic certainty or simplicity, signifies the decentered universe it expresses.

[T]he philosophical implications of expressing a decentered universe imply a problem that has been formulated by philosopher Jacques Derrida as a critical dilemma. In Joyce's case, the problem is technical—the need to find a language to depict a world in which identities are unstable, speakers are deceptive and lack self-knowledge, the point of view is not unified, and the society depicted is anarchic.

Throughout this discussion I have spoken of a dreamer and of the dream of *Finnegans Wake* as though there is indeed a single dreamer and I know exactly who he is. Well, I don't know who he is. To say that Joyce is the dreamer tells us nothing useful. To say that the dreamer is Finn or Earwicker ignores the significance of ambiguous identities in the dream. Wakean figures are interchangeable because characters in dreams are fictions created by the dreamer—including fictions of himself. In other words, the dreamer is invested in all of his characters in certain ways, and the characters that represent himself are no less fictional than any of the others. I suspect that we are to assume a single dreamer, since the same obsessions inform all the themes narrated by the different voices. The different speaking voices may therefore represent different personae of the dreamer relating different versions of the same event. For example, since a single dreamer can be a father, a son, and a brother all at once, he can play out an Oedipal drama in his dream, in which he takes the parts of Laius, Oedipus, and Creon all at once. In this way he can express many conflicting feelings simultaneously. I speculate that it makes no difference whether one supposes a single long dream, with constant repetition of the same theme, or a group of serial dreams, each dealing with the same theme. It seems plausible to suppose that the dreamer is male, since the major conflicts appear to afflict male figures. But sex, like everything else, is mutable in dreams. The question "Who is the dreamer?" is a question properly addressed not to the reader but to the dreamer himself, who discovers in the dream that he is by no means who he thinks he is.

Comic Seriousness and Poetic Prose

Bernard Benstock

As Shem and Shaun, the dual aspects of man's nature, constantly merge and "reamalgamerge" into each other; as Isobel, the Alice-girl, sees her image in her looking glass; so the twin muses of Comedy and Poetry are constantly fusing in the language of *Finnegans Wake*. Essentially they are dual character-istics of Joyce's "Revolution of the Word," which like most revolutionary aspects of the novel (the antithesis challenging the thesis) is actually a *romance* of the word—a synthesis of the comic with the poetic into a single entity of language. As it is often impossible to separate the meaning from the language in *Finnegans Wake*—its form being derived intrinsically from its content—it is equally impossible to segregate the humorous from the poetic. In an attempt to analyze the nature of the comedy and the qualities of the poetry in the *Wake*, it is important to do so primarily in terms of reuniting the dissected parts into its original unity—the synthesis which is the basis of Joyce's harmonic as well as intellectual balance. Its humor is basically verbal since Joyce's universal dream is poetically conceived in terms of "echoes" rather than "images"; it is a purblindman's dream transliterated immediately upon perception into speech patterns capturing the many-leveled irrelevan-cies which dance about the central core of significance in each event.

This is not to imply that *Finnegans Wake* as a comic novel lacks its comedy of situations, but to impress that even its "slapstick" situations are delivered in terms of lingual gymnastics, words falling over each other in comic proces-sions. The strong element of pantomime which, as Atherton indicated,[1] dominated much of Joyce's thinking in his conception of the *Wake*, is equally linguistic. His Harlequins and Columbines wear their splashed profusion of colors in a tumble of linguistic patterns of "rudd yellan gruebleen" (*FW* 23.1), and like players in the early Catholic pageants they can be visualized in "their pinky limony creamy birnies and their turkiss indienne mauves" (*FW* 215.20-21). Actually the pantomime is never *seen* in *Finnegans Wake*; it is there primarily because Joyce alludes to it:

> inseparable sisters, uncontrollable nighttalkers, Skertsiraizde with Donyahzade, who afterwards, when the robberers shot up the socialights, came down into the

From *Joyce-Agains Wake*, Bernard Benstock (Seattle: University of Washington Press, 1965), 108–9, 122–25, 141–43, 154–56, 160–63. Copyright © University of Washington Press, 1965. Reprinted by permission of Bernard Benstock and the University of Washington Press.

[1] James S. Atherton, "*Finnegans Wake*: 'The Gist of the Pantomime,'" *Accent*, XV (Winter, 1955), 14–26.

world as amusers and were staged by Madame Sudlow as Rosa and Lily Miskinguette in the pantalime that two pitts paythronosed, Miliodorus and Galathee (*FW* 32.7–12)

The Gaiety Theatre on Dublin's King Street ("that king's treat house"—*FW* 32.26) and its director, Michael Gunn ("game old Gunne. . . . He's duddandgunne"—*FW* 25.21–24), are also mentioned. But essentially the pantomime as an art form exists in the *Wake* because Joyce characterizes it: "The piece was this: look at the lamps. The cast was thus: see under the clock. Ladies circle: cloaks may be left. Pit, prommer and parterre, standing room only" (*FW* 33.10–12). These sentences describing the pantomime in chapter 9 are in themselves short and jerky, characteristic of the basic pantomime movement, and, like the actors for whom they serve as surrogates, they seem to wear one black sleeve and one white, one checkered leg and one striped, divided as they are down the middle. . . .

Much of the material of the first chapter (the introductory elements of the giant's wake which usher in H.C.E., his successor) revolves around the heroic figure of ancient Ireland, the fallen titan who is destined to wake when Ireland once again requires his services, as well as his stage counterpart, hod carrier Tim Finnegan, who re-enacts Finn's fall and resurrection in the Irish-American vaudeville ballad. The portions of *Finnegans Wake* that deal with Earwicker's heroic ancestor are written in mock-heroic language only duplicated during those portions of the novel in which either Earwicker or *his* deposer, Shaun, fancies himself the titanic hero: Earwicker's defense of the Russian General (*FW* 355–58), Earwicker's self-defense rising up from the body of Yawn (*FW* 534–54), and Shaun delivering his oration before the people (*FW* 407–15). But neither the oligarch Earwicker nor the demagogue Shaun quite manages to recapture the titan's mighty lines.

The opening chapter contains much of the machinery necessary to construct a mock epic. It begins *in medias res*— in midias reeds" (*FW* 158.7)— with a small letter in the middle of a sentence; it echoes the introductory lines of the heroic epic, as well as the chorus of *The Frogs*: "What clashes here of wills gen wonts, ostrygods gaggin fishygods! Brékkek Kékkek Kékkek Kékkek" (*FW* 4.1–2). This ushers in a paragraph dealing with the wars of the Dark Ages as well as the battle in heaven, and ends with the resurrection motif that foreshadows the events of Eden: "Phall if you but will, rise you must" (*FW* 4.15–16). "Of the first was he to bare arms and a name: Wassaily Booslaeugh of Riesengeborg" (*FW* 5.5–6) is another epical introduction to the hero, and it earmarks him as Adam the delver in the Garden of Eden, since Joyce is here parodying the gravedigger in *Hamlet* as he sports with the second clown:

> There is no ancient gentlemen but gardeners, ditchers,
>   and grave-makers; they hold up Adam's profession.
> *Second Clown.* Was he a gentleman?
> *Gravedigger.* 'A was the first that ever bore arms.
>   (V, i, 33–38)

The wake is under way; the keening is heard around the bier of the fallen titan, and the funeral feast is spread. "And they all gianed in with the shoutmost shoviality. Agog and magog and the round of them agrog" (*FW* 6.18–19). Whiskey and stout are served: "With a bockalips of finisky fore his feet. And a barrowload of guenesis hoer his head" (*FW* 6.26–27). The resurrection motif is sounded again: the whiskey will revive the hod carrier, and his "apocalyptic finish" will result in his "genesis" again. Much of this language echoes the Anglo-Saxon heroic poems: "rory end to the regginbrow was to be seen ringsome on the aquaface" (*FW* 3.13–14) is a protracted tetrameter line with the first three stressed words alliterated; *regginbrow* and *aquaface* were probably intended as mock kennings for kingly brow and water.

But whether parodying *Beowulf* or the Bible, Joyce's technique invariably seems to involve verbal humor, "puns, quashed quotatoes, messes of mottage" (*FW* 183.22–23). It is probably with the pun that Joyce does more to achieve his humorous linguistic effect than with any of the other aspects of his comic language.[2] Gillet finds the *Wake* "a linguistic jest, a sort of carnival, a grammatical mardi-gras, a philologist's good-humoured carouse" and cites his ancient precedent for the use of puns in a serious work: "In Homer, Ulysses, when the Cyclops asks his name, replies that he is named Outis, i.e. Noman. Now Ulysses in Greek is Odysseus, or Outis-Zeus (Noman joined to the name of the Deity)."[3] With the *Odyssey*, Shakespeare, and the New Testament (Christ's pun) corroborating the distinguished use of the "lowest form of wit," it remains only for Joyce to elevate the pun to heights of poetic fancy hitherto unknown. Joyce's puns usually have three levels of significance: as serious linguistic manipulations they allow the author to include various concepts, overlapping themes, and levels of meaning in compressed form; as humorous concoctions they grate against our dulled senses—they are the stumbling blocks that make us conscious of every step we take through the *Wake*; as a poetic device they are controlled by a rhythmic logic that creates individual sound patterns at once familiar in rhythm and new in sound. In a statement of the resurrection theme involving Finn MacCool and his comic shadow, Tim Finnegan, Joyce intones: "Hohohoho, Mister Finn, you're going to be Mister Finnagain! Comeday morm and, O, you're vine! Sendday's eve and, ah, you're vinegar! Hahahaha, Mister Funn, you're going to be fined again!" (*FW* 5.9–12). Here basic sounds are repeated in logical fashion: *Finn* becomes *Funn* as well as *Finn again* (the titular pun of the work), while *vine* turns to *vinegar* (another transformation), and the *fine* we had first expected to hear is sounded again in the final sentence. *Comeday* and *Sendday* are both Sunday,

---

[2]Comments on Joyce's punning are most extensive in William T. Noon's chapter, "The Root Language of Shem," in *Joyce and Aquinas*, pp. 144–60, and in Clive Hart's chapter, "Art of Panning," in *Structure and Motif*, pp. 31–38. Additional comments can be found in William York Tindall, *The Literary Symbol* (New York: Columbia University Press, 1955), p. 206; Levin, *James Joyce*, p. 185; Magalaner and Kain, *Joyce*, pp. 236–37.

[3]Louis Gillet, "Mr. James Joyce and his New Novel," *Transition*, XXI (March, 1932), 268.

of course (the Easter Sunday of Christ's resurrection parallels "a trying thirstay mournin" [*FW* 6.14] preceding His crucifixion), while *Comeday* may also be Monday, giving us a full week's progression. The balance Joyce achieves through his language carries not only from *Finn* to *Funn* and *vine* to *vinegar* to *fined*, but is duplicated by his exclamations of *hohohoho* to *hahahaha* and *O* to *ah*.

The extent to which Joyce was capable of carrying an individual pun as a type of leitmotif throughout the *Wake* can be seen by tracing this particular Finn-again through several of its metamorphoses. Each time it changes it remains the Finn-Finnegan motif with a new concept tacked on to give it aptness in a particular situation or new dimension. At the wake, Finnegan's mourners are *thirstay*, so "Sobs they sighdid at Fillagain's chrissormiss wake" (*FW* 6.14–15)—the hero's name becoming a call for refills; when the wife is again mourning her husband at a wake, she is a rather prissy woman and is seen "dragging the countryside in her train, finickin here and funickin there" (*FW* 102.8–9)—Finn-Funn now transformed to fit this finicky Isis who is collecting the parts of Osiris' body (yet another resurrection myth) and is going up and down like a funicular cable-car ("Funiculi, Funicula"). (Her sexual indiscretions are apparent in the obscene pun in *funickin*.) When Anna Livia Plurabelle is seeking a title for her "mamafesta," she puns her initials into Lapp and finds a neighbor of the Lapps to be the Finns; the result is the comic title, "*Lapps for Finns This Funnycoon's Week*" (*FW* 105.21). In toying with the Book of Kells and the amount of minute scholarship that has been spent in poring over that manuscript, Joyce echoes his own preoccupation with sound and sense: "here keen again and begin again to make soundsense and sensesound kin again" (*FW* 121.14–16)—the wailing at the wake is combined with the resurrection . . . .

Joyce is interested in *Finnegans Wake* in a poetic texture that underlies the prose element. He has selected his language carefully and uses lyrical language for various poetic effects—effects integrated with the themes and characters.

The "Anna Livia Plurabelle" section is in itself a comic dialogue between two gossipy washerwomen, yet, in discussing the character and affairs of the most beautiful figure of the work, it manages to rise to many instances of lyrical heights foreshadowing the final rhapsodic soliloquy of the book. Anna Livia's death is already being mourned:

> Wait till the honeying of the lune, love! Die eve, little eve, die! We see that wonder in your eye. We'll meet again, we'll part once more. The spot I'll seek if the hour you'll find. My chart shines high where the blue milk's upset. Forgivemequick, I'm going! Bubye! And you, pluck your watch, forgetmenot. Your evenlode. So save to jurna's end! My sights are swimming thicker on me by the shadows to this place. I sow home slowly now by own way, moyvalley way. Towy I too, rathmine. (*FW* 215.3–11)

Already the river is flowing out to sea; the heroine's death has already occurred, is now occurring, will occur again at the final moments of the *Wake*. The short lines, bits of rhyme, and lyric lilt carry the river along as it flows out to sea. As the descending dusk that transforms the two women had several times already been anticipated—"Murk, his vales are darkling" (*FW* 23.23) and

> shades began to glidder along the banks, greepsing, greepsing, duusk unto duusk, and it was as glooming as gloaming could be in the waste of all peacable worlds. . . . Oh, how it was duusk! From Vallee Maraia to Grasyaplaina, dormimust echo! Ah dew! Ah dew! It was so duusk that the tears of night began to fall, first by ones and twos, then by threes and fours, at last by fives and sixes of sevens, for the tired ones were wecking, as we weep now with them. *O! O! O! Par la pluie!* (*FW* 158.7–24)

—so the "Die eve" poem anticipates Anna Livia's monologue:

> Ho hang! Hang ho! And the clash of our cries till we spring to be free. Auravoles, they says, never heed of your name! But I'm loothing them that's here and all I lothe. Loonely in me loneness. For all their faults. I am passing out. O bitter ending! I'll slip away before they're up. They'll never see. Nor know. Nor miss me. (*FW* 627.31–36).

The rhythms that dominate the earlier farewell to Anna Livia now return to echo that farewell; the short lines and breathless exclamations are echoes in our ears, making us feel that we have heard all this before, that Anna Livia's demise has occurred before. Throughout the *Wake* Joyce is poetically striving for the *déjà vu* experience to emphasize the Viconian continuity. Poetic echoes best serve his purpose; the memorable lines of poetry in the *Wake* reappear often to add to that strange sensation of having been here before.

Although definitions of poetry are not usually subjective—the basic elements of rhythm, meter, rhyme, alliteration, assonance, and so forth, having been objectively outlined—no one attitude toward Joyce's poetic medium can necessarily be universally arrived at; the novelist who is many things to many readers is as individually various as a poet. Margaret Schlauch sees Joyce's poetic language in terms of philological awareness, and finds that Joyce's linguistic variants "can easily be classified by a philologist as examples of reduplication, alliteration, assonance, primitive types of apophony, assimilation, dissimilation, sandhi variants and the like."[4] Harry Levin adds that the reader is "borne from one page to the next, not by the expository current of the prose, but by the harmonic relations of the language—phonetic, syntactic, or referential, as the case may be."[5] Joyce's philological consciousness of words, the shifts of meanings within words, their etymological significances and semantic discrepancies add to the levels of meaning made possible by his skillful handling of language. The philological handling of entomological

[4]Margaret Schlauch, "The Language of James Joyce," *Science and Society*, III (Fall, 1939), 485.
[5]Levin, *James Joyce*, p. 184.

minutiæ in the fable of the Ondt and Gracehoper is very much a case in point. In fact, when asked why he hates his literary brother, Shaun replies, "For his root language, if you ask me whys" (*FW* 424.17), and the tenth thunderclap roaringly follows upon his answer, causing the comment: "The hundredlettered name again, last word of perfect language" (*FW* 424.23–24). But Shaun brags that he too can perpetrate "Acomedy of letters!" (*FW* 425.24). . . .

A handful of critics have cast an eye on the poetic effects of Joyce's language, stopping along the way between the labyrinth of explication and the tower of elucidation, commenting on occasional phrases and sentences. Nor could anyone actually expect any major attempt at an over-all commentary on *effect*, when the most serious problems remain in the area of exegesis, especially when the value of Joyce's poetic techniques exists in the pattern of "sound-sense" created, not in sound alone. In the early *Exagmination* Robert Sage tackles a sentence in Anna Livia Plurabelle:

> She was just a young thin pale soft shy slim slip of a thing then, sauntering, by silvamoonlake and he was a heavy trudging lurching lieabroad of a Curraghman, making his hay for whose sun to shine on, as tough as the oaktrees (peats be with them!) used to rustle that time down by the dykes of killing Kildare, for forstfellfoss with a plash across her. (*FW* 202.26–32)

Sage calls this "a sentence that is pool-like in its lucidity, that is supple and periodic," and goes on to analyze the poetic aspects of it:

> The sentence opens . . . with fifteen one-syllable words, the first eleven being accented, the twelfth and thirteenth hastening the rhythm through their lack of accent and the final two returning to long beats. Through this Joyce suggests the weakness and uncertainty of the stream at its commencement (girlhood). Then comes the stronger three-syllable word *sauntering*, indicating development (adolescence) and leading by a short beat to the epitritus *silvamoonlake*, signifying full growth (maturity), the further associations with the latter stage being sylvan and the silver moon reflected in the lake. The male symbol is immediately introduced in the three ponderous trochees *heavy trudging lurching*, continuing to the molossus *forstfellfoss*, which balances *silvamoonlake* and suggests *first, forest, fell* and *waterfall*, the *foss* coming from the Scandinavian designation of waterfall. The latter part of the sentence, then, completes the introduction of the two symbols by describing the creation of the first cascade through the falling of the tree across the stream.[6]

It is this sort of word-by-word analysis that unearths the hidden beauties of Joyce's language in the *Wake*, the lilt of the string of opening monosyllables, the alliterative onomatopoeia of *forstfellfoss* (echoes of which build toward the grand restatement of chapter 8 in the last chapter: "fond Fuinn feels"—

6Robert Sage, "Before *Ulysses*—and After," in *Exagmination*, pp. 167–68.

FW 427.30; "felt the fall"—*FW* 469.13; "fond floral fray"—*FW* 471.27; and, finally, Anna Livia's "It's something fails us. First we feel. Then we fall"—*FW* 627.11), the "luminous" sounds of *silvamoonlake*, and the comic undertones of the *heavy trudging lurching lieabroad of a Curraghman.* Whether for sheer lyricism, as in "Veil, volantine, valentine eyes" (*FW* 20.34), or for comic sounds, as in the hollow echoing noises coming from the Egyptian dummy, "valiantine vaux of Venerable Val Vousdem" (*FW* 439.17–18), Joyce can manipulate his alliteration of consonants and variations of vowels to create individually pertinent patterns of meaning.

Nor would a charge of poetic "formalism" be at all appropriate against Joyce in his *Wake,* as the analysis by Sage indicates: it is impossible to investigate Joyce's language without explicating meaning interwoven with that language. Form and content in the *Wake* are an interinvolved entity, with poetic patterns revealing ideas once those patterns are looked at closely, and Joyce's meaning engendering a type of language concomitant with the poetic form. It is only through the language in the sentence Sage investigates that one can learn that the Viking's seduction of the Irish nymph engenders the next generation of sons. Earwicker is colloquially "taking advantage of the girl" when he is "making hay while the sun shines," as is indicated by *his hay;* and *sun* suggests son in this context, thus *shine on* equals Shaun, Earwicker's chosen successor; but the brother conflict is never far from the surface as *oaktrees* conjures up Shem, *peats* indicating petrification from tree to stone, as well as the hope that peace will eventually be declared between them.

Thus it is through language as a medium of communication, heightened by musical intonations and strengthened by verbal intensity, that a basic series of interwoven myths and tales supplements a thin plot line to create a vast literary unit. "Prose" as hitherto defined could never sustain such a construction which defies the usual gravitational laws of prose composition: instead of the heavy base of plot material underlying a building toward unity and intensity, Joyce has constructed an inverted pyramid of a book, based on a delicate pinnacle but accumulating mass as it soars upward in cohesion and lyricism. . . .

It is perhaps dangerous to overstress the relationship of Joyce's book to musical form and technique, whose structure demands only that a composition have a logical relationship among its own parts—although *Finnegans Wake* certainly does have that. But the *Wake* is patterned so that the musical devices (the poetic language, the structural balance) are consistent primarily with the levels of meaning pertinent to individual portions. Joyce develops variations on his themes not for the sake of variation alone, but to reapply his ideas to new and inclusive situations to broaden the theme itself as a structure composed intrinsically of its own variations. As difficult as it remains for the reader and the critic to derive even a single layer of meaning from every word in *Finnegans Wake,* it nonetheless becomes apparent with continued exegetical research that every word in it has been constructed for the primarily *literary* purpose of meaning rather than as mere musical abstraction.

The language of the Dublin streets and pubs—particularly the pubs—permeates *Finnegans Wake*. In fact, Joyce's use of that vernacular (of an English tongue in a Celtic mouth*) is the basis for the synthesis of poetry and comedy; the sound and sense one would associate with a Dublin bar brogue is the dominant linguistic element in *Finnegans Wake*. Joyce's twin muses of Comedy and Poetry are actually a pair of Celtic maidens plying their trades in the Dublin he knew at the turn of the century; they offer a language and a dialect that contemporary Irish playwrights like Synge, O'Casey, Robinson, and Johnston have exploited for both rich poetic qualities and rich comic delight. Himself well aware of the full extent of this interweaving of the linguistic and comic aspects of the Dubliner, Sean O'Casey commented to me that only an Irishman can understand *Finnegans Wake*—and he would have to be a Dubliner at that!

The opening lines of the portion of the *Wake* that Joyce recorded offer the best example of the Dublin brogue exploited for its richness in both humor and melody: "Well, you know or don't you kennet or haven't I told you every telling has a taling and that's the he and the she of it. Look, look, the dusk is growing! My branches lofty are taking root. And my cold cher's gone ashley" (*FW* 213.11–14). The repetitions, the interrogative statements, the long sigh of complaint, the exclamations of exasperation and weariness are elements of Joyce's colloquial expression. Part after part of the *Wake* falls easily into Irish dialect without the author's attempt to convert spellings or drop letters. It is the rhythm of Dublin speech that is recorded here, and the fact that the whole book is one long gossipy tale told at a hurried pace in a hushed tone behind the back of one's hand adds to the colloquial flavor of its composition. With what else but a brogue would these lines have their accuracy?

> Ah, but she was the queer old skeowsha anyhow, Anna Livia, trinkettoes! And sure he was the quare old buntz too, Dear Dirty Dumpling, foostherfather of fingalls and dotthergills. Gammer and gaffer we're all their gangsters. Hadn't he seven dams to wive him? And every dam had her seven crutches. And every crutch had its seven hues. And each hue had a differing cry. Sudds for me and supper for you and the doctor's bill for Joe John. (*FW* 215.12–18)

All one need do is read Ogden's translation of these lines into Basic English[7] to find them suddenly devoid of poetry and humor. Only by wagging his English tongue in his Celtic mouth does an Irishman produce such lyrical comedy.

---

*A good deal more involved than this of course. To "Limba romena in Bucclis tuscada" (*FW* 518.24–25) Joyce adds "Farcing gutterish" (*FW* 518.25). See also "brain of the franks, hand of the christian, tongue of the north" (*FW* 127.29–30) and "oyne of an oustman in skull of skand" (*FW* 310.30).

7C. K. Ogden, quoted by Levin, *James Joyce*, pp. 196–97.

Joyce, however, delighted in confusing the issue of his creation with a Jove-like whimsy and an unabashed fascination for leg-pulling, being resolutely an "artist" in the Gogartyan sense of the word—a jokester. Although the connotation of "leg-pulling" in modern art is usually highly suspect, some effort should be made to rescue the concept from becoming purely a pejorative: Joyce's "hoax" is a consummate work of literary art, logically constructed, carefully controlled, and aesthetically embellished. But it is not surprising that many readers and critics of serious mien have been unable to swallow "the hoax that joke bilked" (*FW* 511.34). When an admirer managed to understand one level of meaning in a phrase, Joyce was quick to add a second, but when another admirer asked about levels of meaning, Joyce insisted "it's meant to make you laugh."[8] The seeming contradiction is resolved only when we understand that to Joyce the significance and the poetry and the humor of the book were inseparable, and he was quick to correct any impression that would insist upon only a single facet of his prismatic scheme of art.

[8]Ellmann, *James Joyce,* pp. 707, 703.

Vico's "Night of Darkness": *The New Science* and *Finnegans Wake*

John Bishop

Darkness . . . is the material of this Science, uncertain, unformed, obscure. . . . (*NS* 41)*

"Our Family Furbear"

The critical work on *Finnegans Wake* has failed to account fully for Joyce's passionate interest in Giambattista Vico's *New Science*. Working from a sardonic sentence in one of Joyce's letters to Harriet Shaw Weaver ("I would not pay overmuch attention to these theories, beyond using them for all they are worth, but they have gradually forced themselves on me through circumstances of my own life" [*L* I, 241; *JJ* II, 554]), most critics of the *Wake* have remained content to draw on a reading of Vico that had already become gelled, as early as 1950, into a received form destined to be passed on from study to study without much examination or modification. William York Tindall, the last critic to put finishing touches on this orthodox version of Joyce's Vico, tells the story best:

> In each cycle of history there are three ages: the divine, the heroic, and the human, or the primitive, the semi-historic, and the historic. These three ages produce three sacred customs: religion, marriage, and burial, the first a product of the divine age, the second of the heroic, and the third of the human. After circular flux comes reflux. When one cycle is over, another begins, and, as the Phoenix rises from its ashes, history repeats itself. The first divine age that we know about is the period before the Trojan War. With that war, the heroic age began. The human age of Athens and Rome led to the reflux, and from Rome's decay came a new age, as divine, barbarous, and cruel as the first. The feudal period of Europe brought a

From *Joyce's Book of the Dark*, John Bishop (Madison: The University of Wisconsin Press, 1986), 174–76, 180–93, 199–202, 206–15. Copyright © 1986 by The University of Wisconsin Press. Reprinted by permission of John Bishop and The University of Wisconsin Press.

*Thomas Goddard Bergin and Max Harold Fisch, trans. *The New Science of Giambattista Vico* (Ithaca and London: Cornell University Press, 1948). Abbreviation throughout this chapter as *NS* plus the paragraph number.—*Editor's note.*

return to the heroic age. Vico lived in the human age, and it is easy to guess where we are.[1]

There are, of course, other givens: Vico's conjecture that the crack of thunder, first sounded on the first page of the *Wake,* terrified men in a barbarous state of nature into seeking shelter in caves and so into beginning the churning of the wheels of social history; his conjecture that the terrifying thunderclap caused men to try to duplicate its sound and its power by babbling onomato-poeically, thereby beginning the history of human language; and the observation, first made by Beckett in 1929, that Joyce textured *Finnegans Wake* with an array of quadrupartite phrases which evoke the four human institutions informing Vico's history:

> There are numerous references to Vico's four human institutions—Providence counting as one! "A good clap, a fore wedding, a bad wake, tell hell's well": "Their weatherings and their marryings and their buryings and their natural selections": "the lightning look, the birding cry, awe from the grave, everflowing on our times": "by four hands of forethought the first babe of reconcilement is laid in its last cradle of hume sweet hume."[2]

Most of these accounts, however, misrepresent *The New Science.* Vico specu-lates that history may operate cyclically, in fact, in a conjectural conclusion sixteen pages long, appended to a work of four hundred pages;[3] and all of the details with which Tindall clarifies the nature of Vico's human ages can be found in the synoptic fourth book of *The New Science,* a summary which, together with Book Five, comprises only one-fourth of the entire work.[4]

It is—and should be—hard to understand how the Vico portrayed in Joyce studies should have generated "passionate interest" in Joyce long before he began the writing of *Ulysses,* let alone *Finnegans Wake* (*JJ* II, 340n). It makes little sense to suppose that the realist who in *Ulysses* had invested so much care in the portrayal of a single man in a single city on a single day in history should have ended his career writing a book in polyglottal puns in order to transmit the news that the same things happened over and over again in quadrupartite cycles. It is, moreover, difficult to understand how this re-ceived vision of Vico could have caused Joyce to claim that *The New Science* strongly forced itself on his life or that Vico anticipated and yielded richer insights than Freud; indeed, it is hard to see how the established sense of Vico

---

[1]W. Y. Tindall, *James Joyce: His Way of Interpreting the Modern World* (New York: Charles Scribner's Sons, 1950), p. 71. Tindall goes on to note that "the three ages have languages suitable to each. In mute, divine periods, men use hieroglyphics: picture-writing, coats of arms, and fables. A heroic age brings proverbs and metaphor, the language of the imagination. In the human age, language becomes abstract or vulgar. . . . Attracted by Vico's interest in myth, language, and family, Joyce preferred him to other cyclists."

[2]Samuel Beckett, "Dante . . . Bruno. Vico . . . Joyce," in *Our Exagmination,* p. 8.

[3]Book 5 of *The New Science,* "The Recurrence of Human Things in the Resurgence of Nations," 1046–96.

[4]Book 4 of *The New Science,* "The Course of Nations," 915–1045.

bears any relation to Freud at all, or to the night that *Finnegans Wake* reconstructs. Yet when Joyce first conceived of writing a book that would treat the mind in sleep, he also immediately conceived of Vico as a prototype whose work would serve him (*JJ* II, 554). And after *Finnegans Wake* was completed, he remarked in reply to adverse reviews in the Italian press that the whole book was founded on the work of an Italian thinker (*L* III, 463). He seems to have conceived of *The New Science*, in fact, as an intellectual foundation that would underlie *Finnegans Wake* as the *Odyssey* had *Ulysses*; and like the Homeric correspondences in that novel, the references to the four ages of Vichian nature internal to *Finnegans Wake* seem only to be the superficially most apparent outcroppings of a conception fundamental to the book's whole treatment of the dark. Joyce's thinking was never mechanical, and the imaginative transaction by which he brings Vico into the *Wake* proves to be no exception to that rule.

Like the *Wake*, *The New Science* was not much read or understood in its own day, and when it finally was understood, it was rightly perceived as a work that threatened both Christian orthodoxy and the body of mainstream rationalist Enlightenment thinking. Nowadays, historians armed with hindsight—the historian's gift—speak of Vico as a thinker who effected a revolution in the study of history and the human sciences no less profound than that which Galileo effected in the natural sciences; the English translators of *The New Science* find in the book "the germs of all the sciences of social change," and they speak of historiography as "Vichian and pre-Vichian."[5]

The foresightfully radical snap of thought that made Vico unread and misunderstood in his own day—the same decades of the eighteenth century in which Pope wrote his *Essay on Man*—was his supposition that our political forebears, men in a state of nature, were not enlightened rationalists who could agree on social contracts and protective alliances, but semi-bestial clods who had barely thrown off their fur, speechless giants who rutted, bore furry children, and left them to wallow in their own excrement while they themselves roamed off to sate their appetites (*NS* 192ff; 369ff). This was a conception of history that needed a Darwin before it could become at all generally accepted, and it bore in itself a host of corollaries no less radical. Well before the appearance of Hegel's *Phenomenology of Mind*, *The New Science* necessarily implied that human consciousness was an evolutionary variable, changeable with history and society, and that it depended on the whole human past for its definition. The anthropoid giants who formed the first human society in Vico—a huddled, cave-dwelling knot of men and women who only over

---

[5]Max Harold Fisch and Thomas Goddard Bergin, "Introduction" to *The Autobiography of Giambattista Vico* (Ithaca: Cornell Univ. Press, 1944), p. 20. Here I should acknowledge a general indebtedness to Fisch and Bergin's wonderful "Introduction" to *The Autobiography.* Other works I have found useful are *Giambattista Vico's Science of Humanity,* ed. Giorgio Tagliacozzo and Donald Phillip Verene (Baltimore: The Johns Hopkins Univ. Press, 1976); and *New Vico Studies* 1 (1983).

generations would begin even dimly to grasp the concept of a family—these forebears had a consciousness radically alien from our own, largely by having none at all; the people born ten generations later had a slightly more articulated consciousness than these forebears; and those born later still in Homeric Greece had an even different consciousness yet. To discover the genesis of rational consciousness in "our family furbear (*FW* 132.32) is one whole struggle of *The New Science*, which tries scientifically to determine how beasts driven into caves by the crash of thunder happened to make themselves over generations into learned Enlightenment thinkers capable of building and governing the great nations of the world. Vico's premise, of course, completely breaks with such forms of Enlightenment belief as Cartesian rationalism and Lockean empiricism, both of which regarded "Reason" as an eternal manifestation of laws of nature determined if not by a benevolent deity then by a transcendental order; and implicitly, but not explicitly, it therefore breaks with the world-view out of which rationalism evolved.[6]

The inherent threat that *The New Science* posed both to Christian thought and to the newly rising force of rationalism will explain why Vico had inevitably to refer to "Divine Providence" in *The New Science* and also why he preserved sacred history by locating the Hebrew race outside of the secular world—and essentially beyond the scope of his history—at a region of earth isolated by deserts and centuries from the rest of humanity; for according to the orthodox thought of his age. Adam came to earth already equipped with a language and an innately rational, if fallible, moral sense. As opposed to the sacred history of the Hebrew race, Vico's "gentile history" treats of the "gentile races"—of Egypt. Greece, Rome, Teutonic Germany, and the pagan Mid-East—whose forebears are born to earth wrapped in nothing but animal appetites and fears. Although Vico claims that a Divine Providence secretly guides the gentile races, his own evidence suggests that the "famblings" (*NS* 582.5 [or "families"]) of which these races are composed merely stumble forward in blind, godless "fumblings"; "gentile" history is made by men descended from animals, and not always well.[7] If the academics of Vico's Italy

---

[6]Compare to Vico's evolutionary account of consciousness these representative views of others who wrote at his time: . . . Thomas Hobbes, *Leviathan*, in *The English Philosophers from Bacon to Mill*, ed. Edwin A. Burtt (New York: Random House, 1939), p. 163; . . . René Descartes, "Discourse on the Method of Rightly Conducting the Reason and Seeking the Truth in the Sciences," in *The Philosophical Works of Descartes*, trans. Elizabeth S. Haldane and G. R. T. Ross (New York: Dover, 1955), pp. 81–82; and . . . John Locke, "An Essay Concerning the True Original, Extent and End of Civil Government," *Two Treatises of Government*, in *The English Philosophers from Bacon to Mill*, pp. 404–5. Vico's, of course, was not the only interesting deviation from the mainstream Enlightenment thinking represented in these passages.

[7]Vico, in fact, has to provide an elaborate account to explain how his first men arrived in a bestial state of nature, since ideological orthodoxy held that all mankind descended from a rational Adam. In order not to violate "sacred history" in his "gentile history," Vico supposes that after the Flood, Noah's sons wandered from the culture of their father and roved in the wild for centuries, until they reverted to animalistic beasts void of any property of mind but sensation (*NS* 192ff).

failed to understand his work, then, it was because, like Descartes and Locke, they supposed that reason and enlightened thought of the kind perceptible in the examples of classical Greece and Rome and in the Book of Genesis were natural, transhistorical attributes of the human mind: Enlightenment thinkers were accustomed to referring to the sage examples of Homer, Aesop. and other figures of antiquity who transcended their historical age; Pope translated the *Iliad*, LaFontaine brought Aesop into French. In Vico, however, rational consciousness appears in human history only during the Age of Reason, and to find it in the past is to project the modern mind backwards over the centuries to a historical age in which people possessed their own modes of consciousness and their distinct social forms. . . .[8]

Joyce also undoubtedly admired Vico's peculiarly modern willingness to admit total unreason along with reason as a motivating force of history. Mainstream rationalist thinking bred in the European social community a hypocritical nineteenth-century politics verbally capable of asserting its alliance with Reason and its aspiration to rise onward and upward to work out the beast, but in fact capable of creating social conditions that would produce in Ireland, for instance, a famine described as "the worst event of its kind recorded in European history at a time of peace."[9] This is essentially the politics described in that section of the *Wake* which Joyce called "Haveth Childers Everywhere" (FW 532–54), where HCE, stuttering constantly with guilt, dubiously justifies the aspirant importance of his work to his family by telling the whole story of civilization and including among his accomplishments a rather large number of mistakes: the slums of London (FW 543–45), the pollution of the Liffey (FW 550), and the ambiguously productive rape of Ireland (FW 547). Nature gives Vico's man the mind of an unconscious animal; Vico's history is the process by which man, of his own blind, stumbling power, slowly builds that natural mind toward consciousness, interdependently with language and civil institutions.

Here, too, Vico's vision of history certainly appealed to Joyce, because it extended into social history processes that Joyce himself had sought to trace in *A Portrait of the Artist as a Young Man*, where, as Stephen's personality evolves in time from infancy to young adulthood, the language and consciousness through which he perceives and defines himself also evolve interdependently, all as aspects of one another. Joyce would also have found in Vico, then, a vision of historical growth as intricate as the vision of the personal growth that he represented in *A Portrait*—the struggle of "a bat-like soul

---

[8]"It is another property of the human mind that whenever men can form no idea of distant and unknown things, they judge them by what is familiar and at hand. . . ." "This axiom points to the inexhaustible source of all the errors about the beginnings of humanity that have been adopted by entire nations and by all the scholars. [For, the "conceit of scholars"] will have it that whatever they know is as old as the world" (NS 122–23, 127).

[9]Gifford and Seidman, *Notes for Joyce*: An Annotation of James Joyce's "Ulysses" (New York: E. P. Dutton, 1974), p. 24.

waking to the consciousness of itself in darkness and secrecy and loneliness
. . ." (P 183). The phrase, descriptive both of Ireland's and of Stephen's
individual development in *A Portrait,* defines equally well the evolutionary
development of human history in *The New Science.* It is not entirely clear, in
fact, whether Joyce came to admire Vico because he found the vision of
human growth presented in *A Portrait* confirmed in *The New Science*; or
whether it was Vico who helped cause Joyce to scrap *Stephen Hero* and to
rework it into the form that would come to be *A Portrait.* All we know of the
original transaction that would cause Joyce to champion *The New Science*
throughout his literary career and through all the pages of the *Wake* is that he
first read and expressed passionate interest in Vico during his years in Trieste
(1904–15); that he worked hard on *Stephen Hero,* abandoned it completely,
and rewrote it as *A Portrait* during the same period;[10] and that Vico's vision of
growth of the soul of mankind shares many affinities with Joyce's vision of the
growth of the soul.

Poetic Wisdom

This comparison suggests a final radical corollary to the propositions on
which *The New Science* is predicated—the corollary most interesting to a
reader of the *Wake.* Since Vico argues that the language, consciousness,
society, and problems of any moment in history develop as consequences of
decisions made in a historical past in which the pressures of the immediate
moment far outweigh those of any speculative future; and since he assumes
that human history begins in the minds of bestial giants in a state of nature,
he puts himself into the difficult position of having to account for "social"
choices made by irrational beings who cannot know what "choice" and
"society" are. If the language, consciousness, and civil institutions of Europe
grew by a process of internal dialectic out of forests in which barbaric,
terrified animals scrambled for shelter at the sound of thunder, then a
knowledge of the process by which European civilization came to exist
depended on a knowledge of how those wholly irrational beings thought. His
enterprise, then, is identical to that of *Finnegans Wake* in that it entails a
willed abandonment of reason and a sympathetic entry into unconsciousness:

> But the nature of our civilized minds is so detached from the senses . . . by
> abstractions corresponding to all the abstract terms our languages abound in, and
> so refined by the art of writing. and as it were spiritualized by the use of numbers
> . . . that it is naturally beyond our power to form the vast image of [the world
> perceived by the first men]. . . . It is equally beyond our power to enter into the

---

[10]See Herbert Gorman, *James Joyce* (New York: Rinehart & Co., 1948), p. 32, and *JJ* II, 306–
7; Ellmann additionally notes that Joyce's "decision to rewrite *Stephen Hero* as a *Portrait* in five
chapters occurred appropriately just after Lucia's birth" (*JJ* II, 296).

vast imagination of those first men, whose minds were not in the least abstract, refined, or spiritualized, because they were entirely immersed in the senses, buffeted by the passions, buried in the body. . . . we can scarcely understand, still less imagine, how those first men thought who founded gentile humanity. (*NS* 378)

The problem that Vico addresses in this passage is not one that he despairs of solving; indeed, in the central and most lengthy book of *The New Science*, "Poetic Wisdom," he tries to reconstruct the "scarcely imaginable" minds of those aboriginal first men in order to account for the history that grows out of them. "Poetic Wisdom" is the linch-pin of Vico's history, the studied and labored piece of evidence upon which he builds his science.

Our treatment [of history] must take its start from the time these creatures began to think humanly. In their monstrous savagery and unbridled bestial freedom there was no means to tame the former or bridle the latter but the frightful thought of some divinity, the fear of whom . . . is the only powerful means of reducing to duty a liberty gone wild. To discover the way in which this first human thinking arose in the gentile world, we encountered exasperating difficulties which have cost us the research of a good twenty years. [We had] to descend from these human and refined natures of ours to those quite wild savage natures, which we cannot at all imagine and can comprehend only with great effort. (*NS* 358)

In a direct and substantial way, the mind that Joyce sought to reconstruct in *Finnegans Wake* was equivalent to the aboriginal mind that Vico sought to comprehend in Book II of *The New Science;* what Freud called "the dreamwork" and "the unconscious," Vico, lacking psychoanalytic terminology, simply called "poetic wisdom" and "ignorance":

But these first men who later became the princes of the gentile nations, must have done their thinking under the strong impulsion of violent passions, as beasts do. . . . Hence poetic wisdom, the first wisdom of the gentile world, must have begun with a metaphysics not rational and abstract like that of learned men now, but felt and imagined, as that of these first men must have been, who, without power of ratiocination, were all robust sense and vigorous imagination. This metaphysics was their poetry, a faculty born with them (for they were furnished by nature with these senses and imaginations); born of their ignorance of causes, for ignorance, the mother of wonder, made everything wonderful to men who were ignorant of everything. . . . (*NS* 340, 375; see also 399)

In order to substantiate his dialectical account of history, essentially, Vico had to invent an elaborate depth psychology—a "metaphysics," in his phrase— that would enable him to comprehend the unconsciousness out of which men made social choices "in the deplorable obscurity of the beginnings" of the human world (*NS* 344):

But in the night of thick darkness enveloping the earliest antiquity, so remote from ourselves, there shines the eternal and never failing light of a truth beyond all question: that the world of civil society has certainly been made by men, and that its principles are therefore to be found within the modifications of our own human mind. Whoever reflects on this cannot but marvel that the philosophers should have bent all their energies to the study of the world of nature, which. since God made it, He alone knows; and that they should have neglected the study of the world of nations, or civil world, which, since men made it, men could come to know. This aberration was a consequence of that infirmity of the human mind by which, immersed and buried in the body, it naturally inclines to take notice of bodily things [i.e., the physical universe], and finds the effort to attend to itself too laborious. . . . (*NS* 331)

When Vico proposes to work his way back into the unconscious mind of these first men by discovering "its principles in the modifications of our own human mind," he is not simply proposing—as the psychoanalytic movement would two centuries later—that a stream of primitive, infantile irrationality, reflected in the myths and fables of the past, underruns our modern civil consciousness. His vision is primarily historical. If consciousness is a man-made property that changes in historical time, then each individual owes the way in which he thinks to the generation of his parents; yet his parents owe their thinking and behavior to the generation of their parents; and so forth, in a chain extending back to the beginnings of the gentile world. Those crude choices made by Vico's giants, then, inform all minds born out of them; and the terrifying irrationalities and encaved social structures that they stumbled into still perpetuate themselves, despite the transformations of generations and generations, "in the modifications of our own human minds"—"the traditions of all dead generations weighing like an Alp on the brains of the living," in one of Marx's psychoanalytic phrases.[11]

This conception of history as a force funneling into and determining anyone's life in the present rang particularly true to Joyce, who was born into a family and a culture morally structured by a Catholicism genetically arising out of the Middle Ages. *"Like a gentile man,"* too (*FW* 150.26), he was born into a nation whose political life had been determined by actions militantly undertaken in the twelfth century, when Henry II, asking the English-born pope of the Vatican for permission to take in hand the immoral Irish, made the city of Dublin the eternal property of the citizens of Bristol.[12] Joyce was born into a culture whose social structures were shaped by the infinitely inheritable superstition of racism, a habit of mind passed on from parent to

---

[11]Karl Marx, "The Eighteenth Brumaire of Louis Napoleon" in *On Revolution*, vol. 1 of the Karl Marx Library, tr. and ed. Saul K. Padover (New York: McGraw-Hill, 1971). p. 245.

[12]The Charter of 1173 in which Henry II granted the city of Dublin to the city of Bristol is quoted at length in the *Wake* (545.14–23), Joyce slightly adjusts the charter's language, however, altering the signature of "Henricus Rex" to "Enwreak us wrecks" and adding to the charter's wording the giant Albion's "Fe Fo Fum" and an economic undertone in "Fee for farm." While Henry II granted Dublin simply to "my subjects at Bristol," finally, the "Enwreak us" of Joyce's modified charter grants Dublin to the citizens of Bristol "that from the farthest of the farther of their fathers to their children's children they do inhabit it and hold it." As Joyce's language here suggests, and as Vico's history reaffirms, single political acts engender consequences that endure through history.

child over generations and extending backwards through linguistic history into a time when the verb "to like" was synonymous with the preposition "like," and when to "like" someone meant that one found the likeness of his own race and blood in them.[13] Joyce was born into a family and a religion that implanted in him a fear of thunder so great that throughout his life he refused to live in cities known for the frequency of their thunderstorms and hid in closets, as Vico's giants did in caves, whenever thunder rent the sky; it was Vico's primitive man who bequeathed to generation after generation the fear of celestial punishment that found its way into Joyce's consciousness. And it was Vico's giants who bequeathed to the minds of all human generations after them the social unit of the encaved private family.

Twentieth-century psychoanalysis proposes to isolate and cure the irrationally disturbed components of personality by analyzing the fears and fixations inherited from parents in an impressionable, irrational infantile past. Vico's axiomatic observation that rationality is a man-made structure historically evolved out of animal unreason will suggest why Joyce would have regarded Freudian theory as a diminution of Vico's insights. Since *The New Science* sees the consciousness into which one grows as the product of a historical development that begins in the terror of thunderstruck "furbear[s]," it complementarily implies that the unconscious conflicts rifting modern minds and societies are historically transmitted over much more than one generation. The individual cannot purge himself of neurotic unhappiness by rethinking his familial past alone, because his parents are largely innocent transmitters of a language and an ideology determined by a history that transcends them and himself both. Fully to understand the irrationalities understructuring his mind, he has to exorcise his parents' parents, and his parents' parents' parents, and the "first men, stupid, insensate, and horrible beasts," who laid down the foundations of human civil life and consciousness (*NS* 374). As a Vichian who had already extensively examined his relations with his mother and father in *A Portrait* and *Ulysses*, the Joyce of *Finnegans Wake* is as deeply interested in the remote determinants of neuroses as in the immediate ones. Action according to this psychological model is evident both in Joyce's life and in his representations of it: "tapping his brow" in the hour of his therapeutic release from the past in *Ulysses*, and muttering that "in here it is I must kill the priest and the King," Stephen Dedalus has to lay to rest not only the irrationalities inherited from a devoutly self-abnegating Catholic mother and a self-destructive, jobless father, but also those inherited from the medieval Catholicism and the English economic policy that made possible that mother and that father (*U* 1961:589; *U* 1986:481; 15–4437). In order to understand how that Church and that feudal economic behavior originated, Joyce in turn had to try to understand, in *Finnegans Wake*, the "furbear[s]" buried in the darkness of

---

13Both the verb and preposition derive from the Middle English *lich* ("body") and its cognate *lik* (adjectival "like"), both in turn from the Germanic root **liko-* ("body, shape, form").

Vico's aboriginality. All of history is in one's parents; and the Oedipal struggle is with the whole of the past.

This understanding so fundamentally informs *The New Science* that it shapes Vico's whole prose style, whose texture is as dense, punning, and polyglottal as that of *Finnegans Wake*. In Vico's "gentile history," man creates over generations his own human nature—and exactly as he also creates human nations. Since human nature and nations evolve interdependently with language, Vico conveys their commutual coming-to-be, their *nascimento*, by weaving through *The New Science* an assemblage of words originating in the same aboriginal root **gen-* ("to come to be")—whose meaning is also its evolution. Uttered in the darkness of prehistory by descendants of Vico's first men, this syllable generates over generations, and in all the nations of the gentile world, a diverse vocabulary whose meaning is the genesis of human nature. . . . On the evolution of vocables like this, and the freight they carry, Joyce succinctly comments in *Finnegans Wake* that "the world, mind, is, was and will be writing its own wrunes for ever, man, on all matters that fall under the ban of our infrarational senses" (*FW* 19.35–20.1)—where the appositional equations of "world," "mind," "man," and his "runes" replicate the vision of *The New Science*. An aspect of his science, as the etymology of Vico's "gentility" will attest, is the conceptual identity of "nationality" and "genitality"; originating in the same source, both words embody the same tensions. It is for this reason, in *Finnegans Wake*, that HCE's encounter with the "cad" (*FW* 35.11; 35.1–36.4 [< Fr. *cadet*, "younger son"]) takes place in the shadows of the Wellington Memorial (*FW* 36.18), the dream-displaced scene of his sexual "crime"; the conflict underlying this encounter, underlined by references to nationalist and generational struggles, is localized in HCE's genitalia. In *The New Science* and *Finnegans Wake*, national and generational struggles are also genital struggles, because they all bring patriarchal authorities and those subjugated to such authority into visceral conflict over issues of power and potency.

Since Vico's "Poetic Wisdom" in its own way strives rationally to reconstruct the minds of those irrational first men whose animal instincts began to determine the subsequent evolution of history and human consciousness, it encompasses the psychoanalytic work that Freud achieved in reconstructing the infantile mind whose fears and pleasure determine the shape of personal history. Here, too, Joyce learned much more from *The New Science* than a principle of eternal recurrence. Vico gave him the dream-work by which he spun out *Finnegans Wake*. What Vico called *"Poetic Wisdom,"* Freud explained two hundred years later as the primary process of the unconscious. But Vico also anticipates Freud, and ultimately contributes to *Ulysses* and the *Wake* by drawing a rich fund of insight from the observation and the memory of human infancy. In trying to understand how the first men thought and oriented themselves towards others in a world void of society, he naturally seeks to fathom the wholly unformed mind of the child. Because Vico's first men are born into a state of nature and differ from their modern descendants largely in lacking the benefits of a long-evolved language and consciousness instilled in children by the process of education. Vico axiomatically assumes that these people thought as infants and children do (*NS* 211–16): according to fears, pleasures, and instincts. What distinguishes the newborn child of the modern world from "the first peoples, who were the children of the human race" is the weight of history preceding his birth (*NS* 498). It is a long, complex history whose main lessons the newborn child learns in the first few years of life when his parents teach him, as in the opening pages of *A Portrait*, language, morality, identity, family, and both the superstitions and the achievements of millennia (*NS* 336). But the mind of an infant not yet tutored into the orders of language, reason, and social customs—not yet able to distinguish anything apart from its pleasures and fears—that is the mind which nature gives to "the children of nascent mankind" in Vico's *Science*, the mind out of which his aboriginal giants crudely act and "reason" (*NS* 376).

In the psychogenesis that Joyce derived from Vico, "our family furbears" spent their entire lifetimes in a state of unconsciousness, and it was out of this unformed, infantile mind that they began to generate the utterances and groupings from which our own language and civilization grew. In "Poetic Wisdom," Vico constructs an elaborate psychology of the Unconscious, or "Ignorance," to explain the dreamlike ways in which this infantile and history-originating mind worked and made choices. His reconstruction begins with a willed, imaginary abandonment both of rationalism and of the man-made Newtonian order in which rationalism found its object:

> From these first men, stupid, insensate, and horrible beasts, all philosophers and philologians should have begun their investigations of the wisdom of the ancient gentiles. . . . And they should have begun [not with physics, but] with metaphysics, which seeks its proofs not in the external world but within the modifications of the mind of him who meditates it. For since this world of nations has certainly been made by men, it is within these modifications that its principles should have been sought. And human nature, so far as it is like that of the animals, carries with it this property, that the senses are its sole way of knowing things. (*NS* 374)

"In the early childhood of the world," however, this sensory "knowing of things" is *not* perceptual, but animal and instinctive (*NS* 69); for "men at first feel without perceiving, then they perceive with a troubled and agitated spirit, finally they reflect with a clear mind" (*NS* 218). Men void of the learned capacity to perceive, who sense nothing but their own feelings, can only stand as giants in proportion to all the rest of the unborn world ("the human mind, because of its indefinite nature, wherever it is lost in ignorance makes itself the rule of the universe in respect of everything it does not know" [*NS* 180–81]). "Born in ignorance of causes, ignorance making everything wonderful to men ignorant of everything," the first men of Vico's "giantle" humanity (*FW* 509.19 ["gentile," "giant"]) accordingly resemble the unconscious hero of *Finnegans Wake*—an "overgrown babeling" who lies "fum in mow" (*FW* 6.31, *FW* 596.6)—by virtue of a gigantic egoism that knows in the world nothing but sensation interior to the body. Vico's "giantle[s]" move organically through the *Wake* because they have the sensibilities both of Joyce's unconscious hero and of unconscious human infants, "in [whose] mental life . . . today," according to Freud, "we can still detect the same archaic factors which were once dominant generally in the primeval days of human civilization."[14]

There are now two ways of regarding the genesis of the world into which this infantile mind awakens. In one, invented by Newton and upheld by scientific rationalism, the world begins when a God immanent in nature occasions an astronomical Big Bang that hurls the inanimate physical matter of billions of galaxies outward into space to form, over eons and in a single star-system, a planet whose molecules will providentially start replicating themselves, in turn to generate animate matter capable of reproduction, and then self-consciousness, and then the inspired writing of revelatory books like Genesis; creation is already there, completely ordered and waiting to be known as the infant grows. In the second version, told in Genesis and upheld both in *Finnegans Wake* and in Vico's *New Science* of nescience, "the world in its infancy" begins when a space-pervading spirit named "I AM" (the Hebrew JHVH) starts gathering the appearances of nature out of a dark and void formlessness, paramount among them the form of an aboriginal man who becomes capable of naming animals, shaping the world, inventing and learning concepts like "matter," and evolving over time a mind like Newton's, trained in the pragmatic fictions of mechanical materialism; creation happens dynamically, from the inside out, as the world continually unfolds in "the modifications of our human mind." If the first of these geneses regards as primary the knowing of external matter, through science (< L-*scio*, "I know"), Vico's genesis regards as primary the not-knowing of the human mind, whose coming-to-be through nescience ("I AM") will ultimately generate the man-made constructs of science and reason. In words taken from what Vico called his " 'new science in negative form,' the form, that is, of a destructive criticism of existing theories":[15]

> . . . as rational metaphysics teaches that man becomes all things by understanding them (*homo intelligendo fit omnia*), this imaginative metaphysics shows that man becomes all things by *not* understanding them (*homo non intelligendo fit omnia*), and perhaps the latter proposition is truer than the former, for when man understands, he extends his mind and takes in the things, but when he does not understand, he makes the things out of himself and becomes them by transforming himself into them. (*NS* 405)

---

[14]Sigmund Freud, *The Question of Lay Analysis*, tr. and ed. James Strachey (New York: Norton, 1950), p. 43; cf. also pp. 46 and 86–87, and *ID*, 588. . . . In his later work, Freud moves psychoanalysis toward this kind of Vichian reconstruction, becoming increasingly absorbed with the collective character of the neurosis and more akin to Vico than Joyce may have supposed.

[15]Fisch and Bergin, "Introduction" to *The Autobiography*, p. 11.

The "giantle" world of Vico's *New Science*, then, originates exactly as the world originates in the Book of Genesis, and exactly as it always and only originates in the minds of human infants. "Lost in ignorance," "buried in the body and immersed in the senses," these impercipient, space-pervading giants, informed by *Jov*(e) or *J*(eh)*ov*(ah), rise from an unconsciousness that only knows "I AM" into "gentile" human "nature" by gathering from dark formlessness the etymologically related property of physical "nature"—animating it and making it sensible according to anthropocentric principles of infantile psychology that Vico elaborates throughout "Poetic Wisdom" (see *NS* 180–7, 211—12):

> The most sublime labor of poetry is to give sense and passion to insensate things [as is] characteristic of children. . . . This philologico-philosophical axiom proves to us that in the world's childhood men were by nature sublime poets. (*NS* 186)

Since Vico's aboriginal man actively creates the world by "making things out of himself," "the first nature" of gentile humanity in *The New Science* is "a poetic or creative nature, which we may be allowed to call divine"; "in the world's childhood" of Vico's Divine Age, "men [are] *by nature* poets," and "the world in its infancy [is] composed of poetic nations" (*NS* 187, 216 [italics mine]). The key terms here—as in all of these quotations and "Poetic Wisdom" as a whole—are "nature" (or "nations") and "poetry"; Vico employs the latter in its etymological sense of "creating" or "making" (from the Gr. *poiêsis*) rather than in the sense of literary production, since the giants who people "the world in its infancy" know no language or writing ("infancy," etymologically, < L- *infans* ["not speaking"]). Just as the limits of his culture's vocabulary cause Vico to adopt the term "ignorance" to denote "unconsciousness," so he uses the term "poetic wisdom" to denote the manifold forms of unconscious thinking that Freud would study more specialistically in his work on infantile sexuality. Treating of "metaphor," "synechdoche," "metonymy," "allegory," and "myth," rather than of "condensation," "displacement," and "indirect representation," Vico's "Poetic Wisdom" is a form of Freudian dreamwork. Organic to the minds of "the children of nascent mankind," poetic wisdom is the unconscious wisdom into which his first men rise from their nescience; it is the unconscious wisdom out of which Enlightenment Europe and its institutions dialectically grow in Vico's social history.

In order to explain how this poetic wisdom arises in giants aboriginally "ignorant of everything" but the sensation of their bodies, Vico necessarily undertakes a reconstruction of unconscious memory comparable to Freud's; for "the world in its infancy" is a "time empty of facts which must really have been full of them" (*NS* 735). Not unlike Freud, he attributes the early genesis of human nature to "the terror of present power," learned with the crash of thunderbolts which rudely teach Vico's infantile giant that he does not fill the universe (*NS* 382). Generating the internal perception of fear in a body aboriginally all appetite, this external sound operates like the thunder of the patriarchal "NO!" in Freud's accounts of the sexual organization and toilet-training of modern infants;

> But the greatest and most important part of physics is the contemplation of the nature of man. . . . the founders of gentile humanity in a certain sense generated and produced in themselves the proper human form in its two aspects: . . . by means of frightful religions and terrible paternal powers and sacred ablutions they brought forth from their giant bodies the form of our just corporature, and . . . by discipline . . . they brought forth from their bestial minds the form of our human mind. (*NS* 692)

Poetic wisdom arises in the minds of Vico's aboriginal giants, then, together with the learning of corporeal control and the human body's limited dimensions. Through poetic wisdom man creates his own body, which is not immanent in the physical universe, and which differs from the bodies of animals because it is humanly made and organized:

> In the prevailing best usage [the Latin verb *educere*] applies to the education of the spirit and [the Latin verb *educare*] to that of the body. . . . education began to bring forth in a certain way the form of the human soul which had been completely submerged in the huge bodies of the giants, and began likewise to bring forth the form of the human body itself in its just dimensions from the disproportionate giant bodies. (*NS* 520)

If this kind of education reduces the space-pervading immensity of Vico's infantile first men by subjecting them to self-imposed disciplinary laws, however, it compensatorily liberates, through a form of "sublimation," a human nature that will generate the world of nations and civil institutions:

> Then, between the powerful restraints of frightful superstition and the goading stimuli of bestial lust . . . [these giants] had to hold in [check] the impetus of the bodily motion of lust. Thus they began to use human liberty, which consists in holding in check the motions of concupiscence and giving them another direction; for since this liberty does not come from the body, whence comes the concupiscence, it must come from the mind and is therefore properly human. (*NS* 1098)

In his reconstruction of the mind at the origins both of social history and of personal history, Vico accordingly developed principles of "infantile regression" that Freud would elaborate two centuries later in his accounts of the dreamwork of sleep. Vico discovered in his aboriginal first men the "Freudian" principles of parental determination, dependency, and oedipality:

> The nature of children is such that by the ideas and names of the men, women, and things they have known first, they afterward apprehend and name all the men, women, and things that bear any resemblance or relation to the first. (*NS* 206)

He discovered that in infancy a child has no solidly established sexual identity and therefore thinks, in a kind of promiscuous abandonment allowing the free association of everyone and everything, out of a mind "polymorphously perverse," as the first men of "giantle" humanity also did:

. . . Orpheus then founds the humanity of Greece on the examples of an adulterous Jove, a Juno who is the mortal enemy of the virtues of the Herculeses. . . . Nor is this unrestrained licentiousness of the gods satisfied by forbidden intercourse with women: Jove burns with wicked love for Ganymede; indeed this lust reaches the point of bestiality and Jove, transformed into a swan, lies with Leda. This licentiousness, practiced on men and beasts, was precisely the infamous evil of the outlaw world [the world of the first men, who lived before the creation of civil law]. (NS 80)

Finally, in an age whose philological authorities were trying to discover how the languages of the gentile nations could have developed historically from the Hebrew spoken by Adam in the Garden of Eden, *The New Science* advanced the radical proposition that human language had its beginnings in the minds of infantile first men who growled, whined, and whimpered in pleasure and pain like animals in caves (NS 63); for the languages of Vico's gentile humanity, their beginnings found "in the modifications of our own human mind," originate not simply in historical time and geographical space, but also—as always and only—inside the bodies of human infants "the first dull-witted men were moved to utterance only by very violent passions, which are naturally expressed in a very loud voice" (NS 461); "articulate language began to develop by way of onomatopoiea, through which we still find children happily expressing themselves" (NS 447):

> Men vent great passions by breaking into song, as we observe in the most grief-stricken and the most joyful. . . . it follows that the founders of the gentile nations, having wandered about in the wild state of dumb beasts and being therefore sluggish, were inexpressive save under the impulse of violent passions, and formed their first languages by singing.
> Languages must have begun with monosyllables, as in the present abundance of articulated words into which children are now born they begin with monosyllables in spite of the fact that in them the fibers of the organ necessary to articulate speech are very flexible. (NS 229–231)

Vico's account of human genesis anticipatorily encompasses Freud's, finally, by understanding that human consciousness, language, and reality genetically unfold from inside the bodies of infants. Although the decorous civilization of Vico's Europe had begun learning to devalue the human body, nothing in the universe known to Vico's gentile man ever happens outside of its space, within which the human world and its knowing aboriginally and always come to be. Since the infantile thinking of Vico's first men is equivalently the unconsciousness of the body not yet tutored into human knowing, the psychology of unconsciousness that Vico develops in *The New Science* also anticipates the account of infantile sexuality given in Freud's theories of genitality. But Joyce, who described the secret pressures of the stomach on rational thinking in the "Lestrygonians" episode of *Ulysses*, the patterns of economic management imposed on consciousness by the evacuatory organs in "Calypso," and the evolved forms of human enterprise made possible by the biological endowment of lungs on mankind in "Aeolus," probably preferred to Freud's theories of genital organization Vico's broader account of how "gentile" human nature rolled up into the head not simply out of the loins but out of the entire body of his aboriginal infant giants. In Vico's *nascimento*, the thinking of the body begins not simply the history of personality, but the history of the West; and "genitality," in this history, is only a late and limited conceptual outgrowth of the broader force of a "gentile nature."

Narratology and the Subject of *Finnegans Wake*

Jean-Michel Rabaté

Can it be that most applications of narratology to *Finnegans Wake* result in self-defeating tactics? We generally agree that any theory, while covering a certain field, also designates by its elaboration a gap, an empty space which it attempts to bridge, to fill in, to recover. In the case of the *Wake*, however, the real object of narratology may prove to be the gap itself: in no other text are the indeterminacies of the speaking voice so dense and overwhelming that the reader has only a blurred impression that something is being told, though he cannot ascertain what or by whom. As soon as we try to pinpoint the "events" of a story, it trails off elsewhere, and we have to discover to our surprise that we are in the middle of another narrative. Nevertheless, we retain a constant and insistent feeling that some kind of storytelling is going on in a text which relies so much on speaking voices to tie up all the fragments of such a huge mosaic. In the struggle between the vocal and the visual media, both voice and look destroy or cancel each other out in the end, achieving not a dialectical synthesis, but the most monstrous hybridization of a "soundsense" masquerading as a dream.

True, we know that Joyce originally drafted the early episodes of his *Work in Progress* as simple narratives. Does this imply that a genetic approach may disclose a key to the actual text and not only to the history of its composition? Do the earliest drafts of straightforward stories, those easy pieces around which the rest was slowly to coalesce, contain a kernel of sense, a conceptual mode, which would not only give us an insight into the general design of the book, but also provide a series of relatively fixed meanings, stably anchored behind further proliferation and obfuscation? It was precisely with such questions in mind that I chose a passage which encapsulates a little "story" of a slightly different kind, one which I came across in a notebook dating from 1926. The story remains relatively undeveloped in the draft, and though there are traces of some rewriting, the tentative alternatives do not condense in the final version:

From *James Joyce: The Centennial Symposium*, eds. Morris Beja, Phillip Herring, Maurice Harmon, and David Norris (Champaign: University of Illinois Press, 1986), 137–46. Copyright © 1986 by the Board of Trustees of the University of Illinois. Reprinted by permission of Jean-Michel Rabaté and the Trustees of the University of Illinois.

genderless man embraces woman
traderep
orsemarines in an idingplace
orseriders in an idingplace
as idinole
iwood idingole
iroad. (Notebook VI.B.19, 95–96)

When we find this vignette on page 581 of *Finnegans Wake*, it remains recognizable, and the first problem which arises is the extent to which its being framed by a narrative of some sort modifies it, adds new characteristics to it, and more broadly allows it to function as a microunit within the text. In order to understand how this comes into play, it is necessary to situate the whole section taken as its context (*FW* 581.01–582.27). This is the end of the longest cinematographic sequence of book 3, chapter 4, which affords a general overview of the sexuality of Earwicker's family, called Porter here. The chapter heralds the dissolution of human age before the ricorso of book 4, which sees the coming of daylight. It exhibits a strange mixture of uncomplicated language, at times closer to conventional English than any other part of the *Wake*, and of really obscure scenes told from different perspectives, clothed in a juridical idiom, which present a bleak view of love-making but also propose a matrix capable of generating all stories.

This passage is not just another recapitulation of all the characters; it is also an elaborate digression bearing on the fictive nature of the text as such. The reader is no doubt ill at ease, unable to find his "zingaways" among constantly shifting personal pronouns which nevertheless retell the same hackneyed story. The reader must then confront a pure structure, with gaps to be filled and with an accompanying commentary on the sad fate of our incapacity to escape from identity:

> Bloody certainly have we got to see to it ere smellful demise surprends us on this concrete that down the gullies of the eras we may catch ourselves looking forward to what will in no time be staring you larrikins on the postface in that multimirror megaron of returningties, whirled without end to end. So there was a raughty . . . who in Dyfflingsborg did. . . . With his soddering iron, spadeaway, hammerlegs and . . . Where there was a fair young . . . Who was playing her game of . . . And said she you rockaby . . . Will you peddle in my bog . . . And he sod her in Iarland, paved her way from Maizenhead to Youghal. And that's how Humpfrey, champion emir, holds his own. Shysweet, she rests. (*FW* 582.16–27)

The spaced-out pattern is a direct echo and continuation of "In Amsterdam there lived a . . . But how?" (*FW* 565.09) in which a narrator is obliged to stop because of the fear he elicits from his auditor who trembles—this is a scene of homosexual seduction, turning the tables on the Cad, no longer Earwicker's attacker, but his friend or son to be won over. The same song marks the opening and the end of the second "position" of discordance in the musical pattern of book 3, chapter 4.[1] Unfinished sentences had already started proliferating in the previous chapter, in which they mimicked the floating voices of a mediumistic trance (*FW* 486.17–18, 23–25), presented easy riddles (*FW* 514.18), or provided the corrupted text of an old manuscript (*FW* 481.12–3). In the instance of the bawdy song quoted here, the gaps can simply be filled in (a raughty tinker/did dwell . . .)[2] since the song is hardly modified.

I started with a story which might have been a conceptual nexus, and I will now deal with a formal matrix, almost devoid of "context," which is only used as a reminder that the reader must do some deciphering in order to make sense of it. *Finnegans Wake* appears hinged between a perpetual recapitulation of what is never fully told, and the anticipation of yet another more complete disclosure. Professor Jones gives a precious hint in an early passage as to the completion of the text by the reader: "The genre of portraiture of changes of mind in order to be truly torse should evoke the bush soul of females so I am leaving it to the experienced victim to complete the general suggestion by the mental addition of a wallop bound . . ." (*FW* 165.17–20). In our passage, the wallaby bound cannot help rebounding in the same place, a place in which "shysweet, she rests." This important, humorous transformation of MacMahon's celebrated phrase during the Crimean war, "J'y suis, j'y reste," states the dominant theme of "semper-identity." Yet the expression revealingly modifies the verbal aspect of the sentence, replacing a first person pronoun by a third person one, and in the feminine.

The entire passage is made up of such transformation of subjects. It starts as a report explaining how the population of Dublin—referred to as "they," with a name given now and then "(Big Reilly was the worst)" (*FW* 581.7)—criticizes a "him" and his family. The anonymous narrator does not reveal an identity but a position in the grammatical scheme when he says "I": "Ah ho! Say no more about it! I'm sorry! I saw. I'm sorry to say I saw!" (*FW* 581.24–25). The dialogue already implicit in the collective "we" with moving boundaries and mediating between "they" and "him" naturally enough creates a second person, implied by the invocation "say no more!" The game the text plays with readers is to have them adopt every subjective position sequentially, moving their places all the time, so that they become Earwicker's fighting sons or schizoid daughter(s): ". . . we may catch *ourselves* looking forward to what will in no time be staring *you* larrikins on the postface in that multimirror megaron of returningties" (*FW* 582.18–20; italics mine).

I would like to pause a little and reflect on this weird multimirror, which changes "us" into "you." This is no doubt an apt metaphor of the complex textuality of the *Wake*, founded, as we know, on the circularity of history and

---

[1]See Jack P. Dalton, "Music Lesson," in *A Wake Digest*, ed. Clive Hart and Fritz Senn.
[2]See the reference to the complete song in Roland McHugh, *Annotations to Finnegans Wake*, 582.

of matter—in a mixture of Vico, Einstein, and Dunne's serial and reversible universe, which is condensed by "returningties." My contention is that such an apparatus frames the divided subject of desire, a divided subject which becomes the locus of a disjuncture between voices and events.

A firm narratological axiom is the link between voices and events: it has to be used as the basis for the identification of intra- or extra-diegetic narrators, positioned in such and such a way relative to their story. In *Finnegans Wake*, we cannot help asking the old question: "Who speaks there?" but it would be begging too many answers to affirm that the voices we have learned to distinguish are real narrators. This grants them too much continuity and substance, and in the above-quoted passage, it would be of no great help to decide that this is Mark the Evangelist who is acting as narrator. Indeed, the whole second section or "position" seems to belong to him, but we must admit that he is either split up into different subnarrators, or just a facet of a more composite figure, able to sum Mark up with the other four in "they were all there now, matinmarked for lookin on" (*FW* 581.21–22).

What is fundamentally at stake behind the ascription of any passage to a narrator is the question of the identity of the subject. If what we have seen in this particular passage does apply to the rest of the book, then we may have to replace the terms we still fondly use when dealing with texts, such as "point of view," "perspective," "narrator," "narratee," and so on, by more radical notions, possibly borrowed from philosophical discourse. The term "subject" will be the moot concept here, since it bears the onus of describing both a syntactical pattern, easily identifiable, and a moving instance of positioning, divided between writing and utterance, prone to becoming the object of its own speech, and the theme of a problematic self-questioning. The split subject tends then to fall back into being an object defined by the shift of verbal patterns, before merging into another voice.

Considered in this light, the narrativity of *Finnegans Wake*, which cannot be denied, becomes exactly what we, as readers, make up in order to escape from the impasses of self-cancelling or mutually excluding alternatives. Narrativity corresponds to our irrepressible effort to bridge the gap between the smaller units which at first appear very promising but which generally frustrate our expectations, and the overall sense of structure, a sense all the more pervasive as we realize that too many structures are superimposed onto a mosaic of discrete items, so that they tend to become all too rewarding for commentators, and, by their very proliferation, become one with the "matter" they were supposed to "inform."

Thus an "imaginary narrative" fulfills the function of mediating between the text and the reader already inscribed within it. The chaos facing us is a "complex matter of pure form" (*FW* 581.29–30), echoing "the matter is a troublous and a peniloose" (*FW* 581.01), and exceeds any meaning not predetermined by the Wakean patterns of guilt, trial, original sin as the sin of the origins, and so on. But at the same time, this chaos escapes from the control of first any narrator, then of even the author, since it is only found in an interaction between the structure of the text and our felicitous misreadings:

> Gives there not too amongst us after all events (or so grants a leading hebdromadary) some togethergush of stillandbutallyouknow that, insofarforth as, all up and down the whole concreation say, efficient first gets there finally every time, as a complex matter of pure form, for those excess and that pasphault hardhearingness from their eldfar, in grippes and rumblions, through fresh taint and old treason, another like that alter but not quite such anander and stillandbut one notall the selfsame and butstillone just the maim and encore emmerhim may always, with a little difference, till the latest up to date so early in the morning, have evertheless been allmade amenable? (*FW* 581.26–36)

All the "events" alluded to are always behind or before; they remain uncertain since the only certainty is that something happened—could it have been a sexual assault, a murder, a political insurrection, a foreign invasion? The reader can find elements which seem to corroborate each hypothesis in turn. The "events" must be contrasted with the "facts" which are the object of an inquiry, doomed in advance due to lack of certainty: "Thus the unfacts, did we possess them, are too imprecisely few to warrant our certitude, the evidence-givers by legpoll too untrustworthily irreperible . . ." (*FW* 57.16–19). The "events" are not of the same nature as facts, ficts, and unfacts; they assert that something has happened and will happen again. The sense of a happening, always slightly deferred, is essential to promote the illusion of a performative action accomplished by the reader-in-the-text. It is closer to Heidegger's intuition that ontological difference is articulated by the bounty of the "be" contained in "Being": *Es gibt Sein*, "there-is-being" is a gift, a giving, a disclosure in language; this is here paralleled by the very German pattern of "Gives there not too amongst us after all events. . . ."

The "sameness" of such a pre-ontological giving underlies the recurrence of history, which, as Bloom's story of his encounter with Parnell in the "Eumaeus" episode of *Ulysses* shows, repeats itself with a difference (*U* 1961:654; *U* 1986:535; 16–1510). This statement acquires bleaker overtones in the *Wake*, since to "the way of all flesh" a *ricorso storico* adds yet another "age" and a perpetual way, which produces a "carnage." However, the opposites of "love and war" are implied in the theme of a bisexual "semperidentity" still explicitly stated by a first draft ("For there is scant hope to escape his or her semperidentity by subsisting upon variables" [*A First-Draft Version of "Finnegans Wake"*, 262]), while our passage immediately sexualizes the opposites, and refers them back to ⋔ and Δ by way of their initials: "Scant hope theirs or ours to escape life's high carnage of semperidentity by subsisting peasemeal upon variables" (*FW* 582.14–16; italics mine).

The slander and abuse leveled at Earwicker and his family is turned into a tongue-in-cheek commendation. The community is constituted by all speaking subjects who have inherited the story of the same, and who nevertheless tell it their own way. The tone is almost one of despair, as if the fate imposed by the cyclical scheme was unbearable, a negation of hope hinting at a sisyphean burden to be carried on. Here the solution lies not in a recourse to variation, but in the proximity of difference, still lurking at the core of identity. We find a sort of semantic chiasmus, since one would generally expect to find peace linked with identity, and carnage or battle with differences. The strategy of Joyce lies precisely in this reversal, which necessitates a deft manipulation of differences, even though sameness is outwardly predominant. These difference are shown at work in the "togethergush" which progresses through a series of expressions miming sameness ("fresh taint and old treason," fresh paint and old treason, as a history of human reason), and also subtly undermining it ("alteregoases"—with a pun on *alter ego*, [FW 576.33], and the Latin word for "other" blended with "age," or the "old man" in German—"but not quite such anander and stillandbut one not all the selfsame . . .").

We shift from a structure full of gaps to a series of little differences which introduce one to a chromatic language—as opposed to a diatonic language, which would be keyed in a normal way. All these musical metaphors are relevant here, for the passage also attempts to retell a history of music, with the "notables," "Sullivan," "betune," and several songs quoted. The question of difference within language is fundamental, for it turns out to be the real criterion for any judgment of Earwicker's "sin."

Earwicker is a "right renownsable patriarch," which means that he can be "renounced" and also "renowned"; he is "re-nounced" as well, his proper name being reborn through common names such as "father" or "ark," both contained in "patriarch." The "man from the nark" blends Earwicker as Noah and as Mark of Cornwall, and fuses this with the picture of a Viking invader who has replaced the ancient Gaelic hero Finn Mac Cool. His new stock plays on the senses of a new family originating a whole line of descent, and of a new vine plant. Nhah, drunk with his wine, represents the mythical link between the eponymous hero and his substitute.

All this constitutes a commerce of nouns and of goods, as well as women (to use Lévi-Strauss's definition of society as a system of exchanges). The sons become tradesmen who profit from the original sin equated with perversion in general, or more precisely the homosexual incest when Noah, drunk and naked, exhibits himself to his sons: "shame, humbug and profit" (FW 582.10). They have become "shareholders," thereby leaving behind the primitive times when they were merely smugglers of bootleg whiskey, or raiders living off bartered goods, and stealing women from native populations—as the Danes did, before they were to settle. Thus, Earwicker is described as having brought his wife from Cork county back to Dublin ("paved her way from Maizenhead to Youghal"). The link between "wine, women and song" is made explicit by the references to "find me cool's moist opulent vinery" and to the play on "wife" and "wine" ("zingaway wivewards"). This alludes to the discovery of Vinland (Newfoundland) by the Vikings, and to the pub as the place of the major events. The small traders who also play the customers are the converted descendants who accompanied the Vikings, settled instead of exploring other territories, took on the customs of the country, and helped to develop trade, coining in silver, cities, roads—which serve as a metaphor for the process of civilization: "carryfour," "aspault," "concrete," references to the Appian Way and Maida Vale in London. Civilization and traffic are associated, because both rely on linguistic transformation and exchange.

The "traders" thus oppose an aging autocrat, Freud's original Father, because he has refused to be converted either to the Lord's laws or to the law of a language which admits of difference. He is "unregendered," that is, "unregenerate" and "genderless," or even "un-engendered," since it is he who "begottom," begot them with his bottom as mythical father's arse. This is developed by the little story with which I began this paper. It tells us about "orsemarines in an idingplace" (cf. *FW* 581.20), just as it was drafted in the notebook. The shift from the legendary corps of the "horsemarines," to whom one generally alludes in a dismissive way because of some legpull ("tell that to the horsemarines!"), to "horseriders" without an "h" permits a series of interrelated puns on languages: ". . . then hemale man all unbracing to omniwomen, but now shedropping his hitches like any maidavale oppersite orseriders in an idinhole" (*FW* 581.18–20). The man in question is "genderless" only because his language does not distinguish between the masculine and the feminine: "whose sbrogue cunneth none lordmade undersiding, how betwixt wifely rule and *mens conscia recti*." This is derived from the use of a Scandinavian language, which only possesses common and neuter to express gender. A letter to Miss Weaver states this reference very explicitly and links it to inversion: "Tristan on his first visit to Ireland turned his name inside out. The Norwegian-Danish language has neither masculine nor feminine; the two genders are common and neuter" (*SL* 306).[3] The same notebook which holds the draft of the little story has another reference to this linguistic trait, and attributes it to the two brothers: Shaun is "common," while Shem is "neuter."[4]

The Norse are hidden beneath the sea-horses and are also Greek soldiers crouching inside the Trojan horse. Such an idiom lends itself very well to perversion, moving from unrestricted Donjuanism which denies women any access to a desire dividing them as subjects, since it alludes to them only as wholes or holes, towards homosexuality, considered as the absence of difference ("undersiding" mixes *Unterschied* in German with "undecided" and "understanding"). When the two brothers are united as ⌒ there is indeed no place for the feminine, except when it looms through the metamorphoses of bisexuality.[5]

---

[3]This letter is dated 27/1/1925, thus slightly anterior to the VI.B.19.

[4] ⋀ Common
  ⊏ Neuter (Notebook VI.B.19, 127).

[5]I develop these points in an article on "Bisexuality in *Finnegans Wake*," *Cahiers de l'Herne, James Joyce*, Spring 1985. I have written a summary of it under the same title in *Eigo Seinen / The Rising Generation, James Joyce Special Number*, Kenkyusha, Tokyo, June 1983, 64–67.

All the sexual terms denoting coition are thus fundamentally ambiguous in pages 581–82: "peniloose" hints of "perilous" but suggests "penis loose" or "penislos" ("penisless" in German). "As long as ever there's wagtail surtaxed to testcase on enver a man" (*FW* 582.11–12) can mean "as long as every man has a penis and testicles" as well as "as long as there is intercourse involving the scrotum" ("wagtail," intercourse; "tail," feminine pudenda; "case," female pudenda in slang). Such an absence of distinction and sexual difference, although wallowing in sexual allusions, leaves any subject "undecided" as to his sexual role; sexuality is predetermined by language patterns, for sex and gender are linked, as was already shown by the passage on bisexuality (*FW* 523–25) which utilized the same term of "excess" as here (*FW* 524.1 and 580.30).

The community requires laws to "assist them and ease their fall" (*FW* 579.26); they want to be free of the guilt attached to perversion and finally to sexuality in general. They indeed wish to replace sex, with its attendant array of anguish and doubt, by grammatical gender which can more easily be controlled. Such laws become in turn the laws of fiction, a fiction whose collective nature is stressed. This is why the rowdy ballad ("There was a raughty tinker / Who in London did dwell / And when he had no work to do / His meat axe he did sell") offers blank spaces for any name to be inserted: what really matters is the structure which distributes the roles. The beginning of the "second position" of discordance is marked by a male voice suggesting homosexual contact to a friehtened child; he is in fact asleep, dreaming a scene of seduction between his father and himself. "In Amsterdam there lived a . . . But how? You are tremblotting, you retchad, like a verry jerry!" (*FW* 565.9–10). In the first occurrence, the sentence is merely interrupted, whereas in the second, the ballad yields nothing but a pattern of gaps which will accept any noun. Difference as such is constantly confronted with the ghost of sexual indifference or undifferentiation; thus "every man" is *enver à man* in Danish, but also *homme à l'envers* ("inverted," "reverse," "wrong man") in French. In the same way, the series of terms defining difference, "another," "alter," "anander," culminate on an undecidable word, mixing *einander* (one another) and *anander* (unmanly). Besides, the fourfold anaphoric *v* is heard as the voice of the four old men attempting to place a wedge between "u" (you and us, readers) and "double yous": "*vehmen's vengeance vective volleying, inwader and uitlander . . . .*"

The juridical nature of the whole episode rests on such a play on sexual difference: ". . . second position of discordance . . . Mark! You notice it in that rereway because the male entail partially eclipses the femecovert" (*FW* 564.1–3). The juridical vocabulary shows that the matter is a question of pure form only if we see it as a play on shifting positions and displacement related to difference (pointing towards "toth's tother's place" in *FW* 570.13). Discordance is not limited to "sodomy" here, since the three notes played are "meseedo" (*FW* 564.4), but takes in the generalized incest described by the Honophrius passage (*FW* 572–73). The hesitation between Mark the Evangelist and Mark the cuckold, Mark of Corn-wall (*corne* is "horn" in French), is an oscillation between witnessing (cf. *Zeuge* in German, related to generation and male organs) and watching, which leads to voyeuristic and onanistic satisfaction. What is seen then? A series of signs and numbers which come down to a "monomyth" (*FW* 581.24): either a "single discourse," or a monolith, like Wellington's monument erected in Phoenix Park. For the park is the locus of all these perversions, acted out by shadowy figures.

The turning point in the text is then manifested through the shift from two juridical terms, "amenable" and "venue." "Amenable" means "liable to be brought to judgment," while "venue" is not simply the issue of Earwicker's stock, but the place as such: "venue" means the place from which a jury is a drawn, the locale of an event brought to jurisdiction, the ground or position of someone in a discussion. It becomes in the end a statement showing that the residence of the parties is such that the proper court or authority is established. What stands out, then, is the relationship between place and authority, and the web of stories produced in the course of a long trial.

Such a trial is the trial of descendance rather than that of paternity: "we" represent(s) all men and women since "We have to had them whether we'll like it or not. They'll have to have us now then we're here on theirspot" (*FW* 582.13–14). One cannot avoid having parents, however unpleasant that admission might be to someone intent on becoming his/her own father or mother. Death may play a key role here, since the question is that of a "demise" which turns "smelly." Demise hints of death and transmission of a heritage, both being committed "willy-nilly," or rather "willynully" (*FW* 582.8), in the same process nullifying differences. As soon as one reaches the place where all the stories are generated, differences start proliferating again. Since the collective discourse hesitates between "mock indignation" and "mock praise" ("mock indignation meeting," [*FW* 581.2], and "preposterose a snatchvote of thansalot," [*FW* 582.2–3]), it will have to turn a "deaf ear" to the song of desperation contained in its universal idiom, its "esperanto" ("turn a deaf ear clooshed upon the desperanto of willynully" [*FW* 582.7–8]). We realize then how faithful Joyce was to be to his original project as sketched in the *Scribbledehobble*: "Arabian nights, serial stories, tales within tales, to be continued, desperate story-telling, one caps another to reproduce a rambling mock-heroic tale (L. G.) Scharazad's feat impossible" (*James Joyce's Scribbledehobble* 25 and Notebook VI.A.23).

Finnegans Wake appears therefore as the consistent realization of this program, as a machine containing matrixes of matrixes of stories, capable of narrating everything, and thus never really narrating one story. This machine will not allow us to gain knowledge or information, no matter how long we ponder the text. On the other hand, this lucid epic of disillusion exploits the pleasure we still take in expecting stories to be told to help us lose our knowledge, shed it gloss after gloss in the bottomless structure of perforated stories. The daring and committed loss we experience brings us back to our division as speaking subjects, facing a text which looks more and more like another speaking subject, formidable, inscrutable, but silently and intently peering into our bewildered and fascinated eyes—each contemplating the other in both mirrors of the reciprocal flesh of therehisnothis fellowfaces.

Works Cited

Dalton, Jack P. "Music Lesson." In *A Wake Digest*. Ed. Clive Hart and Fritz Senn. Adelaide: Sydney University Press, 1968.

A First Draft Version of "Finnegans Wake." Ed. David Hayman. Austin: University of Texas Press, 1963.

The James Joyce Archive. Notebooks VI.A. and VI.B.19. New York: Garland, 1978.

James Joyce's Scribbledehobble: The Ur-Workbook for "Finnegans Wake." Ed. Thomas E. Connolly. Evanston: Northwestern University Press, 1961.

McHugh, Roland. *Annotations to "Finnegans Wake."* Baltimore: Johns Hopkins University Press, 1980.

Two Words for Joyce

Jacques Derrida

It is very late, it is always too late with Joyce, I shall say only two words.[1]

I do not yet know in what language, I do not know in how many languages.

How many languages can be lodged in two words by Joyce, lodged or inscribed, kept or burned, celebrated or violated?

I shall say two words, supposing that words in *Finnegans Wake* can be counted. One of Joyce's great bursts of laughter resounds through this challenge: just try to count the words and the languages I consume! I shall no doubt return to Joyce's laughter, and to his last signature. As for the languages, Jean-Michel Rabaté tells me that the experts have counted about forty.

Two words then, simply to put back into play what Hélène Cixous has been saying: the primal scene, the complete father, the law, *Jouissance* through the ear (*by the ear*, more literally, by the word ear, in the ear-mode,[2] in English, for example, and supposing that coming [*jouir*] by the ear is, for the most part, feminine . . .).

What are these two English words? They are only half English, if you will, if you will hear them, that is, do a little more than hear them: read them. I lift them from *Finnegans Wake* (FW 258. 12):

HE WAR

I spell them out: H E W A R, and sketch a first translation: HE WARS— he wages war, he declares or makes war, he is war, which can also be pronounced by babelizing a bit (it is in a particularly Babelian scene of the book that these words rise up), by Germanizing, then, in Anglo-Saxon, He war: he was—he who was ('I am he who is or who am', says YAHWE). Where

From *Post-Structuralist Joyce: Essays from the French*, eds., Derek Attridge and Daniel Ferrer (Cambridge and New York: Cambridge University Press, 1984), 145–159. Copyright © 1984 by Cambridge University Press. Reprinted with the permission of Cambridge University Press and Jacques Derrida. Translated by Geoff Bennington.

[1]What follows is a transcription of a more or less extemporary talk given at the Centre Georges Pompidou, Paris, in November 1982. Jacques Derrida has preferred to mark the circumstantial nature of the talk by retaining in this printed version references to a talk given by Hélène Cixous on the same occasion [Tr.].

[2]The French text plays here on the homophony of 'le mode oreille' and 'le mot d'oreille' [Tr.].

it was, he was, declaring war, and it is *true*. pushing things a bit, taking the time to draw on the vowel and to lend an ear, it will have been true, *wahr*, that's what can be kept [*garder*] or looked at [*regarder*] in truth.

He, is 'He', the 'him', the one who says I in the masculine, 'He', war declared, he who was war declared, declaring war, by declaring war, was he who was, and he who was true, the truth, he who by declaring war verified the truth that he was, he verified himself, he verified the truth of his truth by war declared, by the act of declaring, and declaring is an act of war, he declared war in language and on language and by language, which gave languages, that's the truth of Babel when YAHWE pronounced its vocable, difficult to say if it was a name . . . .

I stop here provisionally, through lack of time; other transformations are possible, a great number, about which I'll say another two words later.

Coming here, I said to myself that there are perhaps only two manners, or rather two greatnesses, in this madness of writing by which whoever writes effaces himself, leaving, only to abandon it, the archive of his own effacement. These last two words speak madness itself.

Perhaps that's an over-extreme simplification (there are certainly other 'greatnesses'), but I take the risk of saying it so as to say something of my feeling about Joyce.

I do indeed say 'my feeling': that—major—affect which, beyond all our analyses, evaluations, interpretations, controls the scene of our relationship with whoever writes. One can admire the power of a work and have, as they say, a 'bad relationship' with its signatory, at least the signatory as one projects, reconstructs, or dreams him, or when one allows oneself to be haunted by him—or by her. Our admiration for Joyce ought to have no limit, no more than should the debt owed to the singular *event* of his work (I prefer to talk here of an event rather than a work or a subject or an author). And yet I'm not sure I like Joyce. Or more exactly: I'm not sure he's liked. Except when he laughs—and you'll tell me that he's always laughing. That's true, I'll come back to it, but then everything is played out between the different tonalities of laughter, in the subtle difference which passes between several qualities of laughter. Knowing whether one likes Joyce, is that the right question? In any case, one can attempt to account for these affects, and I'm not sure that the matter is a secondary one.

I'm not sure of liking Joyce, of liking him all the time. And it's to explain this possibility that I talked of two greatnesses to measure that act of writing by which whoever writes pretends to efface himself, leaving us caught in his archive as in a spider's web.

Let us simplify outrageously. There is first of all the greatness of s/he who writes in order to give, in giving, and therefore in order to give to forget the gift and the given, what is given and the act of giving, which is the only way of giving, the only possible—and impossible—way. Even before any restitution, symbolic or real, before any gratitude, the simple memory, in truth merely the awareness of the gift, on the part of giver or receiver, annuls the very essence of the gift. The gift must be without return, without a sketch, even a symbolic one, of gratitude. Beyond any 'consciousness', of course, but also beyond any symbolic structure of the unconscious. Once the gift is received, the work having worked to the extent of changing you through and through, the scene is other and you have forgotten the gift and the giver. Then the work is loveable, and if the 'author' is not forgotten, we have for him a paradoxical gratitude, which is however the only gratitude worth its name if it is possible, a simple gratitude without ambivalence. This is what's called love, I'm not saying that it happens, perhaps it never *presents itself*, and the gift I'm describing can doubtless never make a present. One can at least dream of this possibility, and it is the idea of a writing which gives.

As for the other greatness, I shall say, with some injustice perhaps, that for me it's like Joyce's greatness, or rather that of Joyce's writing. Here the event is of such plot and scope that henceforth you have only one way out: *being in memory of him*. You're not only overcome by him, whether you know it or not, but obliged by him, and constrained to measure yourself against this overcoming. Being *in memory of him*: not necessarily to remember him, no, but to be in his memory, to inhabit his memory, which is henceforth greater than all your finite memory can, in a single instant or a single vocable, gather up of cultures, languages, mythologies, religions, philosophies, sciences, history of mind and of literatures. I don't know if you can like that, without resentment and jealousy. Can one pardon this hypermnesia which *a priori* indebts you, and in advance inscribes you in the book you are reading? One can pardon this Babelian act of war only if it happens already, from all time, with each event of writing, and if one knows it. One can pardon it only if one remembers too that Joyce himself must have endured this situation. He was its patient, and what's more that's his theme, or, as I prefer to say here, his scheme. He talks about it often enough for there to be no simple confusion between him and a sadistic demiurge, setting up a hypermnesiac machine, there in advance, decades in advance, to compute you, control you, forbid you the slightest inaugural syllable because you can say nothing that is not programmed on this 1000th generation computer—*Ulysses, Finnegans Wake*—beside which the current technology of our computers and our micro-computerified archives and our translating machines remains a *bricolage* of a prehistoric child's toys. And above all its mechanisms are of a slowness incommensurable with the quasi-infinite speed of the movements on Joyce's cables. How could you calculate the speed with which a mark, a marked piece of information, is placed in contact with another in the same word or from one end of the book to the other? For example, at what speed is the Babelian theme or the word 'Babel', in each of their components (but how could you count them?), co-ordinated with *all* the phonemes, semes, mythemes, etc. of *Finnegans Wake*? Counting these connections, calculating the speed of these communications, would be impossible, at least *de facto*, so long as we have not constructed the machine capable of integrating all the variables, all the quantitative or qualitative factors. This won't happen tomorrow, and in any case this machine would only be the double or the simulation of the event 'Joyce', the name of Joyce, the signed work, the Joyce software today, joyceware.

It is with this sentiment, or one should say this resentment, that I must have been reading Joyce for a long time. And no doubt I'm not the only one. Ellmann has recently quoted the avowals of so many writers, critics, artists, all admirers or friends of Joyce, who expressed something of this malaise. But I'm not sure that one can say 'reading Joyce' as I just have. Of course, one can do nothing but that, whether one knows it or not. But the utterances 'I am reading Joyce', 'read Joyce', 'have you read Joyce?' produce an irresistible effect of naivety, irresistibly comical. What exactly do you mean by 'read Joyce'? Who can pride himself on having 'read' Joyce?

With this admiring resentment, you stay on the edge of reading Joyce—for me this has been going on for twenty-five or thirty years—and the endless plunge throws you back onto the river-bank, on the brink of another possible immersion, *ad infinitum*. Is this true to the same extent of all works? In any case, I have the feeling that I haven't yet begun to read Joyce, and this 'not having begun to read' is sometimes the most singular and active relationship I have with this work.

That is why I've never dared to write *on* Joyce. At most I've tried to mark (you were kind enough to recall this a while ago) in what I wrote of Joyce's scores [*portées*], Joyce's *reaches* [*portées*].[3] Beyond the musical measure that can be recognized in this word *portée*, which speaks too of the proliferating generous multitude of the animal [*portée* as 'litter'], you can also hear this in it: such and such a text *carries* [*porte*] in truth the signature of Joyce, it *carries* Joyce and lets itself be carried by him, or even carried off [*déporter*] in advance. Paradoxical logic of this relationship between two texts, two programmes or two literary 'softwares': whatever the difference between them, even if, as in the present case, it is immense and even incommensurable, the 'second' text, the one which, fatally, refers to the other, quotes it, exploits it, parasites it and deciphers it, is no doubt the minute parcel *detached* from the other, the metonymic dwarf, the jester of the great anterior text which would have declared war on it in languages; and yet it is also another set, quite other, bigger and more powerful than the all-powerful which it drags off and reinscribes elsewhere in order to defy its ascendancy. Each writing is at once the detached fragment of a software and a software more powerful than the other, a part larger than the whole of which it is a part.

---

[3]Derrida plays here and in the following sentence on three senses of the word 'portée': (1) range, reach, or scope; (2) musical staff or stave; (3) litter in the veterinary sense [Tr.].

This is already what *Finnegans Wake* represents with respect to all the culture, all the history and all the languages it condenses, puts in fusion and fission by each of its forgeries, at the heart of each lexical or syntactic unit, according to each phrase that it forges, stamping invention there. In the simulacrum of this forgery, in the ruse of the invented word, the greatest possible memory is stamped and smelted. *Finnegans Wake* is a little, a little what?, a little son, a little grandson of Western culture in its circular, encyclopedic, Ulyssean and more than Ulyssean totality. And then it is, simultaneously, much bigger than even this odyssey, it comprehends it, and this prevents it, dragging it outside itself in an entirely singular adventure, from closing in on itself and on this event. The future is reserved in it. The 'situation' of *Finnegans Wake* is also, because of this, our own situation with respect to this immense text. In this war of languages, everything we can say after it looks in advance like a minute self-commentary with which this work accompanies itself. It is already comprehended by it. And yet the new marks carry off, enlarge and project elsewhere—one never knows where in advance—a programme which appeared to constrain them. This is our only chance, minuscule and completely open.

So, yes (I'm replying to your suggestion), every time I write, and even in the most academic pieces of work, Joyce's ghost is always coming on board. Twenty years ago, in the *Introduction to 'The Origin of Geometry'*,[4] at the very centre of the book, I compared the strategies of Husserl and of Joyce: two great models, two paradigms with respect to thought, but also with respect to a certain 'operation' of the relationship between language and history. Both try to grasp a pure historicity. To do this, Husserl proposes to render language as transparent as possible, univocal, limited to that which, by being transmittable or able to be placed in tradition, thereby constitutes the only condition of a possible historicity; and from this point of view, it is necessary that some minimal readability, an element of univocity or an analysable equivocality, resist the Joycean overload and condensation for there to be a reading, and the work's legacy; something of the meaning of *He war* must cross the threshold of intelligibility, through the thousand and one meanings of the expression, for a history to take place, if at least it is to take place, and at least the history of the work. The other great paradigm would be the Joyce of *Finnegans Wake*. He repeats and mobilizes and babelizes the (asymptotic) totality of the equivocal, he makes this his theme and his operation, he tries to make outcrop, with the greatest possible synchrony, at great speed, the greatest power of the meanings buried in each syllabic fragment, subjecting each atom of writing to fission in order to overload the unconscious with the whole memory of man: mythologies, religion, philosophies, sciences, psychoanalysis, literatures. This generalized equivocality of

[4]*Introduction to 'The Origin of Geometry'*, tr. Edward Leavey (Hassocks: Harvester, 1978), pp. 103ff.

writing does not translate one language into another on the basis of common nuclei of meaning (*Introduction to 'The Origin of Geometry'*, pp. 103ff); it talks several languages at once, parasiting them as in the example *He war* to which I shall turn in a moment. For there will remain the question of knowing what one should think of the possibility of writing several languages at once.

A few years later, I had the feeling that without too much difficulty one could have presented *La Pharmacie de Platon*[5] as a sort of indirect reading of *Finnegans Wake*, which mimes, between Shem and Shaun, between the penman and the postman, down to the finest and most finely ironized detail, the whole scene of the pharmakos, the pharmakon, the various functions of Thoth, th'other, etc. I cannot here reconstitute the extreme complexity of this network. I had to be content with playing, in a single note (*Dissemination*, p. 88), at recalling that, of course, 'as will quickly have been understood', the whole of *La Pharmacie de Platon* was only 'a reading of *Finnegans Wake*'. This double genitive implied that this modest essay was read in advance by *Finnegans Wake*, in its wake or its lineage, at the very moment that *La Pharmacie de Platon* was itself presenting itself as a readinghead or principle of decipherment (in short another software) for a possible understanding of *Finnegans Wake*. There again there is a paradoxical metonymy: the most modest, the most miserable descendant of a corpus, its sample in another language, can appear to be *more capacious* than what it allows to be read.

I pass quickly over *Scribble*,[6] the title of my introduction to the *Eassai sur les hiéroglyphes*, a partial translation of Warburton's essay, where, beyond even the title and the quotations, I constantly refer to *Scribbledehobble: The Ur-Workbook for Finnegans Wake* (1961). And I pass quickly over *Glas*[7] which is also a sort of wake.

Above all, ten years later, *La Carte postale*[8] is haunted by Joyce, whose funerary statute stands at the centre of the *Envois* (the visit to the cemetery in Zurich). This haunting invades the book, a shadow on every page, whence the resentment, sincere and acted, always mimed, of the signatory. He sometimes confides his impatience in his addressee, whom, in the first words of the book, two years earlier, he had conceded was right ('Yes, you were right . . .'):

. . . You are also right about Joyce, once is enough. It's so strong that in the end nothing can resist it, whence the feeling of facility, however deceitful it may be. One wonders what he ended up doing, that guy, and what made him tick. After him, don't start again, draw the veil and let everything happen behind the curtains of language which can't do anything about it. But there's a coincidence; for this seminar on translation I followed all the babelian indications in *Finnegans Wake* and yesterday I wanted to take the plane to Zurich and read out loud sitting on his

---

5'Plato's Pharmacy', in *Dissemination*, tr. Barbara Johnson (Chicago: University of Chicago Press, 1981), pp. 61–171.
6'Scribble (writing-power)', *Yale French Studies*, 58 (1979), 116–47.
7*Glas* (Paris: Galilée, 1974).
8*La Carte postale de Socrate à Freud et au-delà* (Paris: Aubier–Flammarion, 1980).

knees, from the beginning (Babel, the fall, and the finno-phoenician motif, 'The fall (bababadalgh [. . .]. The great fall of the offwall entailed at such short notice the pftjschute of Finnegan [. . .] Phall if you but will, rise you must: and none so soon either shall the pharce for the nunce come to a setdown secular phoenish [. . .]') up to the passage on Gigglotte's Hill and Babbyl Market near the end, passing through 'The babbelers with their thangas vain have been (confusium hold them!) [. . .] Who ails tongue coddeau, aspace of dumbillsilly? And they fell upon one another: and themselves they have fallen . . .' and through 'This battering babel allower the door and sideposts . . .' and the whole page up to 'Filons, filoosh! *Cherchons la flamme*! Fammfamm! Fammfamm!', through this passage which you know better than anyone (*FW* 164) and in which I suddenly find 'the babbling pumpt of platinism', through this other passage about 'the turrace of Babbel', the whole Anna Livia Plurabelle passage, where you will find absolutely amazing things; and then everything that comes around 'A and aa ab ad abu abiad. A babbel men dub gulch of tears.', or 'And shall not Babel be with Lebab? And he war. And he shall open his mouth and answer: I hear, O Ismael . . . And he deed . . .', up to 'O Loud . . . Loud . . . Ha he hi ho hu. Mummum.' I run through the text, as they say of actors, at least up until '*Usque*! *Usque*! *Usque*! Lignum in . . . Is the strays world moving mound or what static babel is this, tell us?' (*La Carte postale*, pp. 257–8)

Elsewhere, in front of Joyce's funerary monument: 'He's read us all—and pillaged us, that guy. I imagined him looking at himself posed there—by his zealous descendants, I suppose' (*La Carte postale*, p. 161). Read and pillaged in advance, then. The whole (scriptural and postal) scenography of *Finnegans Wake* is put back into play, starting with the couple Shem/Shaun, the penman/ the postman, up to the war over the invention of the postage stamp and the penny post which is to be found deposited in Joyce's book (*La Carte postale*, pp. 151, 155). With a whole family of James, Jacques, Giacomo, the *Giacomo Joyce* scans all the *Envois* which are sealed, near the end, by the *Envoy* of G. C.: 'Envoy: love me love my umbrella.' '*11 August 1979* (. . .) James (the two, the three), Jacques, Giacomo Joyce—your counterfeit works wonders, this pendant to the invoice: "Envoy: love me love my umbrella." (. . .) I was forgetting, Giacomo also has seven letters. Love my shadow, it—not me. "Do you love me?" and you, say "me" ' (*La Carte postale*, p. 255).[9]

But I repeat, it is above all the Babelian motif which obsesses the *Envois*, and this is where we get back to the *He war* to which I should like to return in conclusion. If you will permit, I shall read first a fragment of the card which quotes the 'he war':

no my love that's my wake. The day when I was talking about all these pp (private *picture postcard* and *penny post*), I was first struck by this: prepayment institutes a general equivalent which regulates the tax according to the size and weight of the *support* and not the number, tenor or quality of the 'marks', even less on what they

---

[9]'Et toi, dis moi': the absence of the hyphen between 'dis' and 'moi' dictates the translation, but also calls up, by graphic difference, the possibility: 'And you, tell me' [Tr.].

call the meaning. It's unjust and stupid, it's barbarous, even, but immensely important [*d'une immense portée*]. Whether you put one word or one hundred in a letter, a hundred-letter word or one hundred seven-letter words, it's the same price; it's incomprehensible, but this principle is capable of accounting for everything. Let's leave it there. Writing *penny post*, I had also the premonition in my memory that Jean the postman (Shaun, John *the postman*) was not very far away, and nor was his twin brother Shem *the penman*. Another pp fraternal couple at war with each other, *the penman and the postman*. The writer, Shem, is the legatee of H. C. E., Here Comes Everybody, which I translate into my idiom as 'Here comes whoever will have loved me in my body'. So I looked for two hours for the *penny post* and here it is, at least one you could link to an all-powerful 'he war' (YHWH declaring war by decreeing dishemination, deconstructing the tower, saying to those who wanted to make a name for themselves, the shemites, and to impose their particular language as a universal language, saying to them 'Babel', I call myself and I impose my father-name, which you understand confusedly as 'Confusion', try, I beg of you, to translate but I hope you won't be able to, it's my double bind), passing through '*his penisolate war*' and the 'sosie sesthers' of the first page. Here then, on page 307 of *Finnegans Wake*: 'Visit to Guinness' Brewery, Clubs, Advantages of the Penny Post, When is a Pun not a Pun?'. Across, in the margin in italics, the names, you know. Here: 'Noah. Plato. Horace. Isaac. Tiresias'. On the preceding page, I pull out only this, for later: 'A Place for Everything and Everything in its Place, Is the Pen mightier than the Sword?' which pulls the following thread for example (p. 211): 'a sunless map of the month, including the sword and stamps, for Shemus O'Shaun the Post . . .'. Read the sequel round about 'Elletrouvetout' and 'Where-is-he?; whatever you like . . .' etc. Look at them, Sword/Pen.

I've just phoned you, it was impossible, you understood, you have to be naked on the phone. But at the same time it's enough for you to undress for me to see myself naked. Our story is also a twin progeny, a procession of Sosie/sosie Altrée/Thyeste, Shem/Shaun, S/p, p/p, (*penman/postman*) and more and more I metempsychose myself of you, I am with others as you are with me (for better but also, I see clearly, for the worst, I play the same tricks on them). Never have I imitated anyone so irresistibly. I'm trying to shake myself out of it because if I love you infinitely I don't love the whole of you I mean these inhabitants of you with their little hats uniquely each time I love: beyond all that is, you are the one—and therefore the other. (*La Carte postale*, pp. 154–5)

'He war', then. How to read these two words? Are there two of them? More or less? How to hear them? How to pronounce them and pronounce on their subject? The question 'how to hear them' multiplies itself, moreover, and echoes in the whole passage from which I extract these two words with the unjustifiable violence which the situation imposes on us, the little time at our disposal. How to hear them? Everything around speaks to the ear and of the ear: what speaking means but first what *listening* means: lending one's ear (*e ar, he ar*) and obeying the father who raises his voice, the lord who talks loud. What rises so high is laud. This audiophonic dimension of the divine law and its sublime height is announced in the English syllabification of *he (w)ar*, is doubled in the *w* and disseminates, for the seme and the form, on the whole page.[10] The rhythm of Biblical writing is mimed by the 'And . . .' of 'And he war . . .'. I read very aloud:

> And let Nek Nekulon extol Mak Makal and let him say unto him: Immi ammi Semmi. And shall not Babel be with Lebab? And he war, And he shall open his mouth and answer: I hear, O Ismael, how they laud is only as my loud is one. If Nekulon shall be havonfalled surely Makal haven hevens. Go to, let us extell Makal, yea, let us exceedingly extell. Though you have lien amung your posspots my excellency is over Ismael. Great is him whom is over Ismael and he shall mekanek of Mak Nakulon. And he deed.
>
> Uplouderamainagain!
>
> For the Clearer of the Air from on high has spoken in tumbuldum tambaldam to his tembledim tombaldoom worrild and, moguphonoised by that phonemanon, the unhappitents of the earth have tererumbled from fimament unto fundament and from tweedledeedumms down to twiddledeedees.
>
> Loud, hear us!
>
> Loud, graciously hear us!
>
> Now have thy children entered into their habitations. And nationglad, camp meeting over, to shin it, Gov be thanked! Thou hast closed the portals of the habitations of thy children and thou hast set thy guards thereby, even Garda Didymus and Garda Domas, that thy children may read in the book of the opening of the mind to light and err not in the darkness which is the afterthought of thy nomatter by the guardiance of those guards which are thy bodemen, the cherry-boyum chirryboth with the kerrybommers in their krubeems, Pray-your-Prayers Timothy and Back-to-Bunk Tom.
>
> Till tree from tree, tree among trees, tree over tree become stone to stone, stone between stones, stone under stone for ever.
>
> O Loud, hear the wee beseech of thees of each of these they unlitten ones! Grant sleep in hour's time, O Loud!
>
> That they take no chill. That they do ming no merder. That they shall not gomeet madhowiatrees.
>
> Loud, heap miseries upon us yet entwine our arts with laughters low!
>
> Ha he hi ho hu.
>
> Mummum. (*FW* 258.11–259.10)

Let us leave to one side, given the lack of time, numerous intersecting motifs, accumulated or condensed in the immediate context of 'he war' (Fall—'Byfall'; the curtain drops, applause—'Uploud!', 'Uplouderamainagain!'—after the *Götterdämmerung*—'gttrdmmrng'; the double: Garda Didymus and Garda Domas, the two policemen; Vico's ghost everywhere, the children's prayer . . . [*FW* 257–8]), and let us limit ourselves, if one can say this, to all that

---

[10]Along with the sense of 'war', the signalling of the recourse to German, etc., this audiophonic dimension of *he war* is one of the very numerous things which must go by the board in the nonetheless very commendable translation of *Finnegans Wake* by Philippe Lavergne (Paris: Gallimard, 1982), which I did not know when I gave this talk. 'And he war' is 'rendered' by 'Et il en fut ainsi' (p. 278). But let us never malign translations, especially this one. . . .

passes through the voice and the phenomenon, the phenomenon as phoneme: at the centre of the sequence, hear the 'phonemanon'.

It reflects, in a state of extreme concentration, the whole Babelian adventure of the book, or rather its Babelian underside: 'And shall not Babel be with Lebab'. This palindrome which overturns the tower of Babel also speaks of the book, and Philippe Lavergne recalls the two Irish words *leaba*, the bed, and *leabhar*, the book.

A few examples among others: 'The babbelers with their thangas vain have been (confusium hold them!) they were and went; thigging thugs were and houhnhymn songtoms were and comely norgels were and pollyfood fiansees. [. . .] And they fell upong one another: and themselves they have fallen' (*FW* 15.12–19); or again: 'and we list, as she bibs us, by the waters of babalong' (*FW* 103.10–11), 'the babbling pumpt of platinism' (*FW* 164.11), 'the turrace of Babel' (*FW* 199.31), 'Is the strays world moving mound or what static babel is this, tell us?' (*FW* 499.33–4), 'to my reputation on Babbyl Malket for daughters-in-trade being lightly clad' (*FW* 532.24–6), etc. . . .

In the landscape immediately surrounding the 'he war', we are, if such a present is possible, and this place, at Babel: at the moment when YAHWEH declares war, HE WAR (exchange of the final R and the central H in the anagram's throat), and punishes the Shem, those who, according to Genesis, declare their intention of building the tower in order to make a name for themselves. Now they bear the name 'name' (Shem). And the Lord, the Most High, be he blessed (*Lord, loud, laud* . . .), declares war on them by interrupting the construction of the tower, he deconstructs by speaking the vocable of his choice, the name of confusion, which in the hearing, could be confused with a word indeed signifying 'confusion'. Once this war is declared, he was it (*war*) by being himself this act of war which consisted in declaring, as he did, that he was the one he was (*war*). The God of fire assigns to the Shem the necessary, fatal and impossible translation of his name, of the vocable with which he signs his act of war, of himself. The palindrome ('And shall not Babel be with Lebab? And he war . . .') overthrows the tower but plays too with the meaning and the letter, the meaning of being and the letters of being, of 'being',[11] BE,EB (baBEl/lEBab), as it does with the meaning and the letter of the name of God, EL, LE. The names of the father (*Dad, Bab*) are moreover dispersed on the same page, along with those of the Lord and of an Anglo-Saxon god (*Go to*—twice, *Gov*) which can spread out elsewhere into governor and scape*goat*.

This act of war is not necessarily anything other than an election, an act of love. We would have to reread here the prodigious pages around this 'paleoparisien schola of tinkers and spanglers who say I'm wrong *parcequeue* . . .' (*FW* 151.9–10), where we would find the following: '. . . for aught I care

---

11'joue aussi avec le sens et la lettre, le sens de l'être et les lettres de l'être, de "être" ': playing on the homophony 'lettre(s)'/'l'être' [Tr.].

for the contrary, the all is *where* in love as war and the plane where . . .' (*FW* 151.36–152.1). And as in Ponge's *Le Soleil placé en abîme*, the redhead whore is not far from the father, in his very bed she becomes one with him: '*In my Lord's Bed by One Whole* . . .' (*FW* 105.34). This is in the great catalogue introduced by 'Thus we hear of . . .' (*FW* 104.5). But I break off this reconstruction here.

So what happens when one tries to translate this 'he war'? It is impossible not to want to do it, to want violently—and reading itself consists, from its very first movement, in sketching out translation. 'He War' calls for translation, both orders and forbids transposition into the other language. Change me (into yourself) and above all do not touch me, read and do not read, say and do not say otherwise what I have said and which will have been: in two words *which was*. For the 'he war' also tells of the irreplaceability of the event that it is, which is that it is, and which is also unchangeable because it has already been, a past without appeal which, before being, was. So that's war declared: before being, that is being a present, it was: was *he*, the late god of fire.[12] And the call to translate rejects you: thou shalt not translate me. Which will also perhaps be translated in the banning of translation (as 'representation', 'image', 'statute', 'imitation', so many inadequate translations of 'temunah')[13] which immediately follows the moment at which YHWH names himself ('Me, YHWH, your Elohim . . .'). The law enounced in the performative dimension is thus also the ban on the very principle of translation, the ban *in* the very principle of translation, intertranslation as one and the same experience of language: of the one language as one God. And transgression (just as impossible) consists, among other things, in translating that, and, already, in perverting into a description or a constatation (*he war*) a first-person performative, the performative of the first person or rather of the first word.

So what happens—repeat the same question—when one attempts to translate this 'he war'? Nothing, everything. Beyond immense difficulties, a limit remains essential. The difficulties: is it possible to make heard (*hear*) *all* the semantic, phonic, graphic virtualities which communicate with the *he war* in the totality of the book and elsewhere? The essential limit (a repetition of Babel's act of war declared—and not declared!—which Joyce reprints here) pertains to the graft (and without any possible rejection) of one language onto the body of another. In two words of which each is the head, the capital or, if you prefer, the principal member. Imagine the most powerful and refined translation-machines, the most able translation teams. Their very success cannot but take the form of a failure. Even if, in an improbable hypothesis, they had translated *everything*, they would by that very fact fail to translate

---

[12]'feu le dieu de feu': 'feu' placed before the noun means 'late' in the sense of 'deceased' [Tr.].
[13]See Michal Govrine, 'Jewish Ritual as a Genre of Sacred Theatre', *Conservative Judaism*, 36.3 (1983).

the multiplicity of languages. They would erase the following simple fact: a multiplicity of idioms, not only of meanings but of idioms, must have structured this event of writing which henceforth stands as law, and will have laid down the law *about itself*. It *was* written *simultaneously* in both English and German. Two words in one (*war*), and thus a double noun, a double verb, a noun and a verb which are divided in the beginning. *War* is a noun in English, a verb in German, it resembles an adjective (*wahr*) in that same language, and the truth of this multiplicity returns, from the attributes (the verb is also an attribute), towards the subject, *he*, who is divided by it right from the origin. In the beginning, difference, that's what happens, that's what has already taken place, that's what was when language was act, and the tongue [*la langue*] writing. Where it was, *He* was.[14]

The German *war* will only have been true in declaring war on English, and in making war on it in English. The *fact* of the multiplicity of languages, what *was done* as confusion of languages can no longer let itself be translated into *one* language, nor even (I'll come to this in a moment) into *language* [*la langue*]. To translate 'he war' into the system of a single language—as has just been tried in French ('Et il en fut ainsi')—is to erase the event of the mark, not only what it said in it but its very saying and writing, the mark of its law and the law of its mark. The current concept of translation is still regulated according to the *twice one*, the operation of passing from one language into another, each of them forming an organism or a system the rigorous integrity of which remains at the level of supposition, like that of a body proper. The translation of a Babelism involving at least two languages would demand an equivalent which would restore not only all the semantic and formal potentialities of the hapax 'he war', but also the multiplicity of languages in it, the *coition* of that event, in truth its very number, its numerous essence. You can always try. It is not only *Finnegans Wake* which here resembles a too-powerful, outsize calculator incommensurable with any translating machine conceivable today, but already the event which the book translates or mimes, before which it, *Finnegans Wake*, will have presented itself.

For a little while, I've been speaking out loud. In proffering 'he war', I entrust myself to this truth, so often recalled: in this book, in this event worked on by the confusion of languages, multiplicity remains controlled by a dominant language, English. Now despite the need to 'phonetize', despite this book's appeal for reading out loud, for song and for timbre, something essential in it passes the understanding as well as the hearing:[15] a graphic or literal dimension, a muteness which one should never pass over in silence. You can't economize on it, and this book could not be read without it. For the

---

[14]'Là où c'était, *Il fut*': troping against Freud's famous 'Wo es war, soll Ich werden' [Tr.].

[15]'quelque chose d'essentiel y passe l'entendement aussi bien que l'écoute': the connotation of hearing (*entendre*) in 'entendement' (understanding) is carried over in the translation to cover 'éoute' (listening) too [Tr.].

Babelian confusion between the English *war* and the German *war* cannot fail to disappear—in becoming determined—when listened to. It is erased when pronounced. One is constrained to *say* it either in English *or else* in German, it cannot therefore be received as such by the ear. But it can be read. The homography retains the effect of confusion, it shelters the Babelism which here, then, plays between speech and writing. This Anglo-Saxon commerce, these exchanges of a piece of merchandise (*ware*) in two languages, must pass through acts of writing. The event is linked to the spacing of its archive and would not take place without it, without being put into letters and pages. Erase the typeface, mute the graphic percussion, subordinate the spacing, that is, the divisibility of the letter, and you would again reappropriate *Finnegans Wake* into a monolingualism, or at least subjugate it to the hegemony of a single language. Of course this hegemony remains indisputable, but its law only appears *as such* in the course of a *war* through which English tries to erase the other language or languages, to colonize them, to domesticate them, to present them for reading from only one angle. But one must also read the resistance to this commonwealth, not only pronounce oneself but also write oneself against it. Against Him. And this is indeed what happens. Between islands of language, across each island. Ireland and England would only be emblems of this. What matters is the contamination of the language of the master by the language he claims to subjugate, on which he has declared war. In doing so he locks himself in a double bind from which YHWH himself will not have escaped. If it is impossible to sing in German and English at one and the same time, the written form retains polyglossia by placing the tongue at risk.

He war, God's signature. As quotation replays the whole of the world's memory, in *Finnegans Wake*, one can only quote—'mention', the speech-act theorists would say, rather than 'use'—the 'I' which henceforth becomes 'he', Him, or the 'he', a pronoun cited rather than a 'real' subject, aimed at by some direct reference. 'He' and not 'she', he who was he in declaring war. He resounds, he gives himself to be heard, he articulates himself and makes himself heard right up to the end: in opposition to the 'Mummum', to the last murmur which closes the sequence, a maternal inarticulated syllabification which falls as close as can be to the 'hush' [*chut*] or the fall [*chute*] after the last vocalization, the series of expiring vowels, voices out of breath:

Ha he hi ho hu
Mummum.

These are the last 'words', the last word of the sequence. In the series of vowels, the 'he' reappears, a simple second place in the sequence of a general hubbub. And if the page is turned, after a broad blank there is the beginning of Book II, Chapter 2 (I content myself here with letting read and resound):

As we there are where are we are we there   UNDE ET UBI
from tomtittot to teetootomtotalitarian. Tea
tea too oo.   (FW 260.01–03)

The final 'Mummum', maternal syllable right near the end, could, if one so wished, be made to resound with the feminine 'yes' in the last line of *Ulysses*, the 'yes' of Mrs Bloom, of ALP, or of any 'wee' girl, as has been noted, Eve, Mary, Isis, etc. The Great Mother on the side of the creation and the fall. In William York Tindall's book on *Finnegans Wake* I came across the following sentence where the word 'hill' plays more or less innocently with the French personal pronoun 'il', to say nothing of the 'ile': 'As he [HCE] is the hill in Joyce's familial geography, so she is the river [. . .]. This "wee" (or *oui*) girl is Eve, Mary, Isis, any woman you can think of, and a *poule*—at once a riverpool, a whore, and a little hen.'[16]

'I'm not sure I like Joyce . . . I'm not sure he is liked . . . except when he laughs . . . he's always laughing . . . everything is played out in the difference between several tonalities of laughter': that is what I suggested as I started. The question would be this: why does laughter here traverse the whole of the experience which refers us to *Finnegans Wake*, thus not letting itself be reduced to any of the other modalities, apprehensions, affections, whatever their richness, their heterogeneity, their overdetermination? And what does this writing teach us of the essence of laughter if it recalls that laughter to the limits of the calculable and the incalculable, when the whole of the calculable is outplayed by a writing about which it is no longer possible to decide if it still calculates, calculates better and more, or if it transcends the very order of calculable economy, or even of an incalculable or an undecidable which would still be homogeneous with the world of calculation? A certain quality of laughter would supply something like the affect (but this word itself remains to be determined) to this beyond of calculation, and of all calculable literature.

It is perhaps (perhaps) this quality of laughter, and none other, which resounds, very loud or very soft, I don't know, through the prayer which immediately precedes the 'Ha he hi ho hu. Mummum.' at the end:

Loud, heap miseries upon us yet entwine our arts with laughters low![17]

Laugh down low of the signature, calm the crazy laughter and the anguish of

---

[16]William York Tindall, *A Reader's Guide to 'Finnegans Wake'* (London: Thames and Hudson, 1969), p. 4.

[17]I do not know if 'laughters low' can be translated, as Lavergne does, by 'sourire discret'. But how to translate—for example the opposition of the first and last word of the prayer, 'Loud'/'low'? And must one translate? On what criteria will one rely to decide that here one must translate, or at least try, and here not? For example: should one, or should one not, translate 'Ha he hi ho hu', where the 'he' is also the homophone of a 'real' word in the language? But again, does not the question 'must one translate' arrive too late, always too late? It cannot be the object of a deliberate decision. Translation has begun with the first reading, and even—this is the thesis of these two words—before reading. There is scarcely anything but writing in translation, as Genesis tells us. And Babel is also the difference of pitch [*hauteur*] in the voice (loud/low) as well as in space. The erection of the tower is interrupted by the *He War*: 'Let's go! Let's get down! Let's confuse their lips there, man will no longer hear his neighbour's lip' (Genesis 11: 7–8; translated from André Chouraqui's French translation).

the proper name in the murmured prayer, forgive God by asking him to let us perform the gesture of giving according to art, and the art of laughter.

At the beginning I spoke of resentment. Always possible with respect to Joyce's signature. But it was a way of considering, on a small scale, Joyce's revenge with respect to the God of Babel. But the God of Babel had already tortured his own signature; he was this torment: resentment *a priori* with respect to any possible translator. I order you and forbid you to translate me, to interfere with my name, to give a body of writing to its vocalization. And through this double command he signs. The signature does not come after the law, it is the divided act of the law: revenge, resentment, reprisal, revendication *as* signature. But also as gift and gift of languages. And God lets himself be prayed to, he condescends, he leans over (Loud/low), prayer and laughter absolve perhaps the pain of signature, the act of war with which everything will have begun. This is art, Joyce's art, the space given for his signature made into the work. *He war*, it's a counter-signature, it confirms and contradicts, effaces by subscribing. It says 'we' and 'yes' in the end to the Father or to the Lord who speaks loud, there is scarcely anyone but Him, but it leaves the last word to the woman who in her turn will have said 'we' and 'yes'. Countersigned God, God who countersigneth thyself, God who signeth thyself in us, let us laugh, amen.

Chronology of Important Dates

1882   James Joyce born at 41 Brighton Square West, Rathgar, Dublin, on February 2, the first of ten children of John Stanislaus Joyce and Mary Jane Murray.

1888–91   Attends Clongowes Wood College, a Jesuit boarding school, until the family's declining financial status forces him to leave.

1892–98   Receives a scholarship from the Jesuits to Belvedere College in Dublin; wins prizes in the annual national examinations and graduates with a brilliant record.

1898–1902   Attends University College, Dublin, founded by Cardinal Newman. In his first year, he publishes an essay, "Ibsen's New Drama," in the London *Fortnightly Review.* Delivers several papers before the College literary society. Begins writing "epiphanies," 1900. Visits Cork and Mulligar with his father. Meets Yeats in October 1902. Takes degree in Modern Languages, 1902.

1903   In Paris, intending to study medicine, lives by book reviewing and giving English lessons. Returns home when mother dies. Meets Oliver Gogarty. His family's finances seriously deteriorate.

1904   Meets Nora Barnacle and falls in love. The fictional essay, "A Portrait of the Artist," is rejected by *Dana,* but three stories and five poems are published. Considers singing career. Lives briefly with Gogarty in a Martello Tower on the Dublin coast; they quarrel and Joyce leaves. Satirizes the Literary Revival in "The Holy Office." In October Joyce and Nora leave Dublin for the Continent.

1905   In Trieste, teaches in Berlitz school. Delighted by birth of son, Giorgio.

1906   Works as correspondence clerk in a bank in Rome.

1907   Returns abruptly to Trieste; hospitalized with rheumatic fever. Daughter Lucia born. *Chamber Music* published. Completes *Dubliners* with novella, "The Dead," and two additional stories. Begins revising *Stephen Hero* into *A Portrait of the Artist.* Riots at Abbey Theatre, Dublin, over Synge's "Playboy of the Western World."

1908   Death of J. M. Synge.

1909   Returns to Dublin, organizes Cinema Volta. Signs *Dubliners* contract with Dublin publisher Maunsel.

1911   Passes Italian government examination for teaching assignment but is denied recognition of his Irish degree and is rejected.

1912   Joyce's last visit to Dublin. Acrimonious interview with Maunsel's managing editor, George Roberts, who abrogates the contract. Printer destroys *Dubliners* proofsheets but Joyce obtains one copy by a ruse. Writes bitter poem, "Gas from a Burner."

1913   Ezra Pound opens correspondence; enthusiastic over opening chapters of *A Portrait*, which are published as a serial in *The Egoist*.

1914   *Dubliners* published in London by Grant Richards. *Exiles* completed. Three episodes of *Ulysses* finished. *Giacomo Joyce* written. European war begins.

1915   Takes family to Zurich for duration of war. Stanislaus interned as enemy alien. Serial publication of *A Portrait* completed. *Exiles* completed. Sister Eileen marries, leaves Trieste for Prague.

1916   *A Portrait of the Artist* and *Exiles* published. Receives Civil List grant through Yeats's influence.

1917   First glaucoma attack. Receives first of many benefactions anonymously from Harriet Shaw Weaver.

1918   First chapters of *Ulysses* serialized in *Little Review* (New York). Organizes, with Claude Sykes, troupe to produce plays in English. Begins friendship with Frank Budgen. Receives large grant from Mrs. Edith Rockefeller McCormick. European war ends.

1919   Returns with family to Trieste, lives with Stanislaus.

1920   Learns that anonymous benefactor is Harriet Weaver. Meets Pound at Sirmione in June. Moves family to Paris, leaving books and manuscripts with Stanislaus. Meets T. S. Eliot. New York court rules *Ulysses* obscene; *Little Review* publication ends.

1921   Sylvia Beach agrees to publish *Ulysses*. Iritis attack, May. Meets Valery Larbaud, who offers his flat for summer occupancy and gives lecture on *Ulysses* at Sylvia Beach's bookshop in December.

1922   *Ulysses* published February 2, Joyce's birthday; edition sold out in four days. Meets Proust in May.

1923   First pages of *Finnegans Wake* written. Dental operations, April. Attack of conjunctivitis, and eye operation. Meets John Quinn, who buys *Ulysses* manuscript. First fragments of *Finnegans Wake* published as *Work in Progress*; get hostile reception.

1924–25   Additional dental and eye operations. Stanislaus hostile to *Wake*.

1926   *Exiles* produced by Stage Society, London. Visit from Stanislaus. Pirated edition of *Ulysses* serialized by Roth, New York. Stanislaus married in Trieste. International protest on *Ulysses* piracy. Friendship with Jolas begins. Lucia takes lessons in drawing, singing, dancing; shows signs of disturbed behavior.

1927   Hostile criticism from Pound.

1929   George (Giorgio) makes debut as singer. Lucia shows symptoms of schizophrenia. Joyce organizes series of 12 essays explaining *Work in Progress*; published as *Exagmination*.

1930 Tenth and eleventh eye operations. Friendship with John Sullivan, Irish tenor. Friendship with Paul and Lucie Léon begins. Herbert Gorman begins work on biography. Marriage of George to Helen Fleischman, December 30.

1931 Takes residence in London to satisfy residence requirement for legalizing marriage. Civil ceremony, July 4. Lucia's symptoms increase. Contract for American publication of *Finnegans Wake* signed with B. W. Huebsch. Depressed over death of father, December 29.

1932 Grandson Stephen born to George and Helen, February 15. Contract signed with Bennett Cerf and Random House for American publication of *Ulysses*; court test of obscenity planned. Lucia hospitalized briefly, after violent episode; bizarre behavior continues. Refuses nomination to Yeats's newly organized Irish Academy of Letters. Renewed dental trouble.

1933 Judge Woolsey's decision admits *Ulysses* to United States, December 6. Lucia living at home, receives psychiatric treatment.

1934 Lucia hospitalized at Nyon; then at Burghölzli asylum (Zurich); then at Jung's hospital at Kusnacht, twentieth specialist.

1936 Lucia enters mental hospital in Ivry. In Trieste, Stanislaus threatened with expulsion, as new European war threat begins.

1938 Helps German writers escape Nazis; organizes Irish residence for 16 refugees.

1939 First copy of *Finnegans Wake* delivered on birthday, February 2. Gorman biography published. George's wife, Helen, has nervous breakdown. Family moves to La Baule (Brittany) when Lucia's hospital moves there (later to Pornichet), to escape German invasion of Paris. Helen returns to her family in America. Family moves to Saint Gérand-le-Puy.

1940 With Maria Jolas in Saint Gérand-le-Puy. Briefly in Vichy to be near Lucia. Paris occupied by Germans, June. Maria Jolas returns to America. Joyce begins negotiations for moving to Switzerland. Family leaves without Lucia, December 14; arrives Zurich, December 17.

1941 Joyce hospitalized with stomach cramps, January 9; x-ray shows perforated duodenal ulcer. Operation on January 12; Joyce dies at 2:15 A.M., January 13. Buried January 15 in Fluntern cemetery.

1951 Nora dies of uremic poisoning April 10, in Zurich, and is buried in Fluntern but not beside her husband. Both are moved in 1966 to a permanent plot.

Notes on Contributors

BERNARD BENSTOCK, Professor of English at the University of Miami and Past President of the James Joyce Foundation, is the founder and editor of the *James Joyce Literary Supplement*. He is the author of *James Joyce: The Undiscov'rd Country* (1977), and *The Augmented Ninth* (ed., 1988).

JOHN BISHOP, Associate Professor of English at the University of California (Berkeley), is the author of *Joyce's Book of the Dark: Finnegans Wake* (1986). He is an Advisory Editor of the *James Joyce Quarterly* and the *Joyce Studies Annual*.

JACQUES DERRIDA is Directeur d'Études at the École des Hautes Études en Sciences Sociales, Paris. His publications include *Glas* (1974), *Of Grammatology* (1976), and *Carte Postale* (1987).

DENIS DONOGHUE, literary critic and theorist, is Henry James Professor of Letters at New York University. He is the author of *Ferocious Alphabets* (1981) and *We Irish: Essays on Irish Literature and Society* (1986).

MAUDE ELLMANN is Lecturer and Fellow of Kings College, Cambridge. Formerly a Lecturer at the University of Southampton, she has also been on the faculties of Amherst College and Smith College, and was a Fellow at the Radcliffe Institute, Cambridge (Mass.). She has published essays on modern literature, critical theory, and feminism.

RICHARD ELLMANN (1918–1987) was Goldsmiths Professor of English Literature at Oxford and Woodruff Professor at Emory University. He is the author of *James Joyce*, *Ulysses on the Liffey*, *The Consciousness of Joyce*, and *Four Dubliners*. His last book was *Oscar Wilde* (1987).

DAVID HAYMAN, Professor of Comparative Literature at the University of Wisconsin (Madison), has written more than 50 articles and 6 books on Joyce, the most recent being *The Wake in Transit* (1990). He edited 25 volumes of Joyce's manuscripts in the *James Joyce Archive*.

SEAMUS HEANEY is Boylston Professor of Rhetoric and Oratory at Harvard University and a member of the Irish Academy. His poems include *North* (1975), *Field Work* (1979), *Station Island* (1984), and *The Haw Lantern* (1987). In 1975 he received the E. M. Forster Award from the National Institute of Arts and Letters.

CHERYL HERR'S most recent book is *For the Land They Loved* (1990), a study of Irish political melodramas. She is Associate Professor of English at the University of Iowa, from which she was on leave in 1992 as holder of a Guggenheim fellowship and a senior fellowship at the Institute of Irish Studies at Queen's University, Belfast. She is an Advisory Editor of the *James Joyce Quarterly*.

PHILLIP F. HERRING, Professor of English at the University of Wisconsin (Madison), is Associate Editor of *Contemporary Literature* and the author of *Joyce's Uncertainty Principle*. He is currently preparing a biography of Djuna Barnes.

FREDRIC R. JAMESON, Professor of Humanities at Duke University, was formerly Professor of French at Yale University. He is the author of *The Prison House of Language* and *The Political Unconscious*, and his most recent book is *Postmodernism or The Cultural Logic of Late Capitalism*.

HUGH KENNER, Franklin and Calloway Professor of Literature, University of Georgia, is a Fellow of the Academy of Arts and Letters and author of *The Pound Era* and *A Colder Eye*. He has been writing on Joyce and on modern literature for more than 50 years.

KAREN LAWRENCE is Professor of English at the University of Utah and President of the international James Joyce Foundation. She is the author of *The Odyssey of Style in "Ulysses"* (1981) and articles on Joyce, Charlote Brontë, and Virginia Woolf. She is currently working on a book on British women travelers.

A. WALTON LITZ, Professor of English Literature at Princeton University, in 1989–90 held the Eastman Professorship at Oxford University. His publications include *The Collected Poems of William Carlos Williams* (1986) and (with Omar Pound) *Ezra Pound and Dorothy Shakespear: Their Letters 1909–1914* (1984).

JAMES H. MADDOX is Professor of English at George Washington University and Director of the Bread Loaf School of English, Middlebury College. He has published *Joyce's "Ulysses" and the Assault upon Character*, (1978) as well as numerous articles on Joyce and on eighteenth-century fiction.

MARGOT NORRIS is Professor of English and Comparative Literature at the University of California at Irvine. Her publications include *The Decentered Universe of Finnegans Wake* (1977) and *Beasts of the Modern Imagination* (1985). Her latest book, *Joyce's Web: The Social Unraveling of Modernism*, explores the relation of Joyce's earlier fictions to *Finnegans Wake*.

JEAN-MICHEL RABATÉ is Professor of English at the University of Dijon. He is the author of *James Joyce: Portrait de l'Auteur en Autre Lecteur* (1948), which was published in translation in 1990 as *Authorized Reader—Joyce*, and also *Joyce upon the Void* (Macmillan, London, 1991).

MARY T. REYNOLDS is the author of *Joyce and Dante: The Shaping Imagination* (1981). She has been Visiting Lecturer in English at Yale University and serves on the editorial boards of the *James Joyce Quarterly* and *Joyce Studies Annual*.

BONNIE KIME SCOTT, Professor of English at the University of Delaware, has published extensively on feminist topics, including her *James Joyce* (1987). She edited *The Gender of Modernism* (1990) and *New Alliances in Joyce Studies* (1988).

FRITZ SENN, Director of the Zurich James Joyce Foundation and a Trustee of the International James Joyce Foundation, is the author of many articles on Joyce, several of which are collected in his *Joyce's Dislocutions* (ed. John Paul Riquelme, 1984). He is currently working on the narrative treatment of time in Joyce's work.

Bibliography

The Joyce Texts

Works are listed by date of first publication. Standard abbreviation are used throughout the text.

Chamber Music. London: Elkin Mathews, 1907; Cape, 1971. *James Joyce's Chamber Music*, ed. W. Y. Tindall. New York: Columbia University Press, 1954. Abbreviated as *CM*.

Dubliners. London: Grant Richards, 1914. *The Corrected Text*, ed. Robert Scholes. New York: Viking Press, 1968, 1975, 1988. Abbreviated as *D*.

A Portrait of the Artist as a Young Man. New York: B. W. Huebsch, 1916. *The Corrected Text*, ed. Chester G. Anderson. New York: Viking Press, 1964, 1976. Abbreviated as *P*.

Exiles. London: Grant Richards, 1918. Jonathan Cape, 1921, 1967, 1971; New York: Viking Press, 1951; Penguin, 1973. Abbreviated as *E*.

Ulysses. Paris: Shakespeare & Company, 1922.

Ulysses. New York: Random House, 1934, 1946, 1990. Vintage paperback, 1961, 1990. London: Bodley Head, 1937, 1960, 1968. Penguin paperback, 1968. Abbreviated as *U* 1961 + page number.

Ulysses: A Critical and Synoptic Edition, ed. Hans Walter Gabler with Wolfhard Steppe and Claus Melchior. 3 vols. New York and London: Garland Publishing, 1984, 1986.

Uylsses: The Corrected Text, ed. Hans Walter Gabler with Wolfhard Steppe and Claus Melchior. New York: Random House, 1986; London: Bodley Head, 1986. Paperback edition, Penguin, London, and Viking Penguin, New York, 1986. Abbreviated as *U* 1986 + page number, followed by episode number and line number.

Finnegans Wake. London: Faber & Faber; New York: Viking Press, 1939; London: Cape, 1969. Abbreviated as *FW*.

Stephen Hero. New York: New Directions, 1944, 1955, 1963. Abbreviated as *SH*.

Collected Poems. New York: Viking Press, 1957, 1963. Abbreviated as *CP*.

Critical Writings, ed. Ellsworth Mason and Richard Ellmann. New York: Viking Press, 1959. Abbreviated as *CW*.

Giacomo Joyce (Posthumous), ed. Richard Ellmann. London: Faber & Faber; New York: Viking Press, 1968. Abbreviated as *GJ*.

The James Joyce Archive, ed. Michael Groden et al. 63 vols. New York and London: Garland Publishing Co., 1978–1980. Abbreviated as *JJA* + volume number.

Letters. Vol. I, ed. Stuart Gilbert. London: Faber & Faber; New York: Viking Press, 1957. Abbreviated as *Letters* I, or *L* I. Vols. II and III, ed. Richard Ellmann. London: Faber & Faber; New York: Viking Press, 1966. Abbreviated as *Letters* II, III, or *L* II, *L* III.

Selected Letters, ed. Richard Ellmann. (London: Faber & Faber; New York: Viking Press, 1975. Abbreviated as *SL*.

James Joyce's Letters to Sylvia Beach. ed. Melissa Banta and Oscar Silverman. Bloomington: Indiana University Press, 1987. Abbreviated as *Beach*.

Poems and Epiphanies, ed. Richard Ellmann and A. Walton Litz. New York: Viking; London: Faber & Faber, 1990. Abbreviated as *PE*.

Reference

Bowen, Zack and James F. Carens, eds. *A Companion to Joyce Studies*. Westport, Conn., and London: Greenwood Press, 1984.

Connolly, Thomas E., comp. *The Personal Library of James Joyce: A Descriptive Bibliography*. Buffalo, N.Y.: University of Buffalo Bookstore, 1955; 2d ed., 1957.

Deming, Robert H., ed. *A Bibliography of James Joyce Studies*. Boston: Hall, 1964, 1967.

————, ed. *James Joyce: The Critical Heritage*. 2 vols. New York: Critical Heritage Series, 1970.

Gillespie, Michael P. *James Joyce's Trieste Library*. Austin: University of Texas at Austin, 1986.

Groden, Michael, comp. *James Joyce's Manuscripts. An Index*. New York: Garland Publishing, 1980.

Staley, Thomas F. *An Annotated Critical Bibliography of James Joyce*. New York: St. Martin's Press, 1989.

————. "James Joyce." In *Anglo-Irish Literature: A Review of Research*, ed. Richard J. Finneran, 366–425. New York: Modern Language Association, 1976.

————. "James Joyce." In *Recent Research on Anglo-Irish Writers: A Review of Research*, ed. Richard J. Finneran, 181–202. New York: Modern Language Association, 1983.

Journals

James Joyce Broadsheet. Semiannual. (Pieter Bekker and Alison Armstrong, editors. School of English, University of Leeds, Leeds LS2 9JT, England.)

James Joyce Literary Supplement. Semiannual. (Bernard Benstock, editor. University of Miami Department of English, P.O. Box 248145, Coral Gables, Florida 33123.)

James Joyce Quarterly (Robert Spoo, editor. University of Tulsa, Tulsa, Oklahoma 74104.)

Joyce Studies Annual (Thomas F. Staley, editor. Harry Ransom Humanities Research Center, University of Texas, P.O. Box 7819, Austin, Texas 78713.)

Biographical

Bradley, Bruce, S. J. *James Joyce's Schooldays*. Dublin: Gill & Macmillan, 1982; New York: St. Martin's Press, 1982.

Budgen Frank. "Mr Joyce." In *Myselves When Young*, 181–204. Dublin and New York: Oxford University Press, 1970.

Colum, Mary, and Padraic Colum. *Our Friend James Joyce*. Garden City, N.Y.: Doubleday, 1958.

Curran, Constantine. *James Joyce Remembered*. London and New York: Oxford University Press, 1968.

Ellmann, Richard. *James Joyce*. New York and London: Oxford University Press, 1959. Rev. ed., 1982.

Fitch, Noel Riley. *Sylvia Beach and the Lost Generation: Literary Paris in the Twenties and Thirties*. New York: W. W. Norton, 1983.

Joyce, Stanislaus. *The Complete Dublin Diary of Stanislaus Joyce*, ed. George H. Healy. London: Faber & Faber; Ithaca, N.Y.: Cornell University Press, 1971.

———. In *My Brother's Keeper*, ed. Richard Ellmann. New York: Viking Press, 1958.

Lidderdale, Jane, and Mary Nicholson. *Dear Miss Weaver*. London: Faber and Faber; New York: Viking, 1970.

Maddox, Brenda. *Nora*. Boston: Houghton Mifflin, 1988.

Mikhail, E. H., ed. *James Joyce: Interviews and Recollections*. New York: St Martin's Press; Basingstoke: Macmillan, 1990.

Potts, Willard, ed. *Portraits of the Artist in Exile: Recollections of James Joyce by Europeans*. Seattle: University of Washington Press, 1979; New York: Harcourt Brace, 1986.

Power, Arthur. *Conversations with James Joyce*. New York: Barnes and Noble, 1974.

Reynolds, Mary T. "Joyce and Miss Weaver." *James Joyce Quarterly* 19, no. 4 (Summer 1982), 373–404.

———. "Joyce as Letter Writer." In *A Companion to Joyce Studies*, ed. Zack Bowen and Janet Carens, 39–70. Westport, Conn.: Greenwood Press, 1984.

Trilling, Lionel. "James Joyce in his Letters." In *Joyce: A Collection of Critical Essays*, ed. William M. Chace, 143–65. Englewood Cliffs, N.J.: Prentice Hall, 1974.

General Works

Reference Tools

Bauerle, Ruth. *The James Joyce Songbook*. New York: Garland Publishing Company, 1982.

Benstock, Shari, and Bernard Benstock, eds., *Who's He When He's At Home: A James Joyce Directory*. Urbana: University of Illinois Press, 1980.

Bowen, Zack. *Musical Allusions in the Works of James Joyce*. Albany, N.Y.: SUNY Press, 1974.

Hodgart, Matthew J. C., and Mabel P. Worthington. *Song in the Works of James Joyce*. New York: Columbia University Press, 1959.

Critical Studies

Attridge, Derek, ed. *The Cambridge Companion to James Joyce*. London and New York: Cambridge University Press, 1990.

———. *Peculiar Language: Literature as Difference from the Renaissance to James Joyce.* Ithaca, N.Y.: Cornell University Press, 1988.

Attridge, Derek, and Daniel Ferrer, eds. *Post-Structuralist Joyce: Essays from the French.* New York: Cambridge University Press, 1985.

Aubert, Jacques. "From History to Memoires: Joyce's Chateaubriand as Celtic Palampcestor." *Joyce Studies Annual 1991,* 177–200.

Beja, Morris and Shari Benstock, eds. *Coping with Joyce: Essays from the Copenhagen Symposium.* Columbus, Ohio: State University Press. 1989.

Beja, Morris, et al., eds. *The Centennial Symposium.* Urbana: University of Illinois Press, 1986.

Bell, Robert H. *Jocoserious Joyce.* Ithaca, N.Y.: Cornell University Press, 1991.

Benstock, Bernard, ed. *James Joyce: The Augmented Ninth.* Syracuse: Syracuse University Press, 1988.

Bloom, Harold, ed. *James Joyce: Modern Critical Views.* New York: Chelsea House, 1986.

Bowen, Zack, and James F. Carens, eds. *A Companion to Joyce Studies.* Westport, Conn., and London: Greenwood Press, 1984.

Boyle, Robert S. J. *James Joyce's Pauline Vision.* Urbana: University of Illinois Press, 1978.

Brivic, Sheldon. *Joyce between Freud and Jung.* Port Washington, N.Y.: Kennikat Press, 1980.

———. *The Veil of Signs: Joyce, Lacan and Perception.* Urbana: University of Illinois Press, 1991.

Brown, Richard. *James Joyce and Sexuality.* New York: Cambridge University Press, 1989.

Burgess, Anthony. *Joysprick: An Introduction to the Language of James Joyce.* London: Andre Deutsch, 1973.

Chace, William M., ed. *Joyce: A Collection of Critical Essays.* Englewood Cliffs, N.J.: Prentice Hall, 1974.

Cixous, Helene. *The Exile of James Joyce,* transl. Sally A. J. Purcell. New York: David Lewis, 1972.

Cross, Richard K. *Flaubert and Joyce: The Rite of Fiction.* Princeton, N.J.: Princeton University Press, 1971.

Cross, Amanda (Carolyn Heilbrun). *The James Joyce Murder.* New York: Ballentine Books, 1987.

Day, Robert Adams. "Dante, Ibsen, Joyce, Epiphanies and the Art of Memory," *James Joyce Quarterly* 25, no. 3 (1988), 145–51.

Deming, Robert H., ed. *James Joyce: The Critical Heritage,* 2 vols. New York: Critical Heritage Series, 1970.

Dick, Susan, Declan Kiberd, Dougald McMillan, and Joseph Ronsley. *Essays for Richard Ellmann.* Montreal: McGill-Queen's University Press, 1989

Dunleavy, Janet E. *Re-Viewing Classics of Joyce Criticism.* Urbana: University of Illinois Press, 1991.

Dunleavy, Janet E., Melvin J. Friedman, and Michael Gillespie, eds. *Joycean Occasions.* Newark: University of Delaware Press, 1991.

Ellmann, Richard. *The Consciousness of Joyce.* New York: Oxford University Press, 1977.

Garvin, John. *Joyce's Disunited Kingdom and the Irish Dimension.* London: Gill and Macmillan, 1976.

Gillespie, Michael Patrick. *Reading the Book of Himself: Narrative Strategies in the Works of Joyce.* Columbus: Ohio State University Press, 1989.

Goldman, Arnold. *The Joyce Paradox.* Evanston, Ill.: Northwestern University Press, 1966.

Gordon, John. *James Joyce's Metamorphoses.* New York: Barnes and Noble, 1981.

Henke, Suzette, and Elaine Unkeles, eds. *Women in Joyce.* Urbana: University of Illinois Press, 1982.

Herr, Cheryl. *Joyce's Anatomy of Culture.* Urbana: University of Illinois Press, 1986.

Jones, Ellen Carol, and William T. Stafford, eds. *Feminist Readings of Joyce.* Special issue of *Modern Fiction Studies.* West Lafayette, Ind.: Purdue Research Foundation, 1989.

Kenner, Hugh. *Dublin's Joyce.* Bloomington: Indiana University Press, 1956; Boston: Beacon Press, 1962.

————. *Joyce's Voices.* Berkeley: University of California Press, 1978.

Kershner, R. B. *Joyce, Bakhtin and Popular Culture.* Chapel Hill: University of North Carolina Press, 1989.

Levin, Harry. *James Joyce: A Critical Introduction.* Norfolk, Conn.: New Directions, 1941.

Litz, A. Walton. *James Joyce.* Boston: Twayne, 1966; rev. ed., 1972.

Lernout, Geert. *The French Joyce.* Ann Arbor: University of Michigan Press, 1990.

Lobner, Corinna Del Greco. *James Joyce's Italian Connection.* Iowa City: University of Iowa Press, 1989.

Loss, Archie K. *Joyce's Visible Art.* Ann Arbor: UMI Research Press, 1984.

Lowe-Evans, Mary. *Crimes Against Fecundity: Joyce and Population Control.* Syracuse, N.Y.: Syracuse University Press, 1989.

MacCabe, Colin. *James Joyce and the Revolution of the Word.* New York: Barnes and Noble, 1979.

Mahaffey, Vicki. *Reauthorizing Joyce.* New York: Cambridge University Press, 1988.

Manganiello, Dominic. *Joyce's Politics.* London: Routledge and Kegan Paul, 1980.

Martin, Augustine, ed. *James Joyce: The Artist and the Labyrinth.* London: Ryan Publishing, 1990.

Martin, Timothy. *Joyce and Wagner.* New York: Cambridge University Press, 1991.

Nadel, Ira B. *Joyce and the Jews.* Iowa City: Iowa State University Press, 1989.

Noon, William T. *Joyce and Aquinas.* New Haven: Yale University Press, 1957.

O'Shea, Michael. *James Joyce and Heraldry.* Albany, N.Y.: SUNY Press, 1986.

Rabaté, Jean-Michel. *Joyce upon the Void: The Genesis of Doubt.* New York, St. Martin's Press; Basingstoke: Macmillan, 1991.

Restuccia, Frances L. *Joyce and the Law of the Father.* New Haven: Yale University Press, 1989.

Reynolds, Mary T. *Joyce and Dante: The Shaping Imagination.* Princeton: Princeton University Press, 1981.

Riquelme, John P. *Teller and Tale in Joyce's Fiction.* Baltimore: Johns Hopkins University Press, 1983.

Sandulescu, C. Georges. *The Language of the Devil.* Monaco: Princess Grace Irish Library, 1988.

Scott, Bonnie Kime. *James Joyce.* Feminist Readers Series. Atlantic Highlands, N.J.: Humanities Press, 1987.

———. *Joyce and Feminism.* Brighton: Harvester Press, 1987.

Senn, Fritz. *Joyce's Dislocutions*, ed. John Paul Riquelme. Baltimore: Johns Hopkins University Press, 1984.

Verene, Donald P., ed. *Vico and Joyce.* Albany, N.Y.: SUNY Press, 1987.

Watt, Stephen. *Joyce, O'Casey, and the Irish Popular Theatre.* Syracuse, N.Y.: Syracuse University Press, 1991.

Weir, Lorraine. *Writing Joyce: A Semiotics of the Joyce System.* Bloomington: Indiana University Press, 1989.

Wilson, Edmund. *Axel's Castle.* New York: Scribner's, 1932. Reprint editions, 1959, 1969.

The Poems

Anderson, Chester. "James Joyce's 'Tilly.'" *PMLA* 73 (1958), 285–98.

Howarth Herbert. "*Chamber Music* and Its Place in the Joyce Canon." In *James Joyce Today*, ed. Thomas F. Staley. Bloomington: Indiana University Press, 1966.

Jackson, Selwyn. *The Poems of James Joyce and the Use of Poems in his Novels.* Frankfurt: Lang, 1978.

Russel, Myra. "The Elizabethan Connection: The Missing Score of James Joyce's *Chamber Music.*" *James Joyce Quarterly* 18, no. 2 (1981), 133–46.

Scholes, Robert. "James Joyce, Irish Poet." *James Joyce Quarterly* 2 (1965), 255–70.

Spoo, Robert. "Rival Confessors in *Chamber Music*: Meaning and Narrative in Joyce's Lyric Mode." *James Joyce Quarterly* 26, no. 4 (1989), 483–98.

Staley, Thomas F. "The Poet Joyce and the Shadow of Swift." In *Jonathan Swift: Tercentenary Essays*, ed. Winston Weathers and Thomas F. Staley. Tulsa, Okla.: University of Tulsa Monograph Series No. 3, 1967.

Tindall, William York, ed. *James Joyce's Chamber Music.* New York: Columbia University Press, 1954.

Exiles

Adams, Robert Martin. "Light on Joyce's *Exiles*? A New Manuscript, a Curious Analogue, and Some Speculations." *Studies in Bibliography* 17 (1964), 83–105.

Bauerle, Ruth. *A Word List to James Joyce's "Exiles."* New York: Garland, 1981.

Benstock, Bernard. "*Exiles*: 'Paradox Lust' and 'Lost Paladays.'" *English Literary History* 36 (1969), 739–56.

Brown, Carole, and Leo Knuth. "James Joyce's *Exiles*: The Ordeal of Richard Rowan." *James Joyce Quarterly* 17 (1979), 7–20.

MacNicholas, John. *James Joyce's "Exiles": A Textual Companion.* New York: Garland 1979.

———. "The Stage History of *Exiles.*" *James Joyce Quarterly* 19, no. 1 (1981), 9–26.

Shaffer, Brian W. "Kindred by Choice: Joyce's *Exiles* and Goethe's 'Elective Affinities.'" *James Joyce Quarterly* 26, no. 2 (1989), 199–212.

Voelker, Joseph. "The Beastly Incertitudes: Doubt, Difficulty and Discomfiture in James Joyce's *Exiles*." *Journal of Modern Literature* 14, no. 4 (1988), 499–516.

Dubliners

Boyle, Robert, S. J. "Swiftian Allegory and Dantean Parody in Joyce's 'Grace.' " *James Joyce Quarterly* 7, no. 1 (1969) 11–21.
French, Marilyn. "Missing Pieces in Joyce's *'Dubliners.'* " *Twentieth Century Literature* 24 (1978), 443–72.
Füger, Wilhelm. *Concordance to James Joyce's "Dubliners."* New York: Georg Olms, 1980.
———. "Crosslocation in *Dubliners*." *James Joyce Quarterly* 27, no. 1 (1989), 87–99.
Garrett, Peter K., ed. *Twentieth Century Interpretations of "Dubliners": A Collection of Critical Essays.* Englewood Cliffs, N.J.: Prentice-Hall, 1968.
Ghiselin, Brewster. "The Unity of Joyce's *Dubliners*." *Accent* 16 (1956), 75–88, 196–231.
Gifford, Don. *Joyce Annotated: Notes for "Dubliners" and "A Portrait of the Artist as a Young Man."* Berkeley: University of California Press, 2nd ed., 1982.
Kelleher, John V. "Irish History and Mythology in James Joyce's 'The Dead.' " *Review of Politics* 27 (1965) 414-33.
Lane, Gary. ed. *A Word List to James Joyce's "Dubliners."* New York: Haskell House, 1972.
Norris, Margot. "Stifled Back Answers: The Gender Politics of Art in Joyce's 'The Dead.' " *Modern Fiction Studies* 35, no. 3 (1989), 479–503.
Owens, Coilin. "Clay." Published in three parts: (1) "Irish Folklore." *James Joyce Quarterly* 27, no. 2 (Winter 1990), 337–52; (2) "The Myth of Irish Sovereignty." *Ibid.*, 27, no. 3 (Spring 1990), 603–14; (3) "The Mass of Mary and All the Saints." *Ibid.*, 27, no. 3 (Fall 1990), 257–67.
Scholes Robert. "Semiotic Approaches to a Fictional Text: Joyce's 'Eveline.' " *James Joyce Quarterly* 16, no. 1 (1979), 65–80.
Scholes, Robert, and A. Walton Litz, eds. *"Dubliners": Text, Criticism and Notes.* New York: Viking Press, 1969.
Torchiana, Donald T. *Backgrounds for Joyce's "Dubliners."* Boston: Allen & Unwin, 1986.
———. "Joyce's 'Two Gallants': A Walk through the Ascendancy." *James Joyce Quarterly* 6 (1968), 115–27.
Walzl, Florence L. "Joyce's 'The Sisters': A Development." *James Joyce Quarterly* 10, no. 4 (1973), 375–421.

A Portrait of the Artist as a Young Man

Reference Tools

Bidwell, Bruce, and Linda Heffer. *The Joycean Way: A Topographical Guide to "Dubliners" and "A Portrait of the Artist."* Baltimore: Johns Hopkins University Press, 1982.

Gifford, Don. *Joyce Annotated: Notes for "Dubliners" and "A Portrait of the Artist as a Young Man."* Berkeley: University of California Press, 1982.

Hancock, Leslie. *Word Index to James Joyce's "Portrait of the Artist."* Carbondale: Southern Illinois University Press, 1967.

Scholes, Robert, and Richard M Kain, ed. *The Workshop of Daedalus: James Joyce and the Raw Materials for "A Portrait of the Artist as a Young Man."* Evanston, Ill.: Northwesten University Press, 1965.

Critical Studies

Booth, Wayne. "The Problem of Distance in *A Portrait.*" In *The Rhetoric of Fiction*, 232–36. Chicago: University of Chicago Press, 1961.

Buttigieg, Joseph A. *A Portrait of the Artist in Different Perspective*. Athens: Ohio University Press, 1987.

Day, Robert Adams. "The Villanelle Perplex: Reading Joyce." *James Joyce Quarterly* 25, no. 1 (1987), 69–85.

Doherty, James. "Joyce and *Hell Opened to Christians:* The Edition He Used for His 'Hell Sermons.'" *Modern Philology* 61, no. 2 (1963), 109–19.

Epstein, Edmund L. *The Ordeal of Stephen Dedalus*. Carbondale: Southern Illinois University Press, 1973.

Feshbach, Sidney. "A Slow and Dark Birth: A Study of the Organization of *A Portrait of the Artist as a Young Man.*" *James Joyce Quarterly* 1, no. 3 (1967), 289–300.

Fortuna, Diana. "The Labyrinth as Controlling Image in Joyce's *Portrait.*" *New York Public Library Bulletin* 76 (1972), 120–80.

Gabler, Hans Walter. "Towards a Critical Text of James Joyce's *A Portrait of the Artist as a Young Man.*" *Studies in Bibliography* 27 (1974), 1–53.

Hayman, David. "Daedalian Imagery in *A Portrait of the Artist as a Young Man.*" In *Hereditas: Seven Essays on the Modern Experience of the Classical*, ed. Frederic Will. Austin: University of Texas Press, 1964.

Kenner, Hugh. "Joyce's *Portrait*: A Reconsideration." *University of Windsor Review* 1 (1965), 1–15.

Kershner, R. B. "The Artist as Text: Dialogism and Incremental Repetition in Joyce's *Portrait.*" *English Literary History* 53, no. 4 (1986), 881–94.

Lanham, Jon. "The Genre of *A Portrait of Artist as a Young Man* and the rhythm of its Structure." *Genre* 10 (1977), 77–102.

Narremore, James. "Style as Meaning in *A Portrait of the Artist.*" *James Joyce Quarterly* 4, no. 4 (1967), 331–42.

Radford, F. L. "Dedalus and the Bird Girl: Classical Text and Celtic Subtext in *A Portrait.*" *James Joyce Quarterly* 24, no. 3 (1987), 253–74.

Reynolds, Mary T. "Stephen's Villanelle and D'Annunzio's Sonnet Sequence." *Journal of Modern Literature* 5 (1976), 19–45.

Riquelme, John Paul. "Pretexts for Reading and for Writing: Title, Epigraph, and Journal in *A Portrait of the Artist As a Young Man.*" *James Joyce Quarterly* 18, no. 3 (1981), 301–21.

Rossman, Charles. "Stephen Dedalus and the Spiritual-Heroic Refrigerating Apparatus: Art and Life in Joyce's *Portrait.*" In *Forms of Modern British Fiction*, ed. Alan W. Friedman, 101–31. Austin: University of Texas Press, 1975.

Scholes, Robert. "Stephen Dedalus, Poet or Esthete?" *PMLA* 89 (1964), 484–89.

Scott, Bonnie Kime. "Hanna and Francis Sheehy-Skeffington: Reformers in the Company of Joyce." In *James Joyce and His Contemporaries*, 77–85. Westport, Conn.: Greenwood Press, 1989.

Staley, Thomas F., and Bernard Benstock. *Approaches to Joyce's Portrait*. Pittsburgh: University of Pittsburgh Press, 1976.

Thrane, James R. "Joyce's Sermon on Hell: Its Sources and Backgrounds." *Modern Philology* 57 (1960), 172–98.

Tobin, Patricia. "A Portrait of the Artist as Autobiographer: Joyce's *Stephen Hero*." *Genre* 6 (1973), 189–203.

Ulysses

Reference Tools

Delaney, Frank. *James Joyce's Odyssey: A Guide to the Dublin of Ulysses*. New York: Holt, Rinehart & Winston, 1981.

Driver, Clive. *"Ulysses": A Facsimile of the Manuscript*. 3 vols. New York: Octagon Press, 1975.

Gifford, Don, with Robert J. Seidman. *"Ulysses" Annotated*. 2nd ed., revised & enlarged by Don Gifford. Berkeley: University of California Press, 1988.

Hanley, Miles L. *Word Index to James Joyce's "Ulysses."* Ann Arbor, Mich.: Edwards Bros., Inc., 1937, 1944, 1951. Handlist to the 1961 edition.

Hart, Clive, and Leo Knuth. *A Topographical Guide to James Joyce's "Ulysses."* Colchester, England: Wake Newsletter Press, 1976.

Herring, Phillip F. *Joyce's "Ulysses" Notesheets in the British Museum*. Charlottesville: University Press of Virginia, 1972.

———. *Joyce's Notes and Early Drafts for "Ulysses." Selections from the Buffalo Collection*. Charlottesville: University Press of Virginia, 1977.

McCarthy, Jack. Joyce's Dublin: A Walker's Guide to *Ulysses*. Dublin: Wolfhound Press, 1986.

Raleigh, John Henry. *The Chronicle of Leopold and Molly Bloom. 'Ulysses' as Narrative*. Berkeley: University of California Press, 1977.

Rose, Danis and John O'Hanlon, eds. *The Lost Notebook: New Evidence on the Genesis of 'Ulysses.'* Edinburgh: Split Pea Press, 1989.

Schutte, William M. *Index to Recurrent Elements in James Joyce's "Ulysses."* Carbondale: Southern Illinois University Press, 1982.

Steppe, Wolfhard, with Hans Walter Gabler. *A Handlist to James Joyce's "Ulysses": A Complete Alphabetical Index to the Critical Reading Text*. New York: Garland, 1986.

Thornton, Weldon. *Allusions in "Ulysses": An Annotated List*. Chapel Hill, N.C.: University of North Carolina Press 1968, 1982.

Critical Studies

Adams Robert M. *Surface and Symbol: The Consistency of James Joyce's "Ulysses."* New York: Random House, 1966.

Benstock, Bernard. *Narrative Contexts in Ulysses*. Urbana: University of Illinois Press, 1991.

———. *Critical Essays on James Joyce's* "Ulysses." Boston: G. K. Hall, 1989.

Bowen, Zack. *Ulysses as a Comic Novel.* Syracuse, N.Y.: Syracuse University Press, 1989.

Brooks, Cleanth. "Joyce's *Ulysses*: Symbolic Poem, Biography, or Novel?" In *A Shaping Joy; Studies in the Writer's Craft*, 66–86. New York: Harcourt, Brace, Jovanovich, 1971.

Budgen, Frank. *James Joyce and the Making of Ulysses.* Bloomington, Ind.: Midland Books, 1960; new ed., London: Oxford University Press, 1972.

Card, James V. *An Anatomy of Penelope.* Rutherford, N.J.: Fairleigh Dickinson Press, 1984.

Di, Jin. "The Odyssey of *Ulysses* into China." *James Joyce Quarterly* 27, no. 3 (Spring 1990), 447–64.

Ellmann, Richard. *Ulysses on the Liffey.* New York: Oxford University Press, 1972.

French, Marilyn. *The Book as World: James Joyce's "Ulysses."* Cambridge, Mass.: Harvard University Press, 1976.

Goldberg, S. L. *The Classical Temper: A Study of James Joyce's "Ulysses."* London: Chatto & Windus, 1961.

Gose, Elliot B., Jr. *The Transformation Process in Joyce's Ulysses.* Toronto: University of Toronto Press, 1980.

Gottfried, Roy. *The Art of Joyce's Syntax in "Ulysses."* Athens: University of Georgia Press, 1980.

Groden, Michael. *Ulysses in Progress.* Princeton, N.J.: Princeton University Press 1977.

Hart, Clive, and David Hayman, eds. *James Joyce's "Ulysses": Critical Essays.* Berkeley: University of California Press, 1974.

Hayman, David. *Ulysses: The Mechanics of Meaning.* Englewood Cliffs, N.J.: Prentice-Hall, 1972.

Herring, Phillip. *Joyce's "Ulysses" Notesheets in the British Museum.* Charlottesville: University Press of Virginia, 1972.

Kelly, Dermot. *Narrative Strategies in Joyce's Ulysses.* Ann Arbor, Mich.: UMI Research Press, 1988.

Kenner, Hugh. *Ulysses.* London: George Allen and Unwin, 1980; rev. ed. Baltimore: Johns Hopkins University Press, 1987.

Lawrence, Karen. *The Odyssey of Style in "Ulysses."* Princeton, N.J.: Princeton University Press, 1981.

McCarthy, Pat. *Ulysses: Portals of Discovery.* Boston: Twayne Publishers, 1990.

McGee, Patrick. *Paperspace: Style as Ideology in Joyce's Ulysses.* Lincoln: University of Nebraska Press, 1988.

McMichael, James. *Ulysses and Justice.* Princeton, N.J.: Princeton University Press, 1991.

Maddox, James H., Jr. *Joyce's "Ulysses" and the Assault upon Character.* New Brunswick, N.J.: Rutgers University Press, 1978.

Madtes, Richard E. *The Ithaca Chapter of Joyce's "Ulysses,"* ed., A. Walton Litz. *Studies in Modern Literature,* no. 27. Ann Arbor, Mich: UMI Research Press, 1983.

Newman, Robert D., and Weldon Thornton, eds. *Joyce's Ulysses: The Larger Perspective,* Newark: University of Delaware Press, 1987.

Rogers, Margaret. "Decoding the Fugue in 'Sirens.'" *James Joyce Literary Supplement* 4, no. 1 (Spring 1990), 13–20.

Seidel, Michael. *Epic Geography; James Joyce's "Ulysses."* Princeton, N.J.: Princeton University Press, 1976.

Staley, Thomas F., ed. *"Ulysses": Fifty Years.* Bloomington: Indiana University Press, 1974.

Stanford, W. B. *The "Ulysses" Theme: A Study in the Adaptability of a Traditional Hero.* Oxford: Blackwell, 1963.

Steinberg, Erwin R. *The Stream of Consciousness and Beyond in "Ulysses."* Pittsburgh: University of Pittsburgh Press, 1973.

Theoharis, Theoharis C. *Joyce's "Ulysses": An Anatomy of the Soul.* Chapel Hill: University of North Carolina Press, 1988.

Thomas, Brook. *James Joyce's "Ulysses." A Book of Many Happy Returns.* Baton Rouge: Louisiana State University Press, 1982.

Tucker, Lindsey. *Stephen and Bloom at Life's Feast: Alimentary Symbolism and the Creative Process in James Joyce's "Ulysses."* Columbus: Ohio State University Press, 1984.

Van Caspel, Paul. *Bloomers on the Liffey.: Eisegetical Readings of Joyce's "Ulysses."* Baltimore: Johns Hopkins University Press, 1986.

On the 1984 Edition

Gaskell, Philip, and Clive Hart. *Ulysses: A Review of Three Texts.* Totowa, N.J.: Barnes & Noble Books, 1989.

Goldman, Arnold. "Joyce's *Ulysses* as Work in Progress: The Controversy and Its Implications." *Journal of Modern Literature* 15 (Spring 1990), 579–88.

Groden, Michael. "A Response to John Kidd's 'An Inquiry into *Ulysses: The Corrected Text.*'" *James Joyce Quarterly* 28, no. 1 (Fall 1990), 81–110.

Kidd, John. "Gabler's Errors in Context: A Reply to Michael Groden on Editing *Ulysses.*" *James Joyce Quarterly* 28, no. 1 (Fall 1990), 111–51.

Kidd, John. "An Inquiry into *Ulysses: The Corrected Text,*" *Publications of the Bibliographical Society of America.* Vol. 82, no. 4 (1988), 411–584.

Pugliatti, Paolo. "Who's Afraid of the 1984 *Ulysses?*" *James Joyce Quarterly* 27, no. 1 (1989), 41–54. Reply by Wolfhard Steppe, pp. 55–68; "Editing *Ulysses*: A Personal Account," by Peter du Sautoy, pp. 69–76.

Rossman, Charles. "The Critical Reception of the Gabler *Ulysses.*" *Studies in The Novel* 21 (Summer 1989), 154–81.

Sandulescu, C. Georges, and Clive Hart, eds. *Assessing the 1984 Ulysses.* Barnes & Noble Imports, 1986.

"Studies in the Novel" (special issue on editing *Ulysses*), Vol. 22 (Summer 1990), Charles Rossman, guest ed.

Tanselle, G. Thomas. "Textual Criticism and Literary Sociology." *Studies in Bibliography* 44 (1991), 3–13.

"*Ulysses*: The Text. The Debates at the Miami Conference." *James Joyce Literary Supplement* 3 (Fall 1989).

Finnegans Wake

Reference Tools

Atherton James S. *The Books at the Wake.* New York: Viking Press, 1960; expanded and corrected, 1974.

Bonheim, Helmut. *A Lexicon of the German in "Finnegans Wake."* Berkeley: University of California Press, 1967.

Christiani, Dounia B. *Scandinavian Elements of "Finnegans Wake."* Evanston: Northwestern University Press, 1965.

Glasheen, Adaline. *A Third Census of "Finnegans Wake."* Berkeley: University of California Press, 1977.

Gordon, John *"Finnegans Wake": A Plot Summary.* Syracuse: Syracuse University Press, 1987

Hart, Clive. *A Concordance to "Finnegans Wake."* Evanston, Ill. Northwestern University Press, 1962.

Hayman, David. *A First-Draft Version of "Finnegans Wake."* Austin: University of Texas Press, 1963.

McHugh, Roland. *Annotations to "Finnegans Wake."* Austin: University of Texas Press, 1980.

Mink, Louis O. *A "Finnegans Wake" Gazetteer.* Bloomington: Indiana University Press, 1977.

OHehir, Brendan, *A Gaelic Lexicon for "Finnegans Wake."* Berkeley: University of California Press, 1977.

OHehir, Brendan, and John M. Dillon. *A Classical Lexicon for "Finnegans Wake."* Berkeley: University of California Press, 1977.

Rose, Danis: *James Joyce's Index Manuscript: "Finnegans Wake" Holograph Workbook, VI.B.46.* Colchester, England: Wake Newsletter Press, 1978.

Critical Studies

Attridge, Derek. "The Backbone of *Finnegans Wake*: Narrative, Digression, and Deconstruction." *Genre* 17, no. 4 (1984), 375–400.

Beckett, Samuel, et al. *Our Exagmination Round His Factification for Incamination of 'Work in Progress'.* Also published as *James Joyce/Finnegans Wake: A Symposium.* Norfolk, Conn.: New Directions, 1939, 1972.

Begnal, Michael H. *Dreamscheme: Narrative and Voice in "Finnegans Wake."* Syracuse, N.Y.: Syracuse University Press, 1988.

Begnal, Michael, and Grace Eckley. *Narrator and Character in "Finnegans Wake."* Bucknell, Pa.: Bucknell University Press, 1975.

Begnal, Michael H., and Fritz Senn, eds. *A Conceptual Guide to "Finnegans Wake."* University Park, Pa.: Pennsylvania State University Press, 1974.

Benstock, Bernard. *Joyce-again's Wake: An Analysis of "Finnegans Wake."* Seattle: University of Washington Press, 1966.

Benstock, Shari. "Apostrophizing the Feminine in *Finnegans Wake*." *Modern Fiction Studies* 35, no. 3 (1989), 587–614.

Bishop, John. *Joyce's Book of the Dark: "Finnegans Wake."* Madison: University of Wisconsin Press, 1986.

Cheng, Vincent J. *Shakespeare and Joyce: A Study of "Finnegans Wake."* State College: Pennsylvania State University Press, 1983.

Devlin, Kimberly J. *Wandering and Return in "Finnegans Wake": An Integrative Approach to Joyce's Fictions.* Princeton, N.J.: Princeton University Press, 1991.

DiBernard, Barbara. *Alchemy and "Finnegans Wake."* Albany, N.Y.: SUNY Press, 1980.

Eckley, Grace. *Children's Lore in "Finnegans Wake."* Syracuse, N.Y.: Syracuse University Press, 1985.

Ferrer, Daniel. "The Freudful Couchmare of Shem: Joyce's Notes on Freud and the Composition of Chap. XII of *Finnegans Wake.*" *James Joyce Quarterly* 22, no. 4 (1985), 367–82.

Frye, Northrop. "Cycle and Apocalypse in *Finnegans Wake.*" In *Myth and Metaphor: Selected Essays 1974–88*, ed. Robert Denham, 356–74. Charlottesville: University of Virginia Press, 1990.

Hart, Clive. *Structure and Motif in "Finnegans Wake."* Evanston, Ill.: Northwestern University Press, 1962.

Harty, John III, ed. *James Joyce's "Finnegans Wake": A Casebook.* New York and London: Garland, 1991.

Hayman, David. *The "Wake" in Transit.* Ithaca, N.Y.: Cornell University Press, 1990.

Hayman, David, and Elliott Anderson, eds. *In the Wake of the Wake.* Madison: University of Wisconsin Press, 1982.

Lernout, Geert. *"Finnegans Wake": Fifty Years.* European Joyce Studies II. Amsterdam and Atlanta: Rodopi, 1890, 1990.

Levine, Jennifer Schiffer. "Originality and Repetition in *Finnegans Wake* and *Ulysses.*" *PMLA* 94 (1979), 106–120.

McCarthy, Patrick A. *The Riddles of "Finnegans Wake."* Rutherford, N.J.: Fairleigh Dickinson University Press, 1980.

McHugh, Roland. *The Sigla of "Finnegans Wake."* Austin: University of Texas Press, 1976.

———. *The Finnegans Wake Experience.* Berkeley: University of California Press, 1981.

Norris, Margot. *The Decentered Universe of "Finnegans Wake."* Baltimore: Johns Hopkins University Press, 1976.

———. *From Joyce's Web: The Social Unraveling of Modernism.* Austin: University of Texas Press, 1992.

Patell, Cyrus R. K. *Joyce's Use of History in "Finnegans Wake."* Cambridge, Mass.: Harvard University Press, 1984.

Rose, Danis and John O'Hanlon. *Understanding Finnegans Wake: A Guide to the Narrative.* New York: Garland, 1982.

Sandulescu, George C. *The Language of the Devil: Texture and Archetype in "Finnegans Wake."* Chester Springs, Pa.: Dufour, 1988.

Solomon, Margaret C. *Eternal Geomater: The Sexual Universe of "Finnegans Wake."* Carbondale: Southern Illinois University Press, 1969.

Wake Newsletter. Old Series, 1–18: March 1962–Dec. 1963; New Series, 1–17: Feb. 1964–Dec. 1980. Colchester, England: Wake Newsletter Press.